NATIONAL IDENTITY AND THE
AGRARIAN REPUBLIC

To Begin
the World Anew

p16

Modern Economic and Social History Series

General Editor: Derek H. Aldcroft

Titles in this series include:

National Identity and the Agrarian Republic

The Transatlantic Commerce of Ideas between
America and France (1750–1830)

MANUELA ALBERTONE
University of Turin, Italy

ASHGATE

Published by
Ashgate Publishing Limited
Wey Court East
Union Road
Farnham
Surrey, GU9 7PT
England

Ashgate Publishing Company
110 Cherry Street
Suite 3-1
Burlington, VT 05401-3818
USA

www.ashgate.com

British Library Cataloguing in Publication Data
A catalogue record for this book is available from the British Library

The Library of Congress has cataloged the printed edition as follows:
Albertone, Manuela, 1953-
  National identity and the agrarian republic : the transatlantic commerce of ideas between America and France (1750–1830) / by Manuela Albertone.
     pages cm. – (Modern economic and social history)
  Includes index.
  ISBN 978-1-4724-2136-4 (hardcover : alk. paper) – ISBN 978-1-4724-2137-1 (ebook) – ISBN 978-1-4724-2138-8 (epub) 1. Agriculture and state–United States–History. 2. Land tenure–Political aspects–United States. 3. Physiocrats. 4. Economics–France–History. 5. National characteristics, American. 6. United States–Relations–France. 7. France–Relations–United States. I. Title.
  HD1761.A629 2014
  338.10973'09033–dc23

2013029919

ISBN 9781472421364 (hbk)
ISBN 9781472421371 (ebk – PDF)
ISBN 9781472421388 (ebk – ePUB)

Printed in the United Kingdom by Henry Ling Limited, at the Dorset Press, Dorchester, DT1 1HD

*For
Antonello,
Giulia and Giorgio*

Contents

Acknowledgements

The idea of this book goes back twenty years. Over this long period I learned a great deal from conversations with colleagues and friends, and a debt is owed to them and to the work of numerous scholars. My interest in French economic thought, and particularly in Physiocracy, originated in the stimulating atmosphere of the Fondazione Luigi Einaudi in Turin, where as a student I began to read the books in its valuable collection of eighteenth-century economic texts, gather together by Luigi Einaudi. My thanks go to the librarians and staff of the foundation for their helpfulness.

Two Italian national research programmes (Prin 2005 and 2009) funded parts of my work: 'Europe and America in the Eighteenth-Century: The Atlantic Republicanism between History and Historiography' and 'Circulation of Economic and Political Models between Europe and the Americas (Eighteenth and Nineteenth Centuries)'. They enabled me to collect material in Italy, France, Britain and the United States. I shared the interest in investigating the to-and-fro of ideas between America and France with the colleague in charge of these national projects, Antonino De Francesco, and together we gave a new reading to the intellectual history at the heart of the Atlantic world. Several conferences and seminars provided opportunities for stimulating discussions that enriched and widened this topic and offered me the occasion to present my work in progress, and for this I give special thanks to André Tiran, Pierre Serna, Koen Stapelbroek, Seizo Hotta, Allan Potofsky, Nicolas Rieucau, Arnaud Orain, Simone Messina and Gilles Bancarel.

I am also grateful for the generous help of Vieri Becagli, Gino Longhitano, Gianluigi Goggi, Giancarlo De Vivo, Gabriel Sabbagh, Edoardo Tortarolo, Philippe Steiner, Christine Théré and Loïc Charles. Richard Whatmore, with whom I have had extended and fruitful discussions over many years, deserves a particular mention for he read the manuscript of my book, encouraging its publication. He also gave me an advanced opportunity to present the results of my research at the Sussex Centre for Intellectual History.

I would also like to thank the anonymous referees who through their comments and suggestions helped me to improve my original manuscript. In addition, I would express thanks to Matthew and David Armistead for their linguistic support in translation and their help in editing and improving the final text.

I also owe thanks to the librarians and archivists of the Bibliothèque Nationale de France, Archives Nationales, Archives du Ministère des Affaires Etrangères, Bibliothèque de l'Institut de France, Archives Municipales de Mantes-la-Jolie, the British Library, New York Public Library, Bobst Library, Historical Society of Pennsylvania, and the Eleutherian Mills Historical Library.

The arguments used in some of the chapters of this book were developed in the journal *History of European Ideas* (2006), and in the collected volumes *La diffusion internationale de la physiocratie (XVIIIe–XIXe)* (1995), *Rethinking the Atlantic World: Europe and America in the Age of Democratic Revolutions* (2009), *Républiques sœurs. Le Directoire et la Révolution atlantique* (2009), *Jean-Baptiste Say. Influences, critiques et postérité* (2010), and *The Rise of Economic Societies in the Eighteenth Century: Patriotic Reform in Europe and North America* (2012). I am grateful to the editors and publishers who have allowed me to publish them.

Modern Economic and Social History Series
General Editor's Preface

Economic and social history has been a flourishing subject of scholarly study during recent decades. Not only has the volume of literature increased enormously but the range of interest in time, space and subject matter has broadened considerably so that today there are many sub-branches of the subject which have developed considerable status in their own right.

One of the aims of this series is to encourage the publication of scholarly monographs on any aspect of modern economic and social history. The geographical coverage is worldwide and contributions on the non-British themes will be especially welcome. While emphasis will be placed on works embodying original research, it is also intended that the series should provide the opportunity to publish studies of a more general thematic nature which offer a reappraisal or critical analysis of major issues of debate.

Derek H. Aldcroft
University of Leicester

Introduction

The aim of this volume is to outline how, from the mid-eighteenth century to the first decades of the nineteenth, the political implications of the economic analysis carried out in France were received in America. It will show how this reaction offered an original re-examination of French ideas and a significant contribution to the development of an American national consciousness marked by anti-British sentiment. During this time a distinctive vein of French culture, unlike British empiricism, was characterized by a political rationalism derived from the study of economics.

In the confrontation between Thomas Jefferson's Republicans and Alexander Hamilton's Federalists, the ideologists of agrarian democracy – from Jefferson to Benjamin Franklin, to George Logan and John Taylor – found in the early scientific analysis of economics, grounded in the central role of agriculture and formulated by Physiocracy, strong theoretical validation for their plans for economic development. These were developed as an alternative to the British model, and were founded on a belief in the existence of truths in nature that regulated interpersonal relations and were best discerned through the application of the principle of evidence. Through their dealings and personal contact with Physiocratic milieus, both Franklin and Jefferson became deeply convinced of the primacy of agriculture and also of their own sense of national identity. They thus became protagonists in the interchange of ideas between France and America, and I have sought to identify what was new in this with regard to the specific cultures of the two countries.

Franklin was acquainted with François Quesnay, the Marquis of Mirabeau and Du Pont de Nemours, and was close to La Rochefoucauld and Barbeu Du Bourg, while Jefferson met with Condorcet and, after returning to America, enjoyed a valuable correspondence with Du Pont de Nemours until the old Physiocrat's death in 1817. It was Du Pont who collaborated with Jean-Baptiste Say to produce *Bonhomme Richard*, a French edition of Franklin's *Poor Richard's Almanack*. The circuitous intersecting careers of these men make it possible to trace the evolution and transformation of the Physiocratic tradition through the course of the long eighteenth century.

I do not intend to offer here a comprehensive history of French economic thought. Instead, I will identify the insights, the spread of texts and the individual relationships that make it possible to follow the circulation of ideas that contributed to setting out a specific pathway in the development of American identity, in the movement of different cultures into different contexts.[1] In addition

---

[1]   Beyond our specific area of research, suggestions might be found in the recent studies on communication and translatability between different cultures. Cf. Peter Burke and

to the intentions of the authors of the texts in question,[2] attention is focused on the reception in America of the current of French economic thought that, starting out from the Physiocrats, travelled a course of evolution that passed beyond the turn of the eighteenth century to arrive at the *Idéologues*. The accent is therefore placed not on influences, but on original contributions – on an intellectual relationship that, being far from passive, involved a cultural exchange that stimulated the development and refinement of ideas.[3]

Such a perspective regards Physiocracy not as a collection of fixed dogmatic principles, but as a set of thoughts in constant motion in the minds of people and through time. This progressive movement can be discerned in the link between economics and politics and in the political importance of the Quesnay group's project. Thus the mutually enriching dialogue between certain exponents of Physiocracy and their American contacts, be it direct or long-distance, offers an original contribution to the political reinterpretation of Physiocracy that has characterized studies in recent decades.

Long the preserve of scholars of economics, and subjected only to a strictly economic interpretation of their ideas,[4] the Physiocratic writers are now at the heart of studies in which historians and economists are in dialogue with one another, to their mutual benefit. Apart from the received wisdom concerning the interconnectedness of economics and politics in Physiocratic thought,[5] we have now acquired a mature understanding of Physiocracy as a political response to the French context in which it originated.[6]

Ronnie Po-chia Hsia, eds, *Cultural Translation in Early Modern Europe* (Cambridge: Cambridge University Press, 2007); Sanford Budick and Wolfang Iser, eds, *The Translatability of Cultures: Figurations of the Space Between* (Stanford: Stanford University Press, 1996), and in particular the essay by Sacvan Bercovitch, "Discovering America: A Cross-Cultural Perspective."

[2]   Cf. Quentin Skinner, "Meaning and Understanding in the History of Ideas," *History and Theory*, no. VIII (1969): 3–53; James Tully, ed., *Meaning and Context: Quentin Skinner and his Critics* (Cambridge: Polity Press, 1988).

[3]   Hans Robert Jauss, *Toward an Aesthetic of Reception* (Minneapolis: University of Minnesota Press, 1982); Hans Robert Jauss, *Question and Answer: Forms of Dialogic Understanding* (Minneapolis: University of Minnesota Press, 1989).

[4]   Ronald L. Meek, *The Economics of Physiocracy* (London: Allen and Unwin, 1962).

[5]   Cf. Catherine Larrère, *L'invention de l'économie au XVIIIe siècle: Du droit naturel à la phyiocratie* (Paris: PUF, 1992).

[6]   In search of the founding moment of the Physiocracy's political discourse, Gino Longhitano has proposed an original reconsideration of the *Tableau économique* as a political text (Victor Riquetti de Mirabeau and François Quesnay, *Traité de la monarchie*, ed. Gino Longhitano (Paris: L'Harmattan, 1999). Cf. also Keith M. Baker, "Representation," in *The French Revolution and the Creation of Modern Political Culture: The Political Culture of the Old Regime*, ed. Keith M. Baker (Oxford, New York: Pergamon Press, 1987), 469–92. Contributions towards a political rereading of Physiocracy have been made by Italian historians. Cf. those presented during the first meeting of the Italian specialists

Yet even as different analyses and perspectives are presented,[7] there still remain unresolved questions confirming the complexity of a subject that has attracted prolonged investigation. What is meant by Physiocracy? Were the Physiocratic authors intimately tied to traditional society or did they express modern ideas? And did the implications of their ideas speed the fall of the Old Regime, as Alexis de Tocqueville first concluded?[8] How did economics and politics relate in Physiocratic thought, and which was given first place? The pages that follow take their place in the body of work concerning the political ramifications of Physiocracy, and examine the questions that arise when looking through an American lens. From this perspective, it is hoped that this research, which seeks to take into consideration both political and economic viewpoints (as previous emphasis on the political reading has sometimes failed to do) will add something new.

The American reading of Physiocracy, the personal relationships of certain Republican exponents with Physiocratic circles, and the channels used to disseminate texts by Physiocratic authors and those close to them all not only bear witness to the political implications and the proactive value of the French economists' theories regarding economic development, even beyond the context in which they were elaborated, but also reveal how these theories were received by their contemporaries. Beginning from these aspects, it is possible to understand how the weight of Physiocracy was not exhausted in the period of Quesnay's 'writing workshop', and how the names of Franklin, Jefferson and Logan can be added to those close or belonging to the Physiocratic movement.[9] When, in

---

in Physiocracy organized by the Luigi Einaudi Foundation in Turin 2003, published together in "Fisiocrazia e proprietà terriera", ed. Manuela Albertone, special issue, *Studi settecenteschi*, 24 (2004).

[7]   Of fundamental importance for an interpretation of Physiocracy that is attentive to the political implications of the economic theory and to the continuity of a discourse that went as far as the French Revolution and beyond are the works of Philippe Steiner (Cf. Philippe Steiner, *La "science nouvelle" de l'économie politique* (Paris: PUF, 1998); Loïc Charles and Philippe Steiner, "Entre Montesquieu et Rousseau: La physiocratie parmi les origines intellectuelles de la Révolution française," *Etudes Jean-Jacques Rousseau*, no. 11 (1999): 89–159; Philippe Steiner, "Wealth and Power: Quesnay's Political Economy of the Agricultural Kingdom," *Journal of History of Economic Thought*, 24/1 (2002): 91–109). A different interpretation, centred mostly on Quesnay and Mirabeau, which sees Physiocracy essentially as the expression of a theodicy and a catastrophic vision, is given by Michael Sonenscher, *Before the Deluge: Public Debt, Inequality, and the Intellectual Origins of the French Revolution* (Princeton: Princeton University Press, 2007). On an unusual recent interpretation on the role mental processes, imagination and passions paid in the physiocratic authors cf. Liana Vardi, *The Physiocrats and the World of the Enlightenment* (Cambridge:Cambridge University Press, 2012).

[8]   Alexis de Tocqueville, *L'ancien régime et la Révolution* (Paris: Gallimard, 1981; first edition 1856), book III, ch. III.

[9]   On the idea of the writing workshop as the original structure of Quesnay's links with the French court, significant contributions have been made by Christine Théré and Loïc

his *Report on Manufactures* (1791), Hamilton made it clear that the impact of the Physiocratic theory on politics was still seen as a threat (beyond the years of momentum it enjoyed in France under Quesnay's exclusive group), Logan responded with the forthrightness of a political attack made under the banner of Physiocratic principles. It is also possible to follow, through the enduring relationship between Jefferson and Du Pont de Nemours, which was interrupted only by Du Pont's death, the full length of the intellectual journey of the elderly Physiocrat, heir to that 'European party of reform'[10] that he tried to export across the Atlantic. Although Du Pont remained faithful to the principles on which he had been nurtured, he updated his ideas in the light of the tumultuous events of his world and the progress of post-Physiocratic French economic culture – a culture that could ably converse with Americans, as this work will show – firm in the belief, shared by his American correspondent, that from Adam Smith to Jean-Baptiste Say the science of political economy owed a debt to Quesnay.

The strong interest among today's historians in how the science of economics emerged in the eighteenth century as a modern political language, shared by different national realities, allows us to revisit the roots of modern European identity and better appreciate its unity in diversity.[11] This work also shows how political economy became a weapon in the service of the two democratic revolutions of the late eighteenth century. In this context, European political and economic culture was both nourished and challenged by the emergence of the American national identity. Such a wide-ranging line of research transcends the confines of Europe.

Franklin met the Marquis of Mirabeau for the first time in 1767, and Jefferson was in contact with the *Idéologues* and Say up to the last years of his life, and was aware of the specific nature of French economic theory and of a continuity beyond the distinctions made by its protagonists that I have attempted to trace over a period of many years. With a few exceptions, historiography has paid little attention to the impact of French economic culture on American thought, focusing instead on its links with Britain, whose contribution I have taken pains not to underestimate. Nevertheless, the attention paid to the political and social dimension of French

Charles, "The Writing Workshop of François Quesnay and the Making of Physiocracy," *History of Political Economy*, 40/1 (2008): 1–42; Christine Théré, Loïc Charles, "From Versailles to Paris: The Creative Communities of the Physiocratic Movement," *History of Political Economy*, 43/1 (2011): 25–58.

[10]   The first to speak about the Physiocratic movement as a "European reformist party" was the Italian historian Mario Mirri, "Per una ricerca sui rapporti fra 'economisti' e riformatori toscani: L'abate Niccoli a Parigi," *Annali dell'Istituto Giangiacomo Feltrinelli*, 2 (1959): 55–115. On the international dimension of Physiocracy, cf. Bernard Delmas, Thierry Demals and Philippe Steiner, eds, *La diffusion internationale de la physiocratie, XVIIIe–XIXe* (Grenoble: Presses Universitaires de Grenoble, 1995).

[11]   Cf. John Robertson, *The Case for the Enlightenment: Scotland and Naples, 1680–1760* (Cambridge: Cambridge University Press, 2005); Istvan Hont, *Jealousy of Trade, International Competition and the Nation-State in Historical Perspective* (Cambridge MA: Belknap Press of Harvard University Press, 2005).

economic thought – in contrast to the British approach, which had more to do with wealth creation – was a factor that enabled a radical reconsideration by the ideologists of American agrarian democracy, providing them with arms for their political struggle and helping them to define their national identity.

Asking to what extent French economic culture contributed to the development of national identity in eighteenth-century America involves addressing many questions at the heart of contemporary historiographic debate: the connection between politics and economics, the idea of republic, the foundations of representation, the role of Europe in the Atlantic world, and the interaction between national histories and global context.

My intention here is to follow the two-way transatlantic passage of ideas: French economic theory, based on the primacy of agriculture and developed in absolutist France as a model of economic progress, alternative to and competing with the British one, arrived in the United States where it was enriched by American democratic republicanism. It then returned to France where, through the common search for a stable republican system, it made a contribution to French post-Physiocratic thought that was then seeking in political economy a means of consolidating the revolutionary achievements. From this perspective, these pages intend to re-establish France at the heart of transatlantic culture, after the Anglocentric imprint left by the past few decades of research.[12]

As a work of intellectual history, this book also seeks to enrich an Atlantic history that has thus far seen mainly as one of empires and trade,[13] by making the transatlantic circulation of ideas a core theme. The century of cosmopolitanism and enlightenment gave rise to the democratic revolutions of America and France, leaving succeeding centuries with a legacy of original political thought. This did not belong to one country in particular, but was a product of the meeting of several cultures, which can be apprehended only in the interaction between different realities beyond national boundaries. In this sense, the long eighteenth century turns out to be a privileged vantage point from which to respond to the stimulating ideas coming from the contemporary historiography of post-national studies.[14] In particular, the research methodology adopted makes it possible to

---

[12]   A critical reconsideration of the interpretation of the Atlantic world dominated by an Anglocentric perspective even on the level of intellectual history is offered by the essays collected within the volume Manuela Albertone and Antonino De Francesco, eds, *Rethinking the Atlantic World: Europe and America in the Age of Democratic Revolutions* (London: Palgrave Macmillan, 2009).

[13]   Cf. David Armitage and Michael J. Braddick, eds, *The British Atlantic World, 1500–1800* (London: Palgrave Macmillan, 2002); Anthony Pagden, *Lords of All the World: Ideologies of Empire in Spain, Britain and France c.1500–c.1800* (New Haven: Yale University Press, 1995); John H. Elliott, *Empires of the Atlantic World: Britain and Spain in America 1492–1830* (New Haven: Yale University Press, 2006).

[14]   Thomas Bender, *A Nation Among Nations: America's Place in World History* (New York: Hill and Wang, 2006).

reconstruct how American national identity, conceived as an expression of society in economic terms, emerged through a cosmopolitan way of thinking focused on the uniqueness of the new state.[15]

This approach of intellectual history has been adopted in order to highlight the practical needs of men seeking to make changes to the world in which they lived, and to place them in context.[16] In other words, my aim is to take note of the channels through which ideas were transmitted, and the real needs that prompted people to perceive, and to act in accordance with, the connection between agriculture and politics. French economic thought suggested the actions that Americans needed to take and gave those actions theoretical sanction. A similar concern linked President Jefferson and the *Idéologues*, all of whom were working to consolidate their revolutionary accomplishments by using the social dimension of political economy as an instrument for institutionalizing democracy. From the Physiocrats to Jefferson's Republicans it is therefore possible to follow a winding course of thinking on the agrarian class, which was seen as the social fulcrum in the movement towards modernization. These ideas began in France with the overturning of the Old Regime society of orders, and they contributed to the shaping of democracy, first in America and then in France itself. It is hoped that this way of looking at things will enhance the historiography of eighteenth-century revolutions.

Within the expansive discussion initiated nearly 40 years ago by John Pocock's *Machiavellian Moment*, opposition to the 'country ideology' offered by a 'new republicanism' heedful of democratic participation[17] is now an accepted branch of research – to which this book will hopefully provide a further contribution – centred firmly on the link between political economy and republic, particularly in relation to French economic culture.[18] Alongside this established form of investigation,

---

[15]   On the idea of the nation-state, cf. Hont, *Jealousy of Trade*.

[16]   Cf. Jean-Claude Perrot, *Une histoire intellectuelle de l'économie politique (XVIIe– XVIIIe siècle)* (Paris: Editions de l'Ecole des Hautes Etudes en Sciences Sociales, 1992); Donald Winch, *Riches and Poverty: An Intellectual History of Political Economy in Britain, 1750–1834* (Cambridge: Cambridge University Press, 1996).

[17]   John Pocock, *The Machiavellian Moment: Florentine Political Thought and the Atlantic Republican Tradition* (Princeton: Princeton University Press, 1975); cf. Judith Shklar, "Montesquieu and the new Republicanism," in *Machiavelli and Republicanism*, ed. Gisela Bock, Quentin Skinner and Maurizio Viroli (Cambridge: Cambridge University Press, 1990), 265–79.

[18]   Cf. Richard Whatmore, *Republicanism and the French Revolution: An Intellectual History of Jean-Baptiste Say's Political Economy* (Oxford: Oxford University Press, 2000); James Livesey, *Making Democracy in the French Revolution* (Cambridge MA: Harvard University Press, 2001); Paul Cheney, *Revolutionary Commerce: Globalization and the French Monarchy* (Cambridge MA: Harvard University Press, 2010); Jesús Astigarraga, *Luces y Republicanismo: Economía y política en las "Apuntaciones al Genovesi" de Ramón de Salas* (Madrid: Centro de Estudios politicos y constitucionales, 2011); Richard Whatmore, *Against War and Empire: Geneva, Britain and France in the Eighteenth Century* (New Haven: Yale University Press, 2012).

this work will undertake the study of agrarian democratic republicanism, a line of enquiry that has been largely unexplored within the complexity and pluralism of eighteenth-century thought. A modern republicanism, of an economic kind and with its roots set in the political rationalism of the Physiocratic tradition, which is followed in its movements and changes, is here investigated through the encounter of two diverse cultures. During the creation of the American democracy, political economy, as it matured beyond Physiocracy, indicated how the republic was not only the right choice, but the only rational one too: for the ideologists of agrarian democracy the encounter with French economic thought marked a foundational moment for the republic.[19]

Chapter 1 goes to the roots of agrarianism seen as an American characteristic that existed before the creation of the new state and before agrarian democracy was placed at the heart of republican ideology. It focuses on the *Letters from an American Farmer* by the Norman nobleman St John de Crèvecoeur, who had migrated to America before the revolution, and who wrote, in a literary form and with his native sensibility and culture, of his life as an American farmer amid the continent's geographic splendour. This contribution from a Frenchman, made at the time of the emergence of American national identity, is examined through the relationships, social circles and biographical events that made their mark on the imagination of an author strongly influenced by the encounter between his homeland and America.

In the context of eighteenth-century international economy, Chapter 2 outlines the ideal of agrarian ideology, seen as a set of American characteristics, and the nature of the republic–democracy–agriculture correlation, during the advent of an analysis that was at once economic and political. In the clash between Republicans and Federalists, the new social hierarchy founded on the farmer, protagonist in a decentralized system of political participation, was at the heart of the attack on the Whig tradition's principle of deference, through which the Jeffersonians brought the representative republic to its full democratic maturation. In the shift from the Puritan ethic to the lay principle of happiness, enshrined by Jefferson in the Declaration of Independence, the central role of religion in preparing the ground for an economic analysis and a philosophy of agriculture based on the notion of a

---

[19] Key reference points for a modern interpretation of American republicanism are the works by Joyce Appleby and Isaac Kraminick, which however focus more on the individual dimension than the democratic. See Joyce Appleby, *Capitalism and New Social Order: The Republican Vision of the 1790s* (New York: New York University Press, 1984); Isaac Kramnick, "Republican Revisionism Revisited," *The American Historical Review*, 87 (1982): 629–54. With regards to these works, a position searching for balance between the modern individualist interpretation of these authors and the classical republican interpretation is offered by Drew R. McCoy, *The Elusive Republic: Political Economy in Jeffersonian America* (Chapel Hill: University of North Carolina Press, 1980). Cf. Cathy D. Matson and Peter S. Onouf, *A Union of Interests: Political and Economic Thought in Revolutionary America* (Lawrence: University Press of Kansas, 1990).

natural order and a beneficent wealth-creating land came to the fore through the emblematic figure of Pastor Samuel Williams.

Chapter 3 reconstructs, through the progression of ideas, personal contacts and plans of action, the encounter between Jefferson and Physiocracy's political rationalism, which sprang from the economic bedrock of society and the natural and universal character of economic laws. When he arrived in France in 1784 Jefferson had already developed a belief in agrarianism that was intimately associated with his ideas on education, which recognized the pedagogic value of agriculture. His pragmatism made him distance himself from the rigidity of the principles of Physiocratic theory, but its political implications did not escape him, and he remained convinced, albeit modifying his ideas over a long period, of the land's capacity to produce wealth. In France, alongside the *Américanistes*, his sense of belonging to his home nation increased. In the early stage of the French Revolution, while in contact with thinkers influenced by the Physiocratic tradition, Jefferson formulated the principle of constitutional revision, starting from the idea that 'the earth belongs to the living'. And on Jefferson's return to America, this principle became a weapon in his political struggle, and it remained part of the heritage of the eighteenth-century revolutions' democratic ideology of Thomas Paine's *Rights of Man*.

The engagement with Physiocracy of the first American economist, Benjamin Franklin, was pivotal to the to-and-fro of ideas between America and France. Chapter 4 demonstrates how, from his earliest assumption of a mercantilist and populationist position, the land was at the heart of Franklin's economic thought. His meeting with Quesnay and the Marquis of Mirabeau, in the days of Physiocracy's height, was a turning point that marked an accelerated development in his economic thinking, which became anti-British by reason of his rejection of Britain's economic model. The exchange was mutual, since Franklin remained a tireless proponent of the Physiocratic tradition in both France and Britain. For Franklin, who created the myth of the middle class in an agrarian society and later became the symbol of America, by dint of the success in France of *Bonhomme Richard*, the prime importance Physiocracy accorded to consumption in the countryside and the widespread wellbeing of an agrarian economy was attractive. It represented the point of convergence that led to a mutual interchange: a view to be considered in contemporary historical investigations of luxury and consumption in the eighteenth century, which hitherto have centred mainly on urban societies.[20]

The agrarian model as an instrument of open political warfare is considered in Chapter 5, through the reflections and direct action of two ideologists of agrarian democracy, George Logan and John Taylor, respectively the emblematic

---

[20]   Cf. John Brewer and Roy Porter, eds, *Consumption and the World of Goods* (London: Routledge, 1993); Maxine Berg and Helen Clifford, *Consumers and Luxury: Consumer culture in Europe 1650–1850* (Manchester: Manchester University Press, 1999); Maxine Berg, ed., *Luxury and Pleasure in Eighteenth-Century Britain* (New York: Oxford University Press, 2005).

representatives of intellectual circles in the North and South. Logan was an authentic American Physiocrat who used Physiocratic principles in his opposition to Federalist policies (for which he was openly denounced by Hamilton). Quakerism, passion for the French Revolution and economic science fused in him to form a vocation for democracy. For Taylor, who represented the ideals of southern landowners, republic and agriculture were also inseparable and served the political conflict. For him, too, agriculture was not merely a science, but a practical commitment that he discharged as an agronomist and propagator of agrarian knowledge. He read Smith and the Physiocratic authors, discussed Turgot, and learned from Malthus and Say. His original theory of the separation of powers to be applied to guarantee the powers of states was, in its particular American expression, an unprecedented implementation of the economic fundamentals of political rationalism.

The channels through which French economic ideas were spread in America, in an interweaving of science, education and politics, are described in Chapter 6. From outside the ideas and actions of the American agrarian ideologists, this work attempts to identify the various ways in which public opinion was influenced. The free and autonomous agricultural societies, which sought to influence economic policies, were all, despite their dissimilarities, institutionalized forms of public participation based on economics. In different ways Jefferson, Logan and Taylor were active in these societies, handing on their knowledge of economics. As hubs of intellectual sociability, a number of societies and circles, encouraged by the cosmopolitan circulation of ideas, were at the same time centres of discussion about agricultural experiments, political action and the training of farmers. The formation of a popular public opinion in favour of giving agriculture a central position was carried out by almanacs, of which Franklin's *Poor Richard's Almanack* was the standard of comparison. The chapter also looks at the penetration of economic science into American academia, including the creation of the first professorships in political economy in the early nineteenth century and the publication of university handbooks, among which was the 1821 American edition of Say's *Traité d'économie politique*, the first European text annotated for educational use and one of the first such books to be made widely available. The American academic culture, in which Smith, Malthus and Ricardo all feature, continued to display an interest in French economic culture as well, thus taking sides against British classical economics.

Chapter 7 examines the three-way interrelation between France, Britain and America, through which the economic and political rationalism of the Physiocratic school circulated, sometimes by way of indirect channels, and reached America having been enriched by democratic tensions, which made a decisive impact on the development of American economic and political culture. Certain key figures among the British Dissenters were pivotal, and Franklin was a link between French and British circles. Condorcet and Turgot were important focal points in the radicalization of the political implications of French economic thought, which later spread to Britain, and the hopes of 1789 France and the myth of America were shared by different groups within British radicalism. The roundabout routes by which ideas flowed between France and Britain resulted in the remodelling of personal and intellectual relationships in which religion, economics and politics fed radical transatlantic thought. Jefferson derived great benefit from his correspondence with Paine, Priestley, Price and Cooper, and during his successful presidential campaign received strong support from British radicals who migrated to the United States in the 1790s.

Finally, in Chapter 8 the link between economics and politics, the overall characteristic of the reciprocal exchange of ideas between France and America, is traced through the long eighteenth century to beyond the dawn of the nineteenth. The contacts between Jefferson and the elderly Du Pont, who chose America as a land of freedom, Destutt de Tracy, Say and the *Idéologues*, and the strategy of orchestrated publication of translations organized by Jefferson in order to acquaint America with post-Physiocratic French theories that were opposed to Ricardo, were all important factors in the sharing of democratic and republican ideas between France and America which was driven by a belief in the social and political value of economic science.

Chapter 1

What is an American?
St John de Crèvecoeur Between
Agrarian Myth and National Identity

The Origins of Agrarian Ideology

When describing his life as a farmer to an English guest in his home, James, the protagonist of *Letters from an American Farmer*, asked himself and the European: 'Where is that station which can confer a more substantial system of felicity than that of an American farmer, possessing freedom of action, freedom of thoughts, ruled by a mode of government which requires but little from us?'[1] With this language and imagery, St John de Crèvecoeur – who introduced himself to Abbé Raynal (to whom he dedicated his book) as a 'simple tiller of the soil' – marked the beginning of American literature and national consciousness.[2] Written in eighteenth-century epistolary style, the twelve letters that made up the book were presented as an American farmer's replies, couched as essays, to questions posed by an imaginary cultured English visitor keen to know more about life in

---

[1]   John Hector St John de Crèvecoeur, *Letters from an American Farmer*, ed. S. Manning (Oxford: Oxford University Press, 1997), 25. From hereon references will always be made to this modern edition, which is of the second English edition (*Letters from an American Farmer: describing certain provincial situations, manners, and customs, not generally known; and conveying some idea of the late and present interior circumstances of the British Colonies in North America. Written for the information of a friend in England, by J. Hector St. John, a farmer in Pennsylvania* (London: T. Davies, L. Davies, 1782)).

[2]   In 1759, at the age of 24 and having enrolled in the French army in Canada, where he worked as a cartographer, Crèvecoeur moved to the colony of New York, where he specialized as a surveyor. In 1765 he was naturalized as a British colonial subject and changed his name to John Hector Saint John. In 1769 he married the daughter of a loyalist New York family, and settled in a property at Pine Hill, in Orange County, New York, becoming an owner-farmer. In the following decade he began work on the *Letters*, until the Revolution broke out. Suspected of loyalist sympathies, he decided to return to France. Between 1779 and 1780 he was imprisoned under the charge of espionage by the British, his house was destroyed and his wife killed. In 1781 he was the guest of the brother of Turgot, a friend of the family and an expert in agronomic issues. Under the recommendation of Mme d'Houdetot, who introduced him into French intellectual circles and to Franklin, he was appointed French consul to New York, serving between 1783 and 1792. Having returned to France, he lived on the margins of the Revolution and died in 1813.

the colonies. The *Letters* appeared in London during the final year of the conflict that led to the birth of the United States. The intention of the British publishers, Thomas Davies and Lockyer Davis – who in 1781 had published an extract from Book XVIII of Raynal's *Histoire des deux Indes* entitled *Révolution de l'Amérique* – was to serve the Whig cause of promoting reconciliation between the colonies and the mother country.[3] To that end, it was decided to publish only the letters that depicted American life in a favourable light, leaving out the more critical ones included in the material that Crèvecoeur had brought with him when he left America to return to France, a part of which he had sold to publishers in London.[4]

The work enjoyed immediate success, far beyond the publishers' hopes.[5] The *Monthly Review* recognized in it the philosophical spirit of the age, while the *Journal de Normandie* and the *Journal de Paris* praised it for the passion it inspired for a fertile and free land like America. The *Courier de l'Europe* declared that the *Letters*, alongside Raynal's *Histoire*, might play a role in the abolition of slavery, which the emancipated colonies would enforce.[6] Although suspected

---

[3]   On the discussion regarding Crèvecoeur's role in the final decision on the work's structure see David Robinson, 'Crèvecoeur's James: the Education of an American Farmer', *Journal of English and Germanic Philology*, 80/4 (1981): 552–70.

[4]   A large part of the manuscripts, which reveal hostility towards the Revolution, was discovered in France and published in 1925 with the title, *Sketches of Eighteenth Century America*, ed. Henri L. Bourdin, Ralph H. Gabriel and Stanley T. Williams (New Haven: Yale University Press, 1925). However, it is only recently that the critical edition of the 22 manuscripts not included in the *Letters* has appeared, having been purchased by the Library of Congress in 1986: John Hector St John de Crèvecoeur, *More Letters from an American Farmer: An Edition of the Essays in English Left Unpublished by Crèvecoeur*, ed. Denis D. Moore (Athens: The University of Georgia Press, 1995).

[5]   The work was also published in Ireland in the same year (Dublin: J. Exshaw, 1782) and by 1784 there were already four English-language editions in circulation (Belfast: J. Magee, 1783) and (London: T. Davies, 1783). The American edition was not published until 1793, by Mathew Carey in Philadelphia. Crèvecoeur himself undertook the translation into French (*Lettres d'un cultivateur américain, écrites à W S. Ecuyer, depuis l'année 1770, jusqu'à 1781. Traduites de l'Anglois par ****, 2 vols. (Paris: Cuchet, 1784), which was in fact an enlarged version dedicated to Lafayette, in which he openly sided with the American cause, inserting new anti-British letters. Another three-volume edition was published in 1787 (*Lettres d'un cultivateur américain addressées à Wm S...on Esqr. Depuis l'Année 1770 jusqu'en 1786, traduites de l'Anglois*, 3 vols. (Paris: Cuchet, 1787), with material left out of the English edition but made up of sixteen letters, four more than the original, enriched by his experiences as consul. The French edition, which clearly shows the influence of *philosophes* circles, is less compact and lacks the literary incisiveness of the more agile English text. This analysis will therefore refer mainly to the English edition, in which the Crèvecoeur's original ideas can be found, as this was received by American culture.

[6]   Cf. *Monthly Review* (June, August, October 1782) LXVI, 401–405, LXVII, 140–46, 273–77; *Journal de Normandie* (11 August 1787), reproduced in Bernard Chevignard, 'St. John de Crèvecoeur à New York en 1779–1780', *Annales de Normandie*, 33/2 (1983): 162; *Courier de l'Europe, Gazette anglo-française*, XIII, no. 31 (Friday 18 April 1783):

of being loyal to the British, Crèvecoeur was nonetheless castigated for harming British interests, as the *Letters* encouraged emigration at a difficult time for Britain; such was the reaction of Samuel Ayscough, who in his *Remarks* also observed that the author's writing style confuted the French philosopher's attempts to portray himself as an American farmer.[7] Extracts from the *Letters* were in fact used as advertisements to boost emigration with the lure of great opportunities.[8] However, Filippo Mazzei, like Ayscough, reckoned the idyllic pen portraits of American life to be exaggerated and unreliable, while Brissot, who pointed out the ambiguity of Crèvecoeur's neutral position at the start of the Revolution, nonetheless did not hesitate to emphasize the value of the *Letters*, defending them against attacks from Chastellux, who was critical of the Quaker communities being outlined as a social model in the description of the island of Nantucket.[9]

Crèvecoeur's work reconciled Romantic tastes with rational Enlightenment rigour by means of Rousseauian percipience in which the human being, free

---

245–47; *Journal de Paris*, no. 38 (Monday 7 February 1785), 158, and no. 41 (Thursday 10 February 1785), 172.

[7]   Samuel Ayscough, *Remarks on the Letters from an American Farmer; or a detection of the errors of Mr. J. Hector St. John; Pointing out the pernicious Tendency of these Letters to Great Britain* (London: John Fielding, 1783): 8–10. Defending himself from Ayscough's accusations, Crèvecoeur publicly upheld his dual nationality in the *Courier de l'Europe*, declaring possession of more original copies of his work than were in the hands of the British editors. This would seem to confirm his active role in the editorial selection (*Courier de l'Europe*, *Gazette anglo-française*, vol. XIII, no. 9, 37 (9 May 1783), 296).

[8]   Cf. Manasseh Cutler, *Description du sol, des productions etc. de cette portion des Etats-Unis située entre la Pennsylvanie, les rivières de l'Ohio et du Scioto et le lac Erié, traduite d'une brochure imprimée à Salem en Amérique en 1787* (Paris, 1789): 22–29. Crèvecoeur himself, in a letter to the Duke of La Rochefoucauld, written during Crèvecoeur's mission to New York, spoke of the opportunities opened by the Ohio Company, referring to the third volume of the French edition of the *Lettres d'un cultivateur américain*: 'The beginnings of this new Establishment seemed to me so interesting that I've collected all the pieces and all the anecdotes, so that one day we can see how the development of the weakest circumstances, in a country such as this, is rapid and surprising' (letter by Crèvecoeur to La Rochefoucauld, New York, 10 December 1787, Archives Municipales de Mantes-la-Jolie, Fonds Clerc de Landresse, Correspondance entre J. Hector de Crévecoeur et le duc de La Rochefoucauld).

[9]   Cf. Filippo Mazzei, *Recherches historiques et politiques sur les Etats-Unis de l'Amérique septentrionale*, 4 vols. (Colle-Paris: Froullé, 1788): IV, 99–101; Jacques-Pierre Brissot, *Mémoires (1754–1793)*, ed. Claude Perroud, 2 vols., (Paris: Picard, [1910]): II, 48–52; Jacques-Pierre Brissot, *Examen critique des voyages dans l'Amérique septentrionale de M. le marquis de Chastellux* (London, 1786): 16–20, and also the article in *L'Analyse des papiers anglois*, vol. 2, 11 April 1788, 368. Cf. Bernard Chevignard, 'Une Apocalypse sécularisée: Le Quakerisme selon Brissot de Warville et St. John de Crèvecoeur', in *Le Facteur religieux en Amérique du Nord: Apocalypse et autres travaux*, ed. Jean Béranger (Bordeaux: Maison des Sciences de l'Homme d'Aquitaine, 1981): 49–68; Robert Darnton, *George Washington's False Teeth* (New York: W.W. Norton, 2003): 119–36.

and unconstrained, found fertile soil on the American continent. The ideal of an agrarian society of independent freehold farmers, set out by this provincial French nobleman (who belonged to a family related to Mme d'Houdetot), became the first test of the ideas of the *philosophes* carried out *in loco* by an American (albeit one educated in Europe) and was the expression of a 'practised utopia'.[10] Considered by Washington to be the standard work to refer to for an understanding of the American situation and by Jefferson to be a learned presentation of the best aspects of New World society, the *Letters* confirmed the validity of the American model as an alternative to European realities: 'and all the benefits attached to the land, to the constitution and customs of the thirteen United Provinces ... all the happiness that a man can procure through an agreeable independence, hard work, the dedication of a beloved family, the enjoyment of a secure and lawful property'.[11]

This was how the *Correspondance littéraire* reviewed the 1784 French translation, demonstrating the interest in America, among the French, as a political, economic and social ideal, which, starting from the clash between the colonies and the mother country, took the shape of a programme of change inspired by the American experience of democracy rather than the British model. Crèvecoeur's *Letters* also presented colonial society as a unique experience – the antithesis of European privileges and hierarchies – and, even before the colonies split from Britain, linked the image of the farmer as independent landowner to the idea of democracy.[12] As a French-born naturalized American, Crèvecoeur transposed his own experiences as a colonial farmer into the main character of his book. Far from

---

[10]   Cf. Bernard Chevignard, 'Les souvenirs de Saint John de Crèvecoeur sur Madame d'Houdetot', *Dix-huitième siècle*, 14 (1982): 243–62; Bronisław Baczko, *Lumières de l'utopie* (Paris: Payot, 1978).

[11]   *Correspondance littéraire, philosophique et critique par Grimm, Diderot, Raynal, Meister, etc.*, ed. Maurice Tourneux, 15 vols. (Paris: Garnier, 1880), vol. XIV (January 1785), 88. Cf. Washington to Richard Henderson, 19 June 1788, in George Washington, *Writings*, ed. John Rhodehamel (New York: Literary Classics of the United States, 1997): 688; Jefferson to La Vingtrie, 12 February 1788, in Thomas Jefferson, *The Papers*, ed. Julian P. Boyd (Princeton: Princeton University Press, 1950–): vol. XII, 586.

[12]   From the 1960s there has been a revisionist reading of the *Letters*, since the consolidation of the interpretation that sees them as a symbol of the American dream and the optimism of the agrarian myth. Cf. D.H. Lawrence, *Studies in Classic American Literature* (New York: Doubleday, 1923): 20–33. Revisionist perspectives have reviewed the work pessimistically, as an expression of the first criticisms of the contradictions in American society. Among the many studies, cf. Elayne A. Rapping, 'Theory and Experience in Crèvecoeur's America', *American Quarterly*, 19/4 (1967): 707–18; James C. Mohr, 'Calculated Disillusionment: Crèvecoeur's Letters Reconsidered', *South Atlantic Quarterly*, 69 (Summer, 1970): 354–63; Thomas Philbrick, *St. John de Crèvecoeur* (New York: Twayne Publishers, 1970); Steven Arch, 'The Progressive Steps of the Narrator in Crèvecoeur's Letters from an American Farmer', *Studies in American Fiction*, 18 (1990): 145–58; Nathaniel Philbrick, 'The Nantucket Sequence in Crèvecoeur's *Letters from an American Farmer*', *New England Quarterly*, 64 (1991): 414–32.

nursing anti-British sentiments, he was not – as a Frenchman possessing a strong American national awareness even before the Revolution – an opponent of the British, but simply different from them.[13]

The idea of an agrarian democracy that solidified American identity took shape between the late eighteenth century and the early nineteenth as an alternative to the hierarchical societies of the old continent. From the Revolution onwards the economic debate was closely linked to politics, and revolutionary thinkers saw the need to reconcile the economy with Republican principles: Jefferson's ideology rested on an economic interpretation of politics in which the notion of political economy reinforced the Republican concept of the interconnectedness of politics, economics and society. As opportunities arose through the creation of the new State, so the clash between Republicans and Federalists in the 1780s and 1790s led the Jeffersonians to outline a politico-economic vision centred on the farmer as a politically active and economically dynamic producer working in the setting of commercial agriculture, and an extended decentralized participatory democracy aimed at defending the rights of the Confederation's thirteen member states. The Federalists counter-proposed a hierarchy with democratic origins, founded on a strong central power that would promote a development programme based on trade and financial interests; this followed the British system and was considered by the Republicans to be incompatible with personal freedom and the traditional autonomy of the individual American states. As the battle against protectionism was waged in the name of economic freedom – which meant battling against privilege and the merchant aristocracy – a social hierarchy based on the farmer appeared to be anti-British.[14]

Written before the birth of the new state, the *Letters from an American Farmer* helps us to understand how Jeffersonian values became American characteristics. It shows the origins of the agrarian myth to be a peculiarly American phenomenon that existed before independence and before Republican ideology posed agrarian democracy at its base, making the projects of agricultural development and democratic participation inseparable one from another – an occurrence that

---

[13] In 1787 Crèvecoeur, with Brissot, Clavière and Bergasse, founded the *Société Gallo-Américaine*, which aimed at intensifying political and commercial relations between the two countries and symbolized the role of France in countering British commercial power.

[14] Cf. Lance Banning, *The Jeffersonian Persuasion: Evolution of a Party Ideology* (Ithaca: Cornell University Press, 1978); Drew R. McCoy, *The Elusive Republic: Political Economy in Jeffersonian America* (Chapel Hill: University of North Carolina Press, 1980); Cathy D. Matson and Peter S. Onouf, *A Union of Interests: Political and Economic Thought in Revolutionary America* (Lawrence: University Press of Kansas, 1990). The works of Joyce Appleby, which demonstrate a rare attention on the contribution of French economic-political culture, is fundamental. See Joyce Appleby, 'What is Still American in the Political Philosophy of Thomas Jefferson?', *The William and Mary Quarterly*, 39 (April 1982): 287–309; Joyce Appleby, *Capitalism and a New Social Order: The Republican Vision of the 1790s* (New York: New York University Press, 1984); Joyce Appleby, *Liberalism and Republicanism in the Historical Imagination* (Cambridge, MA: Harvard University Press, 1992).

Crèvecoeur detailed in his novel, in spite of his British loyalism. Crèvecoeur was the first to express in literature a fundamental American attribute: the ability to question one's own identity. He did this as an American who, with Rousseauian sensibility and introspection, asked himself the questions that Europeans asked about America, in the knowledge of the differences and peculiarities that divided the old and new worlds.[15]

In the third and most famous of the *Letters*, 'What is an American?' Crèvecoeur defined in economic terms the change that had produced the American national identity, giving rise to a new social hierarchy based on land: 'On it is founded our rank, our freedom, our power as citizens, our importance as inhabitants of such a district ... this is what may be called the true and the only philosophy of an American farmer'.[16] Thus, from the figure of the farmer there emerged a new social stratification, in the name of which were repudiated the principles of dignity and hierarchy, based on tradition and custom, linked to the notion of deference and characteristic of European societies.[17] The social model represented by smallholders in the American interior, midway between the sea and the forests defined a new class, unknown in Europe:

> The simple cultivation of the earth purifies them; but the indulgences of the government, the soft remonstrances of religion, the rank of independent freeholders, must necessarily inspire them with sentiments very little known in Europe among a people of the same class. What do I say? Europe has no such a class of men.[18]

The idea that the earth guaranteed personal independence was therefore at the root of a new social hierarchy founded on agrarianism, justifying the exercise of rights of citizenship and the belief that agriculture was the most dignified activity, and capable of ensuring national prosperity.[19]

---

[15]   On the decentralized perspective of American thought in relation to European debates, and on provincialism as a creative and critical value in the founding fathers' thought, cf. Bernard Bailyn, *To Begin the World Anew: The Genius and Ambiguities of the American Founders* (New York: Alfred A. Knopf, 2003).

[16]   Crèvecoeur, *Letters from an American Farmer*, 27.

[17]   Cf. my essay, Manuela Albertone, 'Gerarchia sociale, repubblica e democrazia: la figura del 'farmer' nell'America del XVIII secolo', in *Il pensiero gerarchico in Europa XVIII–XIX secolo*, ed. Antonella Alimento and Cristina Cassina (Florence: Olschki, 2002): 83–109.

[18]   Crèvecoeur, *Letters from an American Farmer*, 45–6.

[19]   Crèvecoeur, *Letters from an American Farmer*, 43, 54.

Between Economics and Botany

In the first part of the *Letters* we read that, 'It is from the surface of the ground, which we till, that we have gathered the wealth we possess'.[20] Years later, in his *Voyage dans la Haute Pensylvanie* of 1801, Crèvecoeur restated his belief that manufacturing was dependent on agriculture and declared himself in favour of a land tax. A vague concept of expectations was also discernible in his hope that Americans would follow Europe's example of improving agriculture, set on the immense base of nature, for only then 'are the products of the earth sufficient to pay for these improvements'.[21]

Vernon Parrington, who has placed Crèvecoeur among the founders of American literature, defined his thought as Physiocratic, supported by warm humanism and convinced agrarianism.[22] Crèvecoeur dedicated his work to Raynal, and he had read at least the first two editions of the *Histoire des deux Indes* and probably even the third,[23] and had thereby assimilated a synthesis of European,

_____

[20]   Crèvecoeur, *Letters from an American Farmer*, 16. Crèvecoeur continued to express his conviction that agriculture would remain the underlying activity of the American economy for several generations to come, a concept later taken up by Jefferson in the *Notes on the State of Virginia*, ed. William Peden (New York: W.W. Norton, 1954): 165.

[21]   John Hector St John de Crèvecoeur, *Voyage dans la Haute Pensylvanie et dans l'état de New York, par un membre adoptif de la Nation Onéida: Traduit et publié par l'auteur des Lettres d'un Cultivateur Américain*, 3 vols. (Paris: Crapelet, Maradan, an IX-1801), II, 332, 351–52. The work came out of the original plan to add an extra volume to the 1787 French edition of the *Letters from an American Farmer* and was dedicated to Washington, who was likened to Napoleon. Cf. Percy G. Adams, 'The historical value of Crèvecoeur's "Voyage dans la Haute Pensylvanie et dans New York",' *American Literature*, 25/2 (May 1953): 155–68; John Hector St John de Crèvecoeur, *Lettres d'un cultivateur américain, écrites à W.S. Ecuyer, depuis 1770, jusqu'à 1781*, II, 278.

[22]   Vernon L. Parrington, *Main Currents in American Thought: An Interpretation of American Literature from the Beginnings to 1920*, 3 vols. (New York: Harcourt, Brace and Co., 1927–1930): I, 142.

[23]   Dating the *Letters* with precision is a controversial affair. Howard C. Rice maintains that *Letters* two to eleven were written between 1770 and 1774 (Howard C. Rice, *Le Cultivateur Américain: Etude sur l'oeuvre de Saint-John de Crèvecoeur* (Paris: Champion, 1932): 54–7, 229–30). Robert de Crèvecoeur (*Saint John de Crèvecoeur, sa vie et ses ouvrages 1735–1813* (Paris: Librairie des Bibliophiles, 1883): 297) put the first version between 1780 and 1781. More recently Bernard Chevignard has advanced the theory that the text may have been written between 1779 and 1780. (See Bernard Chevignard, 'St. John de Crèvecoeur in the looking Glass: "Letters from an American Farmer" and the Making of a man of Letters', *Early American Literature*, 19/2 (Fall 1984): 173–90.) In any case, in 1781 Crèvecoeur was already fully installed in French *philosophes* circles and, furthermore, was in contact with the editor Davis (who in that year published the *Révolution de l'Amérique*); therefore by this time he was almost certainly acquainted with the third edition of Raynal's *Histoire philosophique*. A letter to Jefferson written on 18 May 1785

particularly French, Enlightenment culture.[24] The valorization of agriculture bound to the image of America as a land of freedom that emerges from the *Histoire*, for Crèvecoeur bore witness to the great favour that the picture of rural community life in America enjoyed in France, in the framework of a conviction that agriculture was the real wealth of the state and that every resource not coming from the earth was inescapably artificial and unstable, both materially and morally.[25] The *Histoire*'s extolment of smallholdings, which Crèvecoeur made a social nonpareil, was the expression of widespread agrarianism. At the same time, it revived ideas from the Marquis de Mirabeau's *L'Ami des Hommes*, a complex and not always consistent work, through which Physiocratic themes were filtered, even through those reflections that lacked the rigour of the French *Économistes*.[26]

The idea that agriculture was a science was nevertheless present in Crèvecoeur:

> I intend my children neither for the law nor the church, but for the cultivation of land, I wish them no literary accomplishments; I pray heaven that they may be one day nothing more than expert scholars in husbandry: this is the science which made our continent to flourish more rapidly than any other.[27]

As a science, agriculture followed the laws of nature that, over and above the pervasive Rousseauian sensibility of the *Letters*, signified an order, the rules of which found expression in the American agricultural landscape, delineated by the rationality of cultivation: 'Every disposition of the fields, fences, and trees,

---

also supports the theory that he began the text after his arrival in Europe (Jefferson, *The Papers*, VIII, 155).

[24]   Cf. David Eisermann, 'La "Raynalisation" de l'"American Farmer": la réception de l'"Histoire des deux Indes" par Crèvecoeur', in *Lectures de Raynal: L'Histoire des deux Indes en Europe et en Amérique au XVIIIe siècle: Actes du Colloque de Wolfenbüttel*, ed. Hans J. Lüsebrink and Manfred Tietz, Studies on Voltaire and the Eighteenth-Century, no. 286 (Oxford: Voltaire Foundation, 1991): 329–39.

[25]   Guillaume-Thomas-François Raynal, *Histoire philosophique et politique des établissemens et du commerce des Européens dans les deux Indes*, 4 vols. (Geneva: J. Pellet, 1780), IV, book XIX, 611. Cf. Michèle Duchet, *Diderot et l'Histoire des deux Indes, ou l'écriture fragmentaire* (Paris: Nizet, 1978); Paul Benhamou, 'La diffusion de *l'Histoire des deux Indes* en Amérique (1770–1820)', in *Raynal: De la polémique à l'histoire*. ed. Gilles Bancarel and Gianluigi Goggi (Oxford: Voltaire Foundation, 2000): 301–12.

[26]   Marquis de Mirabeau, *L'Ami des Hommes, ou Traité de la population*, 6 vols. (Hambourg: Chrétien Hérold, 1760–62): I, 80–81. On the influence of Mirabeau's *L'Ami des Hommes* on the *Histoire des deux Indes*, in particular the first three parts praising small properties and preceding his adhesion to physiocracy, cf. Gianluigi Goggi, 'Filangieri e "L'Ami des hommes" di Mirabeau', *Italianistica: Rivista di letteratura italiana*, 10/2 (May–August 1981), 188–214.

[27]   Crèvecoeur, *Letters from an American Farmer*, 214.

seemed to bear the marks of perfect order and regularity, which, in rural affairs, always indicate a prosperous industry'.[28]

The subject of the eleventh letter – an imaginary visit by a Russian nobleman to the celebrated Pennsylvanian botanist John Bertram – is examined through the lens of natural history; seen in this way, nature, the laws of which can be interpreted and applied universally, implied the order of systematic botany. The attention paid to the natural landscape was moreover aimed at preserving the harmony created by the adaptation of men and plants to America's environmental conditions. Crèvecoeur also meant to use this argument to refute the degeneration theories on which European opinions about a natural American inferiority rested. These views found expression even in Raynal, despite his *Histoire* associating them with the evils of colonialism.[29]

'Men are like plants. The goodness and flavour of the fruit proceeds from the peculiar soil and exposition in which they grow. We are nothing but what we derive from the air we breathe, the climate we inhabit'. More than echoes of Montesquieu, these thoughts about nature and its laws had an economic determinism that was the basis of Crèvecoeur's optimism; they expressed not so much a bucolic idyll as an awareness that only respect for economic conditions would generate prosperity, which was destined to turn into misery should they fail.[30]

Knowledge of botany and natural history was an essential requirement of the educated farmer, represented by the protagonist, James, who boasted, notwithstanding his simulated simplicity of mind and dismissal of academic culture, of his grasp and mastery of American farming techniques.[31] Attentiveness to the natural history in the *Letters* is indispensable to an understanding of the fundamentals of American agrarianism.

In the fourth and fifth letters, in which the organizational model of the island of Nantucket is outlined, Quaker society is described in terms of natural history, as characterized by the topography of land, its produce and its customs, placed outside of time and history: 'I want not to record the annals of the island of Nantucket; its inhabitants have no annals, for they are not a race of warriors'.[32] The perception

---

[28]   Crèvecoeur, *Letters from an American Farmer*, 174.

[29]   Crèvecoeur, *Letters from an American Farmer*, 42–3.

[30]   Crèvecoeur, *Letters from an American Farmer*, 45. This is one of the keys to interpreting the tension between the positive outlook of the early letters and the pessimism of the last, in which the protagonist is overwhelmed by the events of the Revolution (cf. Robinson, 'Crèvecoeur's James').

[31]   Cf. the whole of the first letter, in which the protagonist introduces himself to the English traveller as a simple farmer, guided by nature, 'this is the only line I am able to follow: the line which nature has herself traced for me'. (Crèvecoeur, *Letters from an American Farmer*, 11–23).

[32]   Crèvecoeur, *Letters from an American Farmer*, 85. Cf. Pamela Regis, *Describing Early America: Batram, Jefferson, Crèvecoeur and the Rhetoric of Natural History* (Dekalb: Northern Illinois University Press, 1992).

of the American that Crèvecoeur sought to convey was deliberately timeless and distinguished by an attachment to the land. This was in line with an agrarianism outside of politics, which predated Jefferson's position and Republican ideology while being close to both because, like them, it did not adopt an historic approach.[33] Similarly, the account of how James fled land and home to take refuge among tribes of American Indians when confronted by the violence of the Revolution served to illustrate the desire to lay the foundations of the community in original nature, outside of the historical context.

Precedents for this focus on natural history were to be found in American travel literature, which gave detailed reports aimed at providing its primarily British readership with descriptions and information of colonial territories and their populations.[34] But Crèvecoeur used natural history in a novel way, as an alternative perspective to traditional values, pitting America's unique geography and agricultural reality against the veneration of the Ancients and the classics:

> In Italy, all the objects of contemplation, all the reveries of the traveller, must have a reference to ancient generations, and to very distant periods, clouded with the mist of ages. Here, on the contrary, every thing is modern, peaceful, and benign. Here we have had no war to desolate our fields. Our religion does not oppress the cultivators. We are strangers to those feudal institutions which have enslaved so many. Here nature opens her broad lap to receive the perpetual accession of new comers, and to supply with food. I am sure I cannot be called a partial American when I say, that the spectacle, afforded by these pleasing scenes, must be more entertaining, and more philosophical, than that which arises from beholding the musty ruins of Rome.[35]

---

[33]   'Let historians give the detail of our charters, the succession of our several governors, and of their administrations; of our political struggles, and of the foundation of our towns: let annalists amuse themselves with collecting anecdotes of the establishment of our modern provinces.' (Crèvecoeur, *Letters from an American Farmer*, 66). Cf. Jefferson to John Cartwright, Monticello, 5 June 1824, in Thomas Jefferson, *The Writings*, ed. Andrew A. Lipscomb and Albert Ellery Bergh, 20 vols. (Washington: T. Jefferson Memorial Association, 1903): XVI, 44.

[34]   Robert Rogers, *A Concise Account of North America* (London: J. Millan, 1765); William Smith, *An historical account of the expedition against the Ohio Indians, in the year 1764* (Philadelphia: W. Bradford, 1765); William Stork, *An Account of East Florida, with A journal kept by John Batram of Philadelphia, botanist to His Majesty the Floridas* (London: W. Nicoll and G. Woodfall, 1766); James Adair, *The History of American Indians* (London: E. and C. Dilley, 1775); Jonathan Carver, *Travels through the Interior Parts of North America in the years 1766, 1767, and 1768* (London: J. Walter, 1778).

[35]   Crèvecoeur, *Letters from an American Farmer*, 14–15.

Crèvecoeur's American agrarianism presented itself as modern and alien to the worship of the Ancients.[36] The ideal of economic self-sufficiency, which in Europe concerned only a few, in America assumed democratic importance and was fuelled by a Lockian conception of freedom, tied to the land and outside of history.[37] Far from being imbued with Arcadian values, the agrarianism of the *Letters* represented a modern agricultural system that not only involved the moral regeneration of the farmer, but also economic progress.[38] The landscape so admired by foreign visitors evinced a nature transformed, revealing 'the best husbandry as well as the most assiduous attention', and the presence of farmers well versed in agricultural techniques and committed to increasing land productivity by means that were more agronomic than Physiocratic. The rural landscape was not marked by large holdings, but rather by the highly similar situations of the landowners who held only as much acreage as they were able to cultivate on their own, keeping the remainder as common land, in keeping with Lockian principles.[39] Thus the description of the first Nantucket community offered a template for community agriculture, which stimulated competition between individual farmers.[40]

Economic Thought and Agricultural Experimentation

Not only did Crèvecoeur conduct agricultural experiments on his American estate, but he also made significant contributions to both American and French agronomic

---

[36]   By so doing Crèvecoeur placed himself outside the tradition that tied the pre-eminence of landowners to the classical model. On the protracted debate on classical Republicanism as a category of historic interpretation, a contribution has been made by John Pocock's postscript in the new edition of his *The Machiavellian Moment: Florentine Political Thought and the Atlantic Republican Tradition* (Princeton, Oxford: Princeton University Press, 2003).

[37]   'In the beginning all the World was America' (John Locke, *Two Treatises of Government*, ed. Peter Laslett (Cambridge: Cambridge University Press, 1960), *Second Treatise*, book II, ch. V, 319).

[38]   Cf. Leo Marx, *The Machine in the Garden: Technology and the Pastoral Ideal in America* (New York: Oxford University Press, 1964).

[39]   Crèvecoeur, *Letters from an American Farmer*, 41, 113, 178–9. The same Lockian principle that land was originally man's common patrimony and that property was limited by the needs of the individual was developed by Franklin as a means to re-establish social hierarchies in a letter of 1783 (Franklin to Robert Morris, Passy, 25 December 1783, in Benjamin Franklin, *The Writings*, ed. Albert H. Smyth, 10 vols. (New York, London: Macmillan, 1905–1907): IX, 138; cf. John Locke, *Second Treatise*, book II, ch. V, par. 25. For Crèvecoeur the Lockian principle was at the foundation of the landowner's independence: 'I have never possessed or wish to possess anything more than what could be earned or produced by the united industry of my family. I wanted nothing more than to live at home independent and tranquil'. (Crèvecoeur, *Letters from an American Farmer*, 212).

[40]   Crèvecoeur, *Letters from an American Farmer*, 94–5.

literature. In his treatise on the potato,[41] Antoine-Augustin Parmentier, an authority in the propagation of new agronomic interests in France, commended Crèvecoeur for having imported two new species of potato from New York and for having described how Americans cultivated it. In fact, it was by publishing a treatise on potatoes in the same year as the *Letters*, that Crèvecoeur sought to rebuild his image in society as a French intellectual, promoting the cultivation of the potato in his native Normandy and disseminating information about American methods.[42]

Written with the encouragement of the brother of Turgot, the *Traité de la culture des pommes-de-terre* was published anonymously in Caen with a dedication to the Duke of Harcourt (like Turgot, a pioneer in the testing of new crops), dated 1st January 1782 and signed *Normano-Americanus*.[43] Crèvecoeur capitalized on his experience as a 'a Norman who spent thirty years among the people of America', to write what was essentially an agricultural manual. It gave a comprehensive description of different potato varieties, methods of cultivation, tools and various culinary uses of the plant, along with recipes. However, the book's objective was not exclusively agronomic, but touched on wider issues of political economy. Its standard of comparison was Britain, where the potato had been introduced for the feeding of the population and the rearing of livestock, proving to be invaluable as a dependable means of preventing famines and of increasing cereal exports by reducing their domestic consumption.[44] It pointed to Ireland as perhaps the best case in point. In Normandy the free trade in cereals had led to an increase in land values: 'this freedom has become a source of national prosperity, has made metals more common and increased manufacturing, etc.'.[45] The introduction of the potato in place of buckwheat, which was prevalent in Norman agriculture, further stimulated rising production. The trust placed in free corn trade and in the upturn

---

[41]   Antoine-Augustin Parmentier, *Traité de la culture et les usages des pommes de terre, de la patate et du tapinambour* (Paris: Barrois, 1789), 42, 73, 109–10, 121, 237, 314.

[42]   'Just as a bee, after traveling the distant fields, never comes into the hive without bringing back the portion of honey and wax that the republic demands of him; so any good citizen who travels must return a tribute of enlightened ideas, observations and acquaintances, commensurate with his intelligence' (John Hector St John de Crèvecoeur, *Traité de la culture des pommes-de-terre, Et des différens usages qu'en font les Habitans des Etats-Unis de l'Amérique* (Caen, 1782), 5–6).

[43]   The work, which was 74 octavo pages long, soon became difficult to find. To the best of my knowledge, only two copies conserved at the Bibliothèque Municipale de Caen are available to researchers. Two handwritten letters from Crèvecoeur to the Marshal of Castries confirm the authorship of the work (New York, 1 February 1785: Archives Nationales, Affaires Etrangères, B¹ 909, 25v.), along with another to La Rochefoucauld (New York: 17 February 1787, Archives Municipales de Mantes-la-Jolie) in which he refers to his pamphlet on the potato.

[44]   Crèvecoeur, *Traité de la culture des pommes-de-terre*, 10–11, 20. Crèvecoeur had authoritative support for his praise of the British agrarian model in the figure of Raynal (Raynal, *Histoire philosophique*, IV, book XIX, 606).

[45]   Crèvecoeur, *Traité de la culture des pommes-de-terre*, 23.

of the economy was reinforced by Enlightenment faith, nurtured by an eighteenth-century philanthropic sentiment: 'What good have the Enlightenment thinkers of the 18th century served, if they have not made us see, have not made us adopt everything that the genius of man has invented for the happiness of human society?'[46]

Although Britain was held up as an example of political economy, the American colonies were the place where the cultivation and use of potatoes were most dispersed. Crèvecoeur held that American prosperity and the potato were intertwined, and not simply because Americans ignored European crops in favour of local varieties. Spelling out the merits of the potato became a way of exalting the agriculture and economy of America in general, here deemed superior to those of Europe.[47]

Crèvecoeur expounded in detail his technical knowledge and American experiences knowing that it was in French intellectual circles that he would find convinced supporters of agronomic experimentation, such as the Duke of Harcourt, who was committed 'to naturalising the most useful foreign trees', and the Marquis of Turgot, on whose lands grew what Crèvecoeur claimed to be the finest species of potatoes in France.[48] Nor did he ignore the literature on the potato that preceded his treatise, but he drew on it when, for example, he explained how to obtain flour from potatoes, omitting a complete description 'since a good citizen has already published it'. This was probably another Norman, François-Georges Mustel, who in 1770 wrote the *Lettre d'un citoyen à ses compatriotes au sujet de la culture des Pommes de terre*.[49]

Through the Parisian intellectual circles he frequented, because of his reputation as a French publicist, Crèvecoeur entered by full right into the cultural life of his mother country.[50] He was elected a corresponding member of the Académie des

---

[46]   Crèvecoeur, *Traité de la culture des pommes-de-terre*, 18, 47.

[47]   Crèvecoeur, *Traité de la culture des pommes-de-terre*, 31.

[48]   Crèvecoeur, *Traité de la culture des pommes-de-terre*, I–II, 47, 57.

[49]   Crèvecoeur, *Traité de la culture des pommes-de-terre*, 38. Bernard Chevignard has drawn a comparison between the early passage in which Crèvecoeur likens himself to a bee making its contribution to the hive (see note 42 above) with a similar image in Mustel's work (*ibid.*, 51). See his essay, 'Une pomme de terre à la sauce américaine: le "Traité de la Culture des Pommes-de-terre" de Saint-John de Crèvecoeur (1782)', *Mémoires de l'Académie des sciences, arts et belles lettres de Dijon*, 131, (1992): 45–55. However, only in Crèvecoeur is the beehive compared to a republic. An interest in bees as a model of collective behaviour is in fact also present in the *Letters* (28–29), in the passage in which the reference to the Emperor of China and the sacred nature of agriculture borrowed an image in Raynal's *Histoire philosophique* (see note 107 below). Cf. Raynal, *Histoire philosophique*, IV, book XVIII, 342, and Lawrence, *Studies in Classic American Literature*, 27–8; Robert P. Winston, '"Strange order of Things!": the Journey to Chaos in "Letters from an American Farmer,"' *Early American Literature Newsletter*, 19 (1984): 249–67.

[50]   In 1785, acting on Crèvecoeur's advice, the city of New Haven offered honorary American citizenship to the Countess d'Houdetot, the Duke of de La Rochefoucauld, Condorcet, Turgot, Lacretelle and Saint-Lambert (cf. Howard C. Rice, *Le Cultivateur Américain*, 33).

Sciences and member of the agricultural societies of Caen and Paris, before finally entering the Institut in 1796.[51]

Having been appointed French consul to New York, Crèvecoeur devoted himself with scientific rigour to spreading knowledge of agronomy in the United States by writing articles for American newspapers on maize and potato cultivation, the introduction of new plants, the effect of climate on agriculture and sheep rearing.[52] It was at this time that he began a correspondence with Jefferson to gather information on a liqueur in the south that was extracted from potatoes.[53] However, his focus was never exclusively technical, and he helped to establish American agricultural societies and to support government pro-agriculture policies. He was buoyed by the belief that, despite Britain setting a standard for the advance of agricultural techniques, the differences between the two countries were so profound that they necessitated different farming systems.[54]

At a time of economic expansion and rising land values – which triggered a speculative market that Crèvecoeur watched carefully from the vantage point of

------

[51]   In 1786 Crèvecoeur presented two works on American acacia and on a type of stockpot used to cook potatoes to the Paris Société d'agriculture. See John Hector St John de Crèvecoeur, 'Mémoire sur la culture et les usages du Faux-Acacia dans les Etats-Unis de l'Amérique septentrionale', in *Mémoires d'Agriculture, d'Economie rurale et domestique, publiés par la Société Royale d'Agriculture de Paris* (Paris: Cuchet, 1786): 122–43; John Hector St John de Crèvecoeur, François-Alexandre-Frédeéric de La Rochefoucauld-Liancourt and Antoine-Alexis Cadet de Vaux, 'Rapport sur les usages et les avantages de la Marmite Américaine', in *Mémoires d'Agriculture, d'Economie rurale et domestique, publiés par la Société Royale d'Agriculture de Paris* (Paris: Cuchet, 1786): 107–15.

[52]   *Independent Journal*, no. 3 (March 1784); *Boston Magazine* (May 1784); *Massachusetts Magazine* (February 1785); *Worchester Magazine* (April 1786); *New Jersey Gazette* (28 August 1786); *New York Journal* (19 April 1787); *Independent Chronicle* (12 July 1787); *Columbia Magazine* (December 1787); *American Mercury* (7 May and 8 June 1788); *Newport Herald* (September 1788); *Pennsylvania Gazette* (22 October 1788); *New Jersey Journal* (10 February 1790); *Farmer's Journal* (22 July 1790).

[53]   Crèvecoeur to Jefferson, 23 January, 1 July, 1 September 1784, in Jefferson, *The Papers*, VI, 508–9, VII, 376–7, 413–15. During Crèvecoeur's time in Paris between 1785 and 1787, his relations with Jefferson were intense. From a letter by Morellet we learn that Crèvecoeur collaborated with the Abbé on the French translation of Jefferson's *Notes on Virginia*, and he sent the latter the 1787 edition of his own *Lettres*. Once Crèvecoeur had returned to New York, Jefferson, who from Paris acted as agent for the circulation of European publications in America, sent Crèvecoeur a series of pamphlets to pass on to Brissot (Morellet to Jefferson, 11 January 1787; Crèvecoeur to Jefferson, Paris, 16 April 1787; Crèvecoeur to Jefferson, New York, 20 October 1788, Jefferson, *The Papers*, XI, no. 37, 294–95, XIV, 31). Jefferson himself circulated the 1787 edition of the *Lettres* (Le Mau de L'Eupay to Jefferson, 27 October 1787, *ibid.*, XII, 290).

[54]   John Hector St John de Crèvecoeur, *Letters from an American Farmer*, 24 (*Massachusetts Magazine*, (May 1790)). Cf. Crèvecoeur to Mme d'Houdetot, New York, 20 March 1789, where he defended his work from Mazzei's attacks (Robert de Crèvecoeur, *Saint-John de Crèvecoeur*, 378–9).

the Ohio Company[55] – the picture painted by the *Letters* was one of a commercial agriculture that was part of a system of economic freedom outside mainstream channels. According to the fourth letter, about the island of Nantucket, it was trade that underlay the moral constitution of colonial society, characterized by the simplicity of custom, the spurning of luxury and laxity, the solidity of family ties and agriculture that helped to improve nature. These principles were untouched by the moral evils of economic internationalization, though still at risk of its contamination.[56]

As Crèvecoeur accurately observed in the *Sketches*, one of the defects of American society was the burden of debt that oppressed farmers. He denounced this with arguments redolent of Physiocracy.[57] A closeness to Physiocratic positions was also expressed in the *Letters*, in Crèvecoeur's criticism of paper currency and British financial power, disapproval that was also to be found in the British political press.[58]

Crèvecoeur believed that agriculture would ensure the most virtuous lifestyle, but it was from Raynal that he had drawn the conviction that trade had a civilizing effect and was necessary to the existence of political bodies. As his dedication to the Abbé attests, it was his reading of the *Histoire des deux Indes* that first prompted him to think about international relations: 'I traced the extended ramifications of a commerce which ought to unite, but now convulses, the world'.[59]

Nevertheless, it was not only the events of the Revolution that brought to Crèvecoeur's attention the benefits of trade and its capacity to guarantee social stability, based as it was on man's natural sociability.[60] A broad reflection on the effects of trade on customs was developed in the fourth to the ninth letters. Three kinds of social organizations were outlined: agrarian democracy, represented by the freeholders of the middle colonies; the not exclusively agrarian society on the isle of Nantucket, with its internal forms of self-reliance; and the negative

---

[55] Cf. note 8, above, and also Jean Bouchary, *Les Compagnies financières à Paris à la fin du XVIIIe siècle*, 3 vols. (Paris: Marcel Rivière, 1940–42) and Durand Echeverria, *Mirage in the West: A History of the French Image of American Society to 1815* (Princeton: Princeton University Press, 1957).

[56] Crèvecoeur, *Letters from an American Farmer*, 112. The model of a 'farming and commercial' society, to which Americans had to remain faithful in order to maintain their freedom, was outlined explicitly in Raynal's *Histoire philosophique*, IV, book XVIII, 370, 381–2).

[57] Crèvecoeur, *Sketches*, 144.

[58] Crèvecoeur, *Letters from an American Farmer*, 21–2.

[59] Crèvecoeur, *Letters from an American Farmer*, 7.

[60] From this perspective and under the influence of John Pocock's work Christine Holbo, 'Imagination, commerce and the politics of associationism in Crèvecoeur's "Letters from an American Farmer"', *Early American History*, 32 (1997): 20–65, has proposed a new reading of the *Letters* from a psychological-literary viewpoint, considered to be at the root of commercial humanism.

pattern of commercialized urban society, exemplified by Charles-Town in the ninth letter and made famous by the crude description of the agony of a black slave, imprisoned in a hanging cage.[61]

However, it was in the *Sketches*, which described colonial reality in the harshest way, that the lack of commercial outlets was considered a cause of poverty among American farmers.[62] This explained why, in Crèvecoeur's agrarian model, the city fulfilled an important role in so far as it catered for the needs of the agricultural market. Hence the *Letters*, which displayed a clear grasp of commercial economy governed by the principle of supply and demand, conceived the city to be at the service of agriculture, as well as a constituent of the agrarian composite. The island of Nantucket was a positive example of this, whereas Charles-Town was a negative one, since the city exploited the countryside, destroying the harmony between man and nature.[63]

An Economic and Political Diplomat

Crèvecoeur therefore sought to provide solutions to the problems of political economy that were at the heart of European debate, doing so from a perspective that took into account American conditions, without however pretending that these were wholly positive.[64] His diplomatic career belied the romantic persona of the 'simple tiller of the soil'. As is clear from his consular correspondence of 1783–1790, he took advantage of his consular post to promote trade relations and the exchange of economic expertise between France and the United States.[65]

He bemoaned the poor quality of French products compared to those of British competitors, as well as the tendency of France to export luxury goods for which there was little demand in a young and frugal nation like America. In a

---

[61]   Crèvecoeur, *Letters from an American Farmer*, 163.

[62]   Crèvecoeur, *Sketches*, 150. Cf. Norman A. Plotkin, 'Saint-John de Crèvecoeur Rediscovered: Critic or Paneygyrist?', *French Historical Studies*, 3 (1964): 390–404.

[63]   Crèvecoeur, *Letters from an American Farmer*, 40, 86, 90 (a Physiocratic approach to the city–countryside relationship is also present in the *Histoire philosophique*, IV, book XIX, 611). Cf. James Machor, 'The Garden City in America: Crèvecoeur's Letters and the Urban–Pastoral Context', *American Studies*, 23/1 (1982), 69–83.

[64]   Cf. Bernard Chevignard, 'Andrew et André: quelques variations sur le thème du "self-made man" chez Saint-John de Crèvecoeur', in *Actes du 6e Colloque du Groupe de Recherche et d'Etude Nord Américaines (GRENA). 2–4 mars 1984: 'From rags to riches': Le mythe du self-made man* (Aix-en- Provence: Publications de l'Université de Provence, 1984): 9–21.

[65]   Cf. his article, 'Information to the Merchants of North America, respecting the advantage of a mercantile connection between France and America', *New York Packet and American Adviser* (27 January 1785). In a letter to Jefferson in 1788, Crèvecoeur by now expressed a global economic vision and a clear perception of commercial needs (Crèvecoeur to Jefferson, New York, 20 October 1788, in Jefferson, *The Papers*, XIV, 30).

note sent to the Marshall of Castries in 1784, he recommended the exportation of more useful products, such as gunpowder, paper (much needed by a nation that published so many newspapers), crockery, glasses and hardware. He asked the French government to urge manufacturers to imitate British products and, in order to stimulate American exports to France, to guarantee free trade and the abolition of privileges and monopolies, especially that of the tobacco trade.[66]

In addition to expressing his opinions on these economic issues, Crèvecoeur held firmly to the principle that luxury and democracy were incompatible. In a letter to the Duke de La Rochefoucault – written in 1787, the day after his return to New York following two years in Paris – he welcomed the revival of the city, healed of the scars of war and now the seat of Congress, but lamented the pervasiveness of luxury:

> it is not the Congress that caused us all this harm; it comes to us from the Europeans, and from the weakness of Americans who in their weakness submit to this search for clothing, this luxury food and eventually get a taste for them. We also perceive that those returning from travels in Europe relate many little nuances specific to Democracy; what therefore will become of this union of states which are not yeat attached to each other by coercive links?[67]

The correspondence with La Rochefoucault also revealed that Crèvecoeur did not intend to limit his consular activities to technical matters.[68] At a time when consuls in the United States were particularly important, in that they were a source of information on a little-known country, he added a political dimension to his mission, taking an active part in discussions with his American and European partners on the new constitution.[69] For this reason he drew criticism from the French

---

[66]   John Hector St John de Crèvecoeur, *Commerce de la France avec les Etats-Unis. Idées que je crois utiles et que pour cette raison je prends la liberté d'envoyer à Monseigneur le Marechal de Castries*, 4 November 1784, in Archives du Ministère des Affaires Etrangères, Etats-Unis, Mémoires et Documents, vol. XIV, *Correspondance consulaire de New York par St. John de Crèvecoeur 1783–1790*, 300–309. He ended this note by saying that he felt French, despite being away from his homeland for 28 years.

[67]   Crèvecoeur to La Rochefoucauld, New York, 25 July 1787, Archives Municipales de Mantes-la-Jolie.

[68]   During the last years of the Old Regime consulates were under the jurisdiction of the navy. The position of consulates in the United States was complex and delicate, because France now found herself dealing with a federal state for the first time. Article 29 of the friendship and commerce treaty of 1778 instituted reciprocal consulates between the two countries, with powers fixed by a convention, but this also involved relations between Congress and the states. It was decided that the functions of the consulates were matters for Congress, but powers attributed to them restricted the jurisdiction of the states. A consular convention was not established until 1788. Cf. Maurice Degros, 'L'administration des Consulats sous la Révolution', *Revue d'histoire diplomatique* (1982): 68–111.

[69]   For Crèvecoeur's political opinions cf. below pp. 31–3.

minister de Moustier, who was trying to establish a consulate corps composed of efficient functionaries independent of politics. In his eyes, Crèvecoeur, with his *Letters*, had brought about an

> error in many French emigrants. Having lived too long in a foreign country ... he contracted certain prejudices in favour of the customs and laws of England ... one should, it was argued in Paris, recommend him not to advocate a nation that is already too much admired in America and to be French.[70]

Crèvecoeur's commitment to promoting Franco–American trade nevertheless brought concrete results: he created a maritime postal service between Lorient and New York for the purpose of facilitating regular communications and two-way trade between the two countries. This was appreciated by Jefferson, who believed that Crèvecoeur's presence as consul would ensure its continuity.[71]

Agrarian Myth and Political Thought

Notwithstanding his diplomatic experience and maturing political awareness, Crèvecoeur's reputation remained tied to the *Letters*, the agrarian model and a British loyalist propensity. It was undoubtedly true that the English edition of his work reflected the pre-revolutionary era of America, when there was no clear understanding of the relationship between economic freedom and political freedom.[72] Consequently, although the agrarianism of Crèvecoeur lay at the root of Republican agrarian ideology, it had yet to evolve into a political discourse.

In spite of his awareness of the uniqueness of American society, in the *Letters* Crèvecoeur's attachment to Britain and to British national pride when surveying the colonies' prosperity was patently clear. Also evident was his esteem for 'that government, that philanthropic government, which has collected here so many men and made them happy'.[73] However, though he shared the views of those French who considered Britain to be the land of political freedom, his position might well

---

[70]   *Distribution des Consulats de France dans les Etats-Unis et caractère des differens sujets qui y sont employés, 1788*, Archives du Ministère des Affaires Etrangères, Personnel, vol. 20, ff. 235–43.

[71]   Jefferson to Crèvecoeur, Paris, 22 August 1785, in Jefferson, *The Papers*, VIII, 421. In fact, fearing the end of the six paquebots' service, Crèvecoeur expressed all his concerns for the substitution at the navy of Marshal de Castries (to whom he owed his nomination as consul on 22 June 1783) in a letter to La Rochefoucauld in 1788 (Crèvecoeur to La Rochefoucault, New York, 1 December 1788, Archives Municipales de Mantes-la-Jolie).

[72]   Cf. Matson and Onuf, *A Union of Interests*.

[73]   Crèvecoeur, *Letters from an American Farmer*, 66. The same concept was expressed in Raynal's *Histoire philosophique*: 'It is to the influence of its excellent constitution that they owe the peace and prosperity they enjoy. While the colonies live under to salutary

have been described as 'monarchical anarchism', given that his admiration for the British crown went hand in hand with the belief that the colonial agrarian model must perforce be founded on the abdication of imperial power.[74] American laws emanated from the government, which in turn 'is derived from the original genius and strong desire of the people ratified and confirmed by the crown', a crown that offered security and protection in exchange for modest tributes.[75]

Until the eve of the Revolution few had thought that the colonies would ever separate from the mother country. Crèvecoeur – who probably began to formulate his ideas between 1769 and 1776[76] – thus gave voice to a widely shared position; furthermore, he had an authoritative guide in the moderate Toryism of the first two editions of Raynal's *Histoire philosophique*.[77] The dedication to Raynal in the 1782 edition of the *Letters*, the very year after the parliament in Paris had banned the third edition of the *Histoire philosophique*, heightened the perception that his work belonged in the Anglophile camp;[78] certainly, Crèvecoeur's decision to distance himself from the Revolution may well have been reinforced by Raynal's political stance.[79] Even so, the British sympathies of the *Letters* and the hostility to the Revolution in the *Sketches* were actually more a defence of rural community life and a rejection of violence than a reflection of loyalist sentiments.

---

and mild an administration they will continue to make a rapid progress'. (Raynal, *Histoire philosophique* (Amsterdam: 1770), VI, 420).

[74]   Cf. Myra Jehlen, 'J. Hector St. John Crèvecoeur: A Monarcho-Anarchist in Revolutionary America', *American Quarterly*, 31 (1979): 204–22. As regards the growing awareness of national identity during the reorganization of the British Empire in the second half of the eighteenth century, cf. Timothy H. Breen's essay, 'Ideology and Nationalism on the Eve of the American Revolution: Revisions "Once More" in Need of Revising', in *German and American Nationalism: A Comparative Perspective*, ed. Hartmut Lehmann and Hermann Wellenreuther (Oxford and New York: Berg, 1999): 33–69.

[75]   Crèvecoeur, *Letters from an American Farmer*, 43.

[76]   Cf. note 23 above.

[77]   Cf. Edoardo Tortarolo, 'La réception de l'"Histoire des deux Indes" aux Etats-Unis', in *Lectures de Raynal*, 305–28 and Mathé Allain, 'La révolution américaine dans l'*Histoire philosophique* de l'abbé Raynal', *Studies on Voltaire and the Eighteenth Century*, no. 263 (1989): 277.

[78]   The *Correpondance secrète* (21 January 1781): XI, 51–52) attributed the censorship of the work to Raynal's Anglomania (cf. Carlo Borghero, 'Raynal, Paine e la rivoluzione americana', in *La politica della ragione: Studi sull'illuminismo francese*, ed. Paolo Casini (Bologna: Il Mulino, 1978): 349–81).

[79]   Borghero, 'Raynal, Paine e la rivoluzione americana', 368. Nevertheless we should not forget that the complexity and diversity of the analyses that emerge from the various editions of the *Histoire* were clearly read from an anti-American point of view only after the success of the *Letter to the abbé Raynal* by Thomas Paine (Thomas Paine, *A Letter addressed to the abbé Raynal on the affairs of North America in which the Mistakes in the abbé's account of the revolution of America are corrected and cleared up*, (Philadelphia, 1782)).

To the farmer of the *Sketches* the Revolution looked like a civil war, in which colonial roughs, envious of the freeholders, had destroyed the prosperity of the countryside, whereas in the *Letters* it was seen rather as the crushing of a minority: 'The innocent class are always the victims of the few'.[80] Crèvecoeur separated colonial self-government from independence, a distinction that explains both his aversion to the Revolution, experienced personally as civil war and his move away from Raynal's optimism. 'I am conscious that I was happy before this unfortunate revolution';[81] the tragedy of the war was lived out in the last letter as confusion and uncertainty over which position to take: 'self-preservation, therefore, the rule of Nature, seems to be the best rule of conduct'.[82] And it was this defence of the agrarian model that marked his break from Britain: 'Must I then bid farewell to Britain, to that renowned country? Must I renounce a name so ancient and so venerable? Alas! She herself, that once-indulgent parent, forces me to take up arms against her'.[83]

Despite the attitude of isolation and the incomprehension of the Revolution that pervades the last letter – 'sentiment and feeling are the only guides I know'[84] – the agrarianism of the *Letters* was not devoid of political foundations. For Crèvecoeur, the agrarian model already implied a discussion about personal, economic and political liberty, though without any involvement on his part. His acceptance of the monarchy was engendered by a conception of political power characterized by a weak state presence, in view of which the form of a regime was of secondary importance compared to the stability of a government that asked little of the independent farmer. Seen in this light, the farmer, whose success was linked to steady honesty and sobriety rather than good fortune, would become the power behind Jeffersonian democracy as well as the prototype of Jackson's independent Yankee.[85]

---

[80]   Crèvecoeur, *Letters from an American Farmer*, 191.

[81]   Crèvecoeur, *Letters from an American Farmer*, 191.

[82]   Crèvecoeur, *Letters from an American Farmer*, 193. 'I am a lover of peace, what must I do? I am divided between the respect I feel for the ancient connection and the fear of innovations, with the consequence of which I am not well acquainted, as they are embraced by my own countrymen.' (*ibid.*, 191).

[83]   Crèvecoeur, *Letters from an American Farmer*, 197.

[84]   Crèvecoeur, *Letters from an American Farmer*, 191. The harshness and incomprehension of the conflict for Crèvecoeur is affirmed by the account of his stay in New York, between his release from the British on 17 September 1779 and his departure for Ireland on 1st September 1780: *Esquisse de ma vie depuis ma sortie de prison à New York le 17 septembre jusques à mon retour dans la même ville comme consul de France le 17 novembre 1783*, a manuscript published for the first time in Chevignard, 'St. John de Crèvecoeur à New York', 164–73.

[85]   Crèvecoeur, *Letters from an American Farmer*, 66–7. Cf. Russel B. Nye, 'Michel-Guillaume St. Jean de Crèvecoeur: Letters from an American Farmer', in *Landmarks of American Writing*, ed. Henning Cohen (New York: Basic Books, 1969).

The lawful right to be part of society was attained from property rather than political power: 'This formerly rude soil has been converted by my father into a pleasant farm, and, in return, it has established all our rights. On it is founded our rank, our freedom, our power, as citizens; our importance, as inhabitants of such a district'.[86] The democracy within a family – the primary unit of a society in which the individual was not isolated – came to denote a small republic with a hierarchy of its own and forged an original link between democracy and republic. Furthermore, the *Letters* articulated the idea of representative government as the foundation of a new social hierarchy, the expression of a democracy of freehold farmers: 'Europe contains hardly any other distinctions but lords and tenants; this fair country alone is settled by freeholders, the possessors of the soil they cultivate, members of the government they obey, and the framers of their own laws, by means of their representatives.'[87]

Therefore, while for Crèvecoeur the agrarian ideal had implied at an early stage the concept of representative democracy, his adherence to the revolutionary cause came later, when he was in contact with Parisian circles. His intellectual development alongside the *philosophes* gave rise to a more lively interest in political issues, as is evidenced by the 1787 French edition of the *Letters*, the correspondence as consul with Jefferson and La Rochefoucauld, and the *Voyage dans la Haute Pensylavanie*.

In the years, which were decisive for the United States as they were for France, Crèvecoeur defined his political stance, albeit without losing sight of his colonial experience. While in New York he followed with interest the closing phases of the French Old Regime: he supported the plans for provincial assemblies – expressions of a political debate originating from Physiocratic matrices – and placed his faith in the Assembly of Notables:[88] 'which is similar to the Federal Convention, should heal many wounds, and prevent many ailments'.[89] However, he did not agree with the revolutionary violence and, as a Frenchman, in the *Voyage* he judged the Americans to be 'a people who, more fortunate than us, moved from enslavement

---

[86]   Crèvecoeur, *Letters from an American Farmer*, 27.

[87]   Crèvecoeur, *Letters from an American Farmer*, 55.

[88]   'Who Cou'd have foreseen that the Parliaments Shou'd have Shew'd such a spirit of opposition to the Establishment of Provincial assemblies. It wou'd seem as if they were Jealous of that new Institution. Dont you think that the Time is now come to break those antiquated bodys and with the fragments to Establish Supreme Courts, solely for the Tryal of Causes'. (Crèvecoeur to Jefferson, New York, 9 November 1787, in Jefferson, *The Papers*, XII, 332). On the Physiocratic origins of the discussion regarding provincial assemblies and on the relationship between landowner and right of representation, cf. Manuela Albertone, 'Il proprietario terriero nel discorso fisiocratico sulla rappresentanza', *Studi setteschi*, no. 24 (2004): 181–214; Anthony Mergey, *L'Etat des Physiocrates: Autorité et Décentralisation* (Aix-en-Provence: Press Universitaires d'Aix-Marseille, 2010).

[89]   Crèvecoeur to the Duke of La Rochefoucauld, New York, 27 July 1787, Archives Municipales de Mantes-la-Jolie.

to independence without feeling the bloody fury of anarchy'.[90] He retained a strong American pragmatism and France seemed to him to be an example of the evils that could result from the futile quest for a perfect government.

Crèvecoeur's support for the 1787 American constitution was determined by the openness to innovation that set the *Letters* outside of any Arcadian or nostalgic ideal and aroused his interest in provincial assemblies. As early as the second edition of the *Letters*, and later in the *Voyage*, he addressed American political issues in greater depth, pointing out the weakness of the Confederate government, which led to the new constitution.[91] Similarly, his correspondence with Jefferson and La Rochefoucauld revealed his concern for the inadequacy of the democracy of the states, separated, with conflicting interests and with different trade laws: 'The Confederation may be compared to a bundle of 13 sticks tied by straw'.[92] At the start of the war, the Americans had looked upon Federal government as a power capable of ensuring safety and security. Having won independence, they had chosen to give unconditional support to separate sovereignty, only to then return to the original principle.[93] The letters to La Rochefoucauld emphasized the political maturity that gave Crèvecoeur a perception of the concept of nation much clearer than what was evident in the *Letters*, in which land ownership was not yet the cornerstone of a nation:

> Many more years will pass before the Americans become a nation, it will also be more than a century before we will be able to observe in them the moral and physical traits of homogeneity, which produce these nuances of character and nationality; for, as you know, what we see today is only composed of Europeans placed on different land and under a different climate, and who all come from equally different countries, which have, and can only have no other ties other than those of their needs, and of their small local ambition.[94]

Faced with the threat of the disintegration of the new nation, Crèvecoeur placed his hopes in a constitution grounded not on tradition, but on uniform principles and strong government. For these reasons he hoped for the Federalists' success,

---

[90]   Crèvecoeur, *Voyage*, I, viii–ix.

[91]   Crèvecoeur, *Lettres d'un cultivateur américain,* III, 499; Crèvecoeur, *Voyage*, III, 277–82.

[92]   Crèvecoeur to La Rochefoucauld, New York, 25 July 1787, Archives Municipales de Mantes-la-Jolie. In the same letter, written after his return to America following two years of absence, he declared that he had not yet formed a definitive political opinion, but that he nevertheless looked positively upon the situation in America, 'because I come from Europe, where I have seen the Despotism of Intendants, which dries and discourages, the neverending tax wars, the inequality of wealth, amazing poverty of the Countryside, where man is degraded by deepest ignorance and the weight of poverty'. (*ibid.*)

[93]   Crèvecoeur to La Rochefoucauld, New York, 27 July 1787.

[94]   Crèvecoeur to La Rochefoucauld, New York, 1 December 1788.

as he declared to Jefferson in 1788.[95] The same dread of break-up and anarchy, expressed in the *Letters,* led him to support the constitution and the political forces that championed it, but, beyond these alignments, what re-emerged as the most pressing concern was his need of solidarity and security. To be sure, his contact with the Parisian scene had added a marked elitism to his democratic convictions,[96] but when the clash over the French Revolution intensified the conflict between Federalists and Republicans, defining two distinct parties, Crèvecoeur's deep-seated pragmatism remained and could not fully conceal his political scepticism: the parties, as he wrote in the *Voyage*, had no influence 'on the progress of tillage of internal colonies, nor those of trade . It is still more committed to seek the favors of fortune, than what is said and what is done in the halls of Congress'.[97]

Economy, Society and Politics

Solidarity and security as priority values in political choices signified for Crèvecoeur a concept of democracy that presupposed a special relationship between the economy and society. In this sense, the *Letters* represented the appropriation of the central place that the founding groups had held in the colonies. The farmer's individualism did not lead to isolation, since a new form of community sprang from the family structure that was its base.[98] In this perspective, therefore, James, the protagonist of the *Letters*, exemplified the yeoman who constituted the social dynamism of the Revolution, the superseding of pre-colonial community reality: thus Crèvecoeur depicted a social figure that played a key role in Republican ideology.

In the America of the second half of the eighteenth century, when commercial agriculture was on the rise in a period of urban expansion and an increasing European demand for American grain, the *Letters* faithfully represented an aspect of the American economy that regulated relationships between families who were outside of the large trade networks, though still part of the growing market.

---

[95]   Crèvecoeur to Jefferson, New York, 20 October 1788, in Jefferson, *The Papers*, XIV, 29. Cf. also in *ibid.* the letters to Jefferson, New York, 9 November 1787, XII, 332; New York, 5 January 1789, XIV, 416.

[96]   'There is no country in the world where so many people can read and write, but it is impossible for a nation to find legislators among its merchants and labourers ... unfortunately independence has persuaded these good people, that they would become their own Sovereigns, that's why there are so many people here who meddle in politics, and therefore a large number of malcontents, as a member of one of these legislatures, who has never opened a book in his life, is attached to his opinion in proportion to his ignorance.' (Crèvecoeur to the La Rochefoucauld, New York, 1 December 1788, Archives Municipales de Mantes-la-Jolie).

[97]   Crèvecoeur, *Voyage*, III, 320.

[98]   Crèvecoeur, *Letters from an American Farmer*, 25–6.

Crèvecoeur's honest, self-reliant and independent farmer personified the social figure that would emerge during the Revolution and claim an active political role. Here was the origin of a new democracy composed of individuals, but not of atomistic individualism, because the spirit of the founding community survived in the family. The American yeoman, living in a world that had not known feudalism,[99] did not fit into an agricultural hierarchy, but was an expression of a society of independent producers, working for familial autonomy within local trading systems. The protagonist of the *Letters* thus embodied the Republican ideal of a landowner whose own independence was based on the autonomy that was to be found outside the confines of large-scale commercial channels.

In the guise of an epistolary novel, Crèvecoeur's work recorded a particular aspect of the American transition to a market economy by spotlighting a mode of production characterized by exchanges between family units, a trade system which was at once local and part of the country's developing economy.[100] Besides profit, the aim of this trade was the maintenance of the community's social relations, based on the interaction of families, the patriarchal structure of which was affected by the greater involvement of women.[101] The organization of labour on a domestic basis consequently perpetuated family values.[102]

As the hub of agricultural production, the family consolidated the farmers' aspirations. Against the background of dynamic growth in the American economy, the increase in the value of land, consequent upon population growth and rising agricultural prices (both in the colonies and in Europe), augmented the benefits that accrued to smallholders from the lands that had been purchased with no prospect of financial gain. Colonial agrarian individualism therefore did not yet correspond to a capitalist outlook, though it did predispose to it, in much the same way as the evolving familial community ties favoured the maturation of democracy in accordance with a process common to all eighteenth-century societies, which saw in families the catalyst for the transformation or the break-up of traditional

---

[99]   On the question of a revival of feudalism in the eighteenth-century American colonies cf. Rowland Berthoff and John M. Murrin, 'Feudalism, Communalism and the Yeoman Freeholder: The American Revolution Considered as a Social Accident', in *Essays on the American Revolution*, ed. Stephen G. Kurz and James H. Hutson (Chapel Hill: University of North Carolina Press, 1973): 256–88; Allan Kulikoff, 'The Transition to Capitalism in Rural America', *The William and Mary Quarterly*, 3d ser., 46 (1989): 120–44).

[100]   On the issue of the transition to capitalism in North America, cf. Kulikoff, 'The Transition to Capitalism', 133 onwards).

[101]   Crèvecoeur, *Letters from an American Farmer*, 141. As regards how the *Letters* dealt with the changes in the structure of puritan patriarchal families and also the role of the woman, cf. Anna Carew-Miller, 'The Language of Domesticity in Crèvecoeur's "Letters from an American Farmer"', *Early American Literature Newsletter*, 28 (1993): 242–54.

[102]   Cf. James A. Henretta, "Families and Farms: 'Mentalité' in Pre-Industrial America', *The William and Mary Quarterly*, 3d ser., 35 (1978): 3–32.

structures.[103] From this perspective, the dangers – underscored by Crèvecoeur – inherent in the aggressive and antisocial individualism of the race to the frontier were symptomatic of the political thinking that rejected the individual freedom that placed itself outside a collective dimension and that in the 1780s typified the policy of Congress on the colonization of the West.[104]

American Identity and the Enlightenment

The value of the agrarian model of the *Letters* lies therefore in its faithful representation of the economic and social reality of the colonies, as perceived through the medium of European culture. In dedicating his work to Raynal, Crèvecoeur openly declared his intention of participating in the French Enlightenment debate, with respect to its cosmopolitan significance: 'There is, no doubt, a secret communion among good men throughout the world; a mental affinity, connecting them by a similitude of sentiments. Then why, though an American, should not I be permitted to share in that extensive intellectual consanguity?'[105] As a synthesis of European Enlightenment, the *Histoire des deux Indes* had revealed to Crèvecoeur how in the eyes of the *philosophes* America served as a political and social laboratory: 'You viewed these provinces of North America in their true light: as the asylum of freedom; as the cradle of future nations, and the refuge of distressed Europeans.'[106]

The *Histoire* may therefore be seen as a kind of metatext, which offered Crèvecoeur a template on which to set out his own narrative: 'I conceived

---

[103] Joyce Appleby's works, which have highlighted the importance of socio-economic elements and the modernity of the American agrarian development project in the eighteenth century, emphasize an individualism that did not fully value the new collective idea of Republican agrarian ideology and all the democratic implications inherent in it (cf. Appleby, *Capitalism and a New Social Order*; Appleby, *Liberalism and Republicanism*); the discussion in 'How Revolutionary Was the Revolution? A Discussion of Gordon S. Wood's "The Radicalism of American Revolution"', *The William and Mary Quarterly*, 3d ser., 51 (1994): 677–83, by the same author, is more open to democratic issues.

[104] Crèvecoeur, *Letters from an American Farmer*, 51–2. With regard to the policy towards the West and the debates at the Congress in 1784–1785 concerning the need to inspect landed property against speculators, to impose the government's actions cf. Peter S. Onuf, 'Liberty, Development, and Union: Visions of the West in the 1780s', *The William and Mary Quarterly*, 3d ser., 43 (1986): 179–213.

[105] Crèvecoeur, *Letters from an American Farmer*, 7–8. Cf. Eisermann, 'La "Raynalisation" de l'"American Farmer"'. For an unusual reading of Raynal's presence, centred on the relation between theories of the imagination and society, which places Crèvecoeur in rapport with the *Histoire* and Edmund Burke's idea of the sublime, cf. Holbo, 'Imagination, Commerce and the politics of associationism'.

[106] Crèvecoeur, *Letters from an American Farmer*, 7.

your genius to be present at the head of my study'.[107] From this viewpoint, the *Letters*, too, represented a synthesis of the subjects at the heart of eighteenth-century culture: echoes of Montesquieu, pervasive Rousseauian sensibility and Physiocratic arguments that emerge in the unfolding of recurring Enlightenment themes, namely the interconnection between passion and reason; the centrality of the concept of nature; the ideal of an intermediate stage of development between the state of nature and civilization, realized by the American agrarian model; the existence of law of nature, the knowledge of which guaranteed cultural and material progress; philanthropy and the rejection of slavery; the critique of aristocratic societies and ecclesiastical power; the ideal of the melting pot. The simulated spontaneity of the protagonist of the *Letters* concealed Crèvecoeur's intention to address a specific audience of educated Europeans. Thus, in the English edition of the *Letters*, the proposed American agrarian system acted as a denunciation of the Old Regime while, in the French versions, it assumed a revolutionary character, reflecting the position of the *philosophes*.[108]

In addition to aligning Crèvecoeur with moderate political positions through its dedication to Raynal, the *Letters* expressed for the first time the need to compare the Enlightenment vision with the unique situation of the colonies.[109] Raynal's *Histoire* considered their revolutionary experience to have universal importance, but it ignored their specific circumstances.[110] In contrast, the *Letters* was the first reflection on American identity, formulated from a European – and particularly French – cultural point of view, but with first-hand knowledge of the new state. Regardless of how the *Letters* used the American experience to criticize European realities, Crèvecoeur's attention no longer concentrated on Europe itself: his criticisms of Europeans were in fact intended to be a means of enabling Americans

---

[107]   Crèvecoeur, *Letters from an American Farmer*, 7. Crèvecoeur's work also owes its use of recurrent figures in eighteenth-century political literature to Raynal. An example of this is the portrayal of the Emperor of China, who publicly honoured agriculture each year by ploughing the soil before his people, used by Crèvecoeur to exalt the farmer (*Ibid.*, 28; cf. Guillaume-Thomas-François Raynal, *Histoire philosophique*, I, book I, 104 (Amsterdam: 1770), I, 33).

[108]   On the importance that Crèvecoeur's depiction of America had in revolutionary France among the Girondins, in particular through links with Brissot, cf. Plotkin, 'Saint-John de Crèvecoeur Rediscovered', 393–5.

[109]   Nevertheless, the *Letters* do not show a clear position taken by Crèvecoeur on the question of the legitimacy of the colonial insurrection as tackled in the first two editions of the *Histoire des deux Indes*.

[110]   In the same year as the publication of the *Letters*, Thomas Paine, in his *Letter to the Abbé Raynal*, denounced the European viewpoint of the *Histoire*, which showed little attention to the peculiarity of American events (cf. Alfred O. Aldridge, "La signification historique, diplomatique et littéraire de la 'Lettre addressée à l'abbé Raynal' de Thomas Paine," *Etudes anglaises*, 8 (1955): 223–32; Borghero, 'Raynal, Paine e la rivoluzione americana'; Edoardo Tortarolo, 'La réception'.)

to become aware of their own identity and to outline a model different from the proposals that came from the old continent.

The origins of the *Letters* – which mark the first literary expression of American consciousness – sprang from Crèvecoeur's need to question his own identity.[111] This new identity was all the stronger as it paralleled, without overpowering, Crèvecoeur's French identity: in all his adversities, James put the validity of systems that came out of European culture to the test. Crèvecoeur defined the change which would lead to the American sense of identity in economic terms and revealed it in the figure of the farmer, and so personal identity and national identity fused together through the economic perspective:[112] 'the sentiments I have expressed are also the echo of those of my countrymen', he wrote at the end of his dedication to Raynal.[113]

The peculiarity of James's experience stemmed from his special relationship with the landscape of the unique natural splendour of America and these were the exceptional preconditions for the realization of the American agrarian model.[114] In the second and third letters, which threw light on the freehold farmer's situation, individual experience, the economic system and the natural environment began to merge. American identity was thus defined by participation in a certain economic order and the transformation from farmer to American was determined by changes to the landowner's economic, social and political circumstances: 'From being the slave of some despotic prince, to become a free man, invested with lands, to which every municipal blessing is annexed! What a change indeed! It is in consequence of that change that he becomes an American.'[115] The unspoilt beauty of the American cultivated countryside, as described by James to his European guest evoked a social feeling, a sense of citizenship and national pride. The sociability celebrated in the *Letters* was not however the product of an historical process, nor did it take

---

[111] In a letter to Jefferson he expressed the hope that his work might improve the image of America in the eyes of Europeans (Crèvecoeur to Jefferson, New York, 18 May 1785, in Jefferson, *The Papers*, VIII, 156) and in the already cited handwritten memorandum to the Marshall of Castries in 1784 he declared that he felt himself French despite his 28-year absence (*Commerce de la France avec les Etats-Unis*). From the rough copies of letters of the Ministry for Foreign Affairs, one can nevertheless see information on Crèvecoeur's efforts to prolong his stay in France in 1785 and then 1790. In 1791 he swore a civic oath, until, on 5 November 1792, he was relieved of his consular duties in the administrative restructuring that followed the proclamation of the first republic (Archives Nationales, *Minutes des lettres ministerielles concernant l'Amérique 1785–1793*, AE, B III, 439, ff. 9, 33, 95bis, 192, 306, 325, 366).

[112] On the emergence of collective identity from individual identity, of which Franklin's autobiography and Crèvecoeur's *Letters from an American Farmer* represent the first examples in American literature, cf. Philip D. Beidler, 'Franklin's and Crèvecoeur's "Literary" Americans', *Early American Literature*, 13/1 (Spring 1978): 50–63.

[113] Crèvecoeur, *Letters from an American Farmer*, 8.

[114] Crèvecoeur, *Letters from an American Farmer*, 19.

[115] Crèvecoeur, *Letters from an American Farmer*, 59.

on a universal value, but it was a reflection of a natural society that responded to the unrivalled geography of America:

> We are a people of cultivators, scattered over an immense territory, communicating with each other by means of good roads and navigable rivers, united by the silken bands of mild government, all respecting the laws, without dreading their power, because they are equitable. We are all animated with the spirit of an industry which is unfettered and unrestrained, because each person works for himself.[116]

The personal experience of St John de Crèvecour, set in the exceptional American environment and shaped by the literary success of the *Letters from an American Farmer* provided the context that made the reception of French economic ideas in America worthwhile. As a native Frenchman transplanted for a period of his life to America, Crèvecoeur assimilated the French Enlightenment and became acquainted with the agrarian myth through Raynal's *Histoire des deux Indes*, and with French ideas about America's status as a laboratory of innovation and the central economic role of agriculture. Beyond the scientific analysis carried out by the Physiocrats, key elements of the primacy of agriculture became widespread in the eighteenth-century culture assimilated by Crèvecoeur. Nevertheless, his apolitical way of thinking could not turn his agrarian myth into the political project of agrarian democracy that emerged later, with the struggle between Republicans and Federalists in the 1790s.

---

[116]   Crèvecoeur, *Letters from an American Farmer*, 41.

Chapter 2
Republicanism and Agrarian Democracy

Agrarian Ideology

Transformed from myth into a revolutionary ideology that expressed a political culture based on a unique American approach to republicanism and democracy, farmers – from the 'tillers of the earth' in Crèvecoeur's *Letters* to the 'chosen people of God' of Thomas Jefferson's *Notes on the State of Virginia*[1] – were the inspiration and the heart of the American agrarian project. In the exceptional geographic conditions, and in response to the opportunities offered by an international market in which higher prices were paid for agricultural products, agrarian ideology also represented a set of values, in the name of which the incomparability of American nature legitimized the idea of the primacy of laws of nature over governments, setting nature against hierarchical societies. The economy, meanwhile, was seen as a natural order that required minimum intervention from governments.[2] 'The whole landed interest is republican', Jefferson wrote to Filippo Mazzei, denouncing the Federalists as the 'Anglican monarchical aristocratical party',[3] while Benjamin Franklin defined agriculture as 'the most honorable, because the most independent, of all professions'.[4] The revolutionary ideal of a race of landowners turned republicanism and agrarianism into values that were profoundly American and established the agrarian project as an anti-British economic model.[5] Indeed, for Jefferson's Republicans the fight against Britain signified not only a political separation, but also rejection of its economic system.[6] The farmer, the republican patriot par excellence, came to

---

[1]   'Those who labour in the earth are the chosen people of God, if ever he had a chosen people, whose breasts he has made his peculiar deposit for substantial and genuine virtue' (Thomas Jefferson, *Notes on the State of Virginia*, 164–5).

[2]   Cf. Gilbert Chinard, 'Eighteenth Century Theories on America as a Human Habitat', *Proceedings of the American Philosophical Society*, 91 (1947): 27–57.

[3]   Jefferson to Filippo Mazzei, Monticello, 24 April 1796, in Thomas Jefferson, *The Writings*, ed. Bergh, vol. IX, 335–6.

[4]   Franklin to Lafayette, Philadelphia, 17 April 1787, in Benjamin Franklin, *The Works*, ed. Jared Sparks, 10 vols., (London: Benjamin Franklin Stevens, 1882), vol. X, 300.

[5]   Cf. Paul B. Thompson and C. Hildge, eds, *The Agrarian Roots of Pragmatism* (Nashville: Vanderbilt University Press, 2000).

[6]   Cf. the essay by Sidney Sherwood, which continues to be useful for the clarity of its thesis that the American political economy was essentially a protest against the

personify a republicanism whose essence, in America, took also the form of a reflection on political economy.

Between 1785 and 1815 the new American nation found itself choosing which economic path to follow, and the economy assumed the form of a political project. Jefferson and the theorists of agrarian ideology – Franklin, George Logan and John Taylor – based their thinking on the relationship between economic and political freedom, linking the agrarian model to democracy. The notion of economic development serving a democratic purpose became an American principle. Although neither Jefferson's party nor its exponents were always uniform in their principles,[7] on the whole, Jeffersonianism revealed an awareness of the economic foundations of politics and the educational value of economic principles in a democratic context.

The economic and political significance of agrarian democracy was manifest in the 1790s in the clash between Jefferson's pro-French Republicans and Hamilton's pro-English Federalists, which began after the outbreak of the French Revolution.[8] The interaction between republic, agrarianism and democracy allows us to understand the specific nature of American economic-political thought, noting how it differed from the British tradition. The Republicans' American patriotism was anti-traditional[9] and attached to universal values.[10] Furthermore, for the theorists of agrarian democracy the relationship between political economy and moral philosophy implied a consideration of economic-political issues that was normative as well as descriptive. Such an approach highlighted the relationship between ideology and private interests,[11] in that the agricultural economic project and the republican model sought to reconcile individualism with the common good.

---

universalism of the English model, *Tendencies in American Economic Thought* (Baltimore: The John Hopkins Press, 1897).

[7]   On the need to overcome the impasse between an idea of the Jeffersonians as competitive individualists and the classical republicans as promoters of an organic hierarchy, cf. Richard Ellis, *American Political Cultures* (Oxford: Oxford University Press, 1993); John Ashworth, 'The Jeffersonians: Classical Republicans or Liberal Capitalists?' *Journal of American Studies*, 18/3 (1984): 425–35; Michael P. Zuckert, *Natural Rights and the New Republicanism* (Princeton: Princeton University Press, 1994).

[8]   Cf. Lance Banning, *The Jeffersonian Persuasion*.

[9]   'The Gothic idea that we are to look backwards instead of forwards for the improvement of the human mind, and to recur to the annals of our ancestors for what is most perfect in government, in religion and in learning, is worthy of those bigots in religion and government.' (Jefferson to Joseph Priestley, Philadelphia, 27 January 1800, in Thomas Jefferson, *The Writings*, ed. Merrill D. Peterson (New York: Library of America, 1984): 1073).

[10]   Cf. Thomas Pangle, *The Spirit of Modern Republicanism: The Moral Vision of the American Founders and the Philosophy of Locke* (Chicago: The University of Chicago Press, 1988).

[11]   Apart from the works by Bernard Bailyn and Gordon Wood, cf. Richard R. Beeman, Stephen Botein and Edward C. Carter, eds, *Beyond Confederation: Origins of the Constitution and American National Identity* (Chapel Hill: University of North Carolina Press, 1987).

A stable economic foundation was needed to support the democratic republic: Jefferson found it in the farmer, member of a 'chosen people' composed not of the whole nation but of a class – the farmers – providentially favoured by virtue of its customs rather than a predetermined historical role.[12]

The study of American agrarian ideology and the variations its theorists gave it permits us to piece together an intellectual history – not detached from the study of political practice – which emphasizes this democratic juncture:[13] for the first time, in America, a democratic government became reality, and it did so by means of the republican and agrarian model, thus accentuating the political importance of the economy in its construction.[14] Their awareness of the economic underpinnings of the modern republic led the Jeffersonians to focus the political discourse on representative democracy, through the development of forms of participatory democracy that took into account the individual experiences of the states and the cultural and religious traditions of the American colonies, which were construed as mechanisms ensuring security and prosperity in a commercialized society and a vibrant economy.[15]

In the debate on the constitution, the anti-Federalists contended that local control over the economy had to take precedence over political interference from the government. The central role of the farmer reinforced this argument.[16]

---

[12] Cf. Tuveson E. Lee, *Redeemer Nation: The Idea of America's Millennial Role* (Chicago: University of Chicago Press, 1968).

[13] Cf. Martin van Gelderen and Quentin Skinner, eds, *Republicanism: A Shared Heritage*, 2 vols. (Cambridge: Cambridge University Press, 2002). Regarding the American Revolution, one of the first efforts to synthesize liberalism and classical republicanism remains the work of Drew R. McCoy, *The Elusive Republic: Political Economy in Jeffersonian America.*

[14] Cf. Paul A. Rahe, *Republics Ancient and Modern: Classical Republicanism and the American Revolution* (Chapel Hill: University of North Carolina Press, 1992).

[15] Cf. Biancamaria Fondana, ed., *The Invention of the Modern Republic* (Cambridge: Cambridge University Press, 1994), and in particular the essay by John Dunn, 'The Identity of Bourgeois Liberal Republic', 206–29; John E. Dunn, *The Economic Limits to Modern Politics* (Cambridge: Cambridge University Press, 1990); David Wootton, 'The Republican Tradition: From Commonwealth to Common Sense', in *Republicanism, Liberty and Commercial Society, 1649–1776*, ed. David Wootton (Stanford: Stanford University Press, 1994): 1–41.

[16] Jefferson did not want to be seen as an anti-Federalist: 'I am not of the party of federalists. But I am much farther from that of the Antifederalists. I approved from the first moment, of the great mass of what is in the new constitution, the consolidation of the government, the organization into Executive, legislative and judiciary, the subdivision of the legislative, the happy compromise of interests between the great and little states by the different manner of voting in the different houses'. (Jefferson to Francis Hopkinson, Paris, 13 March 1789, in Jefferson, *The Papers*, vol. XIV, 650). Cf. James H. Hutson, 'Country, Court and Constitution: Antifederalism and the Historians', *The William and Mary Quarterly*, 3d ser. 38 (1981): 337–68.

Melancton Smith and the *Letters from the Federal Farmer* are testimony to this link between the key figure of the farmer and the discussion about political representation.[17]

Produced during the time of the ratification of the constitution,[18] the writings and public interventions of this merchant and New York lawyer, who was one of the most vocal anti-Federalists, expressed a desire not to reject the constitution, but to improve it precisely on the issue of political participation. At the heart of the *Letters*, published between 1787 and 1788, was not so much the possibility of an increase in central power posing a threat to the states as that of the right of representation, which he believed could not be guaranteed by a single central government in such a vast country. The constitution provided for a representative for every 30,000 citizens, whereas the states guaranteed one for every 1,500. Smith identified three categories of representatives: the natural aristocracy, popular demagogues and the respectable part of democracy, which he saw in the middle class, made up of farmers:

> A representative body, composed principally of respectable yeomanry, is the best possible security to liberty. When the interest of this part of the community is pursued, the public good is pursued, because the body of every nation consists of this class, and because the interest of both the rich and the poor are involved in that of the middling class.[19]

The agrarian economic project of the Jeffersonians was for the most part inseparable from the political revolution with which, in the 1790s, they subverted the principle of deference. Starting from the ratification of the constitution in 1787, which marked the success of the Federalists in the substantial powers granted to Congress, and continuing until Jefferson's election to the Presidency in 1800, the Republican attacks targeted European hierarchical structures, particularly

---

[17]   *Observations Leading to a Fair Examination of the System of Government Proposed by the Late Convention ... in a Number of Letters from the Federal Farmer, November 1787: An Additional Number of Letters from the Federal Farmer to the Republican, May 1788*. On the attribution of these works to Melancton Smith, after they had previously been attributed to Richard H. Lee, cf. Gordon Wood, 'The Authorship of the "Letters from the Federal Farmer,"' *The William and Mary Quarterly*, 3d ser., 31 (1974): 299–308. Cf. Robert H. Webking, 'Melancton Smith and the "Letters from the Federal Farmer,"' *The William and Mary Quarterly*, 3d ser. 44 (1987): 510–28.

[18]   Cf. Gordon S. Wood, *The Creation of the American Republic, 1776–1787* (Chapel Hill: The University of North Carolina Press, 1969); '"The Creation of the American Republic, 1776–1787': A Symposium of Views and Reviews," *William and Mary Quarterly*, 3d.s., XLIV, no. 3 (July 1987), 549–640.

[19]   *The Debates in the Several State Conventions on the Adoption of the Federal Constitution*, ed. Jonathan Elliott, (Philadelphia: 1826), vol. II, 248.

the British ones to which the Federalists looked.[20] In the same years, Republican support for the French Revolution brought into the discussion on social hierarchy the political cultures of America, France and Britain.[21] While ostensibly relating to a real danger, the Jeffersonians' accusation that the Federalists aimed to establish a monarchy in the United States was in fact intended to incapacitate the Federalist elite by undermining the idea of deference on which its electoral circuit depended. The Republicans contrasted this with their principle of political representation.

The defeat of the concept of deference, which made way for the full democratic development of the representative republic, concurred with the success of the Republicans as a party, signalling their severance from the Whig roots of the American political and economic culture.[22] On the basis of the concept of representation derived from eighteenth-century Whig tradition, the many accepted a limitation of personal participation in government and gave, with a sense of deference, power to those few deemed worthy of representing the interests of the majority by dint of their social position. Against this the Republicans counter-proposed the farmer as a symbol of a new social stratification, in the name of which the principles of dignity and hierarchy founded on tradition and custom and tied to the idea of deference were rejected.[23] Individual independence also encouraged landowners to reject those forms of social subordination on which deference rested,[24] and, on the strength of their grounding in local realities, to demand active political participation.[25] In this picture, the proliferation of democratic societies in the 1790s manifested a form of democracy in which individuals were linked by shared group interests, and this marked the decline of the forms of protection based on relationships of patronage and of family that were ingrained in a deferential society.[26]

---

[20]   The 1787 constitution (article 1, section 9) expressly forbids any title of nobility to be awarded within the United States.

[21]   Cf. Joyce Appleby, *Capitalism and a New Social Order*, 51 ff.

[22]   Cf. Ronald P. Formisano, 'Deferential-Participant Politics: The Early Republic's Political Culture, 1789–1840', *American Political Science Review*, 68/2 (1974): 473–87.

[23]   Cf. John B. Kirby, 'Early American Politics – The Search for Ideology: an Historiographical Analysis and Critique of the Concept of 'Deference'',' *Journal of Politics*, 32 (1970), 808–38; Jack R. Pole, *Political Representation in England and the Origins of the American Republic* (Berkeley: University of California Press, 1969); Richard Buel, 'Democracy and the American Revolution: A Frame of Reference', *The William and Mary Quarterly*, 3d ser., 21 (1964): 165–90; Bernard Bailyn, *The Ideological Origins of the American Revolution* (Cambridge, MA: Harvard University Press, 1966).

[24]   The unusual nature of the American deferential society has been explained by the absence of a feudal period in the life of the colonies. On this controversy cf. Rowland Berthoff and John M. Murrin, "Feudalism, Communalism and the Yeoman Freeholder".

[25]   Cf. Richard R. Beeman, *The Varieties of Political Experiences in Eighteenth-Century America* (Philadelphia: University of Pennsylvania Press, 2004).

[26]   Cf. Gordon S. Wood, *The American Revolution: A History* (New York: The Modern Library, 2002). On the efforts within American political culture to differentiate itself from the European tradition, cf. Henry Steele Commager, *The Empire of Reason: How Europe*

In the clash with the Federalists, Jefferson's Republicans thus set in motion a twofold revolution: economic, outlining a proposal for agrarian development, and political, subverting the principle of deference. In doing so they perpetuated the anti-British spirit of the struggle for independence, waged not only against the British monarchy, but also against the British model of political economy, based on privilege and mercantilist trade practices.

The new social hierarchy was thus understood to be a national particularity, in that it was the abundance of land that made the farmer the embodiment of the national interest, conferring reality on the myth of the independent landowner living in the environment of a commercial economy.[27] A free-trade order that was able to secure overseas markets for American agricultural surpluses also secured the Jeffersonians the support of those anti-Federalist entrepreneurs who called for complete freedom of movement.[28] The rapid growth of the American population, the expansion of agricultural production and the opportunities resulting from increased European demand for American grains gave the landowner a central economic role. So, while in Europe the rise in population laid the foundations for the creation of a proletariat, in America it enhanced the 'farmer', perceived as modern and dynamic, unlike the 'planter', 'who follows the ancient track of his ancestors'.[29] Moreover, the agrarian project of the Republicans provided the expanding nation with a social framework, albeit still within a vision of freedom and democracy that recognized only the rights of the white man.[30] In the uniqueness of American conditions, with land that seemed inexhaustibly abundant, it was the society founded on the farmer that seemed to correspond most to nature, and the idea of a necessary natural order constituted a powerful instrument with which to oppose the arbitrary power spawned by British corruption.[31] Faced with the various options for the development of the new state, the Republicans proposed

---

Imagined and America Realized the Enlightenment (Garden City, NY: Anchor Press, Doubleday, 1977). On the value of the European republican tradition, cf. Franco Venturi, *Utopia and Reform in the Enlightenment* (Cambridge: Cambridge University Press, 1971).

[27]   Cf. Joyce Appleby, *Capitalism*; Isaac Kramnick, 'Republican Revisionism Revisited', *The American Historical Review*, 87/3 (June 1982): 629–64.

[28]   McCoy, *The Elusive Republic*.

[29]   This is the distinction contained in the work by William Tatham, *Communications Concerning the Agriculture and Commerce of the United States* (London: J. Ridgway, 1800): 46, which is recalled in the article by Joyce Appleby, 'Commercial farming and the "Agrarian Myth" in Early Republic', *Journal of American History*, 68/4 (1982): 833–49.

[30]   Cf., among the plentiful literature, David B. Davis, *The Problem of Slavery in the Age of Revolution, 1770–1823* (Ithaca: Cornell University Press, 1975), which investigates the many ideas that supported the antislavery movement. Cf. also the recent summary by Gordon Wood, *The American Revolution*.

[31]   Cf. Joyce Appleby, 'Republicanism in Old and New Contexts', *The William and Mary Quarterly*, 3d ser., 43 (1986): 20–34. On contemporaries' perception of the United States as champions of free trade, cf. the essay by Koen Stapelbroek, "Neutrality and Trade in the Dutch Republic (1775–1783): Preludes to a Piecemeal Revolution," in *Rethinking the*

the agrarian model and economic freedom as the most democratic possibilities and those best qualified to prevent the formation of aristocracies that were inherent in mercantilist trade politics, combining commercial freedom and republican government. General Warren wrote in the *American Museum* in 1787:

> Agriculture has long been a favourite object with me. In a philosophical view, it is great and extensive; in a political view, it is important, and perhaps, the only firm and stable foundation of greatness. As a profession, it strengthens the mind, without enervating the body. In morals, it tends to increase virtue, without introducing vice. In religion, it naturally inspires piety, devotion, and a dependence on providence.[32]

The author underlined the universal need for agriculture, yet at the same time highlighted–America's particular predisposition towards it.[33] In a 1789 article from the *American Museum* the superiority of agriculture over manufacturing was asserted: 'mechanic arts may be justly considered, as the offspring of that plenty, which agriculture begets'.[34]

By the eve of the Revolution there was a strong conviction that the independence of the colonies would remove the obstacles to economic freedom, ensuring political participation, or, more precisely, that economic freedom would lead to democracy via equal opportunities.[35] The situation of the farmer thus came to guarantee greater equality, seen as specifically American, by warrant of the universal principle of equality enshrined in the Declaration of Independence.[36] As such, the hierarchy of the new state was opposed to European social structures, which rested on the corporate interests of separate groups as well as on poverty. The denunciation of European misery, which was juxtaposed with the wellbeing

---

Atlantic World: Europe and America in the Age of Democratic Revolutions, ed. Manuela Albertone and Antonino De Francesco (London: Palgrave Macmillan, 2009), 100–19.

[32]   'Observations on agriculture, its advantages, and the causes that have in America prevented improvements in husbandry. By General Warren, of Massachusetts', *American Museum or Universal Magazine* (2 October 1787): 344.

[33]   *Ibid.*, 345.

[34]   'Whether it be [sic] most beneficial to the United States, to promote agriculture, or to encourage the mechanic arts and manufactures? From a discourse, pronounced by John Morgan, M.D.F.R.S, at a meeting of the Shandean Society of New-Bern, North Carolina, March 15, 1789', in *American Museum or Universal Magazine* (July 1789): 72.

[35]   Cf. Banning, *The Jeffersonian Persuasion*.

[36]   In argument with the interpretative paradigm put forward by classical republicanism, Michael Zuckert traced the origins of a new American, universalistic and egalitarian republicanism to a reading of Locke (Zuckert, *Natural rights*). Cf. also Pangle, *The Spirit of Modern Republicanism*.

of American democracy, was a recurring theme in the descriptions that Americans made of Europe.[37]

Puritan Ethics and Republic: Samuel Williams

The hierarchy founded on the farmer implied a notion of social harmony that had deep religious roots in the Puritan tradition and thus undermined hierarchy based on deference in favour of a notion of providential design and an aversion to a discordant model of society.[38] Tocqueville placed the Puritan political innovations at the base of American constitutionalism and the principle of popular sovereignty and political participation, arguing that, while they had made the colonists British subjects, they had also made them democrats and republicans.[39] After the Great Awakening, the subject of democratization became central to the development of American Christianity, joining evangelical fervour to popular sovereignty. The religious challenge of traditional authority thereby came to define a singular relationship, compared to the tension in Europe, between Enlightenment culture and religion.[40]

Among the different revolutionary discourses it was Puritanism that helped to determine a democratic and radical language and favoured its popular reception. This was seen in the success of Thomas Paine's *Common Sense*, which harnessed the power of the sermon so familiar to the colonial public to secularize the Puritan

---

[37]   Franklin to Joshua Babcock, London, 13 January 1772, in B. Franklin, *The Papers*, ed. W.B. Willcox (New Haven: Yale University Press, 1959–), vol. XIX, 7; Jefferson to John F. Watson, Monticello, 17 May 1814, in T. Jefferson, *The Writings*, ed. Bergh, vol. XIV, 136.

[38]   Cf. Edmund S. Morgan, 'The Puritan Ethic and the American Revolution', *The William and Mary Quarterly*, 24 (1967): 3–43, here, 4; James T. Kloppenberg, 'The Virtues of Liberalism: Christianity, Republicanism, and Ethics in Early American Political Discourse', *Journal of American History*, 74/1 (1987): 9–33.

[39]   Alexis-Henri-Charles de Clérel de Tocqueville, *La Démocratie en Amérique* (Paris: Gallimard, 1951), Part 2, ch. IX, 131–3. Cf. Sanford Kessler, 'Tocqueville's Puritans: Christianity and the American Founding', *The Journal of Politics*, 54/3 (1992), 776–92. Cf. also: Edmund S. Morgan, ed., *Puritan Political Ideas: 1558–1794* (Indianapolis: Bobbs-Merrill, 1965); John P. Diggins, *The Lost Soul of American Politics, Virtue: Self-Interest, and the Foundations of Liberalism* (New York: Basic Books, 1984); Ellis Sandoz, *A Government of Laws: Political Theory, Religion, and the American Founding* (London: Baton Rouge, 1990); James H. Hutson, *Religion and the Founding of the American Republic* (Washington: Library of Congress, 1998); J. Hutson, ed., *Religion and the New Republic: Faith in the Founding of America* (Lanham, MD: Rowman and Littlefield, 2000).

[40]   Nathan O. Hatch, *The Democratization of American Christianity* (New Haven: Yale University Press, 1989); Barry A. Shain, *The Myth of American Individualism: The Protestant Origins of American Political Thought* (Princeton: Princeton University Press, 1994); Frank Lambert, *The Founding Fathers and the Place of Religion in America* (Princeton: Princeton University Press, 2003).

spirit of liberty by appealing to a universal reason as the source of moral authority.[41] Similarly, Franklin, as a journalist and editor, in his *Poor Richard's Almanac* successfully channelled the force of such Puritan virtues as industriousness and frugality to penetrate popular opinion.[42]

By extolling a moral inclination towards social harmony, eighteenth-century Puritan ideology reinforced the concept of economic exchange and wealth creation against the static image of enrichment possible only at the expense of others. In doing so, it commended the creative potential of the individual and contributed to the project of building a national economy independent of Britain, which would preserve American virtue and simplicity.[43] The idea of an economy with ethical foundations and with the ideals of thrift and hard work, which belonged to republican thought, thereby succeeded in harnessing together the evangelical principles of the Founding Fathers, who had wanted to create a different society from that of the Britain they had left behind.[44]

Between the 1780s and 1790s, the period in which agrarian ideology was defined, though not within the inner circle of its theorists, the Reverend Samuel Williams, pastor in Bradford between 1765 and 1780, member of the Philosophical Society and author of religious sermons and a *History of Vermont*, typified an encounter between religious ethics, republicanism and agrarianism in the setting of a cosmopolitan culture. His work eulogized agriculture:

> The wealth drawn from agriculture, is permanent and durable ... The people that thus live by their own agriculture are independent of other nations, and need not be affected by their wars, revolutions, or convulsions; but they always have the means of support and independence among themselves ... Agriculture is the art ... which supports, supplies, and maintains all the rest. It ought therefore to be esteemed the primary, the fundamental, and the most essential art of all.[45]

---

[41]   Harry S. Stout, 'Religion, Communications, and Ideological Origins of the American Revolution', *The William and Mary Quarterly*, 3d ser.ies, 34 (1977): 519–41.

[42]   Benjamin Franklin, *Autobiography*, ed. J.A. Leo Lemay and P.M. Zall (New York: W.W. Norton and Company, 1986): 9. Cf. Whitney Griswold, 'Three Puritans on Prosperity', *New England Quarterly*, VII (1934), 475–93.

[43]   Alan Heimbert, *Religion and the American Mind: From the Great Awakening to the Revolution* (Cambridge, MA: Harvard University Press, 1966); John E. Crowley, *This Sheba, Self: The Conceptualisation of Economic Life in Eighteenth-Century America* (Baltimore: The John Hopkins University Press, 1974).

[44]   Isaac Kramnick, '"The Great National Discussion": The Discourse of Politics in 1787', *The William and Mary Quarterly*, 3d ser., 45 (1988): 3–32.

[45]   Samuel Williams, *The Natural and Civil History of Vermont*, 2 vols. (Burlington, VT: Samuel Mills, 1809): II, 355. The 1809 edition is an enlarged version of the first edition of 1794. Passages also appeared in the article 'Agriculture', published in the *Massachussetts Magazine* (November 1794): 690–92.

This was not only a convinced and general profession of agrarian faith by a critic of luxury and trade[46] who was adept at using the 'rhetoric of accusation' of the English dissenters against vice and corruption.[47] There was also the conviction, expressed in terms that echoed Physiocratic arguments, of the exclusive productivity of agriculture, 'the art which produces, and nourishes all the rest'. Other economic activities, although useful, 'do not of themselves, add any thing to the wealth of nations'.[48] He hoped that manufacturers would remain confined to the domestic sphere and that, in any case, all their activities would be in the service of agriculture. Similarly, he praised the pacifism and independence linked to agriculture.[49]

Williams was nurtured by a cosmopolitan culture, particularly that of France. He knew Raynal and Montesquieu, whom he quoted in a sermon that extolled the relationship between religion and happiness on earth. In the same text he also referred to the *Histoire des Deux Indes* as authoritative evidence of the hopes that were resting on America's future.[50] Enlightenment and religion thus coexisted in the pastor's thoughts, and he had already drawn up, using his religious approach, an image of social harmony in which he placed his later reflections on political economy and agriculture.[51] *The Influence of Christianity on Civil Society* recognized the role of religion in promoting civil and temporal progress, and it linked faith to democracy. The influence of religion on the government needed to be exercised through 'the dominion of equal laws, made by common consent, as the basis of their government', to ensure the rights, property and freedom of all.[52]

Within this influence of French culture, the pastor drew a picture in which the peace and happiness of men were secured by religion. These were in fact the same qualities of the men who received God's blessing in order to determine progress in the civil and temporal sphere. The truth of the gospel and the principle of usefulness were closely related in Williams's vision of religion that saw in the agrarian model and Republican government the way that led to the full realization of the individual.[53] Williams believed that agriculture, which made it possible to avoid repetitive toil, was correlated to morality and virtue. The ethical dimension

---

[46]   Samuel Williams, *The Influence of Christianity on Civil Society, Represented in a Discourse Delivered November 10, 1779* (Boston: John Boyle, 1780): 8.

[47]   Cf. John P. Diggins, *The Lost Soul*.

[48]   Williams, *The Natural and Civil History*, vol. II, 355. For a Physiocratic reading of Williams's reasoning, see Chester E. Eisinger, 'The Influence of Natural Rights and Physiocratic Doctrines on American Agrarian Thought During the Revolutionary Period', *Agricultural History*, 21 (1947): 13–23.

[49]   Williams, *The Natural and Civil History*, vol. II, 355.

[50]   Williams, *The Influence of Christianity*, 15–16.

[51]   Williams, *The Influence of Christianity*, 15–16.

[52]   Williams, *The Influence of Christianity*, 12–13.

[53]   Williams, *The Influence of Christianity*, 19. Williams, *The Natural and Civil History*, vol. II, 387.

of agriculture also indicated a more general focus on the political value of culture and its dissemination and a religion devoid of superstition and ignorance.[54]

The American form of government was praised for its specific nature and was set against the British system:

> On what is the whole system of American Republicanism founded? Does it in fact depend on a system of political checks, balances and arrangements; artificially contrived not to set the machine in motion, but to prevent its going wrong? ... Will not these be unavoidably connected with their circumstances, situations, and employments? And will not agriculture go further to form the desires, opinions, and habits of men, than any other employment?[55]

The special situation of America thus made clear the close interconnection between agriculture and republicanism, a bond moreover that presupposed the rejection of every distinction and privilege:

> When the body of the people are the owners of the lands, and do the labor of husbandry, is there not an extensive and permanent cause for republicanism, in such a situation and employment? Will not such men always be in favour of so much government as will do justice, protect property, and defend the country? And will they not always be averse to the distinctions of monarchy, nobility, the powers of the established church, and army? May we not then venture to say that the American republics will last, as long as the body of the people own lands, and do the labors of agriculture themselves. And that the republican system can no where take place, when the lands are in the hands of a few wealthy men? ... I believe we may venture to say the American system of agriculture and republicanism, have such an affinity to each other, that they will both flourish or decline together.[56]

The principle of representation as an expression of modern republicanism was recognized as the foundation of American governments:

> This kind of government seems to have had its form and origin, from nature. It is not derived from any of the histories of the ancient republics. It is not borrowed from Greece, Rome, or Carthage. Nor does it appear that a government founded in representation ever was adopted among the ancients, under any form whatever. Representation thus unknown to the ancients, was gradually introduced into Europe by her monarchs; not with any design to favour the rights of the people, but as the best means that they could devise to raise money.[57]

---

[54] Williams, *The Natural and Civil History*, vol. II, 387.

[55] Williams, *The Natural and Civil History*, vol. II, 358.

[56] Williams, *The Natural and Civil History*, vol. II, 358–9.

[57] Williams, *The Natural and Civil History*, vol. II, 392.

Williams thus asserted the superiority of the representative governments of republics, and in particular the modern American one. And it was indeed the United States, with the newness of their political experience, which could give rise to an authentic representative government, since the absence of privileges made a system 'derived from nature and reason' possible.[58] A national identity founded on nature was thus perceived as unique to America, and this was a cultural terrain well suited to the planting of the agrarian model, the theory of which had been developed by the Physiocrats and which Jefferson's Republicans had then turned into a political project. The same patriotism had for the reverend a natural foundation that was religious in character.[59] Reading Montesquieu reinforced his arguments, at the point where he recognized in virtue, and not in fear, as in despotic governments, the principle of a just society: 'this virtue is the Love of our country'.[60]

Williams had embraced this kind of patriotism, blended with cosmopolitanism, and in which nature and grace came together, even before independence – as one can see from the *Discourse on the Love of our Country*, of 1774, where love of homeland and virtue were the same thing: 'a free government, which of all others is far the most preferable, cannot be supported without Virtue. This virtue is the Love of our country'.[61] The nation as the chosen place of nature had found expression in the self-government of the colonies, 'free and equal', a position that even for Williams was not initially incompatible with the bond with the mother country, as he openly admitted here, citing Franklin as authoritative legitimization of the relationship between the colonies and Britain.[62]

Religion as an important element of patriotism fostered the political evolution of the reverend, who came in his more mature work to link republic, virtue and the agrarian model, in the extolment of representative government, 'the American System of Government' as he defined the new republic, distinguishing it from monarchy, aristocracy and democracy (in the pejorative eighteenth-century sense of the word). A product of public opinion, the government, 'built upon the rational and social nature of man', was not, however, exempt from degeneration. It was from this perspective that Williams, by now an ardent Republican, hoped that conventions would be held periodically to allow each generation to exercise their constitutional will:

> conventions shall be called at certain periods of time, to alter, amend, and
> improve the present form and constitution of government ... And no policy

---

[58]   Williams, *The Natural and Civil History*, vol. II, 393.

[59]   Samuel Williams, *A Discourse on the Love of our Country; delivered on a Day of Thanksgiving, 15 December 1774* (Salem: S. and E. Nall, 1775): 11.

[60]   Williams, *A Discourse on the Love of our Country*, 11–13.

[61]   Williams, *A Discourse on the Love of our Country*, 12–13.

[62]   Williams, *A Discourse on the Love of our Country*, 15–25.

would appear more puerile or contemptible to the people of America, than an attempt to bind posterity to our forms.[63]

The Secular Idea of Happiness

From the Great Awakening onwards, a new link between religion and democracy, as in the example of Samuel Williams, set out the idea of progress as a religious sentiment that was not inconsistent with the pursuit of happiness. Within this perspective, the transition from a religious to a secular idea of happiness placed the agrarian model at the heart of natural and divine harmony.

In this context, the battle against traditional hierarchies, mercantilist practices and British corruption, and against the economic model of the former motherland thus became the moral cause of a virtuous people. Republican virtue, religious virtue and liberal virtue; the example of the classics, divine admonition, the yearning for individual redemption: the many aspects and facets of American virtue came together in agrarian ideology to define a modern virtue in economic terms, the virtue of a republic that sought to give stability to a new and vast state entity through the relationship between economics and morality. The redefinition of the concept of virtue, imbued with economic substance, was one of the original contributions of Jefferson's Republicans: 'Poverty often deprives a man of all spirit and virtue', declared Franklin, for whom virtue resided not in self-sacrifice but in industriousness, and for whom utility was the guiding light of moral sense.[64] The virtue of the farmer, in its various forms, became the integrative element of society and social solidarity, in which property denoted God's election to produce the common good. 'Cultivators of the earth are the most valuable citizens', Jefferson wrote from Paris in 1785. 'They are the most independent, the most virtuous, and they are tied to their country and wedded to its liberty and interests by the most lasting bands'.[65] And Franklin in an article for the *Éphémérides du citoyen* wrote: 'Fraternity is a country child. How could those who receive blessings from the Creator refuse them to other men? How can they be avaricious, those men whose expenditure has always produced wealth?'[66]

---

[63]   Williams, *The Natural and Civil History*, vol. II, 396. With difficulty Jefferson, but more likely Paine, could have been the inspiration for the principle that it is not legitimate for a generation to tie the next generation to its political choices, one of the cornerstones of the ideology of the eighteenth-century democratic revolutions. On the origins of Jefferson's idea and his relationship with Paine, see below p. 93–8.

[64]   Benjamin Franklin, *The Way to Wealth* (1757), in *The Works*, ed. Sparks, vol. II, 101.

[65]   Jefferson to John Jay, Paris, 23 August 1785, in T. Jefferson, *The Papers*, vol. VIII, 426.

[66]   Benjamin Franklin, 'Lettre de Mr. H. à l'Auteur des Ephémérides, au sujet du Pays florissant qui n'a point de Villes, dont il a été parlé dans le troisième volume de cette année', *Ephémérides du citoyen, ou Bibliothèque raisonnée des sciences morales et politiques*, 8/1 (1769): 44.

Inherent in the American concept of virtue was the idea of a set of common economic interests that were opposed to the British economic model. In American republican ideology the opposition between virtue and corruption thus assumed an importance that was economic rather than ethical, and an attack against corruption thus became one against the unproductiveness of an aristocratic society that was economically disadvantageous, since privilege itself was unproductive.[67] In contrast to this was an idea of benevolence linked to personal independence and moral responsibility: 'I think agriculture the most honorable of all employements, being the most independent. The farmer has no need of popular favor, nor the favor of the great, the success of his crops depending only on the blessing of God upon his honest industry.'[68] Agrarian economy was therefore deemed to be of great assistance to the Republican government, a standard of behaviour and a social plan.

The concept of virtue was complemented and later overtaken by the principle of happiness, which Jefferson outlined in the Declaration of Independence.[69] The pursuit of happiness in fact scaled down the centrality of virtue, since it also involved the search for material wellbeing. By substituting in the Lockean triad of life, liberty and property, the principle of happiness for that of property, Jefferson gave space to a new social hierarchy, in which property for Americans came to be a means rather than an end, and took on political significance as the foundation of republicanism. For Jefferson, property meant land, with all its economic, political and social potential, and it was not deemed a natural right. American republicanism called for a widespread distribution of land, a realistic prospect in the geographic conditions of the new state and essential for stability. It therefore promoted the ideal of a non-pyramidal social hierarchy, in which distinctions did not originate in laws and traditions but were economic, arising from wealth acquired through

---

[67]   Cf. Kramnick, 'Republican Revisionism Revisited'.

[68]   Franklin to Catherine Greene, Philadelphia, 2 March 1789, in Franklin, *The Works*, vol. X, 386–7. On the origins of American virtue, the historiography has challenged itself through a debate that looked comprehensively at the relationship between liberalism, republicanism and religion. Cf. Kloppenberg, *The Virtues of Liberalism*; Joyce Appleby, 'Liberalism and the American Revolution', *New England Quarterly*, 49 (1976): 3–26; Crawford B. Macpherson, *The Political Theory of Possessive Individualism: Hobbes to Locke* (Oxford: Clarendon Press, 1962). For an interpretation of Locke's liberalism from more than simply an individualistic perspective, cf. John Dunn, *Rethinking Modern Political Theory: Essays, 1979–83*, (Cambridge: Cambridge University Press, 1985). On the vital role of Scottish philosophy in the formation of the American political culture, cf. Morton White, *The Philosophy of the American Revolution* (New York: Oxford University Press, 1978); Richard K. Matthews, *The Radical Politics of Thomas Jefferson: A Revisionist View* (Lawrence: University Press of Kansas, 1984). On the transformation of English religious virtue into American secularized virtue, cf. Gertrude Himmelfarb, *The Roads to Modernity: The British, French and American Enlightenments* (New York: Random House, 2004).

[69]   On the European origins of Jefferson's concept of happiness, cf. Forrest McDonald, *Novus ordo seclorum: The Intellectual Origins of the Constitution* (Lawrence: University Press of Kansas, 1985).

labour. Property was not championed by Jefferson for itself, but as a base that gave solidity to the republican government:

> It is a moot question whether the origin of any kind of property is derived from nature at all, it would be singular to admit a natural and even an hereditary right to inventors. It is agreed by those who have seriously considered the subject, that no individual has, of natural right, a separate property in an acre of land, for instance. By an universal law, indeed, whatever, whether fixed or movable, belongs to all men equally and in common, is the property for the moment of him who occupies it; but when he relinquishes the occupation, the property goes with it. Stable ownership is the gift of social law, and is given late in the progress of society.[70]

As a means and not an end, it was thought that property fostered a concept of individual freedom that could expand a person's potential, something that made education a key political issue.[71] In 1778 Jefferson wrote a *Bill for the More General Diffusion of Knowledge*, in which education was presented as the foremost safeguard for the people against governments.[72]

'An enlightened nation is always most tenacious of its rights', wrote Samuel Smith, a Jeffersonian, in his *Remarks on Education,* which declared that the republic, education and virtue were inseparable.[73] The winner in 1797 of the prize launched by the American Philosophical Society on the most suitable system of education for a republic, Smith shared with Jefferson a respect for the freedom of every generation:

---

[70] Jefferson to Isaac McPherson, Monticello, 13 August 1813, in Jefferson, *The Writings*, 1291.

[71] On the evolutionary concept of freedom and the acceptance given to it by Crawford B. Macpherson (*Democratic Theory* (Oxford: Clarendon Press, 1973): 117–19), on the basis of a different conception of property and education in Locke and Jefferson, see David M. Post, 'Jeffersonian Revisions of Locke: Education, Property-Rights, and Liberty', *Journal of the History of Ideas*, 47 (1986): 147–57. Cf. also Stanley N. Katz, 'Thomas Jefferson and the Right to Property in Revolutionary America', *Journal of Law and Economics*, 19 (1976): 467–88.

[72] 'Whereas it appeareth that however certain forms of government are better calculated than others to protect individuals in the free exercise of their natural rights, and are at the same time themselves better guarded against degeneracy, yet experience hath shewn, that even under the best forms, those entrusted with power have ... perverted it into tyranny; and it is believed that the most effectual means of preventing this would be, to illuminate, as far as practicable, the minds of the people', (Thomas Jefferson, *A Bill for the More General Diffusion of Knowledge*, in *Papers*, vol. II, 526).

[73] Samuel H. Smith, 'Remarks on Education' (1798), in *Essays on Education in the early Republic*, ed. Frederick Rudolph (Cambridge: The Belknap Press of Harvard University, 1965), 170. Samuel Smith, a journalist, was also the editor of the *National Intelligencer*, the official publication of Jefferson's administration.

A system of education adapted to a republic should either possess the capacity of original reflection or that of improving, without adopting the ideas of others ... He should look upon the sentiments of the dead with distrust and oppose with intrepidity the prejudices of the living.[74]

It was in keeping with this idea of freedom, distinct from property and realized through education, that in 1776 Jefferson included in the draft constitution of Virginia a proposal to allocate 50 acres of land to every white adult citizen, to guarantee them the right to vote and thereby make the poor man independent and able to exercise his right to govern.[75] Jefferson's preference for small and medium landowners was aimed at levelling conditions, not so much in the first instance for an urgent need of equality – hardly a priority goal in a country with an abundance of land – as for an aspiration for liberty that ensured equivalent economic and political opportunities for all men. With this in mind, he committed himself directly in the fight against privilege, personally promoting the abolition of the right of primogeniture in Virginian society.[76]

The republican synthesis, which reconnected American thought to the British political tradition with new threads, has highlighted the debt that revolutionary thought owed to 'country ideology'.[77] Jefferson and the Republicans found powerful tools in the language of British opposition to the English financial system and, more generally, against the corruption of political power.[78] Similarly, the moral sense of the Scottish philosophers, the various interpretations of Locke and the arguments of Puritan religious dissent all filtered into their thoughts. Again, in a century characterized by the circulation of ideas, among the many and varied political discussions the theorists of agrarian ideology found in France a modern language that combined economics and politics, rejected tradition and proposed a development plan focused on agriculture that ran counter to the British system. Its highest expression was achieved by Physiocracy, which, between the mid-1750s and the 1770s, made the earliest scientific analysis of the economic process. With Physiocracy François Quesnay and his followers intended to give a political as well as economic response to the French crisis, exacerbated by the Seven Years War, in the clash with Britain for international dominance.

---

[74]   Smith, 'Remarks on Education', 169.

[75]   Thomas Jefferson, *The Virginia Constitution: Third Draft*, in *The Papers*, vol. I, 356. Cf. Stanley N. Katz, 'Thomas Jefferson and the Right to Property in Revolutionary America'.

[76]   Thomas Jefferson, *Autobiography* (1743–1790), in *The Works*, ed. Paul L. Ford, vol. I, 77–8; Cf. Thomas Jefferson, *A Bill Directing the Course of Descents*, in *The Papers*, vol. II, 391–3.

[77]   Cf. Shalhope, Robert E., 'Toward a Republican Synthesis: The Emergence of an Understanding of Republicanism in American Historiography', *The William and Mary Quarterly*, 3d ser. 29 (1972): 49–80.

[78]   Cf. Diggins, *The Lost Soul*.

Economics conceived as the modern language of politics – in particular the reflection on the relationship between land ownership and right of representation,[79] with which different personalities of Quesnay's group responded to the demands for reform in the final decades of the Old Regime – survived beyond the 15-year period of Physiocracy's widest expansion. Immediately before the French Revolution, it stimulated political planning of various formulations within the circle of *Américanistes* that – together with Turgot, Du Pont de Nemours, Condorcet, Lafayette, the Count of Mirabeau and La Rochefoucauld – looked to the American experience as an alternative political model to that of Britain, and by its opposition to the *Anglomanes* reproduced in France on the eve of 1789 the duality that existed in America between the Republicans and the Federalists.[80] Discussion of the events of the American Revolution and the circulation of press reports (the censorship of which was avoided by the Franco–American alliance), gave these men a chance to criticize the French state of affairs and to advance their programme of reforms, thereby weakening the structure of the Old Regime. Simultaneously, it allowed direct participation in American debates.[81]

The right time for the publishing of the *Defence of the Constitutions of Government of the United States* was set, as John Adams himself admitted,[82] by the *Lettre au docteur Price* (1778), in which Turgot criticized the American

---

[79]   Cf. Manuela Albertone, 'Il proprietario terriero nel discorso fisiocratico sulla rappresentanza', in *Fisiocrazia e proprietà terriera*, ed. Manuela Albertone, special issue of *Studi settecenteschi* 24 (2004): 181–214.

[80]   Cf. Joyce Appleby, 'America as a Model for the Radical French Reformers of 1789', *The William and Mary Quarterly*, 3d ser., 28 (1971): 267–86; Frances Acomb, *Anglophobia in France 1763–1789: An Essay in the History of Constitutionalism and Nationalism* (Durham, NC: Duke University Press, 1950).

[81]   Regarding the *Américanistes* group's passionate interest in American affairs, David Humphreys wrote to Jefferson in 1786: 'There was however something at the Marquis de la Fayette's which put one in mind of the freedom of investigation in America: it was an assemblage of such friends of America as these, the Duke de Rochefoucault, the Marquises Condorcy and Chattelus, Messrs. Metza, Crevecoeur etc. to hear a discussion on American politics and commerce by a Mr. Warville; the tendency of whose performance is good, some of the observations new, many of them just and ingenious: but perhaps there is too much declamation blended with them' (David Humphreys to Jefferson, Paris, 17 March 1786, in Jefferson, *The Papers*, vol. IX, 329–30).

[82]   John Adams, *A Defence of the Constitutions of Government of the United States of America* (Philadelphia: Hall and Sellers, 1787): 4. Only later would the book receive its subtitle: 'against the attack of M. Turgot in his Letter to Dr. Price' (Cf. Correa M. Walsch, *The Political Science of John Adams* (New York: Putnam's Sons, 1915): 18). On the influence of the *Anglomanes* circle on Adams's thought, see Joyce Appleby, 'The New Republican Synthesis and the Changing Political Ideas of John Adams', *American Quarterly*, 25 (1973): 578–95.

constitutions, denouncing them as imitations of the British model with a system of a balance of powers that betrayed the principle of the unity of sovereignty:[83]

> I observe that by most of them the customs of England are imitated, without any particular motive. Instead of collecting all authority into one center, that of the nation, they have established different bodies … They endeavour to balance these different powers, as if this equilibrium, which in England may be a necessary check to the enormous influence of royalty, could be of any use in Republics founded upon the equality of all the Citizens.[84]

Making it his own, Condorcet had in turn expounded his master's plan for provincial assemblies in his *Vie de Turgot*, published in 1786, the same year in which Adams began to draft his work. He made clear the political significance of a decentralized form of representation founded on landowners, which had been presented in 1775 in the *Mémoire sur les municipalités*, the result of collaboration between the then controller general close to the Physiocrats – albeit from an independent position – and Du Pont de Nemours:

> M. Turgot often said: *I have never known a truly republican constitution*, that is to say, a country where persons of property had an equal right to concur in the formation of laws, to regulate the constitution of the assemblies which digest and promulgate these laws, to give a sanction to them by their suffrage, and to alter by a regular deliberation the form of every public institution. Wherever these rights do not exist in a legal manner, it is not a republic but an aristocracy, more or less corrupt to which we give the name.[85]

A few years later, on the eve of the French Revolution, Condorcet had marked, with his *Essai sur la constitution et les fonctions des assemblées provinciales*, the move from the Physiocratic discussion on representation

---

[83]   Written to Richard Price in 1778 the *Lettre au docteur Price sur les constitutions américaines* was published for the first time in Price's *Observations on the importance of the American Revolution and the means of making it a benefit to the world* in 1784. The first English edition of 1785 (Dublin: L. White, 1785) contained the English translation. See below p. 210.

[84]   For this quotation, see the edition of 1785, 113–14. Cf. Anne-Robert-Jacques Turgot, *Lettre au docteur Price sur les constitutions américaines*, in *Oeuvres*, ed. Gustave Schelle, 5 vols. (Paris: Alcan, 1913–23), vol. V, 534–5.

[85]   Jean-Marie-Antoine-Nicolas Caritat de Condorcet, *The Life of M. Turgot, Controller General of the Finances of France, in the years 1774,1775 and 1776* (London: J. Johnson, 1787): 340–41. (see Condorcet., *Vie de Turgot* in *Œuvres*, ed. Arthur Condorcet O'Connor, François Arago, 12 vols. (Paris: F. Didot frères, 1847–9): vol. V, 209–10). On the constitutional and economic foundations of modern republicanism, cf. *The Invention of the Modern Republic*, ed. Biancamaria Fontana (Cambridge: Cambridge University Press, 1994).

to the idea of representative democracy, noting the point when he turned from reflecting on the rights of landowners to focusing on the rights of the citizen, from monarchy to republic, in defence of free political participation that went beyond economic freedom.[86]

Unicameralism, administrative decentralization, liberalism, modernization of the economy, the central role of agriculture, rejection of the British model, faith in progressive opposition to the cult of the past and tradition, the critique of Montesquieu and his admiration for the British constitution and the balance of powers: these were the points that the *Américanistes* put forward for the transformation of France, and that, as a consequence of the American experience, they considered to be achievable.

In opposing Adams and the British model, which had been given a new lease of life by the success of the Genevan Jean-Louis De Lolme's[87] *Constitution de l'Angleterre*, Condorcet, Du Pont de Nemours and Filippo Mazzei borrowed from the critique of De Lolme made by John Stevens,[88] an American. In January 1789, after blocking the publication of a French edition of Adams's work,[89] they attended to the French translation of Stevens's *Observations on Government*, amplifying it with voluminous footnotes. The *Examen du gouvernement d'Angleterre, comparé aux Constitutions des Etats-Unis*, which paraded the uniqueness of the American experience, was an editorial venture with precise political goals undertaken by French intellectuals well informed of the American situation and committed to spreading knowledge of the new republic in order to stimulate changes in France.

---

[86]   On the relationship between Jefferson and Condorcet, cf. below p. 83 ff..

[87]   Jean-Louis de Lolme, *Constitution de l'Angleterre* (Amsterdam : E. Van Harrevelt, 1774). Originally published in French in 1771, the work was published in English in 1775, followed by three other editions, up to the revised edition of 1784, on which all subsequent editions are based.

[88]   John Stevens, *Examen du gouvernement d'Angleterre, comparé aux constitutions des Etats-Unis. Où l'on réfute quelques assertions contenues dans l'ouvrage de m. Adams intitulé: 'Apologie des constitutions des Etats-Unis d'Amérique', et dans celui de m. Delolme intitulé: 'De la constitution d'Angleterre'. Par Un cultivateur de New-Jersey* (London and Paris: Froullé, 1789). Madison sent the pamphlet to Mazzei in winter 1787. Cf. Filippo Mazzei to James Madison, 4 February 1788, in Richard C. Garlick, *Philip Mazzei, Friend of Jefferson: His Life and Letters* (Baltimore: Johns Hopkins Press, 1933), 117; Filippo Mazzei, *Memoirs of the Life and Peregrinations of the Florentine Philip Mazzei, 1730–1816* (New York: Columbia University Press, 1942), 278–9.

[89]   Cf. Joyce Appleby, 'The Jefferson–Adams Rupture and the First French Translation of John Adams' *Defence*', *American Historical Review*, 73/4 (April 1968): 1084–91. The news of the imminent publication of a translation of the *Apologie des constitutions des Etats-Unis d'Amérique* was given by Filippo Mazzei in the *Recherches historiques et politiques sur les Etats-Unis de l'Amérique septentrionale*, 4 vols. (Colle, Paris: Froulé, 1788): vol. IV, 213–14. On Adams and his difficult relationship with the Turgot–Condorcet group on his arrival in Paris in April 1778, cf. Zoltan Haraszti, *John Adams and the Prophets of Progress* (Cambridge, MA: Harvard University Press, 1952).

This was the moment in which Physiocratic political rationalism received one of its most mature endorsements in a note by Du Pont de Nemours:

> They have not said *lawmaker* [legisfaiteur], which would have indicated the power to make arbitrary laws, but they said *legislator* [legislateur], the bearer of law, which demonstrates that the one who is assigned this honourable duty has no other right than to take the law from the vast repository of nature, justice and reason, where it was all made, and to carry it, to lift it, to present it to the people. Ex natura jus, ordo et leges. Ex homine, arbitrium, regimen et coërtio, [From nature justice, order and law. From man absolute authority, control and coercion] as the profound thinker Quesnay said.[90]

The year before, Mazzei had been personally involved, with the support of Jefferson, in correcting mistaken images and judgments of America that appeared in the *Recherches historiques et politiques sur les Etats-Unis de l'Amérique septentrionale*, which was presented as being written 'by a citizen of Virginia' and was an exaltation of American representative democracy.[91]

Jefferson read these works and knew their authors, who made up his circle of friends between 1784 and 1789 when he was in Paris as the American representative at the French court, charged with strengthening trade links between the two countries.[92] Franklin had preceded him, covering the same role and staying in France on several occasions between 1767 and 1785.[93] Both men facilitated in first person the spread of French political and economic culture in America, and both found in France – Britain's traditional rival – a scientific analysis of economics and a development model based on agriculture that offered an alternative to the British one and reinforced their sense of national identity.

The use of agrarian ideology as a way to shape American national identity and establish democracy was nourished by the political struggle of the 1790s when the Republicans identified in their opponents' plans the British economic and political model. Some American characteristics combined to provide propitious conditions: attacks against the principle of deference, the progressive secularisation of the American idea of happiness, an harmonious vision of God, an appreciation of nature and a sentiment of patriotism, properly represented by reverend Samuel Williams's agrarian convictions. In the eighteenth-century circulation of ideas,

---

[90]   John Stevens, *Examen du gouvernement d'Angleterre, comparé aux constitutions des Etats-Unis. Où l'on réfute quelques assertions contenues dans l'ouvrage de m. Adams intitulé: 'Apologie des constitutions des Etats-Unis d'Amérique', et dans celui de m. Delolme intitulé: 'De la constitution d'Angleterre'. Par Un cultivateur de New-Jersey* (London and Paris: Froullé, 1789), note XIX, 179.

[91]   Mazzei, *Recherches historiques et politiques*, vol. II, 30. Cf. Jefferson to Gijsbert K. van Hogendorp, Paris, 25 August 1786, in Jefferson, *The Papers*, vol. X, 299.

[92]   Cf. below, p. 85 ff.

[93]   Cf. below, p. 115 ff.

and among different intellectual traditions – from the English country ideology and John Locke's thought, to the Scottish philosophy and the British Dissenters – the ideologists of the agrarian democracy found the scientific legitimization of their project in the original link between economics and politics developed by Physiocracy and (later) the Physiocratic rationalist tradition over a long period.

Chapter 3

The Cosmopolitan Vocation of the Agrarian Model: Thomas Jefferson

As a political and economic project, Jeffersonianism derived from its founder an original set of ideas that combined a strong sense of national identity with a cosmopolitan cultural approach. This approach to shaping the American spirit rested on the new way Jefferson linked politics with economics, reinforced also through his lifelong intellectual and personal contact with the French economists. In the context of the bitter political opposition of the 1790s, the Physiocratic arguments used by Jefferson's Republicans against Hamilton's Federalists were aimed at demolishing the reasoning of their opponents.

Faced with the depression and commercial crisis of the 1780s, the myth of America's youthful vigour and the certainty that foreign trade could ensure a predominantly agricultural future for the new nation were being called into question. The Federalists' response to this, which expressed the opinions of the more populous parts of New England, where Hamilton lived, called for the emphasis on agricultural development to be replaced by one on manufacturing and protectionist measures, in the belief that exports of agricultural products could no longer support the prosperity of a country now obliged to be increasingly self-reliant. It was a solution that undermined the ideal of a people of landowners, which had been at the heart of the revolutionary spirit of 1776.[1]

On 5 December 1791 Alexander Hamilton presented the American Congress with his *Report on Manufactures*. In it, he made not only the practical but also the theoretical case for manufacturing. Hamilton was aware of the strong counterarguments, derived from the central role of agriculture in the American economy, which included the country's lack of skilled workers, the high cost of labour given the attraction of easily available land and the widespread arguments against state intervention in the economy, expressing the risk that this might result in monopolies. The document bore witness to the importance given to Physiocratic theories in the United States during those years –theories considered dangerous by those who campaigned for a national programme of manufacturing expansion.

The first part of the report is the most interesting from a theoretical perspective. Hamilton was aware of the opposition to his belief in manufacturing, in the context of an American economy characterized by a great availability of land. He was also well aware that the authority of the French economic theories strengthened the positions of his political opponents. In articulating his political argument with

---

[1]   Cf. Drew R. McCoy, *The Elusive Republic*.

force and clarity, Hamilton showed that he understood economic science and was an attentive reader of Smith, Postlethwayt, Steuart, Hume, Montesquieu and Necker, all points of reference for his arguments, although his political realism and pragmatism led him to deny the universal validity of their economic theories. It was in fact to Smith's principle of the division of labour that Hamilton turned to demonstrate how the dearth of international free trade required the United States to focus on manufacturing.[2] He was aware, however, that the resistance to his plan drew its reasoning from a theory of economics, and he believed this had to be refuted vigorously:

> It has been maintained that agriculture is not only the most productive, but the only productive, species of industry ... Labor bestowed upon the cultivation of land produces enough not only to replace all the necessary expenses incurred in the business, and to maintain the persons who are employed in it, but to afford, together with the ordinary profit on the stock or capital of the farmer, a net surplus or rent for the landlord or proprietor of the soil.[3]

The Physiocratic principles of the exclusive productivity of agriculture, and of the net product, to which Hamilton referred explicitly, were applied 'with peculiar emphasis' to the United States, finding ready interest 'on account of their immense tracts of fertile territory, uninhabited and unimproved'.[4] We have no certain evidence that Hamilton read the Physiocratic authors directly,[5] but what is essential is that the framework of his views on their works was set in an anti-Physiocratic intellectual context or, in any case, in one that was critical or foreign to Physiocracy. Though he made no direct reference to the French economists, he criticized the premises of their theories and paraphrased many passages from Adam Smith's *Wealth of Nations* to summarize their principles;[6] further, he used those parts of Necker's works where the Swiss banker and director-general of the French public finances (and the manifest enemy of the controller-general Turgot and the other Physiocrats) offered support for Hamilton's own assessment by providing a negative summary of many of the views held by Physiocratic authors.[7]

---

[2]   Alexander Hamilton, *The Papers*, ed. Harold C. Syrett (New York: Columbia University Press, 1966): vol. X, *Report on Manufactures*, 239, 249–50.

[3]   Hamilton, *Papers*, vol. X, 236. On the debt owed by the *Report* to Smith, see Donald Winch, *Riches and Poverty: An Intellectual History of Political Economy in Britain, 1750–1834* (Cambridge: Cambridge University Press, 1996): 162.

[4]   Hamilton, *Report*, 231.

[5]   Hamilton, *Report*, cf. the note of the editor, 231–2.

[6]   For a detailed analysis of all the references in the *Report* taken from Smith's *Wealth of Nations*, see the editor's notes to *Report*.

[7]   Hamilton, *Report*, 231–2; (Jacques Necker, *Oeuvres*, 4 vols. (Lausanne: J.-P. Heubach et Compagnie, 1786): III, 204); Hamilton *Report*, 240 (Necker, *Oeuvres*, IV, 99, 102–3); Hamilton, *Report*, 243 (Necker, *Oeuvres*, IV, 82).

In this way he challenged the claim that the labour of the 'classes of artificers' – the Physiocratic *classes stériles* – did not create wealth, arguing to the contrary that their contribution, when added to that of agriculture, converged in the 'total amount of the consumption and production', and that it was only the 'artificers' who could accumulate savings, making the case already stated by Turgot.[8] He also rejected Smith's distinction between productive and unproductive labour and estimated the productivity of the 'artificers' to be the highest, since a division of labour could more easily be adopted by them than by farmers. While recognizing land 'as the primary and most certain source of national supply', and using the notion of capital, he held that manufacturing and agriculture were both productive activities and that, precisely in order to bolster American agriculture, an increase in former was needed at that time.[9] In support of a protectionist economic policy, he rebutted with similar resolve the principle of non-interventionism by the state in the economy and attacks on monopolies.[10]

Repudiation of the exclusive productivity of land, recognition of an active role for the state in the economy, a call for an increase of manufacturing and a protectionist economic policy: these were the key points of Hamilton's programme, which in terms of economic theory was aimed at disproving the principles of the *Économistes*, while at a political level it targeted Jefferson and the Republicans' project of agrarian democracy. The *Report on Manufactures* was in fact a firm response to and a point-by-point rebuttal of the Physiocratic positions held by George Logan who, with his *Letters addressed to the Yeomanry of the United States*, had, a year earlier, attacked the Federalist economic policy of using import duties to repay the public debt.[11] In opposing this American Physiocrat, one of the theorists of agrarian democracy, Hamilton in fact declared the reasons for a protectionist approach and for a conception of liberty that were intended to dispel that resistance to manufacturing which restated Physiocratic arguments against monopolies and government economic intervention.

Jefferson and Jeffersonianism

Jefferson's and Hamilton's projects were in profound conflict, since the Secretary of State, having been moved by insights strengthened by the Physiocratic scientific analysis, believed that the United States, a large country and a modern republic, needed to find its international legitimacy as a champion of free trade and force

---

[8]   Hamilton, *Report*, 236–8.

[9]   Hamilton, *Report*, 235–6.

[10]   Hamilton, *Report*, 232–3.

[11]   George Logan, *Letters Addressed to the Yeomanry of the United States: Showing the Necessity of Confining the Public Revenue to a Fixed Proportion of Net Produce of Land; and the Bad Policy and Injustice of Every Species of Indirect Taxation and Commercial Regulations* (Philadelphia: E. Oswald, 1791). On George Logan cf. below, pp. 139–50.

Britain to accept the same principle.[12] In contrast, the Secretary of the Treasury centred his plans on the formation of a national bank and on funded debt, and his protectionist policy and entire economic model was derived from the British example. Making use of the rivalries among European nations, Jefferson looked towards France and its economic culture and saw its revolution as a turning point that would compel Britain to abandon its economic strategy. Thus, both the Hamiltonians and the Jeffersonians pursued economic independence, but their international views diverged, as Jefferson and the Republicans believed that Britain needed America as an economic partner, and made the case for revolutionary France as a champion of liberty.

On his return home after five years spent in France (1784–9) as the United States' representative to the court of Louis XVI, Thomas Jefferson had been appointed Secretary of State by George Washington, who at the same time made Hamilton head of the Treasury. Compared to when he had left the country, Jefferson found that his Anglophile and aristocratic political adversaries were now a strongly consolidated group. The bitter political struggle of the 1790s thus also turned into a direct clash between him and Hamilton.

Foreign policy and the economy were the central themes of this conflict, which, as well as being a confrontation between two men of different characters, was more generally a collision between two profoundly dissimilar political cultures. In identifying his intellectual reference points, Jefferson had experienced a decisive moment of clarification during his stay in France. In 1792, speaking out against the work of Hamilton, he wrote to Washington:

> His system flowed from principles adverse to liberty, and was calculated to undermine and demolish the republic ... You will there see that my objection to the constitution was that it wanted a bill of rights securing freedom of religion, freedom of the press, freedom from standing armies, trial by jury, and constant Habeas corpus act. Colo. Hamilton's was that it wanted a king and house of lords.[13]

During his years in France Jefferson had reinforced his republican convictions and his rejection of monarchy, and he brought his personal experience as an observer of life in Europe to bear in the attacks on the alleged monarchical aims of the Federalists.[14] Indeed, while still in Paris, in stating his agreement with the new constitution,[15] he had expressed a conception of political representation diametrically opposed to that of the Hamilton's party, who supported a strong

---

[12]   Cf. Richard Whatmore, *Against War and Empire: Geneva, Britain and France in the Eighteenth Century* (New Haven: Yale University Press, 2012).

[13]   Thomas Jefferson to George Washington, Monticello, 9 September 1792, in Thomas Jefferson, *Papers*, vol. XXIV, 353–5.

[14]   Jefferson to G. Washington, Paris, 2 May 1788, in *Papers*, vol. XII, 128.

[15]   Jefferson to J. Madison, Paris, 20 December 1787, in *Papers*, vol. XII, 440.

executive: 'it is my principle that the will of the Majority should always prevail'.[16] As Secretary of State, but one directly involved in the political clash, Jefferson interpreted the hostility of Hamilton and the Federalists towards France and its Revolution from both the economic and political perspectives. In 1793, a few days before the execution of Louis XVI, he wrote:

> There are in the U.S. some characters of opposite principles; some of them are high in office, others possessing great wealth, and all of them hostile to France and looking to England as the staff of their hope ... The successes of republicanism in France have given the coup de grace to their prospects, and I hope to their projects.[17]

Jefferson identified the Republicans with agrarian interests and believed they represented not a party but the entire nation: 'the whole landed interest is republican'.[18] Their opponents were 'weak in numbers, but powerful' speculators, bondholders and bankers bound to traders and British capital.[19] In this light, he set out his thoughts on the value of agriculture, not so much as an economics scholar as a political thinker.

By recognizing the economic foundation of politics, Jeffersonianism placed itself, from the 1790s onwards, at the heart of the ideology of American agrarian democracy, discerning in the relationship between economic and political freedom the bases of a republican economy capable of supporting the principles of the new state that had emerged from the Revolution. The Republicans targeted the economic and political project of the Federalists and the model of Britain in a conflict aimed at defining the American economic identity in an international context.

The Republicans feared that the economic policies of their adversaries might cause the country to contract to a neo-colonial level. Jefferson therefore defied Hamilton's policies, which favoured links with Britain, proposing instead a programme of extended trade relations and the pursuit of national autonomy through, among other things, the development of a domestic market and territorial expansion towards the West, even though he did not reject a policy of retaliation,

---

[16]   *Papers*, vol. XII, 442. For Jefferson, the opposition between political groups was always clear and universal: 'Liberals and Serviles, Jacobins and Ultras, Whigs and Tories, Republicans and Federalists, Aristocrats and Democrats, or by whatever name you please, they are the same parties still, and pursue the same object. The last appellation of Aristocrats and Democrats is the true one expressing the essence of all'. (Jefferson to Henry Lee, Monticello, in 10 August 1824, in Thomas Jefferson, *The Writings*, ed. Bergh, vol. XVI, 73–4).

[17]   Jefferson to William Short, Philadelphia, 3 January 1793, in Thomas Jefferson, *Papers*, vol. XXV, 15.

[18]   Jefferson to Filippo Mazzei, Monticello, 24 April 1796, in Thomas Jefferson, *The Writings*, ed. Bergh, vol. IX, 335–6.

[19]   Jefferson to William Duane, Monticello, 28 March 1811, in *The Writings*, ed. Bergh, vol. XIII, 29; to Mazzei, Monticello, 24 April 1796, vol. IX, 336.

when commercial reciprocity was not guaranteed. The distance between the two programmes was extreme and the union between government and money, with which the Federalists attempted to consolidate their power through the creation of a national bank, and the use of public debt and financial wealth, found in Jefferson both an economic and political critic:[20]

> It is true that a party had risen up among us, or rather has come among us, which is endeavouring to separate us from all friendly connection with France, to unite our destinies with those of Great Britain, and to assimilate our government to theirs. Our lenity in permitting the return of the old tories, gave the first body to this party; they have been increased by large importations of British merchants and factors, by American merchants dealing on British capital, and by stock dealers and banking companies, who, by the aid of a paper system, are enriching themselves to the ruin of our country ... they have raised up an Executive power which is too strong for the legislature.[21]

Jefferson saw a direct link between all the objects of his attacks on Hamilton and the Federalists: the aversion to France, the example of Britain, commercial and financial power tied to Britain, a banking system, the centrality of paper currency and a strong executive power. Economics, politics and international relations were closely correlated in a project entirely different from that of the Republicans.[22]

The country ideology critique of the British financial system undoubtedly added a potent polemic language to American revolutionary discourse.[23] The aversion to public credit, to the banks and to paper currency was a constant in Jefferson's thought: 'Agriculture, commerce, and everything useful', he wrote in 1792, 'must be neglected, when the useless employment of money is so much more

---

[20]   Cf. Richard E. Ellis, 'The Political Economy of Thomas Jefferson', in *Thomas Jefferson: The Man, His World, His Influence*, ed. Lally Weymouth (London: Weidenfeld and Nicolson, 1973): 81–95; McCoy, *The Elusive Republic*; Matson and Onuf, *A Union of Interests*. Opposed for constitutional reasons to the first Bank of the United States in 1791, Jefferson, during his presidency and under the guidance of Albert Gallatin, who became his Secretary of the Treasury in 1801, was induced to appreciate the services that the bank could offer to the financial operations of the government. On Gallatin's fiscal programme, which was focused on both the reduction of expenses and the public debt, as well as the weakening of the fiscal situation, cf. Alexander Balinsky, *Albert Gallatin: Fiscal Theories and Policies* (New Brunswick, NJ: Rutgers University Press, 1958) and Edwin G. Burrows, *Albert Gallatin and the Political Economy of Republicanism 1761–1800* (New York: Garland, 1986).

[21]   Jefferson to Alexander Campbell, Monticello, 1 September 1797, in Jefferson, *The Writings*, ed. Paul L. Ford, 10 vols. (New York: G.P. Putnam's Sons, 1893–9): vol. VII, 169–70.

[22]   'This exactly marks the difference between Colo. Hamilton's views and mine, that I would wish the debt paid tomorrow; he wishes it never to be paid, but always to be a thing wherewith to corrupt and manage the legislature'. (Jefferson to Washington, Monticello, 9 September 1792, in Jefferson, *The Papers*, vol. XXIV, 355).

[23]   Cf. Pocock, *The Machiavellian Moment*; McCoy, *The Elusive Republic*.

lucrative'.[24] Many years later, corruption produced by the financial economy and speculative practices, the 'banking mania,' accelerated by the crises consequent upon the War of 1812, once again undermined in his eyes the republican virtue: the notes issued by the Bank of the United States were a 'fearful tax' on the people and the cause of 'usury, swindling, and new forms of demoralization'.[25]

This aversion encouraged Jefferson to develop his own economic theory, albeit not one formulated in systematic thought, but rather one that provided solutions to problems as they arose. In his acceptance of the quantitative theory of money, which made him watchful of the relationship between the amount of money in circulation and price levels, as well as critical of paper currency and the British model of discount banks,[26] he made explicit mention of Smith and his discussions on John Law and the Scottish banks, as well as of Hume and all of French thought, from Physiocracy to Jean-Baptiste Say to Destutt de Tracy.[27]

He was consistent in his metallism,[28] which led him to attribute the Panic of 1819 to the abuse of paper currency, just as on countless occasions he had attacked bankers as manipulators of money, credit and, more generally, the economy, favouring manufacturers to the detriment of agriculture.[29] His resolute opposition to the creation of the Bank of the United States, which he adjudged unconstitutional according to his restrictive definition of the areas of state action, was primarily an attack on all forms of monopoly.[30] From both an economic and

---

[24]   Jefferson to Justin-Pierre Plumard de Rieux, Philadelphia, 6 January 1792, in Jefferson, *The Papers*, vol. XXIII, 27; Jefferson to Archibald Stuart, Paris, 25 January 1786, in *ibid.*, vol. IX, 218).

[25]   Jefferson to Charles Yancey, 16 January 1816, *Jefferson Papers*, Library of Congress, Washington, cited in Robert E. Shalhope, 'Thomas Jefferson's Republicanism and Antebellum Southern Thought', *The Journal of Southern History*, 42/4, (November 1976): 529–56, here 544.

[26]   Jefferson to John W. Eppes, Monticello, 24 June 1813, in *The Writings*, ed. Ford, vol. IX, 394; Monticello, 6 November 1813, in *The Writings*, ed. Bergh, vol. XIII, 409, 431. The whole of this long letter contains observations on John Law and his criticisms of Smith, and it represents a precise approach, through which Jefferson puts forwards his ideas on the theory of prices.

[27]   Cf. Joseph J. Spengler, 'The Political Economy of Jefferson, Madison, and Adams', in *American Studies in Honour of William Kenneth Boyd*, ed. David K. Jackson (Freeport, NY: Books for Libraries Press, 1940): 2–59; Ellis, 'The Political Economy of Thomas Jefferson'; Charles A. Miller, *Jefferson and Nature: An Interpretation* (Baltimore: The Johns Hopkins University Press, 1988). On the influence of post-Physiocratic French thought on Jefferson, see below, Chapter 8.

[28]   Jefferson to John W. Eppes, 6 November 1813, in Jefferson, *The Writings*, ed. Bergh, vol.XIII, 430.

[29]   Jefferson to James Monroe, Philadelphia, 17 April 1791, in Jefferson, *Papers.*, vol. XX, 236. Cf. also Jefferson to John Blair, Paris, 13 August 1787, in *ibid.*, vol. XII, 28.

[30]   Thomas Jefferson, *Opinion on the Constitutionality of the Bill for Establishing a National Bank*, in *ibid.*, vol. XIX, 276.

a political viewpoint, the bank was in point of fact a financial tool in the hands of the government and, through the management of the public debt, was also a force politically attractive to the economic groups linked to the Federalists.

His aversion to public credit, and that of the Treasury Minister Gallatin, was steadfast and decisive throughout his two terms of office. He always favoured the prompt payment of government liabilities, seeking to contain the growth of the state debt burden and to guarantee its amortization. This stance was supported not only by economic theory, but also by a radical political theory that recognized the right of each generation to be left unburdened by the commitments made by its predecessors.[31] The Lockian principle that every individual received the land by right of usufruct for the duration of his life and, on the basis of this, the idea that debt contracted by the state could not be passed on beyond a generation, expressed a revolutionary viewpoint reached by Jefferson during his stay in France, as we shall see.[32] His criticism of Britain, the model of political use of financial interests, was always linked to this.[33]

In a reflection that assumed a constant relationship between economics and politics, opposition to the proliferation of banks and to a strong role for public credit, by means of which central power grew in strength, was linked to the desire not to diminish the powers of the states. For Jefferson, who approved of the constitution of 1787 as a consolidation of the nascent nation, preserving the authority of the states meant the guarantee of a balance of power between centre and periphery, the containment of the executive and the decentralized exercise of democracy, which constituted the essence of the republic and the authentic expression of the representative government:

> The elementary republics of the wards, the county republics, the State republics, and the republic of the Union, would form a gradation of authorities, standing each on the basis of law, holding every one its delegated share of powers, and constituting truly a system of fundamental balances and checks for the government. Where every man is a sharer in the direction of his ward-republic, or of some of the higher ones, and feels that he is a participator in the government of affairs, not merely at the election one day in the year, but every day; when there shall not be a man in the State who will not be a member of some one of its councils, great or small, he will let the heart be torn out of his body sooner than his power be wrested from him by a Ceesar or a Bonaparte.[34]

---

[31]   Jefferson to John Taylor, Monticello, 28 May 1816, in Jefferson, *The Writings*, ed. Bergh, vol. XV, 23.

[32]   Jefferson to John W. Eppes, 24 June 1813, in *The Writings*, ed. Ford, vol. IX, 389. On the events that led Jefferson to reflect in Paris on the rights of generations regarding the public debt, cf. below, p. 93 ff.

[33]   Jefferson to John W. Eppes, 24 June 1813, in *The Writings*, ed. Ford, vol. IX, 394.

[34]   Jefferson to Joseph C. Cabell, Monticello, 2 February 1816, in Jefferson, *The Writings*, ed. Bergh, vol. XIV, 422.

Thus while the decentralized exercise of politics helped to provide a schooling in republican thought,[35] education was the benchmark of this notion of republic, seen as a continuous interaction between local and national power. For Jefferson, author of the *Bill for the More General Diffusion of Knowledge* and founder of the University of Virginia, public education, made available for every level of society and the first duty of the state, was primarily an instrument of popular control and a defence against political power.[36] From elementary school to university, a complete system of public education was seen as intrinsic to the decentralization of the states and their ramified organization.[37]

Jefferson, who sought the help of Joseph Priestley and Du Pont de Nemours for the establishment of the University of Virginia,[38] took an active interest in deciding what disciplines to include in the curriculum, making sure that economics would be among them and giving the teaching of agriculture a special position.[39] The curriculum was also meant to enable students to understand the damage wrought

---

[35]   Jefferson to Joseph C. Cabell, Monticello, 17 January 1814, in Jefferson, *The Writings*, ed. Bergh, vol. XIV, 70.

[36]   Thomas Jefferson, *A Bill for the More General Diffusion of Knowledge*, in Jefferson, *The Writings*, ed. Bergh, vol. II, 526. On Jefferson's ideas and initiatives in the field of education, cf. *Early History of the University of Virginia, as contained in the letters of Thomas Jefferson and Joseph C. Cabell* (Richmond: J.W. Randolph, 1856); Roy J. Honeywell, *The Educational Work of Thomas Jefferson* (Cambridge, MA: Harvard University Press, 1931); Dumas Malone, *Jefferson and his Time*, 6 vols. (Boston: Little, Brown and Co., 1948–81); Gordon C. Lee, ed., *Crusade Against Ignorance: Thomas Jefferson on Education* (New York: Columbia University, Teachers College Press, 1961); David M. Post, 'Jeffersonian Revisions of Locke: Education, Property-Rights and Liberty', *Journal of History of Ideas*, 47 (1986): 147–57; Lorraine S. Pangle and Thomas L. Pangle, *The Learning of Liberty: The Educational Ideas of the American Founders* (Lawrence: University Press of Kansas, 1993).

[37]   Jefferson to Wilson C. Nicholas, 2 April 1816, in James B. Conant, *Thomas Jefferson and the Development of American Public Education* (Berkeley: University of California Press, 1963): 120; Jefferson to Joseph C. Cabell, Monticello, 13 January 1823, in *Early History of the University of Virginia*, 267; Jefferson to Edward Carrington, Paris, 16 January 1787, in Jefferson, *The Papers*, vol. XI, 49; Jefferson to Washington, 4 January 1786, in *ibid.*, 151.

[38]   On Jefferson and Du Pont de Nemours, see below p. 243 ff. Cf. Manuela Albertone, *Fisiocrati, istruzione e cultura* (Turin: Fondazione Luigi Einaudi, 1979): 95–129; Albertone, 'Du Pont de Nemours et l'instruction publique pendant la Révolution: De la science économique à la formation du citoyen', in *Les Physiocrates et la Révolution française*, Revue française d'Histoire des Idées Politiques, no. 20 (2004): 353–71.

[39]   On the project that he set out for the revision of the organization of the College of William and Mary, which Madison presented in 1785, the law teaching included an economic section, divided between politics and trade, and the teaching of agriculture was included amongst the disciplines of natural philosophy (cf. Jefferson, *A Bill for Amending the Constitution of the College of William and Mary, and Substituting More Certain Revenues for Its Support*, in Jefferson, *The Papers*, vol. II, 541–2). In 1814, in the plan for the transformation of the William and Mary College into the University of Virginia, the teaching of political economy was foreseen in the secondary higher teaching as a

by a credit economy.[40] Jefferson's ideas consequently represented a break with the essentially religious ideal of education of New England, which he countered with the republican education of the nascent nation, from common schools[41] to university, set within an ethical framework rooted in nature.[42]

A decentralized democracy, guaranteed by the powers of the states and political participation conceived as a form of republican education that could be accessed through a comprehensive system of schematic national education, were for Jefferson the touchstones of a republic, which the United States was constructing with a strong sense of identity and individuality. He opposed this to Europe, which he perceived as a set of realities – one of which was Britain – opposed to the American model. This was the Europe of cities, aristocracies, powerful churches and societies shored up by privilege, inequality and ignorance all of which made him doubt, in 1823, 'whether the state of society in Europe can bear a republican government':[43]

> At the formation of our government, many had formed their political opinions on European writings and practices, believing the experience of old countries, and especially of England, abusive as it was, to be a safer guide than mere theory. The doctrines of Europe were, that men in numerous associations cannot be restrained within the limits of order and justice, but by forces physical and moral, wielded over them by authorities independent of their will. Hence the organization of kings, hereditary nobles, and priests. Still further to constrain the brute force of the people, they deem it poverty and ignorance.[44]

In denouncing these realities Jefferson commended American representative democracy, which gave a voice to the farmers 'whose interests are entirely agricultural. Such men are the true representatives of the great American interest.'[45] And in combating the Federalists, who spoke for the interests of the cities and

---

subdivision of philosophy (Jefferson to Peter Carr, 7 September 1814, in Conant, *Thomas Jefferson*, 114).

[40]   Jefferson to William C. Rives, Monticello, 28 November 1819, in Jefferson, *The Writings*, ed. Bergh, vol. XV, 229.

[41]   Cf. Merrill D. Peterson, *Thomas Jefferson and the New Nation: A Biography* (New York: Oxford University Press, 1970).

[42]   The existence of the moral sense was a strong conviction for Jefferson, who had been educated in the school of his Scottish masters in the College of William and Mary (Jefferson to Peter Carr, Paris, 10 August 1787, in Conant, *Thomas Jefferson*, 100–01; Jefferson to Thomas Law, Poplar Forest, 13 June 1814, in Jefferson, *The Writings*, ed. Peterson, 1336).

[43]   Jefferson to La Fayette, 4 November 1823, in Jefferson, *The Writings*, ed. Bergh, vol. XV, 491; Jefferson to Joseph Cabell, 2 February 1816, in *ibid.*, vol. XIV, 421.

[44]   Jefferson to William Johnson, 12 June 1823, in *The Writings*, ed. Bergh, vol. XV, 440.

[45]   Jefferson to Alexander Campbell, Monticello, 1 September 1797, in Jefferson, *The Writings*, ed. Ford, vol. VII, 170.

were set on weakening the coordinating functions of local powers,[46] he came to see that defence of the states was a principle superior even to that of national unity.[47]

From the ideal of Virginian humanism to the individualism of the West, from Jefferson to Calhoun and Jackson, agrarian ideology over time shed its links to eighteenth-century cosmopolitanism, which had fuelled the to-and-fro of ideas between Europe and America, but Jefferson's agrarianism replenished the ideology of the South which was profoundly and originally American.[48] The complexity of his thought, the incongruity of his philanthropy coexisting with an acceptance of slavery,[49] and the political realism that never suffocated the radicalism of his reflections, makes him hard to define. He was profoundly American, and Europe helped to make him such through the culture that he assimilated, the perception of the differences between the two political realities, the circulation of ideas and the development of a radical notion of a European ideal of America – with which he came into contact during his years in France when he lived through the opening phases of the Revolution that overthrew the Old Regime.

---

[46] Jefferson to William Johnson, Monticello, 12 June 1823, *The Writings*, ed. Bergh, vol. XV, 443.

[47] The policy of mediation of Jefferson's two terms as president brought about the fragmentation of the Republicans, which became more acute after the War of 1812, setting the Old Republicans of Virginia and North Carolina against the groups that were more open to the market economy. Jefferson, who lost support in fact from the agrarian classes, feared the secession of the South (Jefferson to William Short, Monticello, 13 April 1820, in Jefferson, *The Writings*, ed. Bergh, vol. XV, 247 and also to Joseph C. Cabell, 31 January 1821, to J. Breckenridge, 15 February 1821, to Thomas Cooper, 2 November 1822, to George Ticknor, 16 July 1823). Nevertheless, faced with the economic and cultural decline of Virginia, he came to see in secession the extreme defence against a centralism that betrayed his idea of a republican democracy (Jefferson to William Gordon, Monticello, 1 January 1826, in Jefferson, *The Writings* ed. Ford, vol. X, 358). Cf. Norman K. Risjord, *The Old Republicans: Southern Conservatism in the Age of Jefferson* (New York: Columbia University Press, 1965) and Adam L. Tate, *Conservatism and Southern Intellectuals, 1789–1861: Liberty, Tradition and Good Society* (Columbia: University of Missouri Press, 2005).

[48] Amongst a very rich bibliography, cf. Shalhope, 'Thomas Jefferson's Republicanism'; Eric Foner, *Free Soil, Free Labor, Free Men: The Ideology of the Republican Party Before the Civil War* (New York, Oxford: Oxford University Press, 1971); Ellis, 'The Political Economy of Thomas Jefferson'.

[49] Amongst the rich literature cf. John C. Miller, *The Wolf by the Ears: Thomas Jefferson and Slavery* (New York: Free Press, 1977); Paul Finkelman, *Slavery and the Founders: Race and Liberty in the Age of Jefferson* (Armonk, NY: M.E. Sharpe, 1996); Garry Wills, *Negro President: Jefferson and the Slave Power* (Boston: Houghton Mifflin, 2003), Roger G. Kennedy, *Mr Jefferson's Lost Cause: Land, Farmers, Slavery and the Louisiana Purchase* (New York: Oxford University Press, 2003); Susan Dunn, *Dominion of Memories: Jefferson, Madison and the Decline of Virginia* (New York: Basic Books, 2007).

The Primacy of Agriculture

Balanced between idealism and realism, Jefferson has represented the development of an American identity as it related to the diverse traditions of European culture, from which emerged an original and shared intellectual heritage that – far more than a simplistic affiliation – was the synthesis of the connections, the convergences and the to and fro of a reciprocal exchange.[50] Author of the Declaration of Independence – which he never claimed to be the result of original thinking[51] – Jefferson, who was the first person to coin the term 'Americanism',[52] drew inspiration from the ideas of the cosmopolitan culture of a long eighteenth century. A protagonist in the American Revolution and eyewitness of the outbreak of the French Revolution,[53] he continued to believe in the pivotal importance of France and of its political and economic culture.[54]

---

[50]   In a very extensive literature, the attempt to locate a nucleus in Jefferson's reflection and a coherent link between his thoughts and actions continues to exercise the minds of scholars, without there having emerged a broad consensus on interpretative elements. Various interpretations of, say, a liberal Jefferson influenced by Locke (Louis Hartz, *The Liberal Tradition in America: An Interpretation of American Thought since the Revolution* (New York: Harcourt, Brace and Co., 1955)), or one sympathetic to a communitarian and organic vision of society derived from the Scottish philosophers (Morton White, *The Philosophy of the American Revolution* (Oxford: Oxford University Press, 1978)), or one bound to a tradition of civil humanism in all of its more recent permutations and evaluations (Banning, *The Jeffersonian Persuasion*), or even one who embodied an individualism manifest in the market economy of nascent capitalism (Appleby, *Capitalism and a New Social Order*), have all given substance to the diverse facets of a personality whose contradictions stemmed from combining the radicalism of an intellectual with the pragmatic efficiency of a statesman. A recent reconsideration of the complexity of Jefferson has been offered by Bernard Bailyn, *To Begin the World Anew: The Genius and Ambiguities of the American Founders* (New York: Alfred A. Knopf, 2003): 37–59.

[51]   Jefferson to Henry Lee, Monticello, 8 May 1825, in Jefferson, *The Writings*, ed. Peterson, 1501.

[52]   In opposition to 'Anglomany', the expression can be found in the letter to Constantin-François de Volney, Washington, 8 February 1805, in Jefferson, *The Writings*, ed. Bergh, vol. XI, 68. Cf. Joyce Appleby, 'What is still American in the Political Philosophy of Thomas Jefferson?', *The William and Mary Quarterly*, 3d ser., 39 (1982): 294.

[53]   Cf. James R. Sharp, *American Politics in the Early Republic: The New Nation in Crisis* (New Haven: Yale University Press, 1993).

[54]   Amongst the works that have underlined the importance of French culture in Jefferson's development, apart from the essay by Appleby 'What is still American' and the numerous studies by Gilbert Chinard, cf. also Adrienne Koch, *The Philosophy of Thomas Jefferson* (New York: Columbia University Press, 1943); Daniel J. Boorstin, *The Lost World of Thomas Jefferson* (New York: Henry Holt and Company, 1948). Traceable to the paradigm of civic humanism, John Pocock sees a Rousseaunian aspect to Jefferson's thought (Pocock, *The Machiavellian Moment*, 532–3).

Jefferson's policy reacted over a long period to the domestic and international situation: the debate of 1789–1790 over commercial retaliation, the 1807 Embargo and the War of 1812 all put Jefferson's principles to the test. From agrarianism to free trade, to the notion of commercial reciprocity, to protectionism, to the encouragement of local manufacturers, to the distrust of banks and financial wealth, up to the aversion to public credit, Jefferson's economic culture was the expression of a thought process that responded readily to the contingencies of political and economic reality while not straying from a coherent course of maturation. His formation was influenced by an original reception of French economic thought and its characteristic links between politics and economics, from Physiocracy to Jean-Baptiste Say, a subject that has yet to receive due attention.[55]

The first and only comprehensive formulation of Jefferson's ideas, the *Notes on the State of Virginia* – his only published work, for which he duly received renown as an author – affirmed his convictions concerning the nexus of economics and politics, convictions that never diminished even as he later adapted to changing conditions.[56] Written between the end of 1780 and 1781 as a response to questions posed by François de Marbois, Secretary of the French delegation to Philadelphia, the *Notes* gave Jefferson an opportunity to interpret his country, which he did in the form of a commentary on political economy, making clear throughout his predilection for agriculture.[57]

---

[55]   A specific discussion on the American reaction to French political culture is outside of the scope of this research. For a preliminary approach cf. the works of Henry May, *The Enlightenment in America* (Oxford, New York: Oxford University Press, 1976); Paul M. Spurlin, *Montesquieu in America 1760–1801* (Baton Rouge: Louisiana State University Press, 1940); Paul M. Spurlin, *Rousseau in America 1760–1809* (Tuscaloosa: University of Alabama Press, 1969).

[56]   Cf. Ruth Henline, 'A Study of *Notes on the State of Virginia* as an Evidence of Jefferson's Reaction against the Theories of the French Naturalists', *Virginia Magazine of History and Biography*, 55 (1947): 233–46.

[57]   Written before he left for Europe, the *Notes* were published for the first time nine months after his arrival in Paris, where the manuscript was completed, although not edited. In his autobiography, Jefferson recalled the events around the first edition, which was published in Paris on 10 May 1785 in 200 copies printed by Pierre-Denis Pierres for private circulation, since he feared the repercussions that his thoughts on slavery and the constitution might have had in America: 'It is possible that in my country these strictures might produce an irritation which would indispose the people towards the two great objects I have in view, that is the emancipation of their slaves, and the settlement of their constitution on a firmer and more permanent basis.' (Jefferson to François-Jean de Chastellux, Paris, 7 June 1785, in Jefferson, *The Papers*, vol. VIII, 184.) This first edition was the source of the French translation by Morellet, which Jefferson did not approve of because of the freedom of the translation, characteristic of Morellet (Paris: Barrois l'aîné, 1786), and which led him to republish the work with the publisher Stockdale of London in its first official English edition of 1787 (Thomas Jefferson, *Autobiography*, in *The Life and Selected Writings*, 60). The first American edition was published in Philadelphia in 1788.

A detailed description of the largest agricultural state and the most important economic region of America, the *Notes* was a true natural history of Virginia – as it was later defined – and one that Jefferson had wanted to put in the hands of every student of the William and Mary College.[58] It placed nature at the heart of a reflection that was both economic and political, a nature that could be identified with America and the national spirit and that was set against history. All this was communicated in two different literary registers for, on the one hand, the book provided detailed scientific observations and, on the other, it gave voice to a sense of national identity, doing so with the romantic perceptivity of the description of the Natural Bridge, which brings to mind St John de Crèvecoeur's *Letters from an American Farmer*.[59]

And, in a similar way to the Norman nobleman's *Letters*, Jefferson placed agriculture at the centre of an ideology and a sociology seen as having originated in America:

> The political oeconomists of Europe have established it as a principle that every state should endeavour to manufacture for itself: and this principle, like many others, we transfer to America ... Those who labour in the earth are the chosen people of God, if ever he had a chosen people, whose breasts he has made his peculiar deposit for substantial and genuine virtue ... While we have land to labour then, let us never wish to see our citizens occupied at a work-bench, or twirling a distaff. Carpenters, masons, smiths, are wanting in husbandry: but, for the general operations of manufactures, let our work-shop remain in Europe.[60]

Leaving aside the tones of puritan millenarianism, Jefferson identified the nation with a particular class, the cultivators of land: 'A people which preserve a republic in vigour'.[61] In his plans for the development of the American economy,

---

On the events surrounding the translation see Dorothy Medlin, 'Thomas Jefferson, André Morellet, and the French Version of "Notes on the State of Virginia"', *The William and Mary Quarterly*, 3d ser., 35 (1978): 85–99.

[58]   Charles Thomson to Jefferson, 6 March 1785, in Jefferson, *The Papers*, vol. VIII, 16; Jefferson to James Madison, 11 May 1785, in *ibid.*, vol. VIII, 147–8.

[59]   Cf. above Chapter 1.

[60]   Jefferson, *Notes on the State of Virginia*, 164–5.

[61]   As he himself observed many years later (Jefferson to Benjamin Austin, Monticello, 9 January 1816, in Jefferson, *The Writings* ed. Peterson, 1370–71), the *Notes* were written in a period of still-strong optimism about the impact of American independence on Europe, in the conviction that this would have allowed the United States to find in agriculture a specialization at the level of an international economy. Even by 1804 he still believed a world division of economic activities to be valid, between Europe exporting manufactured goods and America as a producer of agricultural products and raw materials, as he wrote to Jean-Baptiste Say, on receipt of the first edition of his *Traité d'économie politique* (Jefferson to Jean-Baptiste Say, Washington, 1 February 1804, in Jefferson, *The Writings* ed. Peterson, 1144). On the importance that the reading of Say and the post-Physiocratic French economic thought had on the development of Jefferson's positions, cf. below Chapter 8.

the primacy of agriculture was, for Jefferson, correlated to political principles, and it cohered with his modern republicanism. These were set out clearly in the *Notes*: rejection of coercive government, the sacrosanctity of the law of the majority, the legitimacy of the revision of the constitution, the abolition of the principle of primogeniture, respect for press freedom, the emancipation of slaves, the urgent need for a public education system.

'In so complicated a science as political economy, no one axiom can be laid down as wise and expedient for all times and circumstances, and for their contraries',[62] Jefferson wrote to Benjamin Austin in 1816 to justify his acceptance for an increase in American manufactures during the difficult aftermath of the War of 1812. Many shifts have been seen in the economic thought of Jefferson, whose pragmatism was always conveyed in the realism of an intellectual invested with decisive political powers. Thus, some have seen how, following his return from France, his adherence to the ideal of free trade was moderated by the principle of reciprocity; and how, on his arrival at the presidency, he accepted a balance between economic activities that facilitated national reconciliation policies; and how, from 1805, he made a turn towards protectionism in reaction to the Napoleonic wars.[63] Jefferson's economic development plan, which focused on commercial agriculture, was boosted in the United States by a wave of prosperity linked to growth in overseas trade during the late 1790s, a period marked by international conflicts. As a result, the Jeffersonians secured the support of a number of businessmen who, seeking complete freedom of movement, sided with the anti-Federalists. In the long run, however, the contradictions of such a policy proved harmful to the agricultural character of the nation. From the outbreak of the Revolution, trade had proved vital to the new state and was seen by the republicans to be a viable alternative to manufacturing development, but the hopes of creating an international system of free trade would eventually be disappointed, demonstrating that mercantilist policies were still well and truly alive.[64]

In this context and against the background of a thought ever ready to respond to the necessities of circumstance, agriculture always remained a personal passion for Jefferson. It was the central element of his economic reflections, a benchmark of his politics, the foundation of his radicalism and the expression of his national identity.

---

[62]   Jefferson to Benjamin Austin, 9 January 1816, Jefferson, *The Writings* ed. Peterson, 1372.

[63]   Cf. Grampp, 'A Re-examination of Jeffersonian Economics', *The Southern Economic Journal*, 12/3 (1946): 263–82; Ellis, 'The Political Economy of Thomas Jefferson'.

[64]   Cf. McCoy, *The Elusive Republic*; William A. Williams, '"The Age of Mercantilism: An Interpretation of the American Political Economy," *The William and Mary Quarterly*, 3d ser., 15 (1958): 410–25.

Like George Logan and John Taylor, the other theorists of American agrarian democracy, Jefferson was an agronomist as well as a landowner.[65] He meticulously registered the results of his experiments in the *Farm Book* and was an avid researcher of new plant species, which he described in the *Garden Book*. Along with other southern plantation owners, he was well aware of the dire consequences of intensive farming, which impoverished the land, and he pursued a programme of improvements using artificial fertilizers and systems of crop rotation and, of his own initiative, promoted the birth of American agricultural societies.[66] Moreover, he was one of the earliest importers of merino sheep from Spain, he arranged for the first threshing machine seen in America to be sent from Scotland and he introduced viniculture to Monticello, for which he was indebted to Filippo Mazzei. He was also an admirer of Piedmontese rice, which he arranged to have smuggled out of the Savoyard state: 'this seed too, coming from Vercelli, where the best rice is supposed to grow'.[67] In addition, he attempted to cultivate olive trees in South Carolina but, even though he had sent for 500 plants from Aix-en-Provence, this venture was ultimately unsuccessful. He was a connoisseur of French, British and Italian agricultural literature, contributed to the diffusion of agricultural publications and sought to create a course of agricultural science at the University of Virginia.[68]

Apart from this personal passion and a sensibility that extolled American nature within cultivated land, agriculture was always a key factor in Jefferson's thought, even on the economic and political level. This ideal of transformation and regeneration – which found a means of expression even through the models of classical literature[69] – differentiated America from the Europe of the cities: 'I think our governments will remain virtuous for many centuries; as long as they are chiefly agricultural; and this will be as long as there shall be vacant lands in

---

[65]   On Jefferson's passion for agriculture, cf. Jefferson to Augustin-François Silvestre, secretary of the Société d'agriculture in Paris, of which he was a foreign associate member (Washington, 29 May 1807, in Jefferson, *The Writings*, ed. Bergh, vol. XI, 212); Jefferson to John Adams, Monticello, 25 April 1794, in Jefferson, *The Writings*, ed. Ford, vol. VI, 505). Cf. also August C. Miller, 'Jefferson as an Agriculturist', *Agricultural History*, 16 (1942): 65–78; Edwin Morris Betts, ed., *Thomas Jefferson's Farm Book* (Philadelphia: American Philosophical Society, 1953).

[66]   On Jefferson's work for agricultural societies, cf. below pp. 174–8.

[67]   The details of this contraband operation are narrated by Jefferson in his letter to William Drayton, Paris, 30 July 1787 (Jefferson, *The Papers*, vol. XI, 646).

[68]   Cf. the list of agricultural works recommended by Jefferson, contained in a letter published in the *American Farmer*, vol. II, 16 June 1820: 94; Jefferson to David Williams, 14 November 1803, in Jefferson *The Writings*, ed. Bergh, vol. IX, 430.

[69]   Cf. Leo Marx, *The Machine in the Garden: Technology and the Pastoral Ideal in America* (New York: Oxford University Press, 1964); Douglas L. Wilson, "The American Agricola: Jefferson's Agrarianism and the Classical Tradition," *The South Atlantic Quarterly*, 80/3 (Summer 1981): 339–54.

any part of America. When they get piled upon one another in large cities, as in Europe, they will be corrupt as in Europe'.[70]

During his stays in France and Britain Jefferson had been struck by the widespread poverty, which he deemed to be linked to both political and economic factors: the monarchy, the world of privilege and the predominance of commercial and manufacturing interests over agricultural ones. The America of the farmers was an alternative model of economic dynamism or of political solidity, which for him always had strong connotations of anti-Englishness:[71] 'the whole landed interest is republican'.[72]

Jefferson concentrated his political battle in Virginia on the political and social centrality of landed property and on facilitating its wider ownership so that it was not monopolized by a few. This undertaking included the abolition of the law of entails and the right of primogeniture.[73] While conscious of the social responsibility that fell on the large landowners[74] – even if in his own case the issue of slavery remained ambiguous and unresolved – Jefferson's anti-aristocratic and republican convictions led him to favour the smallholding. Moreover, this was a position that, in the American reality of abundant land, did not contradict a tolerance of large properties, which for Jefferson did not in any case necessarily determine monopolistic positions.[75]

As a foundation of the republican government born from the Revolution, Jefferson conceived the legitimacy of land ownership not as a natural right, but as a right derived from society.[76] 'I am conscious that an equal division of property

---

[70]   Jefferson to James Madison, Paris, 20 December 1787, in Jefferson *The Papers*, ed. Boyd, vol. XII, 442. The same image would remain strong up to his late years, cf. Jefferson to William Johnson, Monticello, 12 June 1823, in Jefferson, *The Writings*, ed. Bergh, vol. XV, 442.

[71]   Jefferson to Horatio G. Spafford, 17 March 1814 (Jefferson, *The Writings*, ed. Bergh, vol. XIV, 120).

[72]   Jefferson to Filippo Mazzei, Monticello, 24 April 1796, in Jefferson, *The Writings*, ed. Bergh, vol. IX, 336.

[73]   *The Virginian Constitution: Third Draft of Jefferson*, in Jefferson, *The Papers*, vol. I, 356, 358, 362–3.

[74]   Jefferson to James Madison, Monticello, 13 May 1810, in Jefferson, *The Writings*, ed. Bergh, vol. XII, 389.

[75]   Jefferson to James Madison, Fontainebleau, 28 October 1785, in Jefferson, *The Writings*, ed. Bergh, vol. VIII, 682.

[76]   Cf. Koch, *The Philosophy of Thomas Jefferson*; Lynd Staughton, *Intellectual Origins of American Radicalism* (New York: Pantheon Books, 1968); Katz, 'Thomas Jefferson and the Right to Property in Revolutionary America'; Richard K. Matthews, *The Radical Politics of Thomas Jefferson: A Revisionist View* (Lawrence: University Press of Kansas, 1984); Post, 'Jeffersonian Revisions of Locke: Education, Property-Rights, and Liberty'; McDonald, *Novus ordo seclorum: The Intellectual Origins of the Constitution*. It remains an open question whether Jefferson's thought on property remained anchored to Locke or to Scottish philosophy, or whether the arguments of the English *Dissenters*,

is impracticable. But the consequences of this enormous inequality producing so much misery to the bulk of mankind, legislators cannot invent too many devices for subdividing property'.[77] These thoughts had occurred to him in France, in 1785, as he beheld a country blighted by widespread misery, which he attributed to the unequal division of property. The measures that he proposed were inspired by the politics of redistribution, which had already been at the root of his interventions in Virginia: the equality of successions, fiscal exemptions below a certain threshold of property ownership and progressive taxation. The conventional origin that he attributed to property was based on a reading of Locke[78] and had notable accents of radicalism: 'If, for the encouragement of industry we allow it to be appropriated, we must take care that other employment be furnished to those excluded from the appropriation. If we do not, the fundamental right to labour the earth returns to the unemployed'.[79] Back in the United States, he never again gave voice to such clear-cut views, for of course he had no need to, given the ease of access to land ownership that white men had.[80] However, his conviction that property did not come under natural law[81] remained forever firm, taking its place, as we shall see, at the heart of one of the more original formulations of his political thought, elaborated while he was in Paris.

For Jefferson, land was a fundamental political element of social cohesion and, in addition, a prime constituent of economics. The questions whether his agrarianism had been more marked up to 1790 and whether he moved (with the First Message presented to Congress in 1801) from an economic policy of self-sufficiency[82] to a programme of agricultural specialization,[83] do not invalidate the adaptability and

---

founded on the idea of Locke in a land originally given in common by God to men were stronger in him.

[77]   Jefferson to James Madison, Fontainebleau, 28 October 1785, in Jefferson, *The Papers*, ed. Boyd, vol. VIII, 682. On the impracticability of the common ownership of property, cf. also the letter to Madison of 30 January 1787, *ibid.*, vol. XI, 93.

[78]   'The earth is given as a common stock for man to labour and live on'. (Jefferson, *The Papers*, ed. Boyd, vol. XI, 93).

[79]   Jefferson, *The Papers*, ed. Boyd, vol. XI, 93.

[80]   Cf. Katz, 'Thomas Jefferson and the Right to Property', 481.

[81]   Jefferson to Isaac McPherson, Monticello, 13 August 1813, in Jefferson, *Writings*, ed. Peterson, 1291; Jefferson to Cornelius C. Blatchly, Monticello, 21 October 1822, in Jefferson, *The Writings*, ed. Bergh, vol. XV, 399.

[82]   Jefferson to Gijbert K. van Hogendorp, Paris, 13 October 1785, in Jefferson, *The Papers*, vol. VIII, 633. Cf. Grampp, 'A Re-Examination'.

[83]   The first clear position taken in favour of a commercial agriculture is contained in a letter of 4 May 1787, a month after the circulation of *De la France et des Etats-Unis*, the work by Brissot and Clavière that supported the intensification and specialization of exchanges between the two countries, in view of which the two future Girondin leaders, in collaboration with St John de Crèvecoeur, created in the same year the *Société Gallo-Américaine*. Jefferson, to whom Brissot showed the text before its publication, appreciated the work, which called on the Americans to preserve their agrarian vocation and exalted

the pragmatism of actions that were always directed at protecting the interests of agriculture. When, inspired by Jean-Baptiste Say and post-Physiocratic economic thought – much more than from reading of Smith, from whom he felt distant despite recognizing the importance of his work – Jefferson arrived at the idea of a necessary balance between economic activities, his programme of manufacturing expansion, and his adoption of certain protectionist measures and of the principle of trade reciprocity, were all purposeful and subordinate to agriculture: 'An equilibrium of agriculture, manufactures, and commerce,' he wrote in 1809, 'is certainly become essential to our independence. Manufactures, sufficient for our own consumption, of what we raise the raw material (and no more). Commerce sufficient to carry the surplus produce of agriculture, beyond our own consumption, to a market for exchanging it for articles we cannot raise (and no more). These are the true limits of manufactures and commerce'.[84]

From the positions he had taken in the 1790s to the convictions of his late maturity[85] the centrality of agriculture remained always at the heart of a republican thought based on the economic-political nexus.

Jefferson and Physiocracy

In addition to being of key importance to politics and economics, agriculture – 'a science of the very first order'[86] – was for Jefferson an essential part of a theoretical reflection that led him to keep a keen lifelong interest in the French economists. As we have seen, he, the author of the *Notes on the State of Virginia*, repeatedly professed his faith in agriculture. Indeed, even before arriving in Europe he had strong convictions on its merits and a well-developed core of political thought. In his letters from Paris, in which he continued his fight against the Federalists from a distance, he stressed the superiority of agriculture.[87]

Over the years, and after his experiences in France, his theoretical convictions grew stronger, even though he often had to act with pragmatism. In a 1792

---

their national identity: 'You have properly observed that we can no longer be called Anglo-Americans ... I had applied that of Federo-Americans'. (Jefferson to Brissot, Paris, 16 August 1786, Jefferson, *The Papers*, vol. X, 262; Brissot to Jefferson, Paris, 8 March 1787, Jefferson, *The Papers*, vol. XI, 204–6). Cf. Jacques-Pierre Brissot, Etienne Clavière, *De la France et des Etats-Unis*, preface by M. Dorigny (Paris: Editions du C.T.H.S., 1996).

84   Jefferson to James Jay, Monticello, 7 April 1809, Jefferson, *The Writings*, ed. Bergh, vol. XII, 271.

85   Jefferson to William H. Crawford, Monticello, 20 June 1816, Jefferson, *The Writings*, ed. Bergh, vol. XV, 28.

86   Jefferson to David Williams, Washington, 14 November 1803, Jefferson, *The Writings*, ed. Bergh, vol. IX, 429.

87   Jefferson to John Blair, Paris, 13 August 1787, in Jefferson, *The Papers*, ed. Boyd, vol. XII, 28; Jefferson to G. Washington, Paris, 14 August 1787, *ibid.*, 38.

circular putting the case for agrarianism to Americans he claimed: 'A prosperity built on the basis of agriculture is that which is most desirable to us, because to the efforts of labor it adds the effort of a greater proportion of soil.'[88] In 1805, when working on a new (but never published) edition of the *Notes*, he described what in 1781 had caused him to resist the formation of American manufacturing, 'I had under my eye, when writing, the manufacturers of the great cities in the old countries', yet another confirmation of the superiority of agriculture based on it being supported 'by the creative energies of the earth'.[89] He drew on the same idea in 1813, speaking of labour that was 'employed in agriculture, and aided by the spontaneous energies of the earth'.[90] And three years later, in his famous letter to Benjamin Austin, in which he explained the reasons for accepting manufacturing growth as inevitable, he set out in the following terms the principles that had guided his actions, believing the theoretical premises to be valid even though the real situation had profoundly changed:

> to the labor of the husbandman a vast addition is made by the spontaneous energies of the earth on which it is employed: for one grain of wheat committed to the earth, she renders twenty, thirty, and even fifty fold, whereas to the labor of the manufacturer nothing is added ... This was the state of things in 1785, when the "Notes on Virginia" were first printed ... We were then in peace ... We have experienced what we did not then believe ... We must now place the manufacturer by the side of the agriculturist.[91]

The consistent references to the earth as a creator of wealth prompts us to ask how much Physiocracy influenced Jefferson's economic ideas.[92] As we have seen, the attacks made by Hamilton, in his *Report on Manufactures*, on economic

---

[88] Thomas Jefferson, *Circular to Consuls and Vice-Consuls* (Philadelphia: 31 May 1792), in Jefferson, *The Papers*, ed. Boyd, vol. XXIII, 618.

[89] Jefferson to John Lithgow, Washington, 4 January 1805, in Jefferson, *The Writings*, ed. Bergh, vol. XI, 56.

[90] Jefferson to John Melish, Monticello, 13 January 1813, in Jefferson, *Writings*, ed. M. D. Peterson, 1268.

[91] Jefferson to Benjamin Austin, 9 January 1816, Jefferson, *Writings*, ed. M. D. Peterson, 1370–71. The letter to Austin is the same in which Jefferson made explicit reference to his economic pragmatism.

[92] Between the belief that Jefferson was strongly influenced by Physiocracy, as recognized by Vernon L. Parrington, *Main Currents in America Thought: An Interpretation of American Literature from the Beginnings to 1920*, (New York: Harcourt, 1927–1930) and the denial of any relationship with Physiocracy expressed by Grampp, 'A Re-Examination', there appears to be a much more complex situation, which is not limited only to economic principles, as this chapter will attempt to show. The reserve of American historians in relation to the attention paid by Parrington to French thought is well described in the essay about his work written by Richard Hofstadter, 'Parrington and the Jeffersonian Tradition', *Journal of the History of Ideas* 2 (1941): 391–400.

theories founded on the exclusive productivity of agriculture, were answered by the Jeffersonian group with sound arguments belonging to the works of George Logan, an authentic American Physiocrat.[93] Logan, the American icon of Physiocracy, versus Hamilton (a sort of American icon of anti-Physiocracy) – the Jeffersonian system versus the Hamiltonian system – natural economy versus artificial economy[94] – these were the protagonists of this struggle.

His characteristic prudence and the discretion required by his position in government prevented Jefferson from committing himself openly, despite his support for the campaign conducted against the Secretary of the Treasury. Indeed, it cannot be denied that, in line with his innate pragmatism, on certain theoretical questions he kept his distance from the *Économistes*. These included taxation, the basic principles of property and the central position accorded to smallholdings in both politics and economics.

As stated above, tax exemption on the ownership of land below a certain threshold was part of Jefferson's wider plan for the redistribution of wealth, which aimed to tax 'the higher portions of property in geometrical progression' and to create a simple, straightforward fiscal system.[95] In December 1784, a few months after his arrival in Paris, he questioned the economic viability of taxation applied directly on land, preferring a levy on the sale of agricultural surpluses.[96] Many years after he expressed these convictions, in his correspondence with Du Pont de Nemours – the authoritative interlocutor in a direct dialogue with Physiocracy and one with whom Jefferson was linked until the old economist's death in 1817[97] – he would refute the validity of applying a land tax in the United States, despite recognizing the theoretical rigour of the Physiocrat's arguments.[98] As an alternative, despite sharing Du Pont's emphatic rejection of taxes on consumption, he proposed forms of import tariffs in the belief that they would impact most heavily on the wealthy.[99]

And yet, for Jefferson – who used French economic ideas as a guidepost and who, after his return home, deepened his relations with the *Idéologues* and post-Physiocratic authors – Physiocracy remained the starting point of the science of

---

[93] Cf. below pp. 139–50.

[94] Cf. Jean-François Faure-Soulet, *Economie politique et progrès au 'siècle des Lumières'* (Paris: Gauthier-Villars, 1964).

[95] Jefferson to James Madison, Fontainebleau, 28 October 1785, in Jefferson, *The Papers*, vol. VIII, 682; Jefferson to Madison, 6 March 1796, *ibid.*, vol. XXIX, 6.

[96] Jefferson to James Madison, Paris, 8 December 1784, Jefferson, *The Papers*, vol. VII, 558.

[97] On the relationship between Jefferson and Du Pont de Nemours and the role of mediator played by Jefferson between Du Pont and post-Physiocratic French thought, cf. below Chapter 8.

[98] Jefferson to Pierre-Samuel Du Pont de Nemours, Monticello, 15 April 1811, in Jeffreson, *The Writings*, ed. Bergh, vol. XIII, 37–8.

[99] Jeffreson, *The Writings*, ed. Bergh, vol. XIII, 39.

political economy, for in his reading he came to see the continuity of an intellectual tradition and a unique French attribute. 'Our method in America is proof of the validity of your theory', he wrote to Du Pont de Nemours in 1787, appreciating 'this geometric exactitude of ideas that characterises everything that comes from your pen'.[100]

The political significance of the Physiocratic authors' discourse did not escape Jefferson, who was interested in their political rationalism, which rose from the economic foundations of society and from the natural and universal character of economic laws. It was grounded in the idea that the law consisted in a declaration of immutable truths. This implied the unity of sovereignty and the need to set the limits of legislative power, whose duties could be reduced to the knowledge and implementation of laws existing in the natural order.[101] The spreading of education was one of the fundamental laws of this economic order. The centrality assumed by the landowner, who embodied the universal interest and represented the entire nation, indicated how economic function was essential to defining not only his economic position but also his political role, through the principle of representation.[102] The Physiocratic ideal of the landowner, which marked the emergence of the distinction between political power and society, thus allowed Jefferson to go beyond the Physiocratic idea of legal despotism and to grasp the meaning of a proposition that, especially at a political level, was manifest in the space between the language used and the implications of such ideas. Accordingly, it is possible to understand the reasons that led Jefferson, the ideologue of American agrarian democracy, to act in accordance with the relationship between economics and politics that was peculiar to Physiocracy and French economic culture.

Jefferson's library contained many works by Physiocratic authors: the first edition in two volumes of *Physiocratie* (Leyde, Paris: 1767–8); by Du Pont de Nemours: the *Réflexions sur l'écrit intitulé: 'Richesse de l'Etat'*, the *A messieurs de la Société d'Emulation de Londres*, the *Mémoires sur la vie, l'administration et les ouvrages de M. Turgot*, the *Lettre à la Chambre de Commerce de Normandie sur*

---

[100]   Jefferson to Du Pont de Nemours, 6 November 1787, in Jefferson, *The Papers*, vol. XII, 328–9. In a list of books recommended to Thomas Randolph in 1790, he suggested as texts of political economy, apart from the *Wealth of Nations*, 'some excellent books of Theory written by Turgot and the economists of France'. (Jefferson to Thomas Mann Randolph Jr, New York, 30 May 1790, in *ibid.*, vol. XVI, 449; cf. also the letters to James Madison, Paris 1 September 1785, *ibid.*, vol. VIII, 464 and to Benjamin Rush, New York, 31 July 1790, *ibid.*, vol. XIII, 286–89). On Jefferson's judgements of Smith, cf. below p. 245.

[101]   On the physiocratic critique of the separation of powers linked to this tax, I refer to my essay, '"Que l'autorité souveraine soit unique." La séparation des pouvoirs dans la pensée des physiocrates et son legs: du despotisme légal à la démocratie représentative de Condorcet', in *Les usages de la séparation des pouvoirs*, *The uses of the separation of powers*, ed. Sandrine Baume and Biancamaria Fontana (Paris: Michel Houdiard, 2008): 38–68.

[102]   Cf. Manuela Albertone, 'Il proprietario terriero nel discorso fisiocratico sulla rappresentanza'.

le mémoire qu'elle a publié relativement au traité de commerce avec l'Angleterre, the 1796 edition of the *Philosphie de l'Univers* and the 1809–11 edition that he had edited of the *Oeuvres de Turgot* ; by Baudeau: *Avis au peuple sur son premier besoin*, the *Explication du Tableau économique*, and the *Idées d'un citoyen sur l'administration des finances du Roi*; by Le Mercier de la Rivière: *L'ordre naturel et essentiel des sociétés politiques*; Mirabeau's *Théorie de l'Impôt* and the 1756–8 Avignon edition of *L'Ami des hommes*; and Le Trosne's *De l'ordre social e De l'administration provinciale*.[103]

When, during August 1784, he arrived in France, where he stayed until September 1789, Jefferson quickly became a participant in the discussions that preceded the Revolution thanks to his contacts with the *Américanistes* – including those who met in Mme Helvétius's salon in Auteuil – among whom the political rationalism of the Physiocratic tradition lived on in Condorcet, Du Pont de Nemours and La Rochefoucauld. He was also helped by his relations with Franklin, his predecessor in France, who played an important part in keeping alive the latter *Idéologues*' interest in Physiocracy.[104]

Jefferson and Condorcet

France was the only place outside the United States where Jefferson would ever have wanted to live.[105] His confidence in the country never wavered, even after the advent of Napoleon, when Mme de Staël hoped that America would side with Britain against France: 'Bonaparte will die and his tyrannies with him, but a Nation never dies. The English Government and its piratical principles and practice have no fixed term of duration … the object of England is the permanent dominion of the ocean, and the monopoly of the trade of the world'.[106] Moreover, he had neither shared the widespread anti-French sentiment of the pre-Revolution years in America – a hostility to the Catholic, absolutist country that had fought against

---

[103]   E. Millicent Sowerby, ed., *Catalogue of the Library of Thomas Jefferson*, 5 vols. (Washington DC: The Library of Congress, 1952).

[104]   Cf. Alfred O. Aldridge, *Benjamin Franklin et ses contemporains français* (Paris: Didier, 1963).

[105]   Jefferson, *Autobiography*, 101.

[106]   Jefferson to Mme de Staël, United States of America, 28 May 1813, in "Unpublished Correspondence of Mme de Staël with Thomas Jefferson," introduction by Marie G. Kimball, *North America Review*, CCVIII (July 1918): 67.

the colonies in the Seven Years' War[107] – nor the denunciation of the radicalisation of the French Revolution when this became a political weapon of the Federalists.[108]

His European experiences convinced Jefferson of the superiority of French civilization and culture, as well as its agriculture, over that of the British.[109] His Parisian years were extremely fruitful for him, stimulating, in the midst of the fast-changing political scene, a set of refined theories. This led him not only to reconfirm his rejection of the British political model, but also to accentuate his detachment from British culture through his original interpretation of French political rationalism and its revolutionary implications. Many of his most important positions and opinions were modified and clarified from those years onwards, resulting in a more mature understanding of American national identity and an awareness of how French ideas had contributed to it. These were the years in which he grew increasingly critical of his country's politics, yet nonetheless more optimistic about its future.[110] In this context he also helped to promote French books, which he sent to Americans correspondents. A comparison between the list of books he sent out and the references noted in his *Commonplace Book* shows

---

[107]   After the Seven Years' War, the unpopularity of France gradually diminished because, alongside its undisputed cultural prestige, its role as a balancing power against British expansion grew (cf. Bernard Faÿ, *L'esprit révolutionnaire en France et aux Etats-Unis à la fin du XVIIIe siècle* (Paris: Champion, 1925)).

[108]   Jefferson on several occasions enjoyed remembering his call for prudence on the eve of 1789 and likened in his judgement 'the unprincipled and bloody tyranny of Robespierre, and the equally unprincipled and maniac tyranny of Bonaparte' (Jefferson to Lafayette, Monticello, 14 February 1785, in Jefferson, *The Writings*, ed. Bergh, vol. XIV, 246–7). The Jefferson who in 1787 had not hesitated to write 'The tree of liberty must be refreshed from time to time, with the blood of patriots and tyrants' (Paris, 13 November 1787, in Jefferson, *The Life and Selected Writings*, 403), did not deny the political value of Louis XVI's death sentence: 'We have just received here the news of the decapitation of the king of France. Should the present ferment in Europe not produce republics every where, it will at least soften the monarchical governments by rendering monarchs amenable to punishment like other criminals, and doing away that aegis of insolence and oppression, the inviolability of the king's person'. (Jefferson to Joseph Fay, Philadelphia, 18 March 1793, in Jefferson, *The Papers*, vol. XXV, 402).

[109]   Cf. Jefferson to George Wythe, Paris, 13 August 1786, in Conant, *Thomas Jefferson*, 99; to David Humphrey, 18 March 1789, in Jefferson, *The Papers*, vol. XIV, 677. On 11 April 1787 Jefferson wrote to Lafayette from Nice: 'The soil of Champagne and Burgundy I have found more universally good than I had expected, and as I could not help making a comparison with England, I found that comparison more unfavourable to the latter than is generally admitted. The soil, the climate, and the productions are superior to those of England, and the husbandry as good, except in one point, that of manure'. (*Ibid.*, vol. XI, 284).

[110]   'The writers of this country now taking the field freely and unrestrained or rather revolted by prejudice, will rouse us all from the errors in which we have hitherto been rocked'. (Jefferson to Thomas Paine, 17 March 1789, in Jefferson, *The Papers*, XIV, 672).

clearly how his horizons had widened: there are many more French authors than British ones, more *philosophes* than jurists.[111]

As we have seen, Jefferson had, at the request of the French delegate Marbé Marbois, made clear his agrarianism by writing the *Notes on the State of Virginia* before his arrival in France. In this work, he distanced himself from and rectified the assumptions and errors originating from, the opinions of French authors such as Buffon, Raynal and D'Aubenton, who spoke of American inferiority.[112] His arrival in Europe also coincided with a period in France when there appeared, in rapid succession, a number of important publications that urged America not to abandon its agrarian project. These included the 1780 edition of the *Histoire des deux Indes*, Mably's *Observations sur le gouvernement et les loix des Etats-Unis* (1784), Turgot's *Lettre au docteur Price* (written in 1778 but not published until 1784), and Brissot and Clavière's *De la France et des Etats-Unis*.[113] In France Jefferson discovered the myth of America while at the same time grasping the urgent need to propagate an accurate image of his country, for the dissimilarity of the two continents had in fact given rise to negative views of it. It was this exigency that prompted him to collaborate with the *Encyclopédie méthodique* and thereby correct the misinformation and misjudgements, offering with his *Notes* material of which Démeunier made ample use in his articles on the United States.[114]

Démeunier resented the criticisms the American articles in his work received, and his feelings were further embittered by his awareness that Jefferson's interventions had been orchestrated with the *Américanistes*,[115] who shared the objectives of freeing America's trade from dependency on Britain, reinforcing

---

[111]   Cf. Otto Vossler, *Jefferson and the American Revolutionary Ideal* (Washington: University Press of America, 1980).

[112]   Jefferson, *Notes on the State of Virginia*, 196, 200–01. Cf. Chinard, 'Eighteenth Century Theories on America as a Human Habitat'.

[113]   Cf. Bernard Faÿ, *Bibliographie critique des ouvrages français relatifs aux Etats-Unis, 1770–1800* (Paris: Campion, 1924). Cf. Jefferson's letter to Madison, in which he told him that he had the *Encyclopédie* and recommended him to buy the *Encyclopédie méthodique* (Jefferson to James Madison, Paris, 8 February 1786, in Jefferson, *The Papers*, vol. IX, 265).

[114]   Jefferson to Chastellux, Paris, 7 June 1785, in Jefferson, *The Papers*, vol. VIII, 184–86. Cf. *ibid.* vol. X, 3–55. Démeunier published separately the American entries of the *Encyclopédie* in his *Essai sur les Etats-Unis* (Paris: de l'Imprimerie de Laporte, 1786) and later in *L'Amérique indépendante, ou les différentes constitutions des treize provinces*, 3 vols. (Gand, 1790). Cf. Roberto Martucci, 'Les articles "américains" de Jean-Nicolas Desmeunier et le droit public moderne', in *L'Encyclopédie méthodique (1782–1832): Des Lumières au positivisme*, ed. Claude Blanckaert and Michel Ponet (Geneva: Droz, 2006): 241–64; Edna H. Lemay, 'L'Amérique dans les écrits d'un Parisien franc-comtois: 1776–1795', *Annales de Bretagne et des Pays de l'Ouest*, 84 (1977): 307–315.

[115]   Cf. Jean-Nicolas Démeunier to Jefferson, Paris, 11 February 1788, in Jefferson, *The Papers*, vol. XII, 579; Jefferson to Gijbert K.van Hogendorp, 25 August 1786, *ibid.*, vol. X, 299.

its relations with France and making America the breadbasket of Europe. Filippo Mazzei, who was linked to Jefferson, contributed to the discussion of the constitution of Virginia and was also an agent for that state in Paris. He gave voice to this collaboration with his *Recherches historiques et politiques sur les Etats-Unis*, for which Jefferson passed on the material that Démeunier had not used.[116] Many points made in the work provide evidence of direct contact with Jefferson and a convergence of American republican ideology and French political thinking on economics.[117] The denunciation of an authoritarian retrogression of the United States, with which the *Recherches* concluded, expressed the democratic convictions of Mazzei, Condorcet and Jefferson.[118]

Within a plan aimed at transforming French institutions, which drew on the American political reflections that Turgot's *Lettre au docteur Price* inspired, there is a resonance of a new political culture and its progressive acquisitions, from the America of the Pennsylvania constitution to the initiatives of the group of Mazzei, Du Pont de Nemours and Condorcet, up to Jefferson's contribution from a democratic perspective to post-revolutionary economic thought. It is thus possible to follow the different stages of one of the most fecund periods of political reflection in the era of the eighteenth-century democratic revolutions.[119]

Lafayette, La Rochefoucauld and Condorcet were the people Jefferson met with most often while in Paris.[120] La Rochefoucauld had been one of those who proactively spread news of the American War of Independence, doing so

---

[116]   Jefferson, *Papers*, vol. X, 10. Mazzei sent with much appreciation a copy of the *Notes on the State of Virginia* to Stanislav Augustus of Poland (Mazzei to Stanislav Augustus, King of Poland, Paris, 27 April 1789, in *Lettere di Filippo Mazzei alla corte di Polonia (1788–1792)*, ed. Raffaele Ciampini, vol. I (July 1788–March 1790) (Bologna: Zanichelli, 1937), 121). On Mazzei and his relations with Jefferson and for an accurate reconstruction of the discussions on the American Revolution, cf. Edoardo Tortarolo, *Illuminismo e rivoluzioni: Biografia politica di Filippo Mazzei* (Milan: Franco Angeli, 1986).

[117]   Filippo Mazzei, *Recherches*, vol. IV, 340–46, vol. I, 379. On Jefferson's appreciation see Jefferson to Louis-Philippe de Lormerie, Paris, 27 February 1788, in Jefferson, *The Papers*, vol. XII, 631.

[118]   Condorcet and his wife translated two chapters of the *Recherches*: 'De la société de Cincinnatus' and 'Du général Washington et du marquis de la Fayette, relativement à la société de Cincinnatus' (cf. Richard C. Garlick, *Philip Mazzei, Friend of Jefferson, His life and Letters* (Baltimore: Johns Hopkins Press, 1933): 104–5). On the work of the group cf. above pp. 55–8.

[119]   On 28 August 1789 Jefferson wrote to Madison from Paris: 'It is impossible to desire better dispositions towards us, than prevail in this assembly. Our proceedings have been viewed as a model for them on every occasion' (Jefferson, *The Papers*, vol. XV, 366).

[120]   Cf. Malone, *Jefferson and his Time*. Gouverneur Morris talked of having taken part in Jefferson's last supper before leaving to the United States at the latter's home, where Condorcet, La Rochefoucauld and Lafayette were also present (Gouverneur Morris, *Diary of the French Revolution*, ed. Beatrice Carey Davenport, 2 vols. (Boston: Houghton Mifflin Company 1939): vol. I, 220–21).

mostly through the *Affaires de l'Angleterre et de l'Amérique*, the periodical that between 1776 and 1779, with support from the cabinet of Vergennes, waged an anti-British propaganda campaign.[121] In addition to writing regular news articles, La Rochefoucauld personally translated the constitutions of all the states for the newspaper, which at the end of the conflict were together published as a book.[122]

Jefferson had an affinity with Condorcet that stemmed from sharing the same democratic convictions enhanced by a common faith in the principle of perfectibility.[123] And, like Jefferson's, Condorcet's ideas on ownership favoured the development of the concept of representative democracy, reinforced by the belief that a good administration would accelerate the distribution of property.[124] 'Our republic', Condorcet wrote in his last letter to Jefferson (December 1792), which criticized Lafayette's more moderate tendencies, 'founded like yours on reason, on the laws of nature, on equality, must be your true ally, we should be nothing less than a single people, we have the same interests, and above all the one of destroying all anti-natural institutions'.[125]

In the tradition of a rationalism essentially inspired by the Physiocratic approach to the relationship between economics and politics, Condorcet was among the best informed and most willing of those who sought to gather accurate information on events in America.[126] The experience of America was a strong political stimulus for him, and it was actually between 1786 and 1788, the years of Jefferson's presence in France, that he expounded his constitutional theories, in the form of a discussion on the new state.

---

[121]   The *Affaires de l'Angleterre et de l'Amérique*, 17 vols. (Anvers: 1776–1779) constitute a precious document with which to follow the thread of relations between the French and American intellectual works and the royal courts, cf. below pp. 129–33.

[122]   Louis-Alexandre La Rochefoucauld D'Anville, *Constitutions des Treize Etats-Unis de l'Amérique* (Philadelphia: Ph.-D. Pierres, Pissot, 1783).

[123]   Jefferson to William Green Munford, Monticello, 18 June 1799, in Jefferson, *The Papers*, vol. XXXI, 127.

[124]   Cf. Jean-Marie-Antoine-Nicolas Caritat de Condorcet, *Essai sur la constitution et les fonctions des assemblées provinciales*, in *Oeuvres*, vol. VIII, 133. Cf. Nadia Urbinati, 'Condorcet's Democratic Theory of Representative Government', *European Journal of Political Theory*, 3 (2004): 53–75.

[125]   Condorcet to Jefferson, 21 December 1792, in Jefferson, *The Papers*, vol. XXIV, 761. Gouverneur Morris informed Jefferson from Paris on 1 August 1792 that Condorcet was preparing his escape to America, along with others (*ibid.*, 277).

[126]   Cf. Keith M. Baker, *Condorcet: From Natural Philosophy to Social Mathematics* (Chicago: University of Chicago Press, 1975); Pierre Crépel and Christian Gilain, eds, *Condorcet: Mathématicien, économiste, philosophe, homme politique* (Paris: Minerve, 1989); Jean-Claude Perrot, 'Condorcet: de l'économie politique aux sciences de la société', in *Une histoire intellectuelle de l'économie politique (XVIIe–XVIIIe siècle)* (Paris: Editions de l'Ecole des Hautes Etudes en Sciences Sociales, 1992): 357–76; *Condorcet: Homme des Lumières et de la Révolution*, ed. Anne–Marie Chouillet and Pierre Crépel (Saint-Cloud: ENS Editions, 1997).

With *De l'influence de la Révolution d'Amérique sur l'Europe* Condorcet delivered one of the most damning denunciations of the British model, 'this system of Machiavellianism', with which he contrasted the creativity and potential of the United States.[127] By giving a positive answer to the question posed in 1783, by the Academy of Lyon, on the usefulness of the discovery of America, Condorcet had developed his argumentation on the political, commercial and diplomatic merits of the American Revolution, clarifying the premises of his ideas: the Physiocratic economic theories, to which he was close, his republicanism, the critique of the separation of powers, the principle of freedom for the press and religion, equality, the universal significance of the rights of man. His draft of the Declaration of Rights in 1789 had been inspired by the author of the Declaration of Virginia;[128] however, in the constitution project of 1793 it was the constitution of Pennsylvania that provided an inspirational example for the unicameral system.

Jefferson had a deep admiration for his *philosophe* friend throughout his remaining years.[129] Although his laicism was distant from Condorcet's materialism, he appreciated his moral rigour, placing Condorcet's *Esquisse* alongside Locke's *Two Treatises of Government* among the classic texts of morality.[130] They had a shared interest in public education,[131] in the adoption of the decimal system[132] and in confronting the problem of slavery, which led Jefferson to start the translation of Condorcet's *Réflexions sur l'esclavage des nègres*.[133] Within his ambiguous position on slavery, Jefferson's ideas on blacks were less radical than Condorcet's and Franklin's arguments, since he tended to ascribe their inferiority

---

[127] Condorcet, *De L'influence de la révolution d'Amérique sur l'Europe* (1786), in *Oeuvres*, vol. VIII, 18. Published in 1786, the work was then included within Mazzei's *Recherches* (vol. IV, 237–83). Cf. Durand Echeverria, 'Condorcet's "The Influence of the American Revolution on Europe"', *The William and Mary Quarterly*, 3d. ser., 25 (January 1968): 85–7.

[128] Condorcet, *Idées sur le despotisme, à l'usage de ceux qui prononcent ce mot sans l'entendre* (1789), in Condorcet,*Oeuvres*, vol. IX, 168.

[129] Jefferson, *The Writings*, ed. Ford, vol. X, 145–6.

[130] Jefferson to John Minor, 30 August 1814, Jefferson, *The Writings*, ed. Ford, vol. IX, 481.

[131] On Condorcet and education, I refer the reader to my work, *Una scuola per la rivoluzione: Condorcet e il dibattito sull'istruzione 1792/1794* (Naples: Guida, 1979) and to my essay 'Enlightenment and Revolution: The Evolution of Condorcet's Ideas on Education', in *Condorcet Studies I*, ed. Leonora Cohen Rosenfield (Atlantic Highlands, NJ: Humanities Press, 1984): 131–44.

[132] Jefferson presented to Congress on 4 July 1790 a *Report on Weights and Measures* and translated into English the report that Condorcet had read to the Académie des sciences on 19 March 1791 (Jefferson, *The Papers*, vol. XX, 353–60). In the letter of 26 July 1790 Jefferson asked William Short to send a copy of his *Report* to Condorcet (*ibid.*, vol. XVII, 281). For a deeper analysis of the relations between Condorcet and Jefferson cf. my essay, 'Jefferson et l'Amérique', in *Condorcet: Homme des Lumières et de la Révolution*, 189–99.

[133] Jefferson, *The Papers*, vol. XIV, 494–8.

to natural causes or to the effects of slavery. His official position prevented him from accepting the invitation from his French friends to join the Société des Amis des Noirs.[134] Nevertheless, he supported Condorcet's positions and found in the Physiocratic arguments on the drawbacks of the work of slaves strong rational arguments to overcome his wavering attitude.[135]

Jefferson also promoted Condorcet's works: on 12 September 1786 William F. Dumas sent him four copies of the *Vie de Turgot*, one of which was intended for him and the others for Franklin, Morris and Jay,[136] and on 31 July 1788 he wrote to James Madison: 'I send you also two little pamphlets of the Marquis de Condorcet, wherein is the most judicious statement I have seen of the great questions which agitate this nation at present'.[137] He was referring to the *Lettres d'un Citoyen des Etats-Unis à un Français* and the *Sentiments d'un Républicain sur les assemblées provinciales et les états généraux*. On 12 January 1789, while informing Madison of the explosive nature of the political situation in Paris, he recommended the *Essai sur la constitution et les fonctions des Assemblées provinciales* and sent him a copy of it.[138] Back in the United States in 1790, John Rutledge Jr. sent him the *Réponse à l'adresse aux provinces*.[139] He also became Condorcet's editor and, as such, ensured the publication of the *Observations sur le vingt-neuvième livre de l'Esprit des lois*,[140] which appeared for the first time in English in 1811, as an appendix to the *Commentary and Review of Montesquieu's Spirit of Laws* by Destutt de Tracy.[141]

In 1788, by means of the *Essai sur la constitution et les fonctions des Assemblées provinciales*, Condorcet joined the ranks of the few opponents of the convocation of the Estates-General, suggesting instead a national assembly along

---

[134]   Jefferson to Brissot, 11 February 1788, Jefferson, *The Papers*, vol. XII, 577–8.

[135]   Jefferson to Condorcet, 30 August 1791, Jefferson, *The Papers*, vol. XXII, 99. On Physiocracy and the theoretical foundations of anti-slavery, cf. Marcel Dorigny, 'The Question of Slavery in the Physiocratic Texts: A Rereading of an Old Debate', in *Rethinking the Atlantic World*, 147–62; Pernille Røge, 'The Question of Slavery in Physiocratic Political Economy', in *Governare il mondo: L'economia come linguaggio della politica nell'Europa del Settecento*, ed. Manuela Albertone (Milan: Feltrinelli, 2009): 149–69.

[136]   Jefferson, *The Papers*, vol. X, 354. Cf. also William F. Dumas to Jefferson, 26 September 1786 (*ibid.*, 404).

[137]   Jefferson, *The Papers*, vol. XIII, 441.

[138]   Jefferson, *The Papers*, vol. XIV, 437. Cf. also the letter to James Currie, in which he gave notice of the publication of the *Essai* (Jefferson to James Currie, Paris, 20 December 1788, *ibid.*, 366).

[139]   Jefferson, *The Papers*, vol. XVI, 266–7.

[140]   On the reasons why Condorcet is thought to be the author of the *Observations*, despite the fact that there is no trace of the manuscript amongst his papers, cf. Baker, *Condorcet*, 446.

[141]   On the events surrounding the publication of the work, and on relations between Jefferson and Destutt de Tracy, cf. below pp. 249–51.

the lines of the *Mémoire sur les municipalités*, which Du Pont de Nemours wrote in 1775 in collaboration with Turgot, who reaffirmed the principles set out in the *Lettre au docteur Price*. Thus it was that, on the eve of the French Revolution, Jefferson could appraise directly the democratic evolution of an author who had grasped the political import of the economic discourse of Physiocracy and who already expressed his views with political maturity. Condorcet held certain firm Physiocratic convictions – for instance, recognizing wealth derived from land as the foundation of the unity of the nation – and these were manifest in a detailed scheme for decentralized representative assemblies. This was directly connected to the debate about the creation of provincial assemblies reserved for landowners, which was one of the most significant expressions of Physiocratic reformist planning from the Marquis of Mirabeau to Du Pont de Nemours, to Le Trosne, until its evolution reached Condorcet, in the reality of revolution, as an articulate project of participatory democracy.[142]

As a supporter of the rights of the American states, Jefferson admired the French plans for decentralized political participation, concurring with their attacks on parliaments and the corporate interests of a society of orders: 'This nation is risen from the dust', he wrote in August 1788. 'They have obtained, as you know, provincial assemblies in which there will be a more perfect representation than in our states assemblies'.[143] He had followed Calonne's reformist plans with interest and understood the potential that opened up after the experience of the Assembly of Notables.[144]

In a broader sense, Jefferson found in Condorcet's essay on the provincial assemblies a scientific approach to politics: 'It is not in the positive knowledge of the laws established by man that we should seek to know what one should

---

[142]   The plan for a decentralized form of representation is also included in the *Lettres d'un Bourgeois de New-Haeven*, published in the same year in Mazzei's *Recherches*.

[143]   Jefferson to William St. Smith, Paris, 2 August 1788, in Jefferson, *The Papers*, vol. XIII, 458. Jefferson was aware of the French pre-revolutionary debates on the creation of provincial assemblies; speaking of the Minister of Calonne he wrote in his autobiography: 'The establishment of the Provincial Assemblies was, in itself, a fundamental improvement. They would be of the choice of the people, one-third renewed every year, in those provinces where there are no States, that is to say, over about three-fourths of the kingdom. They would be partly an Executive themselves, and partly an Executive Council to the Intendant'. (Jefferson, *Autobiography*, 69).

[144]   Jefferson to John Adams, Paris, 30 August 1787, in Jefferson, *The Papers*, vol. XII, 67. The same interest for provincial assemblies was expressed by Gouverneur Morris in a letter to John Jay of 1 July 1789: 'The provincial assemblies or Administrations, in other words the popular executive of the Provinces, which Turgot had imagined as a Means of moderating the royal legislative of the Court, is now insisted on as a counter Security against the Monarch when they shall have established a democratic legislative'. (Gouverneur Morris, *A Diary*, 130).

adopt, it is in reason alone'.[145] Thus, in his eyes, the outbreak of the Revolution in France came to clarify a constitutional picture that contrasted with the British model's quest for a balance between powers and their counteractions: 'In drawing the parallel between what England is, and what France is to be', he wrote a year later, 'I forgot to observe that the latter will have a real constitution, which cannot be changed by the ordinary legislature; whereas England has no constitution at all; that is to say there is not one principle of their government which the parliament does not alter at pleasure'.[146]

In Condorcet's political rationalism and in the circles where the particular approach of Physiocracy to the relationship between politics and economics remained strong, the unity of the national interest was seen as a manifestation of the natural laws that regulated politics, as opposed to the weight of history and tradition of the British model passed on by Montesquieu. This was the context that determined an important change in Jefferson's thinking.

Montesquieu featured as the most annotated author in Jefferson's *Commonplace Book* from 1774 onwards, after he had begun studying his work during the previous decade through Blackstone, Voltaire and Beccaria.[147] In 1790 he stated his first critical judgement of the *Esprit des lois* in a letter in which he recommended the Physiocratic authors and Turgot.[148] From then on, criticisms of Montesquieu appeared frequently in Jefferson's letters, and he became the main and almost only detractor in America of a writer who was deemed to be a classic author for American political thought.[149] Jefferson arrived at the rejection of Anglophilia through a critical study of the balance of powers of the British model and the political relativism theorized by Montesquieu. Physiocratic thought offered strong theoretical arguments against this, in the name of the unity of the law, a law that was not created, in so far as it already existed in nature and thus implied the unity of power, understood as a protective authority subordinate to the natural order and limited by it.[150] In 1809, three months after the end of his presidency, he began working towards the publication of the *Commentaire sur Montesquieu* by Destutt de Tracy, sharing its rejection of relativism and the attention given to history and

---

[145]   Condorcet, *Essai sur la constitution et les fonctions des assemblées provinciales*, in *Oeuvres*, vol. VIII, 496.

[146]   Jefferson to Jean Diodati, Paris, 3 August 1789, Jefferson, *The Papers*, vol. XV, 327.

[147]   Cf. Gilbert Chinard, *The Commonplace Book of Thomas Jefferson: A Repertory of His Ideas on Government* (Baltimore: 1926).

[148]   Jefferson to Thomas Mann Randolph Jr., New York, 30 May 1790, in Jefferson, *The Papers*, vol. XVI, 449.

[149]   Jefferson to Nathaniel Niles, 22 March 1801, in Jefferson., *The Writings* ed. Ford, vol. VIII, 24; Jefferson to William Duane, 12 August 1810 in Jefferson, *The Writings*, ed. Bergh, vol. XII, 407–8; Jefferson to Destutt de Tracy, 26 January 1811, in Jefferson, *The Writings* ed. Ford, vol. IX, 305; Jefferson to Thomas Cooper, 10 July 1812, in Jefferson, *The Writings*, ed. Bergh, vol. XIII, 178. Cf. Spurlin, *Montesquieu in America*.

[150]   Cf. Albertone, "'Que l'autorité souveraine soit unique'".

tradition, something that Condorcet had already stated in the same terms and which Jefferson repeated by publishing in the English language, and therefore not only for an American public, the French writer's *Observations sur le vingt-neuvième livre de l'Esprit des lois*.

So it was in contact with Parisian circles that Jefferson became aware of the conflict between his ideas and those of Montesquieu, at a time when the author of the *Esprit des lois* had become the rallying point for American political groups impressed by the British model. From that moment on Montesquieu symbolised for Jefferson the extolment of Britain against the American model.[151] For him, however, the paradoxes and 'inconsistencies' of the *Esprit des lois* were outfaced by the true principle of republicanism, which corresponded to representative government, contained in the political and economic thought of Destutt de Tracy.[152] In the context of this same political culture, his ideas and those of Destutt de Tracy were so in unison that Du Pont de Nemours was led to believe that Jefferson was the author of the *Commentaire*.[153]

According to Jefferson, it was the principle of representative government that made modern political thought superior to that found in classical antiquity.[154] In the *Summary View of the Rights of British America* Jefferson's anti-British sentiment had been nourished by an ideological use of history through the myth of Saxon democracy taken from Whig historiography.[155] Nevertheless, in the transformations of French political rationalism from Physiocracy to Condorcet's social mathematics, and on to the science of the ideas of the *Idéologues*, he discovered the basis of a permanent adherence to the principle of nature as a

---

[151]   Jefferson to William Duane, Monticello, 16 September 1810, in Jefferson, *The Writings*, ed. Bergh, vol. XII, 414.

[152]   Jefferson to William Duane, Monticello, 12 August 1810, in Jefferson, *The Writings*, ed. Bergh, vol. XII, 408. On Jefferson's rejection of the aristocratic implications of Montesquieu's balance of powers, cf. the essay by Appleby, 'What is still American', 288, which sees this as the entire reason for Jefferson's distance from the notion of a civil humanism described in John Pocock's interpretation in the *Machiavellian Moment*.

[153]   Du Pont de Nemours to Jefferson, 25 January 1812, in Gilbert Chinard, ed., *The Correspondence of Jefferson and Du Pont de Nemours* (Baltimore: The Johns Hopkins Press, 1931): 179–80. Cf. below pp. 251–6.

[154]   Jefferson to Isaac H. Tiffany, Monticello, 26 August 1816, in Jefferson, *The Writings*, ed. Bergh, vol. XV, 65–6.

[155]   Cf. H. Trevor Colbourn, 'Thomas Jefferson's Use of the Past', *The William and Mary Quarterly*, 3d ser., 15 (1958): 56–70; H. Trevor Colbourn, *The Lamp of Experience: Whig History and the Intellectual Origins of the American Revolution* (Chapel Hill: University of North Carolina Press, 1965); Bailyn, *The Ideological Origins of the American Revolution*; Joyce Appleby, *Without resolution: the Jeffersonian tension in American nationalism*, an inaugural lecture delivered before the University of Oxford on 25 April 1991 (Oxford: Clarendon Press, 1991).

normative reference that, just as it led him to reject Montesquieu's relativism, also led to his dismissal of Hume's scepticism.[156]

Faced with Hamilton's admiration for Hume, upon his return home in 1807, Jefferson declared unequivocally his strongly felt rejection of the Tory interpretation of the aristocratic value of history in Hume: 'A knowledge of British history becomes useful to the American politician', he wrote in a letter in which he recommended Locke's essays on government, Priestley's *Essay on the first Principles of Government* and Say's *Traité*, 'the elegant one of Hume seems intended to disguise the good principles of government'.[157] In 1805, Jefferson had added John Baxter's *A New and Impartial History of England* to his library, and had written of it as: 'Hume's history republicanised'.[158] During this period he had closer contact with the *Idéologues*, in particular Destutt de Tracy, whose theories on the biological origins of human knowledge were appreciated by Jefferson, who borrowed his critiques of Hume's pyrrhonism.[159]

'The earth belongs to the living'

From this radical ideology, based on a break with the past and the rejection of tradition and history as political points of reference, Jefferson derived one of the cornerstones of his ideas, which was fully formulated during his stay in Paris: the theoretical legitimization of the principle of constitutional revision, starting from the principle that 'the earth belongs in usufruct to the living', as he stated in a letter to Madison on 6 September 1789.[160] His proximity with intellectual circles inspired by Physiocratic culture and men like Richard Gem and Condorcet made him fully conscious of this principle.

---

[156]   As one who knew the English common law and feudal system due to his legal education, a reader of Blackstone and Lord Kames, Jefferson followed, as for Montesquieu, a similar progressive distancing from Hume and his *History of England* (Jefferson to William Duane, Monticello, 12 August 1810, in Jefferson, *The Writings*, ed. Bergh, vol. XII, 405; Jefferson to Duane, Monticello, 16 September 1810, *ibid.*, 413; Jefferson to Horatio G. Spafford, Monticello, 17 March 1814, *ibid.*, vol. XIV, 120).

[157]   Jefferson to John Norvell, Washington, 14 June 1807, in Jefferson, *Writings* ed. Peterson, 1176–7.

[158]   Jefferson, *Writings* ed. Peterson, 1177.

[159]   Koch, *The Philosophy of Thomas Jefferson*, 54–64. Cf. Craig Walton, 'Hume and Jefferson on the uses of history', in *Philosophy and the Civilizing Arts: Essays presented to Herbert W. Schneider*, eds. Craig Walton and John P. Anton (Athens: Ohio University Press, 1974), 103–25; Douglas L. Wilson, 'Jefferson vs. Hume', *The William and Mary Quarterly*, 3d. ser., 46 (1989): 49–70.

[160]   Jefferson to James Madison, Paris, 6 September 1789, in Jefferson, *The Papers*, vol. XV, 392–7.

In the face of the first revolutionary debates on public debt inherited from the Old Regime, Jefferson took a stand against the notion of amortization, on the basis of the principle that a generation was not entitled to burden the succeeding one with its engagements. In keeping with this idea, he also held that a constitution could not remain legitimate after a generation, calculated by Buffon to be nineteen years:

> The question Whether one generation of men has a right to bind another, seems never to have started either on this or our side of the water. Yet it is a question of such consequences as not only to merit decision, but place also, among the fundamental principles of every government. The course of reflection in which we are immersed here on the elementary principles of society has presented this question to my mind.[161]

Above and beyond the various ideas put forward about the origin of a principle at the root of modern political thought, born from the experience of eighteenth-century democratic revolutions,[162] Jefferson's perception of the newness of the question, and of the intellectual stimuli that the French situation gave to a reflection on society's first principles, shows that Paris, where he formulated his ideas, was his key focal point.

The departure from tradition, on behalf of the rights of younger generations, had been at the heart of Jefferson's proposals for the abolition of the right of primogeniture and entails, with which he had intended to undermine the social structure of Virginia, modelled on the British system. His revolutionary ideology found a clear theoretical formulation under the direct influence of the people he frequented in Paris, in particular two figures close to the Physiocrats: Condorcet and Richard Gem.

Jefferson elaborated his thoughts in the first week of September 1789, during a few days' convalescence after a slight indisposition. He was probably encouraged by his personal doctor, Richard Gem – known through Filippo Mazzei[163] – who

---

[161]   Jefferson, *The Papers*, vol. XV, 392.

[162]   The idea that property ended at death and that a generation could not tie another is common within eighteenth-century thought: it can be found in Locke (*Second Treatise*, ed. Peter Laslett, 286 and 346), Blackstone (*Commentaries*, 2: 3, 10–12), Smith (*Lectures on Jurisprudence*, I, 161–62; *The Wealth of Nations*, book III, ch. II), Paine (*Dissertations on Government* (1786), in *The Writings* ed. Moncure D. Conway, 2 vols. (New York: Burt Franklin, 1969), vol. I, t. II, 164–5), Priestley (*Lectures on History and General Policy* (Birmingham: Pearson and Rollason, 1788), 278, 307–308). A question that is more open to debate is whether the origin of the idea for Jefferson could be found in the radical readings of Locke's principle of property, set out by the English dissenters, or within French circles, or else in the context of the English juridical debate on the right of inalienability of the years 1750–1760, linked to the names of John Dalrymple and Lord Kames, authors who can be found in his *Commonplace Book*.

[163]   Mazzei met Gem in London (cf. Garlick, *Philip Mazzei, friend of Jefferson*).

at that very time had sent him a scheme for reflecting on the subject of public debt, then at the centre of discussions which would lead to the nationalization of the property of the clergy and the emergence of assignats and which contained, couched in the same terms, the idea expressed in Jefferson's letter to Madison.[164]

An Englishman, close to the Unitarians and a doctor at the Embassy in Paris during the early 1760s, Gem personified the meeting point between the dissenters and the French *philosophes*. 'A very sensible man, a pure theorist, of the sect called the eoconomists, of which Turgot was considered as the head', was how Jefferson described him.[165] Considered a follower of Physiocracy, Gem was also an ardent and politically active Republican.[166] He translated Condorcet's *Declaration of Rights* into English[167] and personally drafted a declaration inspired by Physiocracy that restricted voting rights to 'landowners', sanctioned 'the complete liberty of industry and commerce' and fixed 'the single land tax [*impôt territorial unique*]'.[168]

---

[164] 'That one generation of men in civil society have no right to make acts to bind another, is a truth that cannot be contested. The earth and all things whatever can only be conceived to belong to the living, the dead and those who are unborn can have no rights of property.' (*Proposition Submitted by Richard Gem*, [ca. 1–6 Sep. 1789], in Jefferson, *The Papers*, vol. XV, 391–2).

[165] Jefferson to James Madison, Paris, 12 January 1789, Jefferson, *The Papers*, vol. XIV, 437. With Quesnay, Gem in Paris cured one of Smith's pupils (Smith to Lady Frances Scott, Paris, 15 October 1766, in Adam Smith, *The Correspondence*, ed. Ernest Campbell Mossner and Ian Simpson Ross (Oxford: Clarendon Press, 1977): 119). Gem was probably the one who passed on news on England's foreign policy, which Jefferson refers to in a letter to John Jay of 11 January 1789: 'The information I most rely on is from a person here with whom I am intimate, who divides his time between Paris and London, an Englishman by birth, of truth, sagacity, and science.' (Jefferson, *The Papers*, vol. XIV, 429). Having returned to the United States Jefferson wrote to Gem expressing his regret that he could no longer enjoy his 'society and instructive conversation', (Jefferson to Richard Gem (New York: 4 April 1790), in Jefferson, *ibid.*, vol. VI, 297).

[166] Cf. *The Monthly Magazine*, or *British Register*, LI, no. 351 (1 March 1821): 139; John G. Alger, *Englishmen in the French Revolution* (London: Marston Searle and Rivington, 1889), 29–31. Gem was imprisoned in October 1793 as an Englishman, but freed in November due to the need for doctors. He died in 1800, leaving his nephew William Huskisson as his heir, a member of the Société de 1789 and author of a *Discours* against the assignats (1790), which took up the positions expressed by Condorcet in his *Sur la proposition d'acquitter la dette exigible en assignats*.

[167] *Déclaration des droits, traduite de l'Anglois, avec l'original à côté* (London, 1789); Jefferson owned three copies of this (Sowerby, *Catalogue*, nos. 2442, 2522, 2568), and he corrected the title in his own hand in: *Déclaration des Droits, par le Marquis de Condorcet traduite en Anglois, par le Docteur Gem avec l'original à côté* (London, 1789). (Cf. Jefferson, *The Papers*, vol. XV, 386–7).

[168] Jefferson, *The Papers*, vol. XIV, 439. During summer 1789 Jefferson's house became a meeting place for French patriots, who asked him to pass judgements and make political proposals (Lafayette to Jefferson, 25 August 1789, *ibid.*, 354). Lafayette sent him his own copy of the Declaration of Rights, inviting him to submit his comments (Lafayette

The layout of Jefferson's letter followed Gem's plan: 'I set out on this ground, which I suppose to be self evident', he wrote, using Lockian words, '"that the earth belongs in usufruct to the living": that the dead have neither powers nor rights over it. The portion occupied by any individual ceases to be his when himself ceases to be, and reverts to society'.[169] In keeping with the idea that the ownership of property was not a natural right, Jefferson maintained that public debt run up by the state should not pass beyond a generation.[170] More than an argumentation, this went back to near-Physiocratic positions: the social centrality accorded to land, the aversion to public debt, the idea that this implied an aggressive foreign policy and rejection of the British model. Furthermore, this reiterated the distinction between natural law and civil law made by Condorcet in 1786 in the *Vie de Turgot* to invalidate every act that made ownership of property intrinsically eternal.[171] Following the principles that Turgot set out in the article 'Fondation' of the *Encyclopédie*, Condorcet contested the complete freedom to make one's will, which he considered unrelated to the principle of property.[172] Du Pont de Nemours had already articulated in 1769, in typically Physiocratic terms and with regard to the defence of private property, the idea that a generation should not bind another to itself.[173] Jefferson went further, recognizing property ownership as a civil right.[174]

---

to Jefferson, 6 and 9 July 1789, *ibid.*, 249 and 255; Archbishop of Bordeaux Champion de Cicé to Jefferson (20 July 1789, *ibid.*, 291). Jefferson annotated and sent Madison Lafayette's and Gem's Declarations of Rights (Paris, 12 January 1789, *ibid.*, 436–40), writing a draft himself (Jefferson to Rabaut de St. Etienne, Paris, 3 June 1789, *ibid.*, vol. XV, 166–8). To the 15 articles in Gem's declaration, Jefferson added one of his own: 'No. 16. All the land of the territories of the political state must be owned by individuals.' (*ibid.*, 440). In Lafayette's draft, Jefferson deleted the reference to property, substituting it with 'the power to dispose of his person and the fruits of his industry, and all his faculties.' (Jefferson to Lafayette, 10 July 1789, *ibid.*, 230–33).

[169]   Jefferson to James Madison, Paris, 6 September 1789, Jefferson, *The Papers*, vol. XV, 392.

[170]   Jefferson, *The Papers*, vol. XV, 395. Jefferson followed almost word for word the terms used by Gem (392). The distinction between natural laws and civil laws, amongst which was included the right to property, is also contained in a letter by Thomas Paine to Jefferson of March 1788 (Jefferson, *The Papers*, vol. XIII, 4–5).

[171]   Condorcet, *Oeuvres*, vol. V, 142.

[172]   The same distinction and the same arguments of the article 'Fondation' are present in note XXIV, *Sur l'étendue et les bornes du droit de tester*, of the translation of the *Examen du gouvernement d'Angleterre* by John Stevens, 210–11, probably written by Condorcet.

[173]   Pierre-Samuel Du Pont de Nemours, *Du Commerce et de la Compagnie des Indes. Seconde édition, revue, corrigée et augmentée de l'Histoire du Système de Law* (Amsterdam, Paris: chez Delalain, chez Lacombe, 1769): 126–7.

[174]   Behind Jefferson's arguments one can see the presence of the reading of the article by Turgot (Jefferson to James Madison, Jefferson, *The Papers*, XV, 396).

In accordance with the principle that the earth belongs by right to the living, in the same letter to Madison, Jefferson asserted the precept according to which a constitution had no legitimacy after a generation:

> On similar ground it may be proved that no society can make a perpetual constitution, or even a perpetual law. The earth belongs always to the living generation. They may manage it then, and what proceeds from it, as they please, during their usufruct. They are masters too of their own persons, and consequently may govern them as they please … Every constitution then, and every law, naturally expires at the end of 19 years. If it be enforced longer, it is an act of force, and not of right.[175]

It was thus during his residence in Paris that Jefferson arrived at a connection between the principles of the rights of generations and the revision of the constitution.[176] In the same period, on 30 August 1789, Condorcet, in the *Lettre à M. le Comte de Montmorency* had reaffirmed the necessity of regular conventions for the amendment of constitutions,[177] restating again the idea expressed in his

---

[175]   Jefferson, *The Papers*, XV, 395–6. As confirmation of this opposition between two different political cultures, Madison in his reply (Madison to Jefferson, New York, 4 February 1790, *ibid.*, 147–50) opposed Jefferson's rationalist and abstract approach with an argument based on the idea that a generation is a fluctuating thing and never has clearly defined confines, according to what Hume had already expressed in 1741 in his *Of the Original Contract* (David Hume, *Of the Original Contract*, in Hume, *Essays Moral, Political and Literary* (London: Oxford University Press, 1963): 463). Jefferson's thoughts on the rights of generations show how even he did not share the evolutionary approach of the Scottish philosophers (cf. Roy Branson, 'James Madison and the Scottish Enlightenment', *Journal of the History of Ideas*, 40 (1979): 235–50).

[176]   The principle of the revision of the constitution is present in the discussions on the declaration of rights of the summer of 1789 (cf. *Archives parlementaires. Recueil complet des débats législatifs et politiques des chambres françaises – Première Série (1787–1799)*, 47 vols. (Paris, 1867–96): vol. 1 (Nendeln: Kraus Reprint, 1969): vol. VIII, 221–2; 256–61; 399–432). In the various drafts of Lafayette's project, the appearance of the idea of the rights of the generations, which in the end became one of the central elements of the principle of revision, is a sign of the collaboration between Jefferson, Lafayette and Gem, as their correspondence testifies (cf. Gilbert Chinard, *La Déclaration des Droits de l'Homme et du Citoyen d'après ses antécédents américains* (Washington: Institut français, 1945); Stéphane Rials, *La déclaration des droits de l'homme et du citoyen* (Paris: Hachette, 1988), Marcel Gauchet, *La Révolution des droits de l'homme* (Paris: Gallimard, 1989).

[177]   Condorcet, *Lettre à M. le Comte de Montmorency. Première Lettre, 30 août 1789*, in *Oeuvres*, vol. IX, 367–76. On 22 September in the *Chronique de Paris* (no. XXX, 117–18) there appeared the essay *Sur la nécessité de faire ratifier la Constitution par les citoyens* (*Oeuvres*, vol. IX, 413–30), in which the limit of the duration of every constitutional law was fixed as the time required for half the citizens who had ratified to be replaced. The work was most probably written on 17 June, because Condorcet refers to the ratification signed

essay on provincial assemblies, in which he had recognized his intellectual indebtedness to the American constitutional models.[178]

Through this intellectual interchange, which went well beyond mere influence, an original idea had arisen, which was the fruit of the encounter between political rationalism and democratic ideology.[179] The principle that 'the earth belongs to the living' remained the bedrock of Jefferson's political reflections.[180] Having returned to the United States, he made republican agrarian ideology a weapon, which he wielded at the heart of contemporary political debates, even beyond American issues.

In 1791 the first part of the *Rights of Man* was published, in which Thomas Paine legitimized, again by warrant of the principle of the rights of generations, the French Revolution and all the revolutionary thought of his century, defying the defence of tradition, history and the British political culture in Edmond Burke's *Reflections of the Revolution in France*:

> The vanity and presumption of governing beyond the grave, is the most ridiculous and insolent of all tyrannies. Man has no property in man; neither has any generation a property in the generation which are to follow. It is the living, and not the dead, that are to be accommodated. When man ceases to be, the power and his wants cease with him.[181]

---

by each separate order. Cf. also his *Réflexions sur ce qui a été fait et sur ce qui reste à faire, lues dans une société d'amis de la paix*, 1789 (*ibid.*, 447–8).

[178]   Condorcet, *Essai*, 223. Mousnier gives the news of discussions on the revision of the constitution that had taken place in Jefferson's home (Jean-Joseph Mousnier, *Exposé de ma conduite dans l'assemblée nationale; et motifs de mon retour en Dauphiné* (Paris: chez Desenne, 1789): 41).

[179]   The same idea, expressed at the same time, can also be found in Le Mercier de la Rivière. (Pierre-Paul-François-Joachim-Henri Le Mercier de la Rivière, *Essai sur les maximes et les loix fondamentales de la monarchie française, ou Canevas d'un code constitutionnel, pour servir de suite à l'ouvrage intitulé: 'Les voeux d'un François'* (Paris, Versailles, Vallat-La-Chapelle: Veillard, 1789): 33).

[180]   Cf. Jefferson to John W. Eppes, Monticello, 24 June 1813, in Jefferson, *Writings* ed. Peterson, 1280–81; to Joseph C. Cabell, Monticello, 17 January 1814, in Jefferson, *The Writings*, ed. Bergh, vol. XIV, 67–8; to John Taylor, Monticello, 28 May 1816, *ibid.*, vol. XV, 18; to Thomas Earle, Monticello, 24 September 1823, *ibid.*, 470; the last time that Jefferson reformulated this idea was in the letter to John Cartwright, Monticello, 5 June 1824 (*ibid.*, vol. XVI, 44, 48).

[181]   Thomas Paine, *Rights of Man*, ed. Henry Collins (Harmondsworth: Penguin Books, 1971): 63–4. Cf. Edmund Burke, *Reflections on the Revolution in France*, ed. Conor C. O'Brien (Harmondsworth: Penguin Books, 1973): 194–5. On the question of whether to attribute the first development of this idea to Jefferson or Paine, cf. Herbert E. Sloan, *Principle and Interest: Thomas Jefferson and the Problem of Debt* (New York: Oxford University Press, 1995).

The reaction to Paine and Burke in the United States pitted Jefferson against the two Adams;[182] this clash concerned not only choices relating to the outcome of the American experiment but, more generally, the collision of two opposing political cultures, which saw 'some Anglomen'[183] attack the concept of a republic that both Jefferson and Paine had elaborated. 'I profess the same principles', Jefferson wrote to Monroe, discussing the *Rights of Man*, 'the principles of the citizens of the U.S'.[184]

When he returned to the United States, fortified by the republicanism of his Parisian contacts, which was taking shape and fuelled political discussions in France, Jefferson met with a burgeoning Toryism, an emergent desire for reconciliation with Britain, a perception of monarchical tendencies as well as a political picture, within which, in the search for a stability that would help consolidate the outcome of the Revolution, the future of the new state would have to be decided. In the decade that saw the clash between the Federalists and the Republicans, Jefferson's theoretical acquisitions, incubated in the period of transition between the Old Regime and the French Revolution, were crucial.[185] The awareness that political economy would be the instrument with which to reinforce the republican idea of the connection between politics, economics and society found in the Physiocratic approach a model for development based on agriculture and a conception of economics as a science, the foundations of which he consistently acknowledged belonged to the French economists. In Paris Jefferson frequented the circles where the Physiocratic tradition, from Du Pont de Nemours to Condorcet, survived in a political rationalism that, through an unprecedented encounter with the American revolutionary experience, had succeeded in identifying the principles of representative democracy. Only after his return home did Jefferson entrust the attacks on the Federalists' economic project to George Logan, who based his arguments on Physiocratic principles. For his part, Jefferson made land, linked as it was to the rights of man, the essential core of a radical ideology that went as far as claiming the right of every generation to rewrite its own constitution: in Jefferson pragmatism and political rationalism

---

[182]   Cf. Jefferson, *The Papers*, vol. XX, 268–313.

[183]   Jefferson to George Washington, Philadelphia, 8 May 1791, Jefferson, *The Papers*, vol. XX, 291.

[184]   Jefferson to James Monroe, Philadelphia, 10 July 1791, Jefferson, *The Papers*, vol. XX, 297; to John Adams, Philadelphia, 30 August 1791, *ibid.*, 310; Jefferson to Thomas Paine, Philadelphia, 19 June 1792, *ibid.*, 312.

[185]   In the review of the *Rights of Man* published in the Condorcet's *Bibliothèque de l'homme public*, it is written about Paine: 'He proves ... that heredity is regarded in England as a safeguard against the most inviolable of the rights of citizens; and that far from basing their claims on abstract principles, such as human rights ... they have always claimed that which was given in patrimony by their ancestors.' (*Bibliothèque de l'homme public; ou analyse raisonnée des principaux ouvrages François et étrangers*, vol. V (1791)).

found a synthesis, cultivated and brought to fruition during the years he spent in France.

The first scientific economic model to be based on the primacy of agriculture gave Jefferson the legitimacy he needed for the anti-British economic and political project that he used as an instrument with which to attack his opponents, without feeling the need to set out a full theoretical discussion of Physiocratic principles. However pragmatic he was, he consistently accepted the idea of land as a source of wealth and never rejected this even when he later accepted the necessity of a development of manufacturing when facing the possibility of an international war. In an earlier political context, before and during the American Revolution, Benjamin Franklin had engaged in a dialogue and collaboration with the French economists that was more fully developed in terms of economic theory and which was inspired by his pronounced interest to the social implications of the agrarian project.

Chapter 4
The Farmer as Common Man: Benjamin Franklin

The Economist of the Colonies

Agricultural society, virtue and republic: these three guiding principles, adopted as the absolute essentials of life, sum up the contribution of Benjamin Franklin, the author of *Poor Richard's Almanack*, to the ideology of American agrarian democracy – a contribution made during an intellectual and political career brought to fruition amidst the ideas and experiences that circulated throughout the eighteenth century, and which made him a role model for several generations of revolutionaries.

As with Jefferson, Franklin's Americanization gathered momentum in France, but even before arriving in Europe he also had developed a strong belief in the great significance of agriculture.[1] His contact with Physiocracy, his contribution to the *Ephémérides du citoyen*, the affinities and the differences between two forceful agrarian and social projects, his good fortune in France, his role as a proponent of Physiocratic ideas, the reciprocal exchange between two economic-political cultures with clearly defined national identities, were all different building blocks which can be used to reconstruct a two-way movement of ideas between Europe and America.

Franklin was the first American economist and, from the 1750s, the theorist of an American agrarian model. Demographic and monetary issues were central themes in his thought. The theory of population, to which he made an original contribution, was the fulcrum on which all his ideas turned, and the central role he assigned to land and the principle of free trade were connected to it by means of the first clear identification of a link between population and subsistence. His interest in the relationship between paper currency and wages, aimed at increasing consumption, led to his becoming an attentive observer of the economic changes that gave rise to the consumer revolution of the eighteenth century. His judgments on luxury made him an original commentator on the interrelation of economics and morality; as a journalist and editor he knew how to make full use of all the force exerted on popular public opinion by the virtues of frugality and industriousness, contributing thereby to the secularization of evangelical principles. As an exponent of an ideal of a happy mediocrity, which made him an early supporter of the middle class, he understood the potency of the relationship between economy, revolution

---

[1]   Gordon S. Wood, *The Americanization of Benjamin Franklin* (New York: The Penguin Press, 2004).

and republic. Through the precepts of *The Way to Wealth*, he was the theorist of a project of social change and a sociologist of economic behaviour, while the success in France of *Les Maximes du Bonhomme Richard* eventually made him the symbol of republican America.

Considered the first significant American economist, and the only one prior to the nineteenth century, Franklin made use in his theoretical reflections of two main reference points: William Petty and Physiocracy.[2] His successful calculation of the population growth rate of the American colonies was used by Smith, Malthus and Godwin, and Marx highlighted his analysis of value.[3] Franklin did not have a systematic way of thinking, and his practical inclination led him to devise his economic proposals in response to specific problems, and to view political economy as a support for political action. Defined from a modern economic perspective as a 'pragmatic classical', it is thought that he was closer to the Keynesian tradition than to supporters of the free market, precisely because of the adaptability of his ideas, which made him a populationist, a free trade partisan, a supporter of active state intervention in economics, and one who was interested in the redistribution of income.[4]

Despite having grown up in Boston, and having remained an 'urban agrarian',[5] Franklin was also, like the other ideologists of agrarian democracy – Jefferson, Logan and Taylor – an agricultural experimentalist, between 1748 and 1757 on the farm he had acquired in New Jersey. In 1743 he presented to the American Philosophical Society a plan to broaden knowledge of agriculture, being convinced that it had an educational part to play. In 1785 he joined the first American agricultural society, the Philadelphia Society for the Promotion of Agriculture,[6] and thus had direct contact with the foremost agronomists of his day. His correspondence with Jared Eliot, which tells of how they exchanged plants, seeds and their experiences of new methods of cultivation, reveals that Franklin helped immensely in fostering a positive reception for the American agronomist, who is

---

[2]   Cf. Vernon L. Parrington, *Main Currents in American Thought*.

[3]   Adam Smith, *An Inquiry into the Nature and Causes of the Wealth of Nations*, ed., R.H. Campbell and Andrew S. Skinner, 2 vols. (Oxford: Clarendon Press, 1976): vol. I, book I, ch. VIII, 88; Thomas Robert Malthus, *An Essay on the Principle of Population* (London: Macmillan, 1966), ch. VI, 105; William Godwin, *Of Population* (New York: August M. Kelley, 1964): book II, ch. I, 119; Karl Marx, *Capital: A Critique of Political Economy*, book I, 'Capitalist production', part I, 'Commodities and Money', chapter 1, 'Commodities', section 3, 'The form and value or exchange value'.

[4]   Cf. Tracy Mott and George W. Zinke, 'Benjamin Franklin's Economic Thought: a Twentieth Century Appraisal', in *Critical Essays on Benjamin Franklin*, ed. Melvin H. Buxbaum (Boston: G. K. Hall, 1987): 111–26.

[5]   Cf. Virgil G. Wilhite, "Benjamin Franklin: Urban Agrarian," in *Founders of American Economic Thought and Policy* (New York: Bookman Associates, 1958): 283–319.

[6]   Cf. Earle D. Ross, 'Benjamin Franklin as an Eighteenth-Century Agricultural Leader', *Journal of Political Economy*, 37 (1929): 52–72.

considered one of the authors who contributed most to the progress of American agriculture. 'I have perused your two Essays on Field Husbandry', he wrote to Eliot, describing the satisfaction he found in testing new farming techniques, 'and think the public may be much benefited by them; but, if the farmers in your neighborhood are as unwilling to leave the beaten road of their ancestors as they are near me, it will be difficult to persuade them to attempt any improvement'.[7] Franklin was recognized as an authoritative agronomist in his own right and it was to him that Henry Pattullo turned, offering his skills to the service of the new nation.[8]

Franklin's first theoretical text, in which he made known his monetary convictions, originated in his decision to side with the agrarian party. It was in Boston, his home town, that in 1690 the government of Massachusetts issued America's first paper money, which gave rise to a heated debate in the press between the minority of merchants and city-based money lenders and their opponents: the debtors, small savers and investors in land.[9] In 1723 came the first issue in Pennsylvania, and in 1729 Franklin wrote *A Modest Enquiry into the Nature and Necessity of a Paper Currency*, in which he outlined his principles on money, 'a medium of exchange, because through or by its means labor is exchanged for labor, or one commodity for another',[10] in line with the quantitative theory of money and the theory of labour value borrowed from Petty:

> Suppose one Man employed to raise Corn, while another is digging and refining Silver; at the Year's End, or at any other Period of Time, the compleat produce of Corn, and that of Silver are, the natural Price of each other; and if one be twenty Bushels, and the other twenty Ounces, than an Ounce of that Silver is worth the Labour of raising a Bushel of that Corn.[11]

---

[7]   Franklin to Jared Eliot, probably in 1747, in Benjamin Franklin, *The Works*, vol. VI, 83. Cf. also the letter of 12 September 1751, vol. VII, 51. Franklin also discussed with Eliot issues more typically related to political economy, and in 1747 expressed his hopes, still from a mercantilist perspective, for an increase in productivity from English manufacturers (Franklin to Eliot, Philadelphia, 16 July 1747, in Benjamin Franklin, *The Papers*, ed W.B. Willcox (New Haven: Yale University Press, 1959–): vol. III, 151).

[8]   Henry Pattullo to Franklin, St Germain en Laye, 12 October 1778, in Franklin, *The Papers*, vol. XXVII, 549. Cf. also the letter sent by Franklin to Jean-Gabriel Montadoüin de la Touche on 26 September of the same year, which included an introduction to a pupil of Jethro Tull who was 'very devoted to the American cause', 466.

[9]   Cf. Parrington, *Main Currents in American Thought*; Lewis J. Carey, *Franklin's Economic Views* (Garden City, NY: Doubleday, Doran and Company, 1928).

[10]   Franklin, *A Modest Enquiry into the Nature and Necessity of a Paper-Currency (1729)*, in Franklin *The Papers*, vol. I, 148.

[11]   Franklin, *A Modest Enquiry*, 149. For the passages taken from Petty, cf. William Petty, *A Treatise of Taxes and Contributions* (London: N. Brooke, 1662): ch. IV, §§ 13–14; ch. V, § 10, par. II.

While he had yet to make the distinction between money and capital, Franklin nevertheless distinguished between metal coinage (which he referred to as 'currency') and precious metal ('bullion'), whose value could be less than that of the circulating medium;[12] and he anticipated Turgot's theory of natural interest on capital.[13] His mercantilist position – inspired by Petty and taken up by Hume some years later[14] – according to which an abundance of money would guarantee a low interest rate that favoured immigration and manufacturing, was aimed at defending the interests of the colonies and their policy of issuing paper money in the face of British resistance,[15] as well as the interests of those colonists – among whom he included himself – who had been hurt by low wages and the decline in agricultural prices and were overburdened by debts made heavier by the undersupply of currency. With an interest, shared by Jefferson, in problems relating to the extension of the western frontiers, Franklin held that the scarcity of money discouraged settlers from cultivating new land and drove them to seek higher incomes elsewhere. At the heart of his analysis was the aim of stimulating the colonies' economy and that of the social groups damaged by a scarcity of paper currency, which gave an advantage to those who were 'Possessors of large Sums of Money, and are disposed to purchase Land',[16] in that they benefited from high interest rates and low land prices.

This focus on money and the trade balance identifies Franklin as a mercantilist. And yet, as he paid heed to the demand and distribution of revenue, he was more sensitive to the qualitative than the quantitative aspects of money, seeing it as an instrument with which to galvanize all social groups and facilitate economic growth. Nevertheless, his pragmatism led him to correct his monetary theories: while in the *Modest Enquiry* he did not think an excess of paper money to be

---

[12]   'Money as Bullion, or as Land, is valuable by so much labor as it costs to procure this bullion … Money as a Currency has an Additional Value by so much Time and Labour as it saves in the Exchange of Commodities' (Franklin, *A Modest Enquiry*, 153). For a contextualization of Franklin's economic principles in relation to the classical economists and Ricardo's monetary theory, cf. William A. Wetzel, *Benjamin Franklin as an Economist* (Baltimore: The Johns Hopkins' Press, 1895) and Mott and Zinke, 'Benjamin Franklin's Economic Thought'.

[13]   Franklin, *A Modest Enquiry*, 154. Cf. also Anne-Robert-Jacques Turgot, *Réflexions sur la formation et la distribution des richesses* (Paris: Flammarion, 1997): § 57–58, 191–92.

[14]   David Hume, *Of Interest*, in Hume, *Writings on economics*, ed. Eugene Rotwein (London: Nelson, 1957): 47. Cf. Franklin's letter to Hume of 27 September 1760, in which he expresses his appreciation for the *Jealousy of Commerce*, in Franklin, *The Works*, vol. VII, 210.

[15]   Against England's ban on paper currency printed by the American colonies, which was never willingly accepted by English merchants, see Benjamin Franklin, *Remarks and Facts Relative to the American Paper Money* (1764), in Franklin, *The Works*, vol. II, 340–54.

[16]   Franklin, *A Modest Enquiry*, 146.

possible, in 1779 he warned Congress against its depreciation,[17] and in *Paper Money of the United States* he blamed the devaluation of money on the failure to control how and when it was issued. He considered this devaluation in every sense to be 'a gradual tax' and 'thus it has proved a tax on money, a kind of property very difficult to be taxed in any other mode; and it has fallen more equally than many other taxes, as those people paid most, who, being richest, had most money passing through his hands'.[18]

Land and population were the pivots around which Franklin's entire argument in the *Modest Enquiry* turned: a low cost of money encouraged investment in land, whose value increased in proportion to the population, which in turn created demand. Land itself was the most secure guarantee for the issuing of paper money.[19]

Land and population were the themes of the *Observations concerning the Increase of Mankind and the Peopling of Countries*, which marked the beginning of Franklin's fame as a demographer and his success among his contemporaries. Published in 1755 but written in 1751, the essay, which calculated that the population of the American colonies would double within 25 years, was written in support of the American call for the creation of manufacturing in the colonies, against British resistance.[20] He elaborated his thesis which argued that the cost of labour would remain high in America for a long time since the land's abundance predisposed it to agriculture, and therefore Britain had nothing to fear from American competition in foreign markets; it was the sheer number of poor people living in misery in a country without land that caused the drive towards manufacturing. He began by confirming the correlation between population and the means of its support, demonstrating that an improved standard of living inhibited population growth, a factor he deemed to be negative, whereas Malthus thought it positive. Sixteen years before meeting the major exponents of Physiocracy, Franklin was aware of the importance of land, which was fundamental to his theory of population.[21]

His whole discourse on manufacturing was conducted in relation to population and, consequent to this, to agriculture. Some years later, further considerations on

---

[17]   Franklin to Samuel Cooper, Passy, 22 April 1779, in Franklin, *The Works*, vol. VIII, 329–30.

[18]   Franklin, *Of the Paper Money of the United States*, in Franklin, *The Works*, vol. II, 424. In February 1765 Franklin had already expressed the opinion that the devaluation of paper currency represented a fair tax, 'the rich who handle most money, would in reality pay most of the tax'. (Franklin, *Scheme for Supplying the Colonies with a Paper Currency*, in Franklin, *The Papers*, vol. XII, 55). Cf. Franklin to Thomas Ruston, Passy, 9 October 1780 (Franklin, *The Works*, vol. VIII, 507).

[19]   Franklin, *A Modest Enquiry*, 143.

[20]   Cf. Wetzel, *Franklin*; Carey, *Franklin's Economic Views*; Alfred Aldridge, 'Franklin as Demographer', *The Journal of Economic History*, 9 (1949): 25–44.

[21]   Franklin, *Observations Concerning the Increase of Mankind and the Peopling of Countries*, in Franklin, *The Papers*, vol. IV, 225–34.

this would lead him to express his concern that population pressure on the land could intensify manufacturing development:

> Manufactures are founded in poverty. It is the multitude of poor without land in a country, and who must work for others at low wages or starve, that enables undertakers to carry on a manufacture ... But no man who can have a piece of land of his own, sufficient by his labour to subsist his family in plenty, is poor enough to be a manufacturer, and work for a master. Hence while there is land enough in America for our people, there can never be manufacturers to any amount or value.[22]

These were the same hopes that Jefferson expressed almost twenty years later in the *Notes on the state of Virginia*.[23] Like Jefferson, it was while travelling in the British countryside that Franklin became convinced that the British economic model generated poverty, in contrast to the prosperity of American democracy. During a visit to Scotland and Ireland, in 1772, he wrote:

> The Bulk of the People Tenants, [are] extreamly poor, living in the most sordid Wretchedness in dirty Hovels of Mud and Straw, and cloathed only in Rags. I thought often of the Happiness of New England, where every Man is a Freeholder, has a Vote in publick Affairs, lives in a tidy warm House ... Had I never been in the American Colonies, but was to form my Judgment of Civil Society by what I have lately seen, I should never advise a Nation of savages to admit of Civilisation.[24]

And also like Jefferson, his denunciation of the disparity between the wealth of the large landowners and the misery of the peasants in Europe was grounded in the principle of the conventional nature of property, expressed in the same Lockian terms of a primordial common ownership of the land:

> All Property, indeed, except the Savage's temporary Cabin, his Bow, his Matchcoat, and other little Acquisitions, absolutely necessary for his Subsistence, seems to me to be the creature of public Convention. Hence the Public has the Right of regulating Descents, and all other Conveyances of Property, and even of limiting the Quantity and the Uses of it. All the Property that is necessary to a Man, for the Conservation of the Individual and the Propagation of the Species,

---

[22]   Franklin, *The Interest of Great Britain considered with Regard to her Colonies and the Acquisitions of Canada and Guadaloupe* (1760), in Benjamin Franklin, *The Writings*, ed. Albert H. Smyth, 10 vols. (New York: Macmillan, 1905–7): vol. IV, 49.

[23]   Jefferson, *Notes on the State of Virginia*, 165.

[24]   Franklin to Joshua Babcock, London, 13 January 1772, in Franklin, *The Papers*, vol. XIX, 7. Cf. Jefferson to James Madison, Fontainebleau, 28 October 1785, in Jefferson, *The Papers*, vol. VIII, 682.

is his natural Right, which none can justly deprive him of: But all Property superfluous to such purposes is the Property of the Publick, who, by their Laws, have created it.[25]

In the first phase of Franklin's theoretical considerations and his activities as a publicist, his originality as a populationist and his peculiar sharing of mercantilist principles found expression in the link between population and manufacturing. This led him to see the creation of manufacturing in the colonies as an incentive for population growth and expansion of the colonial market, to the advantage of the British Empire.

Thus, Franklin's demand for free commerce also revolved around the centrality of population. In the name of an original 'free trade mercantilism',[26] he was in fact convinced that free trade would speed up population growth in America, with a concomitant benefit worldwide, occasioning a decrease of economic conflict internationally. The American market would absorb European goods, and higher European profits would make possible an increase in wages. The importance of space, not only as regards the American situation, and a vision of societies in continuous movement and expansion, vied to define Franklin's ideal of a harmonious order, where attention to the currency, to the population, to the colonial market, to governmental stimulus of the economy, to trade balance, and to the establishment of colonies in unpopulated areas, all came together with firm resistance to monopolies and price-fixing. Although a populationist, as Davenant, Petty and Mandeville had been before him, he nonetheless linked population directly with happiness, in a context in which America itself was a dynamic determinant because of its availability of land and commercialized agriculture.

From his first works on currency and population onwards, Franklin had a clear grasp of the tension between the expanding commercial economy and access to the consumption of goods that could no longer be restricted.[27] In the face of the eighteenth-century consumer revolution, which brought about rapid changes in popular consumption, not least the inundation of the American market by British

---

[25]   Franklin to Robert Morris, Passy, 25 December 1783, in Franklin, *The Writings*, vol. IX, 138. Cf. Jefferson to James Madison, Fontainebleau, 28 October 1785 in Jefferson, *The Papers*, vol. VIII, 682; John Locke, *Two Treatises on Government*, Second Treatise, II, ch. 5, par. 25.

[26]   Paul W. Conner, *Poor Richard's Politicks: Benjamin Franklin and his New American Order* (New York: Oxford University Press, 1965).

[27]   Cf. John Brewer and Roy Porter, eds, *Consumption and the World of Goods* (London: Routledge, 1993); Daniel Roche, *Histoire des choses banales: naissance de la consommation dans les sociétés traditionnelles (17. 19 siècle)* (Paris: Fayard, 1997); Maxine Berg and Helen Clifford eds. *Consumers and Luxury: Consumer Culture in Europe 1650–1850* (Manchester: Manchester University Press, 1999); Timothy H. Breen, *The Marketplace of Revolution: How Consumer Politics Shaped American Independence* (New York: Oxford University Press, 2004).

products, Franklin's sociological awareness led him to concentrate on the social, economic and political value of an improvement in the quality of life of the people. This made him an early supporter of the middle class and of a 'happy mediocrity', siding with Richard Price's view of the study and safeguarding of a 'middle stage between the savage and the refined'.[28]

Prioritized attention on the question of income and its distribution define Franklin's specific contribution to eighteenth-century thought on political economy. The ready supply of currency and the low price of money, the ease of access to land purchase, increased purchasing power, and the rejection of direct taxes, which damaged consumption, were all aimed at raising wages and the quality of life, in accordance with his populationist and free trade convictions. The economy as a means 'to make life better' would be able to turn the American people into good consumers, preserving the autonomy of the settlers.[29]

A fair medium between luxury and poverty could, in Franklin's eyes, ensure responsible access to consumer goods, honest practices and public freedom: 'Poverty often deprives a man of all spirit and virtue. It is hard for an empty bag to stand upright'.[30] The economic foundations of virtue found expression in his exaltation of a new social figure – typically American and of whom he himself claimed to be an example – in whom the evangelical principle of frugality was laicized. At the same time, it was the changing American society itself that allowed a citizen, by warrant of natural law, to enjoy the fruits of his own labour and move from life at basic subsistence level to the enjoyment of a wellbeing that material progress had made attainable to an ever larger number of people; and this was achieved in the name of a mediocrity which implied the claim of a greater equality, not only on a social level.[31]

In the context of the commercialized economy – which for him meant an increased circulation of goods and was, in his view, the way towards social levelling and thus greater equality – Franklin saw, from his standpoint as an American, all the importance of the eighteenth-century discussions on luxury and gave voice to

---

[28]   Richard Price, *Observations on the importance of the American Revolution and the means of making it a benefit to the world. To which is added a letter from m. Turgot ... with an appendix, containing a translation of the will of m. Fortuné Ricard* (Dublin: L. White, 1785), 70. On the characteristics of the English Enlightenment, which encouraged people to enjoy the benefits of urban societies, cf. Roy Porter, 'The English Enlightenment', in *The Enlightenment in National Context*, ed. Roy Porter and Mikuláš Teich (Cambridge: Cambridge University Press, 1981): 1–18.

[29]   Franklin to the Philadelphia Merchants, London, 9 July 1769, in Franklin, *The Papers*, vol. XVI, 174–5.

[30]   Franklin, *The Way to Wealth* (1757), in Franklin, *The Works*, ed. Sparks, vol. II, 101.

[31]   Cf. Franklin's story about how china bowls and silver spoons, symbols of a wellbeing that was spreading through American households, entered into his domestic life (Franklin, *Autobiography*, 65).

the changes in its perception that were to take shape from the middle of the century in relation to new social and economic realities.[32]

In the *Observations Concerning the Increase of Mankind* he had already distinguished between productive and unproductive luxury, and had declared his opposition to the sumptuary laws, decrying the unnecessary expenditure of those who felt compelled to renounce marriage in order to maintain a high standard of living, but considering the extravagance of the wealthy classes useful, in that it stimulated output.[33] Many years later, when faced with the deterioration of American trade, there arose a polemic against luxury and a distrust of foreign trade,[34] in a letter to Benjamin Vaughan written in 1784, he returned to his position, differentiating good consumers from bad and arguing that luxury which fuelled industriousness was helpful.[35] The pursuit of greater wellbeing was a healthy individual right and a social advantage: 'Is not the hope of being one day able to purchase and enjoy luxuries a great spur to labour and industry? May not luxury, therefore, produce more than it consumes?'[36] However, it was the huge availability of land in America that guaranteed the preservation of good practices that were to be found in the countryside, as opposed to the city where the wealth of the rich was concentrated. Moreover, for Franklin the superiority of the agrarian model had by now been demonstrated.[37]

The economic, social, political and moral value of a way of living in which frugality and industriousness were practised in the setting of widespread and egalitarian wellbeing, equidistant from the two extremes of misery and luxury – a median level of life which a commercial economy could ensure and augment – found its ultimate expression in *Poor Richard*, in which Franklin himself became the personification and expression of an economic revolution turned into a political revolution, and whose success became a symbol that spread from America to Europe. Luxury was challenged by the extolment of normality, the wise enjoyment of a calm wellbeing, of a 'way to wealth' that America's profusion of land could guarantee. The farmer's simplicity of life, accompanied by economic security, thus became a model that disseminated from the countryside into all of society.

---

[32]   Cf. John Sekora, *Luxury: The Concept in Western Thought, Eden to Smollett* (Baltimore: Johns Hopkins University Press, 1977); Maxine Berg and Elizabeth Eger, eds, *Luxury in the Eighteenth Century: Debates, Desires and Delectable Goods* (London: Palgrave Macmillan, 2003); Maxine Berg, *Luxury and Pleasure in Eighteenth-Century Britain* (Oxford: Oxford University Press, 2005).

[33]   Franklin, *Observations Concerning the Increase of Mankind and the Peopling of Countries*, in Franklin, *The Works*, vol. II, 317–18. Cf. Aldridge, *Franklin as a Demographer*.

[34]   Cf. McCoy, *The Elusive Republic*.

[35]   Franklin, *On luxury, idleness and industry*, from a letter to Benjamin Vaughan, Passy, 26 July 1784, in Franklin, *Works*, vol. II, 450.

[36]   Franklin, *On luxury, idleness and industry*, *Works*, vol. II, 448–9.

[37]   Franklin, *On luxury, idleness and industry*, *Works*, vol. II, 451.

The series of proverbs that, from 1732, appeared for twenty-five years in the *Pennsylvania Gazette* and in *Poor Richard's Almanack*, which Franklin published and edited, and which in 1758 were published together as *The Way to Wealth*, constitute a discussion on economic conduct, a manual of good behaviour at a time of increased options for consumers, an expression of a normality, wisdom and popular religiosity. 'Industry gives comfort, and plenty, and respect', Poor Richard reminds his interlocutors, giving voice to a Puritanism that disdained excess and debt, and advocated saving, yet knew how to pursue material and earthly happiness.[38] Franklin used simple language to spell out the difference between luxury and comfort, and, when opposing the sumptuary laws, used it again to muster all the forces of emancipation and freedom inherent in the expansion of popular consumption, which the American colonies open to British products were experiencing in those years: 'would you not say that you were free, have a right to dress as you please, and that such an edict would be a breach of your privileges, and such a government tyrannical? And yet you are about to put yourself under such tyranny, when you run in debt for such dress!'[39]

In the figure of Poor Richard – the exemplification of a society in which the distribution of income moulded the actions of the consumer – virtue did not imply self-denial but rather a restrained and rational use of goods, and it delineated a model of bourgeois behaviour that exhibited the qualities of moderation and limit.[40] For Franklin, who was aware of how economic, political and social factors were interlinked, such behaviour became a republican cornerstone of freedom and independence, a political choice, in the desire to build a social actor midway between 'necessity' and 'luxury', an exemplar related to agrarian ideology that would radiate out from the countryside to the city.[41] At the centre of the Protestant work ethic of Franklin and *Poor Richard* was not so much the tension between civic virtue and selfishness, as that between industriousness and idleness, and so a form of Republicanism came into being that had more to do with social behaviour and 'process' than a political project.

In American republican ideology the conflict between virtue and corruption was therefore waged on economic rather than ethical grounds, and an attack on

---

[38]   Franklin, *The Way to Wealth*, in Franklin, *The Works*, vol. II, 97.

[39]   Franklin, *The Way to Wealth*, in Franklin, *The Works*, vol. II, 101. Cf. Joyce Appleby, 'Consumption in early modern social thought', in *Consumption and the World of Goods*, ed. John Brewer and Roy Porter (London: Routledge, 1993): 162–73.

[40]   Werner Sombart, *The Quintessence of Capitalism* (London: Routledge, 1998): 104, 116.

[41]   Franklin can offer a new analytical perspective regarding American agrarian ideology when placed alongside the rich variety of recent works on consumption and the middle class, which mostly focus on British society and urban life. On the attention to the changing nature of consumption and consumer, which Franklin had also understood, cf. Edward P. Thompson, 'The Moral Economy of the English Crowd in the Eighteenth Century', *Past and Present*, 50 (1971): 76–136.

corruption came to be one made against an aristocratic society that provided no economic benefit simply because privilege was unproductive.[42] However, in the original link between religious, republican and liberal discourse, the essential economic value of virtue came to express not the individualism of possession but an idea of benevolence which bound personal independence to moral responsibility and which put itself at the foundations of American popular sovereignty and an economy based on agriculture: 'I think agriculture the most honorable of all employments, being the most independent. The farmer has no need of popular favor, nor the favor of the great, the success of his crops depending only on the blessing of God upon his honest industry.'[43] The egalitarian implications of widening access to consumer goods were also linked in Franklin, as has been shown, to a radicalism that challenged the natural foundations of property.[44]

It would be the American perspective of a free trade that was then more useful to Europe than to America, 'which can very well subsist and flourish without a Commerce with Europe',[45] as he wrote in 1780, that led Franklin to incite the revolt of the colonies against British mercantilist policy, becoming first anti-British then anti-mercantilist. Up to the middle of the 1750s, he remained a loyal British subject, working to cement the union between the colonies and the mother country. The objective of his theories on population – the development of manufacturing, wage increases, the expansion of colonial trade – was the enhancement of the British mercantilist system. A mercantilism without onerous regulations, and harmonious in the sense of having balanced economic interests, would bring a common advantage.

It was Franklin's critique of British economic policy – accelerating his political development and a defiant anti-British spirit in America – that caused him to turn against mercantilism and the economic and political model of Britain that clashed with a republican conception of political economy. In 1760 in the *Interest of Great Britain* he still considered the great availability of American land, American agriculture capable of guaranteeing a 'middle population', and the rise in population, as elements which were 'most advantageous to Great Britain'.[46] However, in 1767 an economic repression precipitated a mood for revolt by now

---

[42]   Cf. Isaac Kramnick, 'Republican Revisionism revisited', 629–64.

[43]   Franklin to Catherine Greene, Philadelphia, 2 March 1789, in Franklin, *The Works*, vol. X, 386–87. Cf. Crawford B. Macpherson, *The Political Theory of Possessive Individualism: Hobbes to Locke* (Oxford: Clarendon Press, 1962); Joyce Appleby, 'Liberalism and the American Revolution', *New England Quarterly*, 49 (1976): 3–26.

[44]   Cf. above p. 106. Franklin's letter to Robert Morris, Passy, 25 December 1783, Franklin, *The Writings*, vol. IX, 138. Cf. Nicolas Hans, 'Franklin, Jefferson, and the English Radicals at the end of the Eighteenth Century', *Proceedings of the American Philosophical Society*, 98 (1954): 406–26.

[45]   Franklin to C. van der Ondermeulen, Passy, 22 June 1780, in Franklin, *The Writings*, vol. VIII, 107.

[46]   Franklin, *The Interest of Great Britain*, (Franklin, *The Writings*, vol. IV, 49).

irrevocable.[47] In 1769 he argued that the settlers should not fight militarily with the British but confront them on the field of economics: 'it is to be a war on the commerce only, and consists in an absolute Determination to buy and use no more of the Manufacturers of Britain'.[48] It was the way of defending the liberty and independence of the colonies, their industriousness and frugality as responsible consumers.[49] Investing not in luxuries but in agriculture became an attack on British mercantilism through the formation of reliable, thrifty and hard-working consumers, and the Puritan ethic thus became a weapon with which to attack British vice, at the same time also preparing the way towards independence on an economic level.[50] It was the exigency of extricating American economic policy from Britain's that prompted Franklin to fashion the image of America as the champion of economic freedom, an alternative to the British model, and thus by this means the new State would determine its international legitimacy.[51]

The Discovery of Physiocracy

In 1757, the year in which *Way to Wealth* was published, Franklin began to intensify his contacts in Europe while on his first overseas mission, working in Britain as a colonial agent for Pennsylvania until 1762. Up to 1775, he would also act as an agent on behalf of Massachusetts, New Jersey and Georgia, before becoming a diplomat in Paris until 1785. In Britain he regularly visited Lord Kames, Hume, Smith and communities of religious Dissenters.

In 1774 Franklin joined with David Williams, a deist and pedagogue, in founding the Society of Thirteen, a group which had social and educational aims and, like corresponding groups in Spain and Italy with which it was in contact, was inspired by Freemasonry. Priestley, Price, Benjamin Vaughan, Paine, Brissot, La Rochefoucauld and Du Pont de Nemours were all connected to the club. At the outbreak of the Revolution, the whole group supported the American cause, and three members, Priestley, Vaughan and John Paradise, migrated to America. Franklin continued to support Williams's deist congregation even during his diplomatic mission to France.

In London he also frequented the Honest Whigs club, which he had helped to found on his arrival there in 1764, and which remained active during the French

---

[47]   Franklin to Lord Kames, London, 11 April 1767 (Franklin, *The Works*, vol. VII, 334).

[48]   Franklin to Jean-Baptiste le Roy, London, 31 January 1769, in Franklin, *The Papers*, vol. XVI, 33.

[49]   Franklin to the Philadelphia Merchants, London, 9 July 1769, in Franklin, *The Papers*, vol. XVI, 175.

[50]   Cf. Edmund S. Morgan, 'The Puritan Ethic and the American Revolution', *The William and Mary Quarterly*, 3d ser. 24 (1967): 3–43.

[51]   Franklin to Richard Price, Passy, 1 February 1785, in Franklin, *The Writings*, vol. VIII, 107.

Revolution. The club had a secret organization called the 'Constitutional Whigs, Grand Lodge of England', clearly inspired by the Freemasons, and the main leaders of the Dissenters as well as Members of Parliament were associated with it. It held discussions that, notwithstanding the prevalence of clergy, dealt not only with religious arguments but also with politics and economics. Franklin, Priestley and Price all joined the organization, and traces of its activities in 1789 are to be found in Jefferson's correspondence.[52]

In 1759 Franklin met with Adam Smith in Edinburgh. Both were subjects of the British Empire but not English, and both were critical of British political economy but had different opinions on the political value of the colonies' struggle. Smith, after all, was not considered a supporter of the American colonies' constitutional demands, despite his attacks on mercantilism lending economic justification to the demands of Paine's *Common Sense*.[53] How much of Smith's economic analysis was owed to Franklin is hard to say.[54] The chapter on the colonies in book IV of the *Wealth of Nations* used Franklin's data on the growth of the American population.[55] His republican and democratic spirit which manifested his feelings of national belonging was not, however, in tune with Smith's language. Instead it was in the circle of French economists – with whom Smith was also in contact and through which he filtered Franklin's ideas – that the author of *Poor Richard* found an organized system matching his own economic views, and on which he modelled his political discourse.

In France Franklin became an anti-British, anti-mercantilist and pro-Physiocratic patriot. Like Jefferson, even before arriving in Europe he was convinced of the central importance of commercialized agriculture, but it was his contact with the French Physiocrats which gave a more systematic form to his

---

[52]   Cf. Hans, 'Franklin, Jefferson, and the English Radicals'; Verner Crane, 'The Club of Honest Whigs: Friends of Science and Liberty', *The William and Mary Quarterly*, 3d ser., 23 (1966): 210–33. Richard Price was in contact with Du Pont de Nemours and Jefferson was an intermediary between the two (Richard Price to Jefferson, Hackney, 26 October 1788, in Jefferson, *The Papers*, vol. XIV, 40).

[53]   Cf. Donald Winch, *Riches and Poverty: An Intellectual History of Political Economy in Britain, 1750–1834* (Cambridge: Cambridge University Press, 1996); Peter S. Onuf, 'Adam Smith and the Crisis of the American Union', in *The Atlantic Enlightenment*, ed. Susan Manning and Francis D. Cogliano (Aldershot: Ashgate, 2008), 149–64.

[54]   Cf. Deborah Norris Logan, *Memoir of Dr. George Logan of Stenton, by his widow* (Philadelphia: The Historical Society of Pennsylvania, 1899): 46–7. Cf. Thomas D. Eliot, 'The relations between Adam Smith and Benjamin Franklin before 1776', *Political Science Quarterly*, 39 (1924): 67–97. Cf. also James Parton, *Life and Times of Benjamin Franklin* (New York: Mason Brothers, 1864).

[55]   On Franklin as the author of the part of Smith's chapter on the colonies that dealt with wages, cf. Wetzel, *Benjamin Franklin as an Economist*, 52; Aldridge, *Benjamin Franklin et ses contemporains français*, 67–8.

ideas, 'half physiocrat before the rise of the physiocratic school'.[56] The discovery of this affinity was reciprocal from the moment when, arriving in Paris in 1767, he met Quesnay in the first week of October, before leaving once more for London[57] whence he sent a letter to an American correspondent a few months later, already writing from a Physiocratic viewpoint:

> This Country is fond of Manufactures beyond their real value; for the true Source of Riches is Husbandry. Agriculture is truly productive of new wealth; Manufactures only change Forms; and whatever value they give to the Material they work upon, they in the mean time consume an equal value in Provisions, &c. so that Riches are not increased by Manufacturing; the only advantage is, that Provisions in the Shape of Manufactures are more easily carried for Sale to Foreign Markets.[58]

In February, a few months before his arrival in Paris, the *Ephémérides du citoyen* had published one of his articles, possibly without knowing its authorship, since it was simply signed 'Arator'. This had appeared in the 27–29 November 1766 edition of the *London Chronicle* under the title *On the Price of Corn, and Management of the Poor*. The article's translator was Morellet[59] and its publication was aimed at discrediting Britain's image at a time of unrest provoked by the high cost of grain.[60] Arguing against British embargoes on grain exports, Franklin pleaded the cause of free trade, highlighted the advantages of having a grain price standard to protect the purchasing power of its producers, denounced

---

[56] Sidney Sherwood, *Tendencies in American Economic Thought* (Baltimore: The Johns Hopkins Press, 1897): 9. More recently, Gordon Wood has also highlighted the importance of his French experience, 'Franklin as the representative American belonged to France before he belonged to America itself' (Wood, *The Americanization of Benjamin Franklin,* 174).

[57] Cf. Willis Steel, *Benjamin Franklin of Paris 1776–1785* (New York: Minton, Boech, 1928); Bernard Faÿ, *Franklin, the Apostle of Modern Times* (Boston: Brown and Company, 1930); Carl van Doren, *Benjamin Franklin* (New York: The Viking Press, 1938); David Schoenbrun, *Triumph in Paris: The Exploits of Benjamin Franklin* (New York: Harper and Row, 1976); Aldridge, *Benjamin Franklin et ses contemporains français*. On the influence of Franklin's physics on physiocratic idea of circulation, cf. Jessica Riskin, *Science in the Age of Sensibility: The Sentimental Empiricists of the French Enlightenment* (Chicago: University of Chicago Press, 2002), 112.

[58] Franklin to Cadwalader Evans, London, 20 February 1768, in Franklin, *The Papers*, vol. XV, 52.

[59] 'Lettre d'un fermier au public anglois, sur les terreurs et les soulevements populaires qu'a occasionnés la cherté des grains; et sur les moyens qu'on a pris pour y remédier', *Ephémérides du citoyen*, vol. II, no. 1 (1767): 5–18. Dorothy Medlin has identified ten of Franklin's works translated by Morellet (cf. Dorothy Medlin, 'André Morellet, translator of liberal thought', *Studies on Voltaire and the Eighteenth Century*, no. 174 (1978): 189–201.

[60] 'Lettre d'un fermier au public anglois', 6.

a misguided assistentialist policy, and extolled the central role of the farmer to counter mercantilist theories that proposed keeping grain prices low for the sake of manufacturers: 'I am one of that class of people, that feeds you all, and at present is abused by you all, in short I am a farmer.'[61] The *Ephémérides* article revealed the contrast between the interests of agriculture and those of commerce and manufacturing, making reference to social figures as landowners and the tenants that were central to the Physiocratic argument even if they were not mentioned in Franklin's work.[62]

The Physiocrats were the first group with whom Franklin came into contact after arriving in Paris. They included the Marquis of Mirabeau, Quesnay, Du Pont de Nemours and Barbeu Du Bourg, who immediately became his supporters. His closest rapport was with Mirabeau, who shared his interest in population.[63] It was apparently the marquis who introduced him to Quesnay.[64] His keenest exchange of correspondence was with Du Pont de Nemours who he had asked after during this first visit but failed to meet. In a letter of apology, sent with a copy of the *Physiocratie* and of *De l'origine et des progrès d'une science nouvelle*, Du Pont expressed his respect for 'the learned man, the geometrician, the physicist, the man whom nature allows to reveal her secrets', adding that he had translated some passages passed to him by Barbeu Du Bourg. He went on to express the hope that the Physiocratic newspaper might enjoy the collaboration of Franklin, whom he believed had the genius and ability to apply in practical ways the principles of economic science, which he thought was politically important as a means of promoting rights and wealth distribution:

> It is in the clear development of all human rights that we will find the basis and the principles of a perpetually thriving government that is equally useful and reliable for its own country as well as beneficial for other countries around it which profit from its love of peace, of liberty, and of the openness and freedom that it will offer to its trade, and the distribution of increased wealth that will come from its agriculture. A genius like yours, sir, is clearly made to make

---

[61]   Franklin, *On the Price of Corn, and the Management of the Poor*, in Franklin., *The Works*, vol. II, 355.

[62]   'Lettre d'un fermier au public anglois', 6.

[63]   Franklin to Du Pont de Nemours, London, 28 July 1768, in Franklin, *The Papers*, vol. XV, 180.

[64]   Samuel Romilly, *Memoirs of the Life of Sir Samuel Romilly*, 3rd ed., 2 vols. (London: J. Murray, 1841): vol. II, 447–58, cited in Aldridge, *Benjamin Franklin et ses contemporains français*, 23. Alexander Small, in a letter from 1777, wrote: 'I dare say the Ami des Hommes, and his friends live in friendship with you' (Alexander Small to Franklin, St Philips Minorca, 15 March 1777, in Franklin, *The Papers*, vol. XXIII, 497–8. Cf. also Victor Riquetti, Marquis of Mirabeau to Franklin, 19 July 1777, in Franklin, *The Papers*, vol. XXIII, 336.

clear these truths which are so useful to mankind and to hasten the happiness of the world.[65]

This language was not alien to Franklin, who thanked Du Pont for the volumes of the *Physiocratie*, 'which I have read with great Pleasure, and received from it a great deal of Instruction', and addressed his own compliments to the 'venerable Apostle Dr. Quesnay' and the 'illustrious Ami des Hommes'. The reply to Du Pont was a declaration of faith in Physiocracy, which brought together freedom, benevolence and welfare in a new vision of economics, the antithesis of the policies of Britain to which he felt he still belonged:

> There is such a Freedom from local and national Prejudices and Goodness mixt with the Wisdom, in the Principles of your new Philosophy, that I am perfectly charm'd with them, and wish I could have staid in France for some time, to have studied in your School, that I might, by conversing with its Founders have made myself quite a Master of that Philosophy ... I am sorry to find, that that Wisdom which sees the Welfare of the Parts in the Prosperity of the Whole, seems not yet to be known in this Country. We are so far from conceiving that what is best for Mankind, or even for Europe, in general, may be best for us, that we are ever studying to establish and extend a separate Interest of Britain, to the Prejudice of even Ireland and our own Colonies! It is from your Philosophy only that the Maxims of a contrary and more happy Conduct are to be drawn, which I therefore sincerely wish may grow and increase till it becomes the governing Philosophy of the human Species.[66]

Franklin was deeply affected by his exchanges with the French economists with whom he rubbed shoulders during the years of the most intense elaboration and systematization of Physiocratic theories. Upon returning to London he began to use Physiocratic principles in support of his own arguments, be they in his written works or his correspondence. He collaborated with the *Ephémérides*, which he received regularly,[67] and in July 1769 he returned to Paris, where he remained until 1 September. Economics and politics were bound ever closer together in his mind as he was faced with the worsening colonial crisis; and, in the growing awareness of the need to separate the American economy from that of Britain, he often turned to Physiocracy for guidance. In 1769, he wrote in the margins to Allan Ramsay's *Thought on the Origin and nature of Government on the colonial dispute* that:

---

[65]   Du Pont de Nemours to Franklin, Paris, 10 May 1768, in Franklin, *The Papers*, vol. XV, 119.

[66]   Franklin to Du Pont de Nemours, London, 28 July 1768, Franklin, *The Papers*, vol. XV, 180–81.

[67]   Cf. Barbeu Du Bourg to Franklin, Paris, 31 May 1772, Franklin, *The Papers*, vol. XIX, 160; Franklin to Du Pont de Nemours, London, 12 August 1772, *ibid.*, 235.

'the Produce of the Earth is the only Source of Revenue'.[68] When discussing a rigidly mercantilist text in 1771, he founded his criticisms on the principle of the exclusive productivity of agriculture:

> When a Grain of Corn is put into the Ground it may produce ten grains: After defraying the Expence, here is a real Increase of Wealth. Above we see that Manufactures make no Addition to it, they only change its Form. So trade, or the Exchange of Manufactures, makes no Increase of Wealth among Mankind in general ... But the clear Produce of Agriculture is clear additional Wealth.[69]

In comparison to the works he produced before arriving in Europe, Franklin, who was now using a clearer and more orderly methodology, somewhat changed his ideas about manufacturing. In the same way, he abandoned the labour theory of value, which in his early works he had adopted from Petty.[70] Faced with the conditions in America, where production was closely linked to the cultivation of land, the fundamental argument of the Physiocratic theory – that agricultural labour was the measure by which to calculate the value of all goods – appeared to him to be more relevant and convincing.[71]

Franklin, who extolled the farmer and created the myth of normality as the 'way to wealth', was quite at ease when approaching the French economic theory regarding large landholdings. Above and beyond the American Republicans' specific agrarian ideology, which was characterized by a distinct convergence of the concerns of small and large landowners, he was driven by a personal sociological intuition that explains his particular interest in Physiocracy as a reflection on economics interpreted as a social science.

As an editor and journalist himself, Franklin shared the Physiocrats' concern with shaping public opinion. The close relationship between morality and economics, and economics construed as a language of politics, were common

---

[68]   Franklin, *Marginalia* to Allan Ramsay, *Thought on the Origin and nature of Government, Occasioned by the Late Disputes between Great Britain and Her Colonies: written in the Year 1766* (London: 1769), in Franklin, *The Papers*, vol. XVI, 315.

[69]   Franklin, *Remarks on Agriculture and Manufacturing*, comment on the eleventh chapter of *Considerations on the Policy, Commerce and Circumstances of the Kingdom* (London: 1771), in Franklin, *The Papers*, vol. XVIII, 274.

[70]   'Those working People seldom receive more than a bare Subsistence for their Labour; and the very Reason why six penny Worth of Flax is worth perhaps twenty Shillings after they have wrought into Cloth, is, that they have during the Operation consum'd nineteen Shillings and sixpence worth of Provision. So that the Value of Manufactures arises out of the Earth, and is not the creation of Labour as commonly supposed'. (Franklin, *Remarks on Agriculture and Manufacturing*, in Franklin, *The Papers*, vol. XVIII, 274).

[71]   Franklin to Lord Kames, London, 21 February 1769, in Franklin, *The Writings*, vol. V, 195. For an analysis of Franklin's ideas on value in relation to agricultural labour, subsequently critiqued by Ricardo, cf. Mott and Zinke, *Benjamin Franklin's Economic Thought*, 120–21.

perspectives in different contexts. In the attempt to show the American colonies a way of development and wellbeing that preserved their individuality and autonomy, Franklin found an anti-mercantilist and anti-British paradigm in Physiocracy that suited his demographic convictions. His meeting with the French economists confirmed his anti-mercantilism, which in turn directed his reflections on British colonial policy and its economy, considered by him to be chained to its insularity and unsuitable for larger territories like France and America.

Whereas Jefferson, with his more pragmatic and political approach, found a method of thought in Quesnay's school, which he acknowledged without entering into theoretical discussion, Franklin confronted the principles of Physiocracy directly, sharing its anti-mercantilist stance rather than the theory as a whole. The vision of a harmonious order, the centrality of agriculture (a belief that, after his personal contacts with Quesnay and Mirabeau, became a conviction in the exclusive productivity of land) and freedom of commerce, opposition to monopolies, the criticism of public debt and price control were all non-negotiable for him. However, his pragmatism led him to be more flexible on the need for duties and indirect taxes, and to insist that a single territorial tax would be impracticable.

In his *Doutes*, addressed in 1777 to Turgot in response to the *Mémoire pour Franklin*, in which the ex-Controller General had attacked indirect taxation that ultimately always fell on landowners, Franklin contended that this analysis could not be applied generally; it was inapplicable, he held, to countries where landowners worked directly on the land and thus found it difficult to calculate their variable net product, as well as to those that depended solely on manufacturing and commerce or those, like the United Provinces, with mixed economies.[72] After the approval of the American Constitution, in the face of high war debts, he would maintain that indirect taxes were more practicable since they were less onerous and easier to levy in a sparsely populated territory.[73]

Republican Virtue and Consumption

Apart from some specific principles, the Physiocratic approach to economics as a social science sat well with Franklin's vision. He had moved close to the new science, shared some of its premises and benefited from its theoretical organization, all in the context of a system whose fixed main purpose was to improve the material

---

[72]   Franklin, *Doutes de Franklin* (1777), in Anne-Robert-Jacques Turgot, *Oeuvres*, ed. Schelle, vol. V, 516.

[73]   Franklin to Morellet, Philadelphia, 22 April 1787, in Franklin, *The Works*, vol. X, 301. See also Franklin to Veillard, 22 April 1788 (*ibid.*, 346). He restated this belief in a letter to Alexander Small, emphasizing, like Jefferson, that Americans found it hard to accept the notion of taxes being finally paid by the land (Franklin to Alexander Small, Philadelphia, 28 September 1787, *ibid.*, 323). Cf. Jefferson to Du Pont, Monticello, 15 April 1811, in Jefferson, *The Writings* ed. Bergh, vol. XIII, 39.

conditions of life. In a letter of 1769 in which he reaffirmed his loyalty to the king and people of Britain – seeing its Parliament as the sole enemy – he set out a way for Americans to escape the crisis. It took the form of an economic programme, clearly inspired by Physiocracy, that would bring widespread prosperity.[74]

Franklin's Puritan ethic was at odds with British moral decadence; and Physiocratic criticisms of manufacturers of luxuries provided him with the economic basis for a political break from Britain. His democratic radicalism could thus appraise the social implications of the economic debate from outside the French monarchical context in which it evolved. In the Physiocratic analysis, the production of luxury goods consumed by the rich elite occurred at the expense of agricultural development and the provision of goods needed by the majority of the population. Heightened poverty and the waste of natural resources damaged the economy, and, in order to support the privileged and unproductive class, workers in both the country and the city were exploited by deleterious political economics that suppressed wages and grain prices to assist the export of manufactured goods. In opposing this situation, Franklin took advantage of the rich potential of the theoretical picture – offered by the *ordre naturel et essential des sociétés politiques* – which ensured a rise in the entire nation's quality of life.

In contrast to the British system, the Physiocrats aimed to centre consumption on the countryside; the corn *juste prix* would bring higher wages, which would increase the demand for goods not only from landowners but also from tenants and peasants. The criticism of luxury thus became an attack not against consumption itself, but rather against expenditure on things that drew the consumer away from acquiring products from the countryside – the centre of production and wealth that made consumption possible. In October 1767, when Franklin's first period in France was drawing to a close, Quesnay published the *Lettre de M. Alpha sur le langage de la science économique* in the *Ephémérides du citoyen*. Continuing the polemic that the periodical had started in relation to Forbonnais's *Principes et observations oeconomiques*, this work clarified the distinction made by the new economic science between 'commerce', which included production and consumption, and the 'profession of dealer, who buys in order to resell'.[75] In these pages Franklin rediscovered the idea of the relationship between the value of goods and the level of subsistence needed by the worker, which led him to abandon Petty's theory.[76] Quesnay's reasoning thus demonstrated to Franklin why he had to distance himself from British mercantilist policies: not only in order to preserve political freedom, but also to protect the productive base of a republican

---

[74]   Franklin to Samuel Cooper, London, 27 April 1769, in Franklin, *The Papers*, vol. XVI, 119.

[75]   François Quesnay, *Lettre de M. Alpha sur le langage de la science économique*, in François Quesnay, *Oeuvres économiques complètes et autres textes*, eds. Christine Théré, Loïc Charles and Jean-Claude Perrot, 2 vols. (Paris: INED., 2005): vol. II, 1117.

[76]   Quesnay, *Lettre de M. Alpha*, in Quesnay, *Oeuvres économiques complètes*, vol. II, 1124.

political economy. The central role that Physiocracy accorded to consumption in the countryside and the widespread wellbeing of an agrarian economy, was well suited to America and its frugal way of life: conscientious, comforting and mythologized in *Bonhomme Richard*, which showed that danger lay in irresponsible consumerism, not in consumer goods themselves.[77] The American reading of Physiocracy carried out by Franklin, a sociologist of the American consumer revolution, who shared American optimism with regard to expanding the material conditions that signified freedom of choice and social mobility, should therefore be interpreted from outside the Old Regime social structure where the Physiocratic theory developed, and also from beyond the immediate political strategy of Quesnay's group.

In the debate on luxury, during which, midway through the century, various reactions to economic expansion and increased consumption were heard,[78] Mirabeau's position had several points in common with that of Franklin, for whom the marquis was the initial connection with Physiocracy. Thanks to the author's enormous success, the criticisms of luxury in his *Ami des Hommes* came to influence Franklin's shift from a moralistic attitude towards luxury to an economic perspective on how to deal with it, in accordance with what Mirabeau emphasized following his conversion to Physiocracy. 'Luxury is not in the thing, it is in the abuse',[79] he had asserted in the second part of the work, where the discussion continued to swing between the traditional critique of the 'reversal' of the social order, provoked by ostentatious spending and spurious honours, and the moralistic attacks on the positive opinions of Melon and Hume. However, a distinction was made between luxury and spending, and 'politeness, industry and the arts' were held in high regard.[80] As regards the central social and economic role of the noble landowner – based on Cantillon – which the *Ami des Hommes* recognized, Mirabeau, like Franklin, distinguished between harmful extravagance and productive consumption, and praised the landowner who produced 'in his life more good for his family, his neighbours, for the poor, for the State, and for his homeland than the finest minds could ever have imagined'.[81] The liberalization of the economy, the abolition of monopolies and the central economic role of

---

[77]   Cf. the analysis of Franklin's position regarding the American consumer revolution in Breen, *The Marketplace of Revolution*.

[78]   Cf. Ellen Ross, 'Mandeville, Melon, and Voltaire: The Origins of the Luxury Controversy in France', *Studies on Voltaire and the Eighteenth Century*, no. 155 (1976): 1897–1912.

[79]   Victor de Riquetti, Marquis de Mirabeau, *L'Ami des hommes, ou Traité de la population*, 5th ed. (Hambourg: chez Chrétien Hérold, 1760): vol. II, 200. Cf. Michael Kwass, 'Consumption and the World of Ideas: Consumer Revolution and the Moral Economy of the Marquis de Mirabeau', *Eighteenth Century Studies*, 37/2 (2004): 187–213.

[80]   Mirabeau, *L'Ami des hommes*, 244.

[81]   Mirabeau, *L'Ami des hommes, ou Traité de la population*, 1st ed. (Avignon: 1758–1760): vol. I, 80.

agriculture would lead to national prosperity and expansion in the market of essential goods. Like Franklin, the *L'Ami des Hommes* disapproved of all forms of sumptuary law.[82]

The theoretical picture of Mirabeau's critique of unproductive luxury is seen more clearly after the beginning of the collaboration with Quesnay. In a wholly economic analysis, Quesnay's distinction between 'luxe de décoration' and 'luxe de subsistance' viewed spending on agricultural products and commodities positively and placed consumption at the centre of the economic process.[83] The *Tableau économique*, which linked production, circulation and consumption, and recognized the importance of raising the quality of life of the whole population through higher wages – not an effect, but the cause of prosperity – offered a strong conceptual defence for Franklin's democratic approach.[84] Quesnay's work contained not only a criticism of the manufacturing of luxury goods, which diverted capital from agriculture, the sole active creator of wealth, but also the theoretical legitimization of expenditure on material goods and agricultural products that all social classes, however rich or poor, had to consume, thus benefiting from the material wellbeing that was the expression of the economy's natural laws.[85]

In the setting of a society of orders based on privilege, which the Physiocratic discourse began to undermine, the role of consumption – in an economic system which reinvested all national income – and of a general improvement in the material conditions of life, came to take on implications aside from the formulations and intentions of its theorists, as an enlargement of popular participation in the market of consumer goods.[86]

---

[82]   *Ibid.*, vol. II, 123.

[83]   François Quesnay, *Tableau économique avec ses explications*, in *Oeuvres*, vol. I, 479. Cf. also Quesnay, *Maximes générales du gouvernement économique d'un royaume agricole*, no. XXII, *ibid.*, 571.

[84]   'The true cause of laziness in the oppressed peasant is his excessively low wage ... poor peasants, poor kingdom', (Maxime XX, in Quesnay, *Oeuvres*, vol. I, 592).

[85]   Victor Riquetti, Marquis de Mirabeau and François Quesnay, *Philosophie rurale, ou Economie générale et politique de l'agriculture*, 3 vols. (Amsterdam: chez les Libraires associés, 1763): vol. II, 16. Cf. Albert Hirschman, *Shifting Involvements: Private Interest and Public Action* (Princeton: Princeton University Press, 1982).

[86]   In this sense the analysis of Physiocracy and consumption can offer new contributions to current historiographical thinking on the relationship between the widening of consumption and the formation of a middle class, which up to now has been confined to the study of British urban classes, and on the role played by the consumer revolution and the economy in general in the origins of the French Revolution. Cf. Sarah Maza, 'Luxury, Morality, and Social Change: Why there was no Middle-Class Consciousness in Pre-Revolutionary France', *The Journal of Modern History*, 69 (1997): 199–229; Colin Jones, 'Bourgeois Revolution Revivified: 1779 and Social Change', in *Rewriting the French Revolution*, ed. Colin Lucas (Oxford: Clarendon Press, 1991): 69–118; Paul Cheney, *Revolutionary Commerce: Globalization and the French Monarchy* (Cambridge: Harvard University Press, 2010).

In the *Philosophie rurale* the 'new Colonies which have grown an abundance of corn in deserted land'[87] were themselves an example of the relation between abundant production and abundant consumption. Le Mercier de la Rivière, who in 1767 provided with *L'ordre naturel et essentiel des sociétés politiques* a synthesis of the new economic science, defined the centrality of consumption in Physiocratic thought: 'Consumption is the proportional measurement of reproduction', a formula that Quesnay had already given in the entry on 'Grains' in the *Encyclopédie*, repeating an idea of other authors, such as Boisguillebert, d'Argenson and Dupin.[88]

In the Physiocratic scheme consumption had a specific meaning in the process of agrarian reproduction, and Mirabeau would define it accurately when formalizing the science of economics in meticulously clear terms. In *Les économiques*, published between 1769 and 1771, he distinguished between 'decorative expenditure'(*dépense de décoration*) and 'expenses of consumption' (*dépense de consommation*), considered the 'opening' (*débouché*) of the economic process,[89] and, albeit in a social context that did not care about inequalities, he emphasized the desirability of stability founded on a common average level of prosperity.[90]

Bearing in mind that the wealth of the nation was to be found in the 'affluency of the people', the particular social awareness (compared with other Physiocratic writers) of the *L'Ami des Hommes* did not fail to consider the economic impact of the changes on the material conditions of the working class, including an improved diet.[91] Notwithstanding the respective contexts and the differences that separated the French marquis from the bourgeois American, in Mirabeau, as in Franklin, responsible behaviour in relation to the spread of consumption, which opened the market to wider social groups, led to judgments being made on luxury on the basis of a socio-economic rationale.[92]

---

[87]   Mirabeau and Quesnay, *Philosophie rurale*, vol. III, 83.

[88]   'When we say that consumption is the proportional measurement of reproduction, we are talking about consumption that benefits those whose work and spending revive productions'. (Pierre-Paul-François le Mercier de la Rivière, *L'ordre naturel et essentiel des sociétés politiques*, 2 vols. (Paris: J. Nourse, Desaint, 1767): vol. II, ch. XXXII, 'Effets et contrecoups des impôts établis par les cultivateurs personnellement', 138–9). Cf. François Quesnay, *Grains*, in Quesnay, *Oeuvres*, vol. I, 162: 'The consumption of the subjects is the source of the sovereign's income'.

[89]   Victor Riquetti, Marquis de Mirabeau, *Les économiques*, 3 vols. (Amsterdam: 1769–71): vol. II, 115–16.

[90]   Mirabeau, *Les économiques*, vol. III, 153.

[91]   Victor Riquetti de Mirabeau, *Réponse aux objections contre le Mémoire sur les Etats provinciaux*, in Mirabeau *L'Ami des hommes*, vol. IV, 158–9.

[92]   Mirabeau, *Réponse aux objections contre le Mémoire sur les Etats provinciaux*, in Mirabeau *L'Ami des hommes*, vol. IV, 315. This is also true of the consumption of the cities, which comes about thanks to the wealth created in the countryside (*ibid.*, 323).

Franklin and the *Ephémérides du citoyen*

The Physiocratic interpretation of society and economy, unified and harmonious in the name of social responsibility, was perceived by Franklin to be opposed to the British model which begat division and competition; and it was to be against the corporate interests of British merchants, which damaged consumers. His interest in this viewpoint can be explained by his realization that in the French economists – who always looked favourably on the American colonies, their development, and economic potential, and who from the outset endorsed their cause (which Smith did not) – he had found a support and a channel through which to transmit information about America.[93]

Franklin contributed articles to the *Ephémérides du citoyen* about economic freedom, the need to raise the wages and increase the spending power of workers, the incomparable situation of the farmers, the fight against protectionism and the advantage of rural life over that in the city. Starting with his first article (published in 1767) on Britain's grain trade, which appealed to the editors for its defence of economic freedom, he centred his discussion on the relationship between high grain prices, farmers' profits and increasing workers' pay on the one hand, and raising the standard of living of the poor on the other. Opposed to all forms of assistentialism, he hoped to attain an improvement of living conditions through economic freedom: 'I think the best way to help the poor, is not to make them live comfortably in their state of poverty, but to pull them out of this state'.[94] His argument agreed on several points with the Physiocratic approach, for he also believed that the impetus for consumption came from the countryside and then fed into the general economy.[95]

The following year Barbeu Du Bourg translated, under the title of *Des Troubles qui divisent l'Angleterre et ses colonies*, Franklin's famous interrogation by the Chamber of Deputies on the colonies' resistance to the *Stamps Act*, which had already been published in the 4–7 July edition of the *London Chronicle*. Franklin

---

[93]   Even before the start of tensions between the American colonies and their mother country, Mirabeau, in the third part of the *L'Ami des hommes*, had praised and defended the spirit of freedom in the way the colonies organized, their ability to offer openings to production, which implied free trade, and their populationist concerns. He had highlighted the republican structure of their institutions and had predicted their independence, as a reaction against Britain's mercantilist policies, just as Turgot had done in 1750 (Mirabeau, *L'Ami des hommes*, vol. III, part 3, ch. VI, 'Des Colonies'; Anne-Robert-Jacques Turgot, *Tableau philosophique des progrès successifs de l'esprit humain*, in Turgot, *Oeuvres*, ed. Schelle, vol. I, 222). On the economic role of the British colonies and the French economists who later supported their revolution, cf. Paul B. Cheney, 'Les économistes français et l'image de l'Amérique: L'essor du commerce transatlantique et l'effondrement du «gouvernement féodal»," *Dix-huitième siècle*, no. 33 (2001): 231–45.

[94]   *Ephémérides du citoyen* (1767): vol. II, no. 1, 16.

[95]   *Ephémérides du citoyen* (1767): vol. II, no. 1, 11.

defended consumer interests and attacked the restrictions on free trade, though in reply to the deputies who wanted to know whether taxation in Pennsylvania was set to disadvantage British goods, he did not openly claim that taxes on trade were more onerous than those on production. The notes added to the translation attempted to show how, behind the cautious language, Franklin supported the idea that taxes on trade fell in the end on cultivators.[96] In addition to damaging Britain's image, the intention of the *Ephémérides* was to present this defence of consumers as an exposition of Physiocratic principles, and Franklin was praised as a disciple of the Quesnay school:

> this wise American was struck, when we spoke with him about it, by the links between those [truths] which for some years have reduced what has been called the art of governing Nations into an exact Science. He quickly became one of the most capable followers of this noble science, which continues to have, in its country of origin, certain contradictions which have not hindered its progress, and its defenders console themselves with the pleasure of making progress of the same weight and merit as that of Franklin.[97]

The publication, in 1769, of the twelve *Positions à examiner*, however, left not a shadow of doubt about Franklin's close relationship with the *Économistes*. Having returned to Britain and remained in contact with Barbeu Du Bourg and Du Pont, who sent him copies of the *Physiocratie*, and having subscribed to the *Ephémérides*, Franklin thought through his ideas in the light of his new contacts. He set them out in a series of aphorisms, which he sent to Lord Kames at the start of the year,[98] and which were published in the *London Chronicle* on 29 June and

---

[96]   *Ephémérides du citoyen*, (1768): vol. VII, no. III, part I, 51. The interview is in pages 34–91 and in vol. VIII, part 3, no. 1, 159–92. Evidence of the collaboration of the Physiocrat group in this translation can be found in Du Bourg's correspondence with Franklin (Barbeu Du Bourg to Franklin, Paris, 8 May 1768, in Franklin, *Papers*, vol. XV, 114).

[97]   *Ephémérides du citoyen* (1768): vol. VII, no. III, part I, 33. Even Du Pont, in the 'Notice abrégée' of the *Ephémérides* of 1769, had reaffirmed the idea that Franklin should be considered assimilated to the 'exact science' of economics and worthy of pronouncing its principles (*Ephémérides* (1769): vol. IX, 67–68). Turgot, in a letter to Du Pont, criticized Franklin's assimilation into Physiocracy as being forced, and his having failed to seize the opportunity to further the discussion on the colonies, given that Franklin also held positions that were favourable to imports. 'You have not yet recovered from the spirit of sect' (Turgot to Du Pont de Nemours, Limoges, 5 August 1768, in Turgot, *Oeuvres*, ed. Schelle, vol. III, 13). Franklin, who shared with him the theory of natural interest, admired Turgot (Franklin to George Washington, Paris, 2 April 1777), and visited him in Paris (Barbeu Du Bourg to Franklin, Paris, 12 March 1777), in Franklin, *The Papers*, vol. XXIII, 551 and 479).

[98]   'To commence a conversation with you on your new subject, I have thrown some of my present sentiments into the concise Form of Aphorisms, to be examin'd between us, and rejected or corrected and confirm'd as we shall find most proper'. (Franklin to Lord Kames, 1 January 1769, in Franklin, *The Papers*, vol. XVI, 4).

then immediately translated into French. The list of principles, which followed the form of Quesnay's *Maximes*,[99] began with 'All Food or Subsistence for Mankind arise from the Earth or Waters'. The value of goods, calculated on the consumption of agricultural products, was expressed in Physiocratic language: 'Manufactures are only another Shape into which so much Provisions and Subsistence are turned as were equal Value to the Manufactures produced. This appears from hence, that the Manufacturer does not in fact, obtain from the Employer, for his Labour, more than a mere Subsistence'.[100] The primacy of agriculture over other activities was reaffirmed in the last maxim in ethical and economic terms:

> Finally, there seem to be but three Ways for a Nation to acquire Wealth. The first is by War as the Romans did in plundering their conquered Neighbours. This is Robbery. The second by Commerce which is generally Cheating. The third by Agriculture the only honest Way; wherein Man receives a real Increase of the Seed thrown into the Ground, in a kind of continual Miracle wrought by the Hand of God in his Favour, as a Reward for his innocent Life, and virtuous Industry.[101]

The commentators of the *Ephémérides* no longer had any need to point out the proximity of Franklin's ideas to the new science; in fact the notes that accompanied the text softened Franklin's highly negative verdict on commerce[102] and his rigid moralistic attitude towards the entrepreneurial spirit. Indeed, in Maxim X he concluded that the price at which a producer could sell a quantity of grain ground into flour was a type of trick – more ingenious than most – that enabled him to save time and effort.[103]

However, Franklin, who had read Quesnay's *Maximes*, had not accepted all its principles, but disregarded those that did not tally with his American and democratic perspective: there is therefore no hint of a determined defence of land ownership, the single land tax and the negative value of savings, or of the preference for large estates.[104]

Franklin contributed other articles to the *Ephémérides*, collaborating with the editors' plan of painting a positive picture of the American colonies.[105] Two articles, published as letters to the paper, commended the scarcity of cities in America and the advantageously widespread distribution of the population which allowed, in

---

[99]   Franklin, *Positions to Be Examined*, in Franklin, *The Papers*, vol. XVI, 107 (*Ephémérides du citoyen* (1769): vol. X). Cf. Quesnay, *Maximes*, I.

[100]   Franklin, *Positions to Be Examined*, in Franklin, *The Papers*, vol. XVI, 108 (*Ephémérides du citoyen* (1769): vol. X, 8).

[101]   Franklin, *Positions to Be Examined*, in Franklin, *The Papers*, vol. XVI, 109 (*Ephémérides du citoyen* (1769): vol. X, 15–16).

[102]   *Ephémérides du citoyen* (1769): vol. X, 15–16.

[103]   *Ephémérides du citoyen* (1769): vol. X, 10–13.

[104]   Cf. Quesnay, *Maximes*, IV, V, VII, XV, XXVI.

[105]   *Ephémérides du citoyen* (1769): VI, no. I, 56–78; (1772): vol. II, no. I, 213–27.

contrast to urban life, a middle state of wellbeing: 'everyone has his house, clean and pleasant, and around this his garden, his fields, and a variety of intelligently chosen crops'.[106] The information given in the first article, which presented the New York colony as an archetype, was subsequently amended whenever Franklin provided new data. The *Ephémérides* were thus able to give one of the earliest realistic descriptions of American life.[107] 'Virginia, the beautiful countries without cities', wrote an anonymous author, perhaps Du Pont de Nemours,[108] in one of the first contributions to the creation of the Virginian myth that would later find full expression in Jefferson's *Notes on the State of Virginia*. Virginia's agrarian economy, which ensured wellbeing, solidarity and independence, was representative of other colonies, and presaged their forthcoming break with the mother country. The article concluded with a series of Physiocratic principles in the name of individual rights and freedoms, and in an international picture the hope was expressed that distinctions made between black and white, American, European and African would be abolished, thereby allowing the colonies to be transformed into a powerful empire within a century.

The *Ephémérides du citoyen*'s support for the American Revolution also involved a plan to carry out translations. This focused on Barbeu Du Bourg, writer of the deist work *Petit code de la raison humaine*, of which the first publication, in 1768, was closely linked to the author's meeting with Franklin, to whom he dedicated the work.[109]

---

[106]   'Lettre de Mr. H. à l'auteur des Ephémérides du citoyen Sur un Pays très florissant où il n'y a point de Villes, Paris, 12 mars 1769', in *Ephémérides du citoyen* (1769): vol. III, no. III, 69–72.

[107]   'Lettre de Mr. H. à l'auteur des Ephémérides, au sujet du Pays florissant qui n' a point de Villes, dont il a été parlé dans le troisième Volume de cette année', in *Ephémérides du citoyen* (1769): vol. VIII, no. 1, 52.

[108]   Alfred Aldridge attributes the two letters to Barbeu Du Bourg, on the basis of the similarity with the preface to his translation of the *Letters from a farmer in Pennsylvania* by John Dickinson (Aldridge, *Benjamin Franklin et ses contemporains*, 36). Gustave Schelle, on the other hand, attributes it to Du Pont de Nemours, in the list of works by Du Pont published in an appendix to his *Du Pont de Nemours et l'école physiocratique* (Paris, 1888). The tone of the discussion and the appeal to rights makes the attribution to Du Pont more realistic. Turgot was critical about the idealization of Virginia; in a letter to Du Pont on 7 November 1769 he wrote: 'what does all this fine praise for Virginia mean? Do you not know that this Virginia is a black colony?' (Turgot, *Oeuvres*, ed. Schelle, vol. III, 70). In relation to this see Manuela Albertone, 'Letture fisiocratiche della Rivoluzione americana: il manoscritto del marchese di Mirabeau sulla *Dichiarazione dei diritti della Virginia* e la risposta di Pierre-Samuel Du Pont de Nemours', in *Governare il mondo: L'economia come linguaggio della politica nell'Europa del Settecento*, ed. Manuela Albertone (Milan: Feltrinelli, 2009): 171–201.

[109]   Cf. Alfred O. Aldridge, 'Jacques Barbeu-Dubourg, a French disciple of Benjamin Franklin', *Proceedings of the American Philosophical Society*, 95 (1951): 331–92.

In 1769 Du Bourg, who was in close contact with the older Mirabeau and who played a role in French foreign policy through his links with Vergennes, translated John Dickinson's *Letters from a Farmer in Pennsylvania*, extracts of which later appeared with a commentary in the *Ephémérides*.[110] In 1771 Du Bourg published, under the false claim that they were translations from the *Pennsylvania Chronicle*, two *Lettres d'Abraham Mansword, Citoyen de Philadelphie, à ses compatriotes de l'Amérique septentrionale*, a constitutional observation of the American situation from a Physiocratic perspective.[111] Five years before the *Common Sense*, Du Bourg predicted the American Revolution and the creation of a federal republic, and presented the draft for a constitution to serve as the basis of representative government and decentralized use of political participation, in compliance with the provincial assemblies' plans. It was one of the most mature proposals of reforms prepared by Physiocratic authors:

> This revolution is in the order of things: considering the size of their territory, fertility of their soil, the benefits of their climate, it is not possible that the English Colonies of North America will fail to quickly establish a numerous and powerful population ... the English Colonies, know how important it is for them to form a single republic, a single society, a single power, and cannot fail to unite with one another to form a good and wise confederation.[112]

Du Bourg's close personal relationship with Franklin and his intention to link Franklin's ideas to Quesnay's principles led to his becoming the editor of the first two-volume French edition of Franklin's works, which appeared in 1773 as a significantly enlarged version of the 1769 fourth edition of the *Experiments and Observations on Electricity made at Philadelphia in America*. In addition to articles on the electrical experiments, the book included writings on economics, demographics and politics. Moreover, it presented the first French translation of *Bonhomme Richard* and the *Observations sur l'accroissement de l'espèce humaine, la Population des Pays*. Du Bourg added explanatory notes and an essay that listed a series of Physiocratic principles purportedly used in Franklin's demographic analysis.

---

[110]   John Dickinson, *Lettres d'un fermier de Pennsylvanie aux habitants de l'Amérique septentrionale*, trans. from English (Amsterdam: aux dépens de la Compagnie, 1769). Franklin's *Observations adressées à la société royale de Londres* appear on pp. 239–58 and the translation of the *Observations concerning the Increase of mankind* is in an appendix. This also appeared in the 1773 edition of Franklin's works.

[111]   *Ephémérides du citoyen* (1771): vol. XI, no. III, 83–4. See Franklin's letter to Du Pont de Nemours of 15 June 1772, in which there are words of appreciation for the publication of the *Lettres d'Abraham Mansword* (Franklin, *Papers*, vol. XIX, 178).

[112]   *Ephémérides du citoyen* (1771): vol. XI, no. III, 91 and 95.

There were two points to this: on the one hand, there was a desire to give a Physiocratic interpretation of the *Observations*,[113] and, on the other, a desire to correct Franklin's errors. Like Franklin, Du Bourg linked population and food resources and – unlike the analyses later developed by Malthus – held that agricultural progress was capable of resolving the problems of population growth. The land's increased productivity, rather than weddings, was deemed to be the driver of demographic increase. Du Bourg also openly challenged both Franklin's mercantilist viewpoint, according to which a country becomes stronger by increasing its population at the cost of its neighbours, as well as the principle that made trade a factor in demographic growth: 'But take care not to forget that there are the same disparities between agriculture and trade as there are between source and capital'.[114]

The French version of the *Way to Wealth*, which appeared in the version edited by Du Bourg,[115] was not as successful as the translation by Quétant that was published a few years later, in 1777, under the title *La science du Bonhomme Richard, ou Moyen facile de payer les impôts* and enjoyed enormous success: four editions were published in two years and another five before the end of the century.[116] There are several possible reasons why *Bonhomme Richard* became the most widely read American work in France: in 1777 the American Revolution had already broken out, and Bonhomme Richard symbolized the just man who was both morally and materially satisfied; Quétant's translation was more free, using language aimed at the common man; and above all there was the fact that Franklin had returned to Paris in December 1776 as a colonial envoy sent to obtain French support for the Revolution, and had been hailed as a hero of democracy:

> Dr. Franklin, who recently arrived in this country from the English Colonies is
> very popular, highly feted by the Learned. He has a fine appearance, sparse hair

---

[113]   Amongst Mirabeau's papers there is an incomplete manuscript copy of the *Observations*, written by an unknown hand, with corrections in another and an annotation by Mirabeau that says: 'Memoir on population by Mr Franklin, given to me by him before he developed his economic ideas and it is evident, 2Xbre 1771'. (Archives Nationales, M 773, no. 2).

[114]   Franklin, *Oeuvres de M. Franklin*, trans. from English 4th ed. by M. Barbeu Dubourg with new annotations, 2 vols. (Paris: chez Quillau, Esprit et l'Auteur, 1773): vol. II, 'Extrait d'une Lettre du Traducteur à M. Franklin', 132. Du Bourg sent these same comments to Franklin, in a letter dated 19 December 1772 (Franklin, *Papers*, vol. XIX, 432–4).

[115]   Following Franklin, Du Bourg wrote *Calendrier de Philadelphie, ou Constitutions de Sancho-Pança et du Bon-Homme Richard, en Pennsylvanie* (1778). This was a presentation of deist principles, centred on the ideas of religious tolerance and political freedom, partly repeated in the *Petit code de la raison humaine*.

[116]   Franklin, *La science du Bonhomme Richard, ou Moyen facile de payer les impôts* (Philadelphie, Paris: chez Ruault, 1777). Two editions appeared in 1777 and another two in 1778.

and a leather bonnet that he wears constantly. He is very modest in public about the news of his country that he loves so much: he says that the sky was jealous of its beauty and sent it the scourge of war. Our great minds have skillfully probed into his religion, and they believe that it is similar to their own, that is to say he has none.[117]

Franklin – 'this old peasant with a noble air', 'this great physicist who has now become a redoubtable political opponent of England'[118] – and his Bonhomme Richard became the symbols of the dignity and industriousness of the new republic.[119] Compared to his two earlier sojourns in Paris, the diplomatic mission (1776 to the mid-80s) that returned Franklin to France cast his activities and ideas in a more political light. It coincided with an intensification of the political activities of the *Américanistes*, supporters of the American cause who were committed to devising a project of reforms for France. And among these were a number, including Franklin himself, who were actively committed to keeping alive the Physiocratic economic-political perspective.

Between France and America

Just as he had provided news about the colonies to the *Ephémérides du citoyen*, so Franklin continued to be a channel of information on the new republics for the *Affaires de l'Angleterre et d'Amérique*. In fact, through him it is possible to discern a continuity of French interest in America as both an economic and political exemplar, which began with the *Ephémérides* and later became a potent propaganda tool in the *Affaires*. As a journalist and editor, Franklin knew what tactics to use to shape French public opinion in America's favour; this he did on each of his stays in France, first in 1767 when he immediately allied himself to the Physiocratic group, then in 1776 when he gathered around him a kind of headquarters in support of the Revolution.

---

[117] *Mémoires secrets pour servir à l'histoire de la république des lettres en France* (London: J. Adaneson, 1777–1780): vol. X, 4 February 1777, 29. In the entry for January 17 we read: 'The current fashion is to have an engraving of Mr Franklin on one's fireplace', (*ibid.*, 11).

[118] Michel-René Hilliard D'Auberteuil, *Essais historiques et politiques sur les Anglois-Américains*, 2 vols. (Brussels, Paris: chez l'auteur, 1782): vol. II, 44–7.

[119] *L'espion anglais* (Paris: L. Collin, 1809): vol. I, 15 January 1777, 450–51. The review in the *Correspondance littéraire* stated: 'The science of Poor Richard leads entirely to this great principle that the taxes that people complain about are far from being the most onerous, that our laziness deprives us of twice as much as the government, our pride three times, and our thoughtlessness four times', (*Correspondance littéraire, philosophique et critique*, vol. XII, November 1777, 29).

Had Franklin not been present in Paris between 1776 and 1783, Vergennes would have lacked a powerful apologist with which to muster French approval for the monarchy's intervention in the American conflict. Edited by Franklin, Court de Gébelin, Robinet, the Duke of Rochefoucauld and Edmé-Jacques Genêt, the *Affaires de l'Angleterre et de l'Amérique*, which first appeared in the spring of 1776 with Vergennes's agreement, provided a means of disseminating anti-British propaganda and, after Franklin's arrival in December of that year, increased its support of the American Revolution.[120] The attention on the American colonies as constitutional laboratories that had already been found in the *Ephémérides* (with the *Lettres d'Abraham Mansword* as one of its highlights) was central to the 'Lettres d'un Banquier de Londres à M***', one of the two sections into which the *Affaires de l'Angleterre et de l'Amérique* was divided, the other being the 'Journal' which gave detailed reports about the theatres of war.[121] It is uncertain whether the decision to publish, from the early issues, large sections of Paine's *Common Sense* and Price's *Observations on the Nature of Civil Liberty* (albeit accompanied by a critical commentary) had been dictated by the veiled intent of using the *Affaires* to carry their message,[122] or by Vergennes's desire to manage the response to them, or whether the anti-British sentiment, which was more nationalist than ideological, was aimed at attracting both a liberal and conservative public readership.[123] But the fact is that from the publication of the Articles of Confederation on

---

[120]   Cf. Paul L. Ford, 'Affaires de l'Angleterre et de l'Amérique', *The Pennsylvania Magazine of History and Biography*, 132 (July 1889): 222–6; Gilbert Chinard, 'Notes on the French Translations of the "Forms of Government or Constitutions of the several United States" 1778 and 1783', *The American Philosophical Society Year Book* (1943): 88–106; Gilbert Chinard, 'Adventures in a Library', *The Newberry Library Bulletin*, 2d ser., no. 8 (March 1952): 223–38; George B. Watts, *Les Affaires de l'Angleterre et de l'Amérique* (Charlotte, NC: Heritage Printers, 1965). Cf. also Bernard Faÿ, *The Revolutionary Spirit in France and America* (London: G. Allen and Unwin Ltd., 1928), 89–91; Frances Acomb, *Anglophobia in France 1763–1789: An Essay in the History of Constitutionalism and Nationalism* (Durham, NC: Duke University Press, 1950), 83–5.

[121]   The main sources of the documentation used were Franklin himself and *The Remembrancer; or, Impartial Repository of Public Events* published in London by John Almon.

[122]   *Affaires de l'Angleterre et de l'Amérique*, vol. I (1776): no. 1, 'Lettres d'un Banquier de Londres à M.***' (London: 4 May 1776), 83–7; no. 4 (June 15, 1776), 33–87; vol. III (1776), no. 12, 45–88; no. 13, 113–76; no. 14, 177–231. The dates refer always to the dating used in the *Lettres d'un Banquier*. The newspaper contains numerous errors in its page numbering and dates.

[123]   The importance of the Declaration of Independence, which was published just over a month and a half later, was nevertheless highlighted (*Affaires de l'Angleterre et de l'Amérique*, vol. II, no. 7 (16 May [sic] 1776), 88–95), and in the following issue it was underlined that the declaration did not in any case constitute 'a general infringement on sovereignty'. The separation of the colonies was nevertheless seen as being inevitable and advantageous for Britain herself (no. 8, 2 September 1776, 91–4).

27 December, a week after Franklin's arrival, the discussion centred on constitutional themes in a line of continuity with the political rationalism of the Physiocrats.[124] Already the comments to the *Common Sense* by the Dutch banker from London – penned perhaps by La Rochefoucauld but even so the result of a team effort – had closely followed the Quesnay group's criticisms of Britain's mixed government, differentiated between monarchy and absolute government, and had recognized the primacy of law and the unity of sovereignty. In the letter of 24 February 1777, a detailed analysis of the Articles of Confederation and the Constitution of Pennsylvania, which at the time were attributed to Franklin and whose single-house system became in France the model of the unity of sovereignty, revealed the paper's constitutional approach. The appreciation for Pennsylvania's 'equal representation'[125] and for the Virginia Declaration of Rights, which placed the origin of positive laws within natural law, was linked to the positive reaction to the Articles of Confederation that guaranteed the decentralization of political administration. This approach agreed with the French reformist politics to which the Physiocratic authors had made a substantial contribution with their plans for provincial assemblies,[126] part of a strategy aimed at conserving the unity of law and sovereignty. Faced with the British and American models Franklin had to arbitrate between two empires.[127]

With Franklin's help, La Rochefoucauld translated the constitutions of the American states for the *Affaires de l'Angleterre et de l'Amérique*, which were then published in 1783 as a semi-official edition entitled the *Constitutions des Treize Etats-Unis de l'Amérique*.[128] Franklin's help with this enterprise was significant, within the larger picture of his programme of political action undertaken in the service of America's economic interests. In a letter of July 1783 to Robert

---

[124]   *Affaires de l'Angleterre et de l'Amérique*, vol. II, no. 15 (27 December 1776), CLXXVIII–CLCII. Some of Franklin's speeches were included even before his return to France (vol. II, no. 6 (11 April 1776), 26–7).

[125]   In a note of comment to the first article of the constitution of Pennsylvania, 'All men are born equal and independent', we read: 'the political meaning of this implies a share in Government, and the right to vote'. (*Affaires de l'Angleterre et de l'Amérique*, vol. 4, no. 17, 24 février 1777, LXVI).

[126]   *Affaires de l'Angleterre et de l'Amérique*, vol. 4, no. 17, 24 février 1777, LIV–LV.

[127]   *Affaires de l'Angleterre et de l'Amérique*, vol. IV, no. 17 (24 February 1777), LIX.

[128]   *Constitutions des Treize Etats-Unis de l'Amérique*, (Philadelphia, Paris: chez Ph.-D. Pierres, Imprimeur ordinaire du Roi, 1783). Edited by Franklin, this was the most complete French edition of the constitutions of the American States. This was preceded by the *Recueil des loix constitutives des colonies angloises, confédérées sous la dénomination d'Etats-Unis de l'Amérique-Septentrionale... Dédié à M. le Docteur Franklin* (Philadelphia, Paris: chez Cellot et Jombert, 1778); another edition from the same year indicates ' en Suisse, chez les Libraires associés' as a location. Cf. Durand Echeverria, 'French Publications of the Declaration of Independence and the American Constitutions, 1776–1783', *The Papers of the Bibliographical Society of America*, 47 (Fourth Quarter, 1953): 313–38. Cf. Gilbert Chinard, 'Notes on the French translations'.

Livingston, he expressed the hope that free trade would be strengthened to the detriment of the British monopoly, thereby giving rise to more abundant goods and greater prosperity for the United States. His decision to collaborate with La Rochefoucauld in the translation project had the precise objective of informing Europe, which wished to trade with America, about 'what sort of people, and what kind of government they will have to treat with'.[129]

The coming together of Franklin and the French group connected with Physiocracy passed beyond economics to take in matters of political theory in the common belief in the unity of sovereignty, to which Physiocratic rationalism had contributed with a critical reflection on the notion of the balance of powers, casting doubt on Montesquieu's authority and the British constitutional model.

In the eulogy pronounced two months after Franklin's death in 1790, La Rochefoucauld invoked him and the Constitution of Pennsylvania in support of the single-house system:

> When I had the honour to present to Franklin my translation of the constitutions of America, people were no better disposed towards it on this side of the Atlantic; and with the exception of Dr. Price in England and Turgot and Condorcet in France, almost everyone with an interest in political ideas disagreed with the American philosopher. I dare say I was one of the few who had been impressed by the beauty of the simple plan he had developed, and I had no reason to change my opinion when ... the National Assembly established as a principal of the French constitution that legislation would be confined to a single body of representatives.[130]

On the eve of the approbation of the 1787 constitution, La Rochefoucauld had urged Franklin to continue following the American constitutional path, independent from Britain, which could serve as a template for the rest of the world.[131] Franklin quickly let La Rochefoucauld and his other French collaborators have the text of the new constitution, defending its value as a means of ensuring a strong power.[132]

---

[129]   Franklin to Robert R. Livingston, Passy, 22 July 1783, in Franklin, *The Works*, vol. IX, 536–43.

[130]   *Extrait du Journal de la Société de 1789. Dans le comité général de discussion, tenu le 13 juin à la société de 1789, M. de la Rochefoucauld député de Paris à l'assemblée nationale, a lu le morceau suivant sur Benjamin Franklin*, 8–9. Cf. also Condorcet, *Eloge de Franklin*, in *Oeuvres*, vol. III, 401–2.

[131]   La Rochefoucauld to Franklin, Paris, 8 February 1786, in Franklin, *The Works*, vol. X, 246. In the letters sent to Franklin after he had returned to America, La Rochefoucauld expressed the hopes that the constitution of America could serve as an example for all of Europe and faith in Franklin's abilities to conciliate the Republicans and Federalists (La Rochefoucauld to Franklin, 30 November 1785 and 8 February 1786, reproduced in Daniel Vaugelade, *Franklin des deux mondes* (Paris: Editions de l'Armandier, 2007), 101–2).

[132]   Franklin to Le Veillard, Philadelphia, 17 February 1788, Franklin, *The Works*, vol. X, 22. In a letter sent a few months later to Du Pont de Nemours, from which we can deduce

The part carried out by Franklin during the entire lifespan of the *Affaires de l'Angleterre et de l'Amérique*, between 1776 and 1779 – his discourses were presented to the French public from the earliest issues and his interrogation in the House of Commons was published in 1778[133] – therefore combined well with the intentions of the editorship to juxtapose France with Britain so as to accentuate the closeness between France and America and to leave in ruins the image of Britain as the land of individual freedom, by conveying the inevitability and the advantages of a constitutional approach, albeit while avoiding direct criticism of French governmental policies.

Thus through the group that revolved around the *Affaires de l'Angleterre et de l'Amérique* Franklin enacted a decisive role in initiating a period of discussion of American issues, which was one of the most creative periods in the development of French politics in the 1780s;[134] and by mingling with the milieu sympathetic to the Physiocratic tradition he found the sympathizers most ready to support his propaganda activities for the American cause.

The Marquis de Mirabeau's admiration for the American revolutionary and his interest in American issues were shared by his son, the Count of Mirabeau, who became Franklin's collaborator. Franklin held the Mirabeau name in high regard (despite the disputes wreaking havoc on the family) and appreciated the Count of Mirabeau's endeavours. In 1777, the younger Mirabeau had taken a stand in favour of the colonies in the *Avis aux Hessois*, and so was willing to assist Franklin with his propaganda programme.[135] In keeping with his father, he believed in the potential of American land and lauded agriculture in a work written with reference to the agrarian myth of St John de Crèvecoeur's *Lettres d'un cultivateur américain*, but which was never published.[136] At the end of 1784, Mirabeau wrote,

---

that the Physiocrat wished to preserve the separate constitutions of the states, Franklin defended the overcoming of the Articles of Confederation, but nevertheless expressed his admiration for Du Pont, at the same time as he tried to overcome his rationalist rigour: 'we must not expect, that a new government may be formed, as a game of chess may played by a skilful hand, without a fault.' (Franklin to Du Pont de Nemours, Philadelphia, 9 June 1788, in Franklin, *The Writings*, vol. IX, 659.)

[133]   *Affaires de l'Angleterre et de l'Amérique*, vol. VIII, nos. XXXV, CCXI–CCLXI.

[134]   Cf. Edoardo Tortarolo, *Illuminismo e rivoluzioni*.

[135]   Franklin did not meet Honoré-Gabriel Riquetti, Comte de Mirabeau during his first two stays in Paris, a period in which the count was a recluse; it was Mme Helvétius who introduced them in 1778. In 1779 Mirabeau also wrote a study of the American Revolution, which reproduced the Declaration of Independence, but which, however, was never published. (*Précis de la révolution des Etats Unis de l'Amérique*, Archives du Ministère des Affaires Etrangères, Etats-Unis, Mémoires et Documents, vol. 1888, feuilles 66–9). During Mirabeau's sojourn in London in 1784, Franklin facilitated his inclusion into radical Presbyterian circles, introducing him to Richard Price, with whom Mirabeau then remained in contact for the rest of his life.

[136]   The work, entitled *Sur l'Amérique*, was probably composed in 1784, the year of the publication of the first French edition of Crèvecoeur's *Letters*, to which it refers frequently

at Franklin's request, the *Considérations sur l'Ordre de Cincinnatus, ou Imitation d'un pamphlet anglo-américain.*[137] This was far more than a simple translation of the pamphlet by the American Aedanus Burke, who had argued against the creation in 1783 of a hereditary military order in the United States, for by merging his own ideas with those on pages written by Franklin, Mirabeau used the work to launch a violent attack on the hereditary principle in pre-Revolutionary France.[138]

Franklin also actively collaborated with Du Pont De Nemours in the common interest of the two countries, and continued to do so into the 1780s. His propaganda campaigns and his contact with Vergennes resulted in the 1778 Franco–American commercial treaty; free trade, to which both he and Du Pont were committed,[139] energized Du Pont's efforts as he worked on the 1786 trade treaty with Britain, which was welcomed by both men as an affirmation of the principles of the new science of economics.[140]

Franklin became the fulcrum of a movement of ideas, and of the attention being given to the link between economics and politics, that, based on Physiocracy and by dint of contributions from two continents, had evolved into a revolutionary

---

(Archives du Ministère des Affaires Etrangères, Etats-Unis, Mémoires et Documents, vol. 1888, feuilles 70–72).

[137]   Honoré-Gabriel Riquetti Comte de Mirabeau, *Considérations sur l'Ordre de Cincinnatus, ou Imitation d'un pamphlet anglo-américain* (London: Johnson and Rotterdam: C.R. Hake, 1785). The editor Johnson, had already edited an edition of Franklin's works, in London in 1779. The work was very successful, with two editions being published in 1784, one in 1785, another again in London in 1785 and one in Philadelphia in 1786. For a detailed explanation of the genesis of the work, through the comparison of the work with a letter by Franklin to his daughter, Sarah Bache, on 26 January 1784, partly drawn on by Mirabeau, see Bernard Faÿ, "Franklin et Mirabeau collaborateurs," *Revue de littérature comparée*, 8 (1928): 5–28.

[138]   In a letter to Vaughn of 7 September 1784, to whom he asked for help in finding an editor for the work, Franklin wrote: 'This will be delivered to you by the count Mirabeau, son of the Marquis of that name, author of *L'Ami des Hommes*. This gentleman is esteemed here, and I recommend him to your civilities and counsels, particularly with respect to the printing of a piece he has written on the subject of *Hereditary nobility*, on occasion of the order of Cincinnati lately attempted to be established in America, which cannot be printed here'. (Cited in Faÿ, 'Franklin et Mirabeau', 15).

[139]   Already in 1769, in his *Du Commerce et de la Compagnie des Indes*, written against commercial monopolies, Du Pont had shared with Franklin, to whom he made explicit reference, an idea of commerce that intended to defend consumption against the interests of the merchants (Pierre-Samuel Du Pont de Nemours, *Du commerce et de la Compagnie des Indes* (Amsterdam, Paris: chez Delalain, chez Lacombe, 1769): 240). Cf. Franklin's letter of thanks, London, 2 October 1770, in Franklin, *The Papers*, vol. XVII, 234.

[140]   Franklin to Alexander Small, 28 September 1787, in Franklin, *The Works*, vol. X, 325. Pierre-Samuel Du Pont de Nemours, *Lettre à la Chambre du Commerce de Normandie, Sur le Mémoire qu'elle a publié relativement au Traité de Commerce avec l'Angleterre* (Rouen, Paris: Moutard, 1788): 248, 261.

ideology.[141] In August 1789 (a month after the death of his father) Mirabeau, reporting to the National Assembly on Emmanuel Sieyès's project for a declaration of rights, restated the Physiocratic principle in whose name men met together and created a society to have the full benefit of the natural laws: 'Everything is in this principle, so great, so liberal, so fruitful, that my father and his illustrious friend, M. Quesnay, consecrated thirty years ago'.[142]

Franklin did not share Jefferson's great passion for France. Before his first stay in Paris he had little trust for 'that intriguing nation'[143] but his taste for comfortable simplicity soon led him to appreciate the courtesy of the French.[144] His pragmatism led him to see the advantages that Vergennes's support offered to the colonial cause, just as the chance to air his views in the *Ephémérides du citoyen* had done, all as part of an orchestrated anti-British political and cultural manoeuvre. His position became official when he joined the diplomatic mission to the French court, where he remained until Jefferson succeeded him. However, his contacts with Physiocratic circles were maintained outside of his working programme.

His house in Passy became the centre of an international interchange of ideas that profited France as well as the United States. He returned to America in 1784, the year in which St John de Crèvecoeur's *Lettres d'un cultivateur américain* was published; the author had been introduced to Franklin by Mme D'Houdetot in 1781.[145] Franklin had already seen in the English edition of the *Letters* that the agrarian image of the Norman nobleman turned American might be used to

---

[141]   Franklin's positions in the first phase of the French Revolution, regarding which he hoped for a constitutional solution, were nevertheless more cautious and always remained less radical compared to Jefferson's (cf. Aldridge, *Benjamin Franklin*, 70).

[142]   *Archives parlementaires de 1787 à 1860. Première Série (1787–1799)*, vol. VIII, 18 August 1789, 453. One unpublished note about Quesnay went so far as to liken Franklin to the founder of Physiocracy: 'Instead of comparing Quesnay to Socrates, we might find a more striking resemblance with Franklin and quite happily reconcile the two celebrated men because of the similarity of their education, to whom they owe nothing but to themselves, and their taste for the sciences, as well as for the similarity of their spirits, good nature and their character, which is so rare and noteworthy a sign of a spirit blessed with wisdom and patience'. The author of the notice was Edme-Joachin Bourdois de la Motte (1754–1835), a doctor in the Faculty of Medicine and the doctor to the Count of Provence and later of the King of Rome. The manuscript text is undated and was probably composed after the Revolution (Académie Nationale de Médecine, Paris, Ms 81 (54), Papiers du Dr Bourdois de la Motte, *Notes sur François Quesnay*, sheets 44–9).

[143]   Cf. Aldridge, *Benjamin Franklin*, 69–87.

[144]   Franklin to Josiah Quincy, Passy, 22 April 1779, in Franklin, *The Writings*, vol. VII, 290.

[145]   On relations between Franklin and Crèvecoeur, cf. Percy G. Adams, 'Crèvecoeur and Franklin', *Pennsylvania History*, 14 (1947): 273–9; Philip. D. Beidler, 'Franklin's and Crèvecoeur's "Literary" Americans', *Early American Literature*, 13/1 (Spring 1978): 50–63; Claude-Anne Lopez, *Le sceptre et la foudre: Benjamin Franklin à Paris, 1776–1785* (Paris: Mercure de France, 1990).

encourage European emigration.[146] James, the protagonist of the *Letters*, and Bonhomme Richard both embodied the myth of a modern, rural and comfortable normality, and of a standard of private life made public, in which the two authors transposed the political dimension of their personal identity in the context of the American reality and the French economic analysis of the agrarian system, which were contrasted with those of Britain.

'I think agriculture the most honourable of all employments', Franklin declared repeatedly in letters to his British and French correspondents.[147] In the to and fro of ideas across the Atlantic, before, during and after the two democratic revolutions of the end of the eighteenth century, he played a key role and helped create the semblance of a link between the ideas of the French *Économistes* and those of the American revolutionaries, toning down the differences both inside France and outside of it.

The influence exerted by the Physiocratic tradition on the shaping of American agrarian ideology passed through a triangulation which had one of its pillars situated in the radicalism of the English Dissenters and which used Franklin as a fixed point of reference. He frequented both Physiocratic circles and radical British religious groups.[148] At Passy he received George Logan, who became his follower, and whom Franklin introduced to French circles. Upon returning to the United States in 1780, Logan launched his campaign as an authentic American Physiocrat in the Jeffersonians' conflict with Hamilton's Federalists for the establishment of a Republican agrarian democracy. Through the 1780s Franklin's legacy continued to exert influence mostly among the *Américanistes*, who included the *habitués* of Mme Helvétius's salon, where future *Idéologues* and the last generation of the *Économistes* shared the anti-British project of establishing commercial and political links with America. Franklin, who frequented this meeting-place, represented a *trait-d'union* between the Physiocratic economic culture and the *Décade philosophique* circle. This circle maintained a strong admiration for the United States· and Jean-Baptiste Say saw Franklin as an important predecessor in his efforts to stabilize the republic and maintain the legacy of the Revolution by providing an economic theorization of the middle class (*classe mitoyenne*).[149]

---

[146]   Cf. Franklin's letter to Lord Buchan, 17 March 1783, in Franklin, *The Works*, vol. IX, 497. In a letter from 1784, Franklin explained the link between agrarian society and political participation in terms that were almost identical to a passage in Crèvecoeur's *Letters* (Franklin to Mrs. Georgiana Hare-Naylor, 25 January 1784, in Franklin, *The Writings*, vol. IX, 159–60) Cf. John Hector St. John de Crevecoeur, *Letters from an American Farmer*, 55).

[147]   Franklin to Lafayette, Philadelphia, 17 April 1787; to Catherine Green, Philadelphia, 2 March 1789; to John Wright, Philadelphia, 4 November 1789, in Franklin, *The Works*, vol. X, 300, 386–7, 402.

[148]   On relations between the British radicals and Physiocratic circles, see below, Chapter 7.

[149]   Jean-Baptiste Say, *Traité d'économie politique, ou Simple exposition de la manière dont se forment, se distribuent et se consomment les richesses*, 2 vols. (Paris: Imprimerie

In America this same middle class had been lionized in the figure of the *Bonhomme Richard* and it was no coincidence that in 1794 Say, along with Du Pont de Nemours, chose to issue a new edition of the translation of Franklin's celebrated book.[150]

Both Jefferson and Franklin found in Physiocracy a valid confirmation to their positions, which strengthened their agrarian republicanism and anti-British attitude. Their pragmatism did not allow them to accept the whole Physiocratic theory, even though both agreed with the idea of the exclusive productivity of agriculture. Among the ideologists of the agrarian democracy it was George Logan who shaped American agrarianism in the terms that were most strictly in adherence with Physiocracy and he attempted to bring together its economic theory with political struggle.

---

de chez Deterville, 1803): vol. II, 383. Cf. also in Say, *Œuvres complètes*, the recent critical edition in two volumes, ed. Claude Mouchot (Paris: Economica, 2006). Cf. Sergio Moravia, *Il tramonto dell'illuminismo. Filosofia e politica nella società francese 1770–1810* (Bari: Laterza, 1968); Sergio Moravia, *Il pensiero degli Idéologues: Scienza e filosofia in Francia (1780–1815)* (Florence: La Nuova Italia, 1974).

[150]   Franklin, *La science du bonhomme Richard; précédée d'un abrégé de la Vie de Franklin, et suivie de son Interrogatoire devant la Chambre des Communes* (Paris: Imprimerie des sciences et des arts, an II). Cf. *La Décade philosophique,* 30 thermidor an II, 150–157. As the owner of the press that printed the work, Say sent a number of free copies to the executive board of public education, proposing the work as a school text, just as Du Pont de Nemours recommended it to elementary schools in the United States (Pierre-Samuel Du Pont De Nemours, *Sur l'éducation nationale dans les Etats-Unis d'Amérique,* 2nd ed., (Paris: Le Normant, 1812): 34).

Chapter 5

The Agrarian Ideology Between Economic Theory and Political Struggle: George Logan and John Taylor

George Logan: An American Physiocrat

As we have seen, having emerged from the cosmopolitan culture of the eighteenth century and its multiple reference points, Jeffersonian ideology, which viewed economics in its international dimension, found in Physiocracy a model of economic development based on agriculture and a scientific conception of economics. Although Jefferson (as well as other Republicans influenced by the Physiocrat authors, such as Franklin) did not share every principle of their theory, he nevertheless found guidelines in their ideas that clarified his understanding of economics: these aimed to establish a state which served as a focal point against unwarranted interference from particularistic economic interests in the political sphere, in the name of a free realization of individual potential. This struggle against corporate interests was the same as that conducted by the Republicans against the owners of state revenues and the Federalists, who in their eyes were guilty of having sacrificed the general interest of the nation to minority financial ones.

The wealth of arguments provided by the Physiocrats – against public debt, finance capital, the banks and protectionist tariffs – was used by Jefferson's group in its economic dimension, and it offered a different language from the traditional one when opposing financial power with the 'country' ideology. Unlike Britain, the rival of the Americans and French, France epitomized a country with a predominantly agrarian economy, not yet oriented towards manufacturing development, and for which the *Économistes* proposed a different economic plan based on the exploitation of natural resources. The French ideal of an agrarian society of freeholders was well received by the American democrats – despite the legal despotism and the position that Francois Quesnay's group had occupied in absolutist France – by virtue of the special relationship between economics and politics designed and developed by the Physiocratic authors for what were sensitive issues for the Americans. These ranged from the question of decentralization, which was tied to Physiocratic plans for the creation of provincial assemblies – an idea not at odds with the idea of the unity of law and national sovereignty – to the importance given to consumption and improving the general material conditions of life.

The Republican struggle against corruption, which characterized the clash of the 1790s, pitted the natural economy against the artificial economy,[1] and thus employed a language profoundly different from that used by British authors of the Commonwealth tradition. At the same time, the reception of Physiocracy in the United States took its place in the context of Puritan ideology, which supported revolutionary thought.

It is possible to reconstruct the reception of Physiocracy within American revolutionary thought by following the sometimes-winding paths of different authors, from Jefferson to Franklin, or from Taylor to Paine. However, among the heavyweight ideologues of American agrarian democracy, only George Logan was an authentic American Physiocrat.[2] His political campaigns made him the direct counterpart of Hamilton; he was a valuable witness to Franklin's impulse to keep the Physiocratic tradition alive; he exemplified the encounter between religious and economic pacifism; and, by way of Physiocracy, he gave an original voice to American radicalism in an attempt to strike a balance between freedom and order, equality and authority.

Born into a well-established Quaker family of Philadelphia, Logan derived two elements from his home environment that helped form his personality: agrarian passion and religious spirit. His grandfather, James Logan, who was the secretary of William Penn, set up the family's landholding at Stenton, where he conducted experiments on Indian corn, the results of which were published at Leyden in 1739.[3] George's father, William Logan, was a rich merchant and innovative landowner, a correspondent of Jared Eliot, a practising Quaker and pacifist, and the author of *Memoranda in Husbandry*.[4]

At the time Logan received his education, Philadelphia was the cultural capital of the American colonies, a hub of scientific knowledge, as New England had once been for literature and theology. The city was led by an intellectual elite that was republican and bourgeois, multi-confessional and progressive – the same elite

---

[1]   Cf. Faure-Soulet, *Economie politique*.

[2]   Henry N. Smith defined Logan as a 'dogmatic Physiocrat' and Chester H. Eisinger also recognized the presence of Physiocracy in Logan's work, albeit alongside a stronger influence from Locke; Joseph Dorfman, despite underlining the particular national circumstances, called him the 'Physiocratic spokesman for commerce'. Cf. Henry N. Smith, *Virgin Land: The American West as Symbol and Myth* (Cambridge, MA: Harvard University Press, 1950): 277; Chester H. Eisinger, "The Influence of Natural Rights and Physiocratic Doctrine', 16; Joseph Dorfman, *The Economic Mind in American Civilization*, 5 vols. (New York: The Viking Press, 1946): vol. I, 295).

[3]   Cf. Frederick B. Tolles, 'George Logan and the Agricultural Revolution', *Proceedings of the American Philosophical Society*, 95 (1951): 589.

[4]   This unpublished work is kept in the Library of the American Department of Agriculture in Washington (cf. Frederick B. Tolles, 'George Logan, Agrarian Democrat: A Survey of His Writings', *The Pennsylvania Magazine of History and Bibliography*, 75/1 (January 1951): 261–2).

that produced the Constitution of Philadelphia so greatly admired by the French *Américanistes*.[5] In the years 1770–1780 Philadelphia was also the American city with the largest French presence, even though some anti-French sentiment persisted from pre-Revolution times.[6] However, France retained all its intellectual prestige: from 1754, on Franklin's initiative, the University of Philadelphia began to teach the French language.[7]

In keeping with Quaker tradition, Philadelphia paid great attention to the study of medicine. It had links with Edinburgh, where young Americans were sent to complete their education. Logan himself went to Scotland and Paris in 1768 to finalize his studies and become a doctor, as Quesnay had been. During his stay in Scotland, he recorded his observations on agriculture, 'the present state and daily improvements in Agriculture through out Scotland highly merit the attention and applause of every traveller'. He praised the rotation of crops emulating new methods practised in England, he cited Scottish authors, and he noted the purchase of a treatise on experimental agriculture written by Lord Kaim.[8]

During his stay in Paris he visited Franklin at Passy, who introduced him to French circles, showing the same generosity that James Logan had shown him in his youth.[9] Logan considered Franklin to be his master; he shared a friendship with him until his death, and in fact helped to bear his coffin.

Back in America, he entered the service of Robert Morris, Superintendent of Finances, and devoted the rest of his life to his two intimately related passions, agriculture and politics. In 1785 he was elected, as a Republican, as Philadelphia's representative to Congress; and from that point on his career was marked by the struggle against commercial and financial wealth, which, in his eyes, was advantaged by the constitution to the detriment of landowners.

Drawing on what he had learned in Europe, Logan implemented new cultivation techniques at Stenton, which in the late 1780s and 1790s became a model estate. It was also a centre for agricultural experiments, the results of which he passed on to the farming community mainly through Mathew Carey's *American Museum*

---

[5]   In 1786 the American Philosophical Society counted 21 Frenchmen among its 54 members, including Condorcet, Cabanis, Chastellux, Lafayette, Lavoisier, Raynal and the Duke of La Rochefoucauld.

[6]   On the ending of anti-French sentiment, cf. Paul A. Varg, 'The Advent of Nationalism 1758–1776', *American Quarterly*, 16 (1964): 169–81.

[7]   Cf. Bernard Faÿ, *L'esprit révolutionnaire en France et aux Etats-Unis à la fin du XVIIIe siècle* (Paris: Champion, 1925) and Howard M. Jones, *America and French Culture 1750–1848* (Chapel Hill, NC: University of North Carolina Press, 1927).

[8]   Historical Society of Pennsylvania, *George Logan Papers*, 'Doctor George Logan's Journal 1775–1779', # 379 # 41, sheets 330–34.

[9]   Logan to Franklin, Philadelphia, 20 September 1780, in Benjamin Franklin, *The Papers*, vol. XXXIII, 314. In her memoirs of her husband Deborah Logan remembered the mornings spent by Logan in Passy and how Franklin recounted to him his relations with Adam Smith. Logan, *Memoir of Dr. George Logan of Stenton*, 36, 46.

and Eleazer Oswald's *Independent Gazetteer and Agricultural Repository*[10] in order to spread knowledge and mould the opinions of the agrarian public.[11] Logan was also an influence on Jefferson, who, because of his abilities as an agronomist, turned to him for guidance and the sharing of information. In 1793 he directed a young planter from Virginia to Logan for advice on how to acquire copies of the works of Arthur Young.[12]

Regardless of his strong anti-British sentiments, Logan worked hard to introduce new agricultural techniques from Britain to America, and to naturalize the revolution in farming introduced by Young and John Sinclair. He used these authors as reference points throughout his works, albeit while recognizing the need to adapt the British systems to American conditions. In the context of the agricultural reform movement of the 1780s, which after the War of Independence assumed a patriotic value, Logan, like many similar farmers in America, united with others around voluntary associations, without recourse to state aid. In this climate he was also an agronomist, a founder, in 1785, of the Philadelphia Society for Promoting Agriculture, as well as a leading figure of the American societies of Agriculture, in which he sought to instil a more emphatic democratic spirit.[13] His work concentrated on the rotation of crops, the use of fertilizers (his name became linked to plaster of Paris)[14] and the rearing of livestock. His specialization in sheep breeding, which led him to become one of the first importers of merino sheep in Pennsylvania, was aimed at encouraging the domestic manufacture of wool to make the American economy independent of British wool products.

In this picture, Logan's interest in Physiocracy was in direct line with the teaching received from Franklin. While managing his lands, he consulted the Physiocratic authors for the political significance of their reflections on agriculture.

---

[10]   Logan kept an account in the most minute detail of the income and expenditure of his holding in Stenton, noting all the agricultural tasks, seeding, harvests and maintenance, along with a record of the farmers' health and the jobs assigned to each of them from day to day (Historical Society of Pennsylvania, *George Logan Papers*, 'George Logan's Stenton Farm Diary 1809–1813', # 379 # 73).

[11]   Cf. Stevenson W. Fletcher, *Pennsylvania agriculture and country life, 1640–1840* (Harrisburg: Pennsylvania Hist. and Mus. Comm., 1950).

[12]   Jefferson to Logan, 1 July 1793, in Thomas Jefferson, *The Papers*, vol. XXVI, 428. He wrote about Logan to Thomas Mann Randolph in 1793: 'He is the best farmer in Pennsylva. Both in theory and practice, having pursued it many years experimentally, and with great attention'. (Jefferson to Thomas Mann Randolph, Jr., Philadelphia, 28 July 1793, Jefferson, *The Papers*, vol. XXVI, 576).

[13]   On Logan's involvement in the agricultural societies, see below pp. 172–4.

[14]   'He was one of the first who used gypsum as a manure, and its success at the beginning was wonderful. Perhaps at no period of his life did he experience greater happiness than at this, his intervals of leisure being employed in reading authors of the greatest utility in agricultural and political science, and he was of the foremost and most zealous advocates in whatever he thought would promote the public good'. (George Logan, *Memoir*, 43).

When he was elected a Republican representative in 1785, he turned his attention 'to such authors as he thought had thrown most light upon political science' – as his wife, Deborah, noted – including 'the French works of Turgot and, I think, Du Trone and Rivière. He read Neckar [sic], but saw vanity and ambition strongly linked with his good qualities'. He also read Smith and 'the Wealth of nations, which he justly appreciated without approving of all the author has advanced'.[15]

The economy was a political language for Logan right from the start of his career, and Physiocracy was a weapon to wield against Hamilton and the Federalists. Thus, he became the ideologue of American democratic agrarianism. In March 1786 he took part, in a balanced way, in the Republican debate against paper currency issued by the Bank of North America, proposing the establishment of a loans office and the involvement of the bank in the interests of farmers.[16] However, 1790, the year in which the Philadelphia Agricultural Society encountered political difficulties, was a turning point.[17] His language then became incendiary and the Physiocratic arguments in his writings became a summation of American agrarian thought.

Physiocracy as a Political Weapon

Between 13 March 1790 and 8 January 1791 Logan published a series of articles in the *Independent Gazetteer*, objecting to the duties with which Hamilton planned to pay the interest on public debt. These were reprinted by Eleazer Oswald as a pamphlet entitled *Letters Addressed to the Yeomanry of the United States: Shewing the Necessity of Confining the Public Revenue to a Fixed Proportion of the Net Produce of the Land; and the Bad Policy and Injustice of Every Species of Indirect Taxation and Commercial Regulations*. The title itself clearly expressed the Physiocratic stamp of the author, who signed his articles with the pseudonym 'A Farmer', borrowed from the famous *Letters from a Farmer in Pennsylvania* by John Dickinson, a cousin of Deborah. The principles of agrarian democracy, the idea that only an independent landowner – the 'American Yeoman' – could be the underpinning of a free republic, were fixed by the central tenets of Physiocratic theory: the single tax, the exclusive productivity of agriculture, the notion of the sterile classes, the advances. These were all principles that challenged Hamilton's defence of taxation, merchants, manufacturers, banks and public credit, and his 'Machiavellian politics': 'a dangerous aristocracy is forming, which if not crushed

---

[15]   George Logan, *Memoir*, 46.

[16]   Mathew Carey, ed., *Debates and Proceedings of the General Assembly of Pennsylvania on the Memorials Praying a Repeal or Suspension of the Law Annulling the Charter of the Bank* (Philadelphia: Printed for Carey and Co. Seddon and Pritchard, 1786): 109–17.

[17]   Cf. below, p. 173.

in the bud will destroy our liberties forever'.[18] This was political language that drew on Locke, Smith, the Physiocrats, Franklin and Jefferson, and fed on the science of political economy, using a rhetoric that differed from the *Cato Letters* of the American revolutionary culture.

The law of nature was the starting point of Logan's thought: a law, clear and simple, which governments had to respect and that everyone should know: 'Governments are instituted to support the laws of nature ... the least acquaintance with the order of science evidences that it is by the most simple truths that men attain the knowledge of those which are less evident'.[19] Logan's Quaker sensibility fitted with the Physiocratic divine order. The gifts of the Creator manifested 'happiness and prosperity ... the laws constituting the social order as making part of the universal and immutable laws of nature'.[20] His definition of political economy accorded with the Physiocratic paradigm: 'by political economy is to be understood, that natural order appointed by the Creator of the Universe, for the purpose of promoting the happiness of men in united society. This science is supported by the physical order of cultivation, calculated to render the soil the most productive possible'.[21] In this natural universe, agriculture was the sole economic activity that created wealth, and the farmer was the social figure that represented the entire national interest: 'The earth being the only productive fund, the cultivation of the earth is the only productive employ'. All other activities could be more or less useful, but never productive.[22]

Logan rejected state intervention in the economy and held that regulation provoked trade wars, as the example of Britain demonstrated. Furthermore, the American Revolution had had its origins in the rejection of British economic policy. He therefore issued a stark warning to his compatriots who, 'infatuated with the false principles of the government of Great Britain', were 'anxious to adopt her wretched system of policy'.[23] The ancients had been ignorant of the truth of economics, the disciples of Machiavelli, Hobbes and Spinoza had seen a warlike nature in man; the science of political economy was modern, 'and the world is alone indebted to a few enlightened men in France for this important discovery', the principles of which had until then been adopted only by the Prince of Baden and the Grand Duke of Tuscany.[24] He used the Physiocratic terms of 'net produce', 'primitive expenses' and 'annual expenses', and declared himself in favour of the single land tax: this, imposed proportionally on the net product, was more equitable than indirect taxes:

---

[18]   Logan, *Letters Addressed to the Yeomanry of the United States* (Philadelphia: E. Oswald, 1791): 32.

[19]   Logan, *Letters Addressed to the Yeomanry of the United States*, 3.

[20]   Logan, *Letters Addressed to the Yeomanry of the United States*, 4.

[21]   Logan, *Letters Addressed to the Yeomanry of the United States*, 11.

[22]   Logan, *Letters Addressed to the Yeomanry of the United States*, 15.

[23]   Logan, *Letters Addressed to the Yeomanry of the United States*, 13–14.

[24]   Logan, *Letters Addressed to the Yeomanry of the United States*, 8, 24.

As all the private and public wealth of a country arises from the land, the revenue necessary for the support of government can only be derived from the proprietors and farmers. ... A direct tax, being confined to a just proportion of the net produce of your farms, can never be oppressive, whilst an indirect tax, preying upon the gross produce of your farms, will destroy the means of future cultivation.[25]

The interests of farmers, 'the most valuable class of citizens', were nevertheless threatened by an aristocracy of merchants who Logan scorned in Physiocratic terminology as 'citizens of the world ... who knew no country but their coffers of gold'.[26] Similarly, Physiocratic language against movable wealth bolstered his attacks against public credit, 'which our politicians esteem of the greatest importance to the government', and instead 'should be regarded as the most unjust and ruinous importation of modern times'.[27]

In a different scientific context, in response to the question posed in 1785 by the Philadelphia Agricultural Society – the cause of his separation from it, a break prompted by the political radicalism that went hand in hand with his agronomic thinking – he had already expounded the Physiocratic concept of advances, classifying agricultural investment costs as 'primitive' expenses connected to land, 'instrumental' expenses and 'annual' expenses for the livelihood of the farmers.[28] Agricultural production was in direct ratio to these expenses. For this reason, moving from the American tradition that extolled smallholdings, he called for the creation of 'larger farms'.[29] Logan was not bound to the interests of the South, his convictions stemmed directly from his theoretical guidelines.

The relation between the economic activities was already evident here: 'A nation can only carry on a permanent commerce, upon the surplus produce of its labours, whether consisting in the produce of the earth, derived immediately from the farmer, or such produce converted by the industry and art of her citizens, into manufactures'.[30] Practice and science came together in his thought; the rotation model was British, and he expounded the results of his experiments, but the approach was theoretical, 'agriculture like other sciences, cannot improve

---

[25]   Logan, *Letters Addressed to the Yeomanry of the United States*, 16–18, 25–6.

[26]   Logan, *Letters Addressed to the Yeomanry of the United States*, 33–4.

[27]   Logan, *Letters Addressed to the Yeomanry of the United States*, 35–6.

[28]   George Logan, *Fourteen Agricultural Experiments, to Ascertain the Best Rotation of Crops: Addressed to the Philadelphia Agricultural Society* (Philadelphia: Bailey, 1797): 31–2. The work had been published as a series of articles in 1791 in the *Columbia Magazine* and in 1792 in the *National Gazette*.

[29]   He advocated this idea in terms of independence, to the extent that 'two hundred acres [the size of his property in Stenton] preserve the independence of the yeomanry', promising an economic and political culture which guaranteed the superiority of landowners. (Logan, *Fourteen Agricultural Experiments*, 33).

[30]   Logan, *Fourteen Agricultural Experiments*, 40–41.

by accident'.[31] However, the link between agriculture and politics was already clear, and he quoted the *Voyage d'un philosophe* by Pierre Poivre in confirmation of it, a chance to reflect on the negative consequences of the policies pursued by France before the Revolution – something that was not welcome by the Philadelphia Agricultural Society.[32]

His profession of Physiocratic faith in the *Letters Addressed to the Yeomanry* signalled the beginning of the duel between the Federalists and Republicans, which was played out mainly around political economics. Hamilton responded to Logan's *Letters* in December 1791 with his *Report on Manufactures*, in which the Republicans' agrarian project was denounced, as we have seen, even in its premise, as an articulation of Physiocratic principles,[33] of which he highlighted all the political dangers since they implied adherence to the French revolutionary cause.

At Logan's home at Stenton a group gathered around him that preserved the legacy of Franklin's science and democratic spirit, which had fuelled the American agrarian project: Jefferson,[34] Franklin Banny Bache (nephew of Benjamin and director of the anti-Federalist *General Advisor* newspaper), David Rittenhouse, an illustrious astronomer, the physician James Hutchison and the lawyer James Dallas. His official position as Secretary of State prevented Jefferson from throwing himself into open political warfare, so it fell to Logan to state the case for the campaign devised by the Jeffersonians. The response to Hamilton and the plan to create the Society for Useful Manufactures – which was meant to bring together a large group of industrialists under the direction of William Duer, a businessman linked to the Treasury Secretary – came in February 1792, in the *Five Letters Addressed to the Yeomanry of the United States: Containing Some Observations on the Dangerous Scheme of Governor Duer and Mr. Secretary Hamilton to Establish National Manufactories*.[35]

In the polarized confrontation of the two parties, which became defined as being either for or against revolutionary France, the agrarian project and the French

---

[31]   Logan, *Fourteen Agricultural Experiments*, 36.

[32]   Logan, *Fourteen Agricultural Experiments*, 37–8.

[33]   Cf. above, pp. 61–3.

[34]   Deborah Logan referred to Logan's friendship with Jefferson again immediately after the formation of the federal government: 'When that gentleman was Secretary of State he used frequently to visit us in a social and intimate manner, sometimes with small parties whose company was agreeable to one another and sometimes alone. His conversation was very pleasing. He had resided at the Court of France, and upon his return appeared in somewhat of its costume, and wore a suit of silk, ruffles, and an elegant topaz ring; But he soon adopted a more republican garb, and was reproached with going to the other extreme as a bait for popularity' (Logan, *Memoir*, 50).

[35]   In addition to its publication as a pamphlet (Philadelphia: E. Oswald, 1792) and as a series of articles in Oswald's *Independent Gazetteer*, the *Five Letters* appeared in the same year in Philippe Freneau's *National Gazette* and Mathew Carey's *American Museum*.

Revolution became fused in Logan and reinforced his democratic arguments. The *Five Letters* opened by quoting the *Déclaration des droits de l'homme et du citoyen*. If the United States had adopted a declaration as 'firm and equitable' as the French one, they would have avoided the negative effect of the mercantile regulations that damaged the interests of landowners, the government securities to the benefit of speculators and banks at the expense of the poor, and the taxes that impacted on farmers.[36]

In opposing 'this dark system of British finance', Logan took the economic-political culture of revolutionary France as his touchstone.[37] In addition to the French political contribution, he cited the second volume of the *Wealth of Nations* against the prohibitions that violated natural rights, and above all the Physiocrat authors:

> the motto of the French economists, 'faire le bien c'est le recevoir' is applicable to nations as to individuals; yet, in this enlightened period, do we observe the most polished nations doing every injury in their power to each other, with the unjust and absurd ideas of deriving advantage to themselves, by circumscribing or destroying the advantages of their neighbours.[38]

In line with American liberalism, Logan's aim was to make the United States economically independent, hence he did not totally rule out the creation of manufactures, so long as this did not hinder agriculture or involve situations of privilege.[39] It was true that personal inequalities were considered positive and inequalities of wealth were necessary to stimulate labour. Logan's radicalism, however, emerged in his steadfast repudiation of the accumulation of riches.[40]

At the start of 1793, his attacks against the National Bank, public credit and Federalist policies once more took shape in the *Letters Addressed to the Yeomanry of the United States, Containing Some Observations on Funding and Bank Systems*. Jefferson's influence was discernible in arguments made against the public debt by the repetition of his celebrated principle 'the earth belongs to the living', which prohibited one generation from bequeathing its

---

[36]   *American Museum*, vol. XII, 160–61.

[37]   *American Museum*, vol. XII, 161–2.

[38]   *American Museum*, vol. XII, 215. Evidence of Logan's careful reading of the Physiocratic texts can be seen in his frequent references to Colbert, a recurring theme in Physiocratic literature, and to the negative effect on the French economy of his policy of regulation: 'When Colbert demanded of an old experienced merchant what steps his master should take to encourage commerce, the answer was – let us alone. The citizens of the United States engaged in agriculture, in manufactures, in mechanics, and ever in the cod fishery, may with justice and propriety give a similar answer to congress'. (*American Museum*, vol. XII, 167, cf. also 215.)

[39]   *American Museum*, vol. XII, 215.

[40]   *American Museum*, vol. XII, 163.

debts to successive ones.[41] Logan took inspiration from the data in Buffon's tables of mortality (which were also used by Jefferson in his famous letter to Madison of 6 September 1789)[42] to demonstrate that state debts which lasted more than nineteen years violated the rights of the next generation. Such a policy had led to the downfall of the French monarchy. Logan's sources were many: apart from the exponents of the 'heaven-born French philanthropy', he cited Smith, Paine, Priestley, Arthur Young and Catherine Phillips, the preacher whose renown and ideas came from Britain via the American Quakers.[43]

In this phase of intense activity, the period of a more radical political engagement, Logan published meticulous, collaborative works with which to attack Hamiltonian policies, and he followed these up with a series of propagandist interventions to influence public opinion more directly.

In June 1793 he became a member of the 'Societé française des amis de la liberté et de l'égalité', in Philadelphia, which was inspired by the Jacobins club and of which only a few Americans were adherents. Stenton then became a centre for supporters of the French Revolution. These included James Monroe, Jean de Marsillac, a French Quaker who had tried to open a school of agriculture in France, Napper Tandy, head of the United Irishmen who was organizing the revolt in Ireland, and Kosciuszko. Coincidentally, with the appearance of the *Five Letters*, Logan organized a debate in the Germantown Society for Promoting Domestic Manufactures, in which he denounced the Society for Useful Manufactures sponsored by Hamilton and, in the name of the principles of the French Revolution and a thoroughgoing transatlantic solidarity between America, France and the English democratic societies, called on the audience of artisans to resist the government's attempts to violate their natural rights.[44]

Subsequently, in January 1794, thanks to his reputation as a republican ideologue, Logan was received into the Democratic Society of Philadelphia, a centre of anti-Federalism. His agrarianism led to a further radicalization of his political positions. On 12 May 1798, in the red-hot climate of the XYZ affair and the Quasi-War, at the Society of the Sons of Saint Tammany, a meeting place for republicans and Irish immigrants, he rallied workers and artisans to join with

---

[41]   'The present generation, even to preserve its own existence, has no right to infringe on the property of posterity … The earth and the fruits thereof belong to the living, by the gift of God'. (Logan, *Letters Addressed to the Yeomanry of the United States, Containing Some Observations on Funding and Bank Systems* (Philadelphia, 1793): 8–9). Published as a pamphlet at the beginning of May, the *Letters* began to appear in the *National Gazette* on 31 January 1793.

[42]   Cf. above, p. 93.

[43]   Logan, *Five Letters*, 20–22.

[44]   Logan, 'At a meeting of the Germantown society for promoting domestic manufactures, on Monday the 13th of August 1792', *The American Museum*, vol. XII, part II (July to December 1792), Appendix II, *22–*23. The intervention was also published in the *National Gazette*, 25 August 1792.

farmers in a non-violent action against the danger of the return of the monarchy. It was in the framework of a social hierarchy and a physical, religious order based on the farmer, that he issued this call in the name of freedom and equality brought about by the two revolutions, French and American.

Even in the extremism of his language, the guiding principles of Physiocracy continued to give substance to Logan's position as an agrarian democrat, even in the direct re-use of passages from the *Five Letters*. The farmers, to ensure their independence, also became artisans and thus cooperated with manufacturing workers 'for the surplus produce of their industry'.[45] The science of economics and his Quaker faith merged in the recognition of the perfect order of the physical world. God's laws had established the 'perfectibility of the nature of Man' and it was only when men 'destroy the natural order of things, in the moral or physical world, [that] confusion and distress must be the consequence'.[46]

That same year Logan, true to his Quaker pacifism and his family tradition, left for Paris on his own initiative with the intent to avert the threat of war between France and the United States. He was received by Talleyrand and Merlin, head of the Directory, and obtained the lifting of the embargo and the authorization for the free movement of American ships.[47] This action, however, met with negative reactions at home, prompting Congress to pass the Logan Act, which forbade unauthorized citizens from negotiating with foreign governments, in 1799.[48]

In 1801 Logan was elected to the Senate, at the same time as Jefferson became President. He had worked hard for Jefferson's victory and in February wrote to him: 'Your election in February has relieved my mind from great anxiety, respecting my Country. You have an arduous task before you. I pray God that you may be enabled to select Men of the strictest honor and probity to assist you'.[49] He concurred with Jefferson's domestic policies and, despite being, like him, a convinced supporter of agrarianism, encouraged him to develop a manufacturing sector to liberate the United States from economic dependence on Britain: 'As long as we are dependent on Great Britain for our cloathing and other necessaries; we must be influenced

---

[45]   George Logan, *An Address on the Natural and Social Order of the World, as Intended to Produce Universal Good; Delivered Before the Tammany Society, at their Anniversary on 12th of May 1798* (Philadelphia: B. Franklin Bache, 1789): 9.

[46]   Logan, *An Address on the Natural and Social Order of the World*, 11.

[47]   On that occasion Du Pont de Nemours wrote to Jefferson: 'Dr. Logan will tell you that he found good and zealous friends of America in France and you will not be surprised that my son and I were amongst that number' (Du Pont de Nemours to Jefferson, Paris, 10 Fructidor of Year VI [27 August 1798], in Jefferson, *The Papers*, vol. XXX, 501).

[48]   Cf. Frederick B. Tolles, 'Unofficial Ambassador: George Logan's Mission to France, 1798', *The William and Mary Quarterly*, 3d ser., 7 (1950): 3–25.

[49]   Logan to Jefferson, Lancaster, 27 February 1801, in Jefferson, *The Papers*, vol. XXXIII, 93.

by her baneful politics'.[50] In the prevailing difficult international situation, he had become more convinced – as had Jefferson – of the need for American economic self-sufficiency. For all that, he remained an advocate of free trade and upholder of the democratic force of a free and developed agriculture, which could ensure the independence and popular participation: 'This is that constitutes what is called Patriotism'.[51] The American agrarian model, by virtue of the specific geography and polity of the United States, was an alternative to the systems of European countries where the first signs of the industrial revolution could already be seen:

> Still less are we desiderous of introducing in this happy Country, that baneful system of European Management which dooms the human Faculties to be smothered, and Man be converted into a Machine. We want not that unfeeling plan of Manufacturing Policy, which has debilitated the Bodies, and debased the Minds, of so large a Class of People as the Manufactures of Europe.[52]

On the other hand, Logan, a pacifist by conviction, was critical of the President's foreign policy. Their strategies were different: while Logan advocated entente and diplomacy, to ensure peace in any way, Jefferson pressed for economic retaliation, in the name of the principle of reciprocity.[53] Thus in 1810 Logan embarked on another peace mission, to avert war with Britain, but this time without success.

As the conflict drew closer, Logan abandoned politics, left his office as Senator and returned to being a farmer, re-establishing his relationship with the Quaker community from which he had distanced himself after his first trip to Europe. At the end of his intellectual journey he rediscovered the value of religious faith as a foundation of agrarian democracy, and in his last paper he extolled the pacifism of the Moravian community.[54] They were the epitome of a faith that, as a national asset, had led him to an authentically American elaboration of Physiocracy.

---

[50]   Logan to Jefferson, Lancaster, 27 February 1801, in Jefferson, *The Papers*, vol. XXXIII, 93.

[51]   Logan to Jefferson, Lancaster, 27 February 1801, in Jefferson, *The Papers*, vol. XXXIII, 93.

[52]   George Logan, *A letter to the Citizens of Pennsylvania, on the necessity of promoting Agriculture, Manufactures and the useful Arts* (Philadelphia: Patterson and Cochran, 1800): 9.

[53]   Jefferson to Logan, Washington, 21 March 1801, in Thomas Jefferson, *The Papers*, vol. XXXIII, 390–91.

[54]   Logan, *Address on the Errors of Husbandry in the United States* (Philadelphia: 1818), cited in Frederick B. Tolles, *George Logan of Philadelphia* (New York: Oxford University Press, 1953): 316.

John Taylor: The Philosopher of Jeffersonian Democracy

The American agrarian ideology unfolded through a theoretical and political elaboration to which different positions and personalities contributed. It lay at the heart of the Republicans' model of democracy in their battle with the Federalists. Jefferson was the focal point and embodiment of the republican project by dint of his two terms as President. Yet, apart from the *Notes on the State of Virginia*, it is not in his work that we find the exposition of the fundamentals of agrarian democracy in its connection between economics and politics, but rather in that of John Taylor of Caroline, landowner, agronomist and quintessential Virginian who was educated at the William and Mary College. 'There is a spice of fanaticism in my nature upon two subjects, agriculture and republicanism', Taylor wrote to Jefferson in 1795, knowing that he would find a strong correspondence of sentiments in his interlocutor.[55]

Taylor was the philosopher of Jeffersonian republicanism, by warrant of the cornerstones of his thinking: property and sovereignty of the nation. He held an unusual position among the Anti-Federalists, being far from Thomas Paine's radicalism but hostile to the Federalists' hierarchical system. Like Jefferson, Taylor did not entirely resolve the question of the slavery. As a Southern plantation owner, he accepted the practice, and his arguments were less radical than Jefferson's, despite believing that it was damaging to agriculture: 'Negro slavery is a misfortune to agriculture, incapable of removal, and only within the reach of palliation' and a problem that America had to confront and resolve with a gradual transfer of the slaves to Africa. Two essays are dedicated to the question in *Arator*, and practical advice is given on the handling of slaves: 'Negro slavery is an evil which the United States must look in the face. To whine over it, is cowardly; to aggravate it, criminal; and to forbear to alleviate it, because it cannot be wholly cured, foolish'.[56]

All the characteristics of Jeffersonianism were summed up in him: agrarian convictions, hostility towards banks and finance, the defence of the power of the states, an aversion to the British system. He represented the ideals of the Southern landowners who felt threatened by the North and was apprehensive about what America eventually became after 1860: an industrial, urban society guided by a protectionist economic policy. In opposition to the British political and economic model, he advocated an agrarian republic and the defence of traditional American values. As an Old Republican, he grew disillusioned with Jefferson's conciliatory

---

[55]   Taylor to Jefferson, Caroline, 5 March 1795, in Jefferson, *The Papers*, vol. XXVIII, 293; cf. also Jefferson to Taylor, Monticello, 16 July 1816, in Jefferson, *The Writings*, ed. Bergh, vol. XV, 44.

[56]   John Taylor, *Arator*, ed. Melvin E. Bradford (Indianapolis: Liberty Classics, 1977): 180. Cf. Keith M. Bailor, 'John Taylor of Caroline: Continuity, Change and Discontinuity in Virginia's Sentiments toward Slavery, 1790–1820', *Virginia Magazine of History and Biography*, 75 (1967): 290–304.

policies towards divergent national interests, and the course he took led him to become the 'prophet of secession'.[57] He denounced Federalist policy as a project conceived at the expense of the South: land and labour would be used to pay the debts of the government, taxes would fund credit and protectionist mercantilism would damage agriculture: 'the best markets of our agriculture lie in foreign countries, whilst the best markets of our manufactures are at home. Our agriculture has to cross the ocean, and encounter a competition with foreign agriculture on its ground'.[58]

For Taylor, agriculture and republic were inseparable, and, in a similar way, his thinking moved on two levels, the science of economics and political theory, and he made original contributions to both. He used the discourses of traditional British political opposition, but the guidelines of his ideas were always the science of economics and politics. To depict him as an exponent of 'country' ideology is therefore to commit an injustice against an author who challenged the British political culture and its system.[59] With this point in mind, a re-reading of Taylor's work presents a clear picture of the key ideas on which the reception in America of an entire eighteenth-century tradition of political rationalism was founded. These were the unity of sovereignty, the criticism of the British model, the centrality of nature and the links between agriculture and politics.

Taylor's attacks against Hamilton, which made him a champion of the anti-Federalist campaigns in the 1790s, have perpetuated the image of an author known chiefly for the oppositional stamp of his reflections, and this casts a shadow on the importance of his constructive and creative ideas.[60] In truth, his ideas on agriculture, on the relationship between economics and politics and on the division of powers, mark him out as one of the most original exponents of American republicanism.

Having fought alongside Lafayette, as a colonel in the Virginia militia, and having been a lawyer until 1792, when he retired to his holding in Hazlewood to devote himself exclusively to agriculture and politics, Taylor was a senator three times between 1792 and 1822, and his commitment as a Republican was the wellspring of his writings, the principles of which always came to the surface through contingent political controversies.[61]

---

[57]   Cf. William Dodd, 'John Taylor of Caroline, Prophet of Secession', *The John P. Branch Historical Papers of Randolph-Macon College*, vol. II, nos. 3–4 (June 1908): 214–52.

[58]   Taylor, *Arator*, 75.

[59]   One interpretation in this direction emerges from F. Thornton Miller's introduction to John Taylor, *Tyranny Unmasked* (Indianapolis: Liberty Fund, 1992): x–xii. Cf. also Banning, *The Jeffersonian Persuasion*, 192–3.

[60]   Duncan Macleod was the first to underline the need to go beyond the polemic value of the thoughts of Taylor. Cf. Duncan Macleod, 'The Political Economy of John Taylor of Caroline', *Journal of American Studies*, 14/3 (1980): 387–405.

[61]   Cf. Henry H. Simms, *Life of John Taylor: The Story of a Brilliant Leader in the Early Virginia State Rights School* (Richmond: W. Byrd, 1932).

His early writings, produced in 1794, were a condemnation of Hamilton's banking and financial policies, which aimed to create an aristocracy of money that would prove damaging to the democratic government.[62] These interventions were part of an offensive strategy agreed with Jefferson.[63] In *Definition of Parties* Taylor denounced the laws enacted in favour of financial wealth, the paper interest, a form of political and unnatural property: 'Land cannot be increased by law – paper money may. Land, being incapable of an artificial multiplication, cannot by increasing its quantity, strengthen its influence – with paper the case is different. Land cannot in interest be at enmity with the public good – paper money is often so'.[64]

To expel the 'stock-jobbing paper interest' in all its forms was a priority for the restoration of the foundations of representative government.[65] Already present in this work were some of the issues that would remain central in his works of later years: the Bank of the United States (seen as the axis of an entire financial system that aimed to restore kings, lords and commoners), the negative consequences of tariffs and of a protectionist economic policy, the threat of political factions, the striving after privilege. He countered these by proposing political and economic freedom, which, to his mind, were interconnected and involved the limited presence of a state subordinated to the economy.

His economic knowledge was rich, and he exhibited a thorough understanding of the European economists. Smith, the Physiocrats and Steuart provided the theoretical support for his *Argument Respecting the Constitutionality of the Carriage Tax* (1795), an uncompromising attack on indirect taxation levied in accordance with Hamiltonian policy. The economic material he gathered was applied from the political – particularly constitutional – perspective of the American revolutionary tradition: 'representation and taxation ought to be fairly apportioned, and all who impose, ought to share in the burden'.[66] The authority of the Physiocrats was considered to be more pertinent to that of Smith since it centred on land and not income, so it was this that he invoked to legitimize his reflection on taxation:

> Mr Smith uses the terms 'directly and indirectly', in stating the difficulty of taxing revenue in proportion. To revenue he applies them. And he might with equal propriety have applied them to any other object. Though he holds up

---

[62]   John Taylor, *A Definition of Parties: or the Political Effects of the Paper System Considered* (Philadelphia: Francis Bailey, 1794); John Taylor, *An Enquiry into the Principles and Tendency of Certain Public Measures* (Philadelphia: Dodson, 1794).

[63]   Jefferson to Madison, Monticello, 15 May 1794, in Jefferson, *The Writings*, ed. Ford, vol. VI, 511.

[64]   Taylor, *A Definition of Parties*, 9.

[65]   Taylor, *A Definition of Parties*, 15.

[66]   John Taylor, *An Argument Respecting the Constitutionality of the Carriage Tax; Which Subject was Discussed at Richmond, in Virginia, in May 1795* (Richmond: A. Davis, 1795): 25.

revenue as the sole object of taxation, yet the same station might have been filled by land, with equal, if not greater propriety; for this idea the economists of France contend by powerful arguments. Or persons might as plausibly have placed in the niche, and such a system would have approached nearer to the principle of the Constitution.[67]

He discussed Smith, but he did not fully share his thesis, believing that his analytical perspective remained European and that, on the subject of taxation, he had not arrived at a 'substantial political difference' between direct and indirect taxes. The American lens through which this defender of the interests of the states viewed things came to mark the disparity between his thoughts and those of European authors. He thus used his economic viewpoint to argue that taxes should be set and levied proportionately not on the income of individuals, but on that of each state[68] and fiscal policy should be based on the taxation of land.[69]

Taylor cannot be considered, like Logan, a follower of Physiocracy – from which he differed on essential points of theory such as that of value and land rent, which he considered equivalent to interest paid on loans – and we have no certain evidence that he directly read the Physiocratic authors. Nonetheless this Southern landowner, who accepted slavery but was not convinced of its economic effectiveness, knew their theories, filtered through the evolution of their economic ideas and those of Smith in Jean-Baptiste Say and Malthus, and was mostly stimulated by the political implications of French economic culture.

His fame as a political thinker and writer on economics came later than these first circumstantial interventions, with the success of *Arator* in 1813 and *An Inquiry into the Principles and Policy of the Government of the United States* in 1814, but his basic ideas and coordinates remained unaltered. In the mid 1810s he continued to be the mouthpiece of the eighteenth-century political and economic culture and to propose an agrarian model for America that was incompatible with the development of manufacturing. Of his two most important works Taylor wrote: 'Agriculture and politics are primary causes of our wealth and liberty... *Arator* is chiefly confined to agriculture, but it contains a few political observations. The *Inquiry*, to politics; but it labours to explain the true interest of the agricultural class'.[70]

His attitude towards agriculture was political, scientific and practical. For him, agriculture had a patriotic significance, in that it consolidated the republic through a direct link with the land, which ensured a decentralized participation and made it possible to maintain at once a local and national perspective. This was an

---

[67]   Taylor, *An Argument Respecting the Constitutionality of the Carriage Tax*, 26.

[68]   Taylor, *An Argument Respecting the Constitutionality of the Carriage Tax*, 28.

[69]   'All, or nearly all taxes, must be ultimately paid by agriculture, and ought of course to be inflicted by her, if the doctrine is true, that the payer is the only imposer of taxes' (Taylor, *An Inquiry into the Principles and Policy of the Government of the United States* (Fredericksburg: Green and Cady, 1814): 333).

[70]   Preface to the fourth edition (1818), of Taylor, *Arator*, 50.

urgent matter given that the land, especially in the South, had been impoverished and exhausted by single-crop farming. His attitude also had a strong element of national identity in it, which drove him to promote an alternative to the British economic model: 'because a system is practicable in England, it does not follow that it is practicable here. That which is allowable for the ends of sustaining a monarchy or an aristocracy, may be tyrannical in a republic'.[71]

For Taylor agriculture was not only a topic for discussion, but was also a reality. He was one of the greatest agricultural experimenters in America, the first president of the Virginia Agricultural Society, and strongly committed to joining together in patriotic wedlock the practical dimension and political vocation of the American agricultural societies.[72] This dual focus gave birth to *Arator, Being a Series of Agricultural Essays, Practical and Political*, a collection of articles – previously published in a Georgetown newspaper in 1803 – on trials carried out on his lands to counteract their continuous impoverishment. Using capital acquired through agriculture to fund the fertilizing of the land and labour-saving, was the main theme of the essays.[73] The work was centred on farming, with special attention given to rotation systems and to fertilizers, which made it, with its eight editions, one of the most successful American texts on agronomy, especially in the South.[74]

Overall, however, *Arator* also dealt with the social order of an agrarian republic and other factors relating to agriculture: the American economy, politics, and those enemies of the republic, dealers and bond-holders, banking and manufacturing.[75] In the opening pages of the collection, before agronomic issues were discussed, a section dealt with 'The Political State of Agriculture' and another – 'The Pleasures of Agriculture' – considered the patriotic impulses conferred by the cultivation of the earth and the riches of the mind, as well as the body, that it procured.[76]

Taylor bemoaned the lack of an agrarian literature in America and recognized the merits of Britain in the field of agricultural progress, but he insisted that its model was inapplicable to the American reality.[77] The decline in the fertility

---

[71]   Taylor, *Tyranny Unmasked*, 166.

[72]   On Taylor as an economist cf. Avery O. Craven, 'The Agricultural Reformers of the Ante-bellum South', The *American Historical Review*, 33/2 (January 1928): 302–14; William D. Grampp, 'John Taylor: Economist of Southern Agrarianism', *The Southern Economic Journal*, 11/3 (1945): 255–68; MacLeod, 'The Political Economy of John Taylor of Caroline'. On Taylor's role in the agricultural societies, cf. below, pp. 178–80.

[73]   Taylor, *Arator*, 131.

[74]   'It was the first original agricultural work (worthy to be called) which had ever been published in Virginia, or in the southern states; and it appeared at a time when agricultural improvement was still neglected by the men of intelligence and wealth... Almost every intelligent land-holder became a reader of Arator' (Edmund Ruffin's judgment appears in the *Farmer's Register*, VIII, no.12 (31 December 1840): 703).

[75]   Taylor, *Arator*, 98.

[76]   Taylor, *Arator*, 314–15.

[77]   Taylor, *Arator*, 60.

of American agriculture was caused not so much by poor management as by specific political choices, which was to say the protectionist measures of Hamilton's policies.[78]

If his interest in agronomic literature was always practical, his reflections on agriculture formed part of a wider scientific dimension. The centrality of agriculture was derived from both its status as a natural activity performed on the land and the way it represented the interests of the greater part of the nation,[79] which made the farmer 'the fountain from which all those benefits must flow'.[80]

Despite his more mature works being published in the opening decades of the nineteenth century, Taylor did not fit well in the furrow ploughed by American economic authors, from Daniel Raymond to McVickar, Thomas Cooper, George Tucker and Jacob Cardozo, whose ideas were stimulated by the publication in America of Ricardo's *Principles* in 1819. Taylor's economic culture was still that of the long eighteenth century.

Just as agriculture was combined with the republic, so Taylor was inseparable from the idea of economic freedom. In *Tyranny Unmasked*, written in 1822, which was the first articulated American argument against protectionism – the first attack against the 'American System' – he set the republic and liberalism against despotism and mercantilism.[81] In this framework, in which he distinguished between natural and artificial wealth, agriculture was recognized as the fount of all profit: 'land is the only, or at least the permanent source of profit; and its successful cultivation the encourager of all other occupations, and the best security for National prosperity'.[82] For confirmation of this, he turned to Malthus and his *Principles of Political Economy*, published two years earlier, from which he cited long passages and pointed out how his own ideas paralleled those of the English author:

> that land only can yield permanent and sometimes profits, in the United States especially; that manufacturing in the present state of the world must yield lower profits; that arbitrary depressions of wages are necessary to obtain these low profits; that the products of good land, well cultivated, will bestow spirit and Energy both on domestick and foreign commerce; that an increase of foreign commodities will both augment and enhance the price of domestick productions; that the freer are exchanges the more industry is encouraged; that restrictions

---

[78]   Taylor, *Arator*, 74.

[79]   Taylor, *A Definition of Parties*, 8.

[80]   Taylor, *Arator*, 61.

[81]   Taylor composed the work as a timely response to Henry Clay's attempt to breathe new life into Hamilton's plan to encourage commerce and manufacturing. After the War of 1812, certain protective measures had been passed to defend the nascent American industries from cheaper British goods.

[82]   Taylor, *Tyranny Unmasked*, 157.

upon this freedom produce stagnations of labour and check the progress of wealth.[83]

Here was an economic culture that already had clear notions of productive consumption and profit, and of how capital was as necessary for manufacturing as for agriculture, albeit only the latter was a safe investment.[84] Taylor did not believe in the exclusive productivity of agriculture, but deemed the earth to be the most dependable source of wealth. Once again he appealed to Smith and Malthus for corroboration of his conviction that 'it is therefore impossible that a mechanical surplus, should contribute more to the prosperity of a nation, than an agricultural surplus, even where they are equally attained'.[85] There is in Taylor a theory of labour and value drawn from Smith which, although not scientifically rigorous, was deduced empirically from American conditions: without labour land became impoverished, and Taylor set himself, as an absolute priority, the task of ensuring the stability of the traditional social order, in the face of the race to the West.[86]

With his writings on economics Taylor meant not only to destroy the strongholds of moneyed interest, but also to extend a scientific and practical status to the agrarian model.[87] He had faith in the moral impulses of the rural life, and his democratic political philosophy was based on a vision of the agricultural structure of society.[88]

Agriculture, the Rights of the States and the Separation of Powers

Although not egalitarian, but rather a typical representative of agricultural interests in which he saw no tensions, which was made clear from his attitude as a major plantation owner,[89] Taylor believed in the centrality and unity of national

---

[83]   Taylor, *Tyranny Unmasked*, 161–2.

[84]   Taylor, *Tyranny Unmasked*, 164–5.

[85]   Taylor, *Tyranny Unmasked*, 187.

[86]   Cf. Bernard Drell, "John Taylor of Caroline and the Preservation of an Old Social Order', *The Virginia Magazine of History and Biography*, 46 (1938): 285–98.

[87]   A different reading of Taylor's ideas on agriculture, which sees in them a pastoral model, in keeping with the classical tradition of civic humanism, was given by Robert E. Shalhope, *John Taylor of Caroline: Pastoral Republican* (Columbia: University of South Carolina Press, 1980). Cf. also the introductory essay by Melvin E. Bradford, 'A Virginia Cato: John Taylor of Caroline and the Agrarian Republic', in the previously cited edition of *Arator*, 11–43, and William C. Hill, *The Political Theory of John Taylor of Caroline* (Rutherford: Fairleigh Dickinson University Press, 1977).

[88]   Taylor, *Arator*, 324.

[89]   Taylor gave this definition of the majority: 'They are composed of men, excluding women; of adults, excluding minors; of landowners, excluding those who have no land; and in a multitude of ways' (Taylor, *An Inquiry*, 1–15).

sovereignty through the decentralization of powers.[90] An ideologue of the rights of the states, he gave one of the most original and consistent formulations of the separation of powers, in relation to both Britain and France, developing his ideas independently of the system of checks and balances and Montesquieu's theory. Moreover, he was one of the first Americans to be aware of the specific nature of such a system and of how it compared with the European theories of the balance of power.

The economic character of political decentralization and of the unity of sovereignty was constantly asserted by Taylor.[91] He denounced the economic format of the factional spirit of the parties, which undermined national unity;[92] and he declared that the divisions in the Virginia Assembly arose 'from the interests of banking – a system, spreading and forming a monied party'.[93]

The expression of this particular form of constitutionalism was grounded in political rationalism, which led him to make an original contribution to the debate on nature and the American constitutional patterns, opposing Turgot's *Lettre au docteur Price* to the *Defence of the Constitutions of Government of the United States of America*, by John Adams. *An Inquiry into the Principles and Policy of the Government of the United States* was published in 1814, but Taylor had begun writing it as far back as 1794, in the midst of the anti-Hamiltonian campaign, as a response to Adams's *Defence*.[94] The work thus belongs to the culture of the eighteenth century and is testimony to the continuity of the author's reflections.

No monopoly was legitimate for Taylor, either in economics or in politics, and the most effective antidotes were agriculture on the one hand and the power of the states on the other. Economic discourse was at the root of his political theory, which was based on property as a natural law and on national sovereignty. Two long chapters, 'Funding' and 'Banking', were devoted to explaining the perverse effects that financial power, public credit, moneyed interests and the banks and

---

[90]   Cf. Manning J. Dauer, 'John Taylor: democrat or aristocrat?', *The Journal of Politics*, 6 (1944): 381–403.

[91]   Historiography has read Taylor's thought from a predominantly political and constitutional perspective, paying less attention to the economic dimension of his work, limited to the agronomic sphere (cf. Benjamin F. Wright, 'The Philosopher of Jeffersonian Democracy', *The American Political Science Review*, 22/4 (November 1928): 870–92; Eugene T. Mudge, *The Social Philosophy of John Taylor of Caroline: A Study in Jeffersonian Democracy* (New York: Columbia University Press, 1939); Maurice J. Vile, *Constitutionalism and the Separation of Powers* (Oxford: Clarendon Press, 1967); Charles W. Hill, *The political theory of John Taylor*. For an economic reading of the *Inquiry* cf. Charles A. Beard, *Economic Origins of Jeffersonian Democracy* (New York: Macmillan, 1915).

[92]   Taylor to Vice-President, 25 June 1798, in John Taylor, *Correspondence*, in *The John P. Branch Historical Papers*, II (1908): 274; Taylor to Vice-President, 14 October 1799, in *ibid.*, 283.

[93]   Taylor to Monroe, 27 February 1806, in Taylor, *Correspondence*, 291.

[94]   Taylor to Monroe, Caroline, 8 November 1809, in Taylor, *Correspondence*, 301–2.

holders of public securities had on the nation's political structure, determining the divisions, clashes between factions and the pursuit of privilege.[95] The lack of economic freedom was seen as having direct repercussions on political freedom, and the concentration of power was hostile to political decentralization.

In this panorama, Taylor criticized Adams and his *Defence* for identifying nation with government as was done in Britain, whereas America was in reality characterized by the distinction it made between the nation, formed of individuals, and the government, considered in its abstract sense.[96] Taylor differentiated between 'democratic republicanism' and 'monarchical republicanism', to which he believed Adams adhered.[97] His *Inquiry* opened with a repudiation of the existence of a natural aristocracy and of a system of artificial orders, into which Adams condensed the structure of the American constitutions, offering 'too much respect to political skeletons, constructed with fragments torn from monarchy, aristocracy and democracy', distinctions which Taylor thought fictitious.[98] The discussion in which he took part, contrasting democracy and a system of separate institutions, was one of the highest moments of encounter between the political cultures of Britain, France and America.

At the start of his voluminous work, Taylor recalled that the source of Adams's book was Turgot's *Lettre au docteur Price*, and he quoted a long passage from the English translation of this work,[99] from the section in which the American constitutions were deemed to be too levelled down to the British political model: 'Turgot condemns a balance of power, and different orders of men, and approves of collecting all authority into one centre, the nation'.[100] Turgot's political rationalism, which had been nourished by the Physiocratic notion of the union of the economic law and the critique of the balance of powers,[101] was put forward once more by Taylor, who aimed at an equitable distribution of power through a groundbreaking form of representative government.

Taylor's most original and typically American idea appears in his criticisms of both Adams and Turgot. Adams was wrong to attack Turgot's preference for the unity of authority, opposing it with a defence of the balance of powers. Turgot made the mistake of considering the American form of government to be a mixture of monarchy and aristocracy.[102] Their common error was that of failing to consider

---

[95]   Cf. also Taylor to Vice-President, 25 June 1798, in Taylor, *Correspondence*, 271–6.

[96]   Taylor to Monroe, Caroline, 25 March 1798, in Taylor, *Correspondence*, 269.

[97]   Taylor to Daniel Carrol Brent, Caroline, 9 October 1796, in Taylor, *Correspondence*, 260–61.

[98]   Taylor, *An Inquiry*, V.

[99]   Taylor, *An Inquiry*, 86–7. Anne-Robert-Jacques Turgot, 'Translation. To Dr. Price, London. Paris, 22d March, 1778', in Richard Price, *Observations on the Importance of the American Revolution*, 113–14.

[100]   Taylor, *An Inquiry*, 89.

[101]   Cf. M. Albertone, '"Que l'autorité souveraine soit unique"'.

[102]   Taylor, *An Inquiry*, 88–9.

any form of government other than the traditional ones. America was a completely new type of democracy, founded on the unity of sovereignty and the division of powers, entrusted to the states:

> Instead of balancing power, we divide it and make it responsible, to prevent the evils of its accumulation in the hands of one interest … Instead of monarchy, which excites evil qualities, our division (not a balance) of power, renders it responsible, and brings good qualities out of governors; and instead of a tumultuary nation, election, by division also, is filtered of its worst vice, and brings good qualities out of the mass of the people.[103]

The defence of the rights of the states thus came to combine a territorial presence, useful to a rural economy, and the exercise of a national sovereignty, not by different bodies but by the sum of all individual components.

In 1820, as the ideologue of the rights of the states, thanks to a mature and original grasp of eighteenth-century political culture, Taylor deepened his thinking on the limits of the government, in *Construction Construed and Constitutions Vindicated* – a tirade against the renewal of the authorization for the Bank of the United States by the Supreme Court – which propounded his theory on the unity of sovereignty as a defence of the powers of the people against the governors, and of the states against Congress. Two years later, in *Tyranny Unmasked* he mounted the defence of the states against nationalism and its corollary, mercantilism, in the name of a notional unitary nation founded on decentralized power to ensure popular sovereignty.

Taylor supported Jefferson's presidential campaign, and in his inaugural speech of 1801 the President took up some of the Taylor's fundamental themes.[104] In 1805, Taylor published *A Defence of the Measures of the Administration of Thomas Jefferson*, in support of the Louisiana purchase and the President's policy. With his constitutionalism, he exercised a powerful influence on Jefferson, and was an important interlocutor for him on agronomic issues.

Their intense correspondence abounds with long letters exchanging news of their agricultural activities and the latest methods of cultivation; in this, Taylor, the agronomist, acted as Jefferson's tutor.[105] For his part, in the concrete, technical framework of his interest in farming, Taylor re-echoed in the *Arator* the agrarian

---

[103]   Taylor, *An Inquiry*, 88.

[104]   Jefferson, *Inaugural Address*, in Thomas Jefferson, *The Life and Selected Writings*, ed. Adrienne Koch and William Peden (New York: Random House, 1993): 300.

[105]   Jefferson to Taylor, Monticello, 29 December 1794, in Jefferson, *The Writings*, ed. Bergh, vol. XVIII, 192. Cf. also Jefferson to Taylor, 13 April 1794, in Jefferson, *The Papers*, vol. XXVIII, 326–27; Jefferson to Taylor, 15 April 1795, *ibid.*, 328; Jefferson to Taylor, 8 June 1795, *ibid.*, 383–84; Jefferson to Taylor, 8 October 1797, vol. XXIX, 545–46; Taylor to Jefferson, 14 October 1797, *ibid.*, vol. XXIX, 553–55; Taylor to Jefferson, 19 November 1797, *ibid.*, 573–74.

myth of the 'chosen people of God' from the *Notes on the State of Virginia*: 'The divine intelligence which selected an agricultural state as a paradise for its first favourites has here again prescribed the agriculture virtues as the means for the admission of their posterity into heaven'.[106] The exchange of letters became more frequent from 1794 onwards, after Jefferson had left the post of Secretary of State and settled in his 'new occupation of a farmer'.[107] However, in those years the agronomic discussions were mixed with political strategies.[108]

After the publication of the *Inquiry* this political dialogue became even more animated, and Taylor played an influential role in the last phase of Jefferson's life. The day after reading the work, Jefferson wrote Taylor a long letter in which he gave one of his clearest arguments on the idea of republic. Both interpreted the constitution in the same way and had always fought side by side against the power of the banks and bondholders, in the name of the principle that one generation must not burden the next.[109] 'You have successfully and completely pulverized Mr. Adams' system of orders', Jefferson told Taylor, who he believed had debunked a vague notion of republicanism encompassing different situations, from Holland to Switzerland, to Genoa, Venice and Poland. He then clarified his definition thus: 'It means a government by its citizens in mass, acting directly and personally, according to rules established by the majority'. Representative government denoted a direct exercise of democracy, which defined the republican form as he, in accord with Taylor, perceived it: 'The further the departure from direct and constant control by the citizens, the less has the government of the ingredient of republicanism'.[110]

The ideas of a central government limited by the exercise of the states' powers and of the primacy of popular sovereignty on the constitution was given greater room in Jefferson's political thought in his last decade. He appreciated *Constructions Construed* and recognized how this helped change his views.[111] However, he did not share the Southern sectarianism that Taylor came to exhibit, and he feared the break-up of national unity, a unity he had worked hard to realise during two terms as President and that set him at odds with the consensus of the Old Republicans, including Taylor.

Notwithstanding their shared republican commitment and the points of convergence of their political strategies, the differences between Taylor and

---

[106]   Taylor, *Arator*, 314.

[107]   Jefferson to Taylor, Monticello, 1 May 1794, in Jefferson, *The Writings*, ed. Ford, vol. VI, 505.

[108]   Jefferson, *The Writings*, ed. Ford, vol. VI, 507.

[109]   Jefferson to Taylor, Monticello, 28 May 1816, Jefferson, *The Writings*, ed. Bergh, vol. XV, 18; 23. Cf. Taylor, *An Inquiry*, 248.

[110]   Jefferson to Taylor, Monticello, 28 May 1816, *The Writings*, ed. Bergh, vol. XV, 19–23.

[111]   Jefferson to Spencer Roane, Monticello, 27 June 1821, Jefferson, *The Writings*, ed. Bergh, vol. XV, 327.

Jefferson remained, and it was these that marked out the former's role in the development of American agrarian ideology.[112] Taylor, for whom property was always a natural law, did not share Jefferson's radicalism. However, his criticisms of Jefferson's work as President not only were made in defence of the interests of the South, they also originated from the coherent uniqueness of his agrarian democracy.[113]

Over the course of thirty years Taylor's thought underwent no modification. He was characterized as a philosopher of American agrarian democracy who did not understand the intellectual movements of the times and could not accept the commercial aspects of agriculture or the need for balance between economic activities – ideas that Jefferson made his own through contact with French economic thought, from Say to Destutt de Tracy, and with ideas from the British radical emigration, from Paine, to Priestley, to Cooper. In Taylor Jefferson found a pristine agrarian ideology, untouched by either circumstances or the passage of time.

Taylor's political theory was based on the economic dimension, in the belief that men were motivated by self-interest and that the spirit of faction and privilege had originated from a reprehensible distribution of property. He did not distinguish between faction and party, another sign of an eighteenth-century culture that rejected all corporate interest. His vision was at once economic and political, and it had its fulcrum in farming. The widespread rearing of crops and animals and the vastness and accessibility of land comprised the democratic prerequisites of a political project that made the rural economy the expression of the interests of the majority. Against the forms of aristocracy he attacked – the feudal aristocracy that had existed in Europe and that of financial capitalists in America – agrarian democracy and the separation of powers through the exercise of the functions of the states constituted the bedrock of Taylor's unique American model.

Both ideologists of the American agrarian democracy and Hamilton's strong opponents, Logan and Taylor represented two different approaches to the French culture coming from the North and the South. Logan, a Quaker from Philadelphia, a convinced Physiocrat and a passionate democrat, followed Physiocratic principles along with the progressive radicalization of his thought and his support to the French Revolution. Taylor, a Southern landowner, approached the French economists and conceived a modern idea of republic rooted in agriculture, but he was mostly inspired by suggestions coming from political rationalism characteristic of the French economic tradition proceeding from Physiocracy and the idea of the unity

---

[112]   On the differences between Jefferson, 'commercial agrarian democrat' and Taylor, 'agrarian democrat', cf. Grant Mc Connell, 'John Taylor and the Democratic Tradition', *The Western Political Quarterly*, 4/1 (1951): 17–31.

[113]   'There were a number of people who soon thought, and said to one another, that Mr. Jefferson did many good things, but neglected some better things; and who now view his policy, as very like a compromise with Mr. Hamilton's. ... The mixture of federal and republic policy gained no federalists and disgusted many republicans' (Taylor to Monroe, Caroline, 26 October 1810, in Taylor, *Correspondence*, 310).

of sovereignty. The ideologists of the agrarian democracy, Jefferson, Franklin, Logan and Taylor were all engaged in agricultural experiments and in spreading agrarian innovation. Within the plurality of institutions and the channels through which agriculture was put at the heart of political and economic discussions, these men played a leading role, testifying to the different means of penetration – from practical to academic milieus – of French economic culture and its contribution to the shaping of a new and larger type of republic in which economics and politics were intertwined and which was in search of its own national identity.

Chapter 6

Channels for Disseminating the Economic Culture

Organizing Agricultural Progress

In the aftermath of the American Revolution and in the context of the clash between the Republicans and the Federalists, the agricultural societies of America developed in a unique way. They flourished particularly between 1785 and 1830, the period in which agricultural societies also proliferated in other countries. Faced with making strategic choices for the new nation, Thomas Jefferson and the Republicans encouraged the American societies' growth as a means of augmenting their political and economic plans. Jefferson and all other ideologists of agrarian democracy, including Benjamin Franklin, George Logan and John Taylor, were in some way involved in the societies, and they all used French economic thought as a point of reference.

To understand better the driving force and endeavours of the new institutions, it is necessary to place their experiences in their national and international economic context. The societies developed after the American Depression of the mid 1780s, and they were connected to the resurgence of agriculture during the post-revolutionary period, up to the collapse of American cereal and tobacco exports to Europe at the end of the century. While the first and most important agricultural societies were established in the northern cities – first of them all was the Philadelphia Society for the Promotion of Agriculture and Agricultural Reform, in 1785 – their growth in the South was accelerated by the move towards isolationism after the War of 1812.[1]

The new American agrarian spirit coincided with the years of the Revolution, between 1775 and 1790, and so the composition of the agricultural societies had a notable prevalence of progressive members, some of them protagonists of revolutionary events and some employed in the new political administration. In 1789, after the war with Britain, America with its unique geography had reasons to focus on agriculture, in that it needed urgently to recover economically.[2]

---

[1]   Cf. Percy W. Bidwell and John I. Falconer, *History of Agriculture in the Northern United States, 1620–1860* (Clifton: A.M. Kelley, 1973) (first published 1925); Lewis Cecil Gray, *History of Agriculture in the Southern Unites States to 1860*, 2 vols. (Clifton: A.M. Kelly, 1973) (1st ed. 1933).

[2]   'An address to the public, from the South Carolina Society for promoting and improving agriculture and other rural concerns', *The American Museum*, V (January 1789): 41–2;

Before 1800 the foremost agricultural societies were, in addition to the Philadelphia one, the New York Society for Promoting Agriculture, Arts and Manufactures (1791) and the Massachusetts Society for Promoting Agriculture (1792), though others sprang up in Charleston, South Carolina, Hallowell, Maine and New Haven.[3] Far from being farmers' clubs in which help and practical experience were shared, these were associations for rich landowners who belonged to the liberal professions, an elite of doctors, lawyers and clergymen, who lived in the city but wished to improve the running of their estates. They had no direct contact with the farming population but, brought up on classical culture and a Virgilian agrarian myth, much like that of the educated classes of Europe, they were moved by the desire to introduce and spread new agricultural techniques, particularly those from Britain, since they were aware of both the backwardness of American agriculture, which had been deprived of experimentation during the colonial period, and of the country's rare and rich physical features. The landowners therefore represented an ideal of agriculture that was not Arcadian, but modern and dynamic: 'Much useful knowledge in husbandry is to be acquired from the treatises which have been published on that subject; but as they are mostly calculated for climates, in many respects varying from ours, it is only by experiments made here that we can venture, with safety, to apply their principles'.[4]

Many of the members of the agricultural societies – and by no means only the most famous, such as Jefferson, Washington, Logan, Taylor and Franklin – were personally engaged in agricultural experiments. They had direct experience of the latest European methods of cultivation and knowledge of British agronomists, and were active in the exchange of plants, seeds and new breeds of livestock.[5] Both Jefferson and Washington corresponded with Arthur Young and John Sinclair, who in 1797 had pushed for the creation of a national board of agriculture in Philadelphia, on the lines of the British model, of which seven Americans became honorary members. Young was a direct point of contact in American trials and

---

'Observations on agriculture, its advantages, and the causes that have in America prevented improvements in husbandry. By General Warren, of Massachusetts', *The American Museum*, II (October 1787): 345.

[3]   Rodney H. True, 'The early development of Agricultural societies in the United States', *Annual Report of the American Historical Association, for the year 1920* (Washington: Government Printing Office, 1925): 295–306; Margaret W. Rossiter, 'The Organization of Agricultural Improvement in the United States 1785–1865', in *The Pursuit of Knowledge in the Early American Republic: American Scientific and Learned Societies from Colonial Times to the Civil War*, ed. Alexandra Olesen and Sanborn C. Brown (Baltimore: John Hopkins University Press, 1976): 284–7.

[4]   *Rules and Regulations of the Massachusetts Society for Promoting Agriculture* (Boston: Thomas Fleet, 1796): 3–4.

[5]   Rodney C. Loher, 'The Influence of English Agriculture on American Agriculture, 1775–1825', *Agriculture History*, 11 (January 1937): 3–15.

his *Annals of Agriculture* were widely known among American agriculturalists.[6] Before the success of Young and Sinclair, the English agricultural revolution of Jethro Tull, which was based on tillage, had already found a channel of distribution in America through Jared Eliot and Franklin, whose merits as pioneers of agricultural experiments are often forgotten.[7]

The prime exemplar of the learned societies, which inspired the agricultural societies, was the American Philosophical Society, through which in 1743 Franklin, one of its founders, encouraged the expansion of agricultural knowledge by setting in operation a section entitled 'Husbandry and American improvements.' This fitted in well with the aims of the society – which elected Franklin as its president in 1769 and then Jefferson in 1796 for a period of nineteen years – to create a network of similar associations in order to cement the union between North and South through the pursuit of two basic Enlightenment objectives: the spread of education and the improvement of the material conditions of life.[8] In 1798 Jefferson presented the designs for his famous plough to the society. Research in the fields of botany, chemistry, mechanics, trade and agriculture did not, however, preclude a keen interest in politics, and topics like 'What form of government contributes most to the public weal?' appeared on the agenda alongside more practical items.

The American Philosophical Society was among the most important avenues through which French thought gained access to America; it was a point of interchange between the revolutionary cultures of the two countries. Jefferson, Franklin and St John de Crèvecoeur made themselves directly responsible for this by means of their personal contacts and, during their stays in France, by acting as intermediaries for the distribution of works by French authors. There was a high number of French members in the societies, including Buffon, Lavoisier, Daubenton, Lafayette, Chastellux, Brissot, Volney and Cabanis, and not a few were linked to Physiocratic circles: Du Pont de Nemours, Condorcet, Barbeu Du Bourg and La Rochefoucauld. In 1789, Quesnay de Beauregard, nephew of

---

[6]   John Taylor to George W. Jeffrey, 16 August 1816, *American Farmer*, vol. II (16 June 1820): 93.

[7]   Jared Eliot, *Essays upon Field Husbandry in New England and Other Papers 1748–1762* (New York: Columbia University Press, 1934). Eliot confided that agricultural progress would have cemented both the unity between the colonies and the spirit of cooperation with Britain. Moreover, his plan for intensive agriculture was in harmony with the British colonial policy of restricting the expansion into land in the West. Cf. Christopher Grasso, 'The Experimental Philosophy of Farming: Jared Eliot and the Cultivation of Connecticut', *The William and Mary Quarterly* 50 (1993): 502–28; Earle D. Ross, 'Benjamin Franklin as an Eighteenth-Century Agricultural Leader', *Journal of Political Economy*, 37 (1929), 52–72; Richard Bridgman, 'Jefferson's Farmer before Jefferson', *American Quarterly*, 14 (1962): 567–77.

[8]   *Proceedings of the American Philosophical Society*, vol. III, quoted in Oscar Hansen Allen, *Liberalism and American Education* (New York: Octagon Press, 1965): 105.

François Quesnay, presented his plan for the strengthening of cultural and scientific ties between America, France and other European countries to the Academy of Sciences and Belles Lettres, based in Richmond.[9] The American Philosophical Society and, more generally, the learned societies were thus forums for discussion for the agricultural societies, the practical orientation of which marked them out from the start as institutions more directly linked than others to local realities.

Imitating the example set by European societies, American agricultural improvement programmes awarded prizes for essays on set themes and held competitions for farmers at agricultural shows and livestock fairs, where all the latest things were on display. The first livestock fair, in Pittsfield, Massachusetts, came into being through Elkanah Watson, an enterprising New Englander who, taking full advantage of his journeys in Europe, introduced merino sheep to America in 1807.[10] The sponsored techniques were aimed at promoting intensive farming methods by means of crop rotation, the reduction of single-crop farming, the introduction of new varieties of plants and the use of fertilizers, gypsum and lime. Dissertations, reports and transactions informed an educated public of the results achieved. Among other goals of the programmes were the establishment of specialized libraries to house agricultural works from Europe, and the broadcasting of information and shaping of public opinion through a specialized press.

The agricultural societies published their papers and proceedings in the specialized periodicals, which also republished British texts on agriculture and kept up-to-date lists of fluctuating agricultural prices. The first such periodical, the *Agricultural Museum*,[11] made its debut in 1810, and 1819 saw the birth of John Skinner's *American Farmer*, which became the mouthpiece of the Agricultural Society of Albemarle, promoted and planned by Jefferson and Madison, and a point of focus for national calls for agricultural renewal. Others followed: the *New England Farmer* in 1822, *The New York Farmer* in 1826, *The Genesee Farmer* in 1831, *The Cultivator* in 1834 and *The Maine Farmer* in 1835. The *Farmer's Register*, founded in 1832 by Edmund Ruffin of Virginia, an agricultural experimenter, became a central point of interest for farming in the South. The *Register* published articles by Taylor, who allied himself to Ruffin's campaigns against the power of the banks – campaigns that hastened the periodical's demise in 1842 – and to his cultural and political project of an agrarian South opposing the North. These positions distanced the Old Republicans from the balanced,

---

[9]   Joseph G. Rosengarten, 'The early French members of the American Philosophical Society', *Proceedings of the American Philosophical Society*, 46 (1907): 87–97.

[10]   Cf. Bidwell and Falconer, *History of Agriculture in the Northern United States*, 187–8.

[11]   Claribel R. Barnett, '"The Agricultural Museum": An Early American Agricultural Periodical', *Agricultural History*, 2 (1928): 99–102.

unifying politics of Jefferson's presidency and paved the way taken by the South that ultimately led to the Civil War.[12]

Another objective of the agricultural societies was that of exerting social control and applying the brakes to migration to the West, by people in search of fertile land. The programmes of intensive agriculture, based on British techniques, which the societies sought to implement, clashed with the traditional methods of cultivation practised by the farmers who, due to the immense availability of low-priced land, tended to exhaust their acres then move to more fertile ones. Moreover, before 1800 the strong demand for grain in the East kept prices high, so farmers had no interest in increasing the productivity of their holdings.

The same resistance could be found in the South. The system of plantations, the vastness of land and high labour costs encouraged extensive farming that impoverished the land,[13] against which Taylor fought in his campaign for the use of fertilizers. However, in the same period the migration of white farmers towards the South weakened the aristocracy of the plantation owners.[14] It was in this climate that the campaigns against the abolition of the right of primogeniture (in which Jefferson was involved) took place, endeavours that aided the movement against slavery, to which the echoes of the French Revolution gave added impetus.

This conflict between the American reality and the objective of intensive agriculture based on the European model explains why the agricultural societies declined. The high point was reached between 1820 and 1825 with the rapid spread of the county societies, which had a greater practical impact – in 1819 Watson estimated that there were at least 100 in the United States – thanks in part to the financial support of the states, particularly Massachusetts, New York and Pennsylvania.[15] Starting out at a time of price rises, the societies underwent a phase of swift collapse, and farmers saw their hopes dashed, especially when public funding began to fall. Even so, improvements were encouraged here and there by agricultural societies and competitions, as agricultural and livestock shows helped to democratize, educate and inform. These, however, did not follow the course of the profound changes in American agriculture between 1790 and 1830, which were characterized by westward migration by farmers who preferred to seek new lands rather than adopt the revolutionary farming methods promoted by the reformers, which thus remained the preserve of the wealthy landowners.

---

[12]   Avery O. Craven, 'The Agricultural Reformers of the Ante-bellum South', *The American Historical Review*, 33/2 (January 1928): 302–14; Norman K. Risjord, *The Old Republicans: Southern Conservatism in the Age of Jefferson* (New York: Columbia University Press, 1965).

[13]   George Washington, *Letters on Agriculture*, ed. Franklin Knight (Washington: The editor; Philadelphia: W.S. Martien, 1847).

[14]   Cf. Richard Bridgman, 'Jefferson's Farmer before Jefferson', 567–77; D. Allan Williams, 'The Small Farmer in Eighteenth-Century Virginia Politics', *Agricultural History*, 43 (1969): 91–102.

[15]   Cf. Bidwell and Falconer, *History of Agriculture*.

In the main the American agricultural societies did not operate within a state programme, even though they formed part of a national design. In 1776 the continental Congress had called for a 'society for the improvement of agriculture, arts, manufactures, and commerce' to be set up in every colony, looking forward to coordination between them.[16] However, when the war against Britain ruled out the implementation of these plans, it was only after 1787, with the creation of the national market, that they were followed through.

The experiences of the agricultural societies therefore prove to be an instructive lens through which to study the ties between the intellectual elites and the government. Considered within the relationship between states and central power, they represented, in the national composite, the local components.

Jefferson was a staunch defender of the autonomy of the agricultural societies: in 1811, he put forth a plan for their organization, spelling out what their function, objectives and structure ought to be. Though formulated for the society of Albemarle, Virginia, the plan was intended to provide a blueprint nationally. It called for the creation of a central society for every state to serve as the communication hub for all the county organizations. The function of the governing structure was merely to facilitate such communication and not to manage activities:

> I have on several occasions been led to think on some means of uniting the state agricultural societies into a central society: and lately it has been pressed from England with a view to a co-operation with their board of agriculture. You know some have proposed to Congress to incorporate such a society. I am against that, because I think Congress cannot find in all the enumerated powers any one which authorizes the act, much less the giving the public money to that use.[17]

Towards the end of his second presidential term, he perceived the essential distinguishing quality of the agricultural societies to be their cosmopolitan aspect. In confirmation of this he could boast of his contacts with the societies of Paris and London, of which he was a member, his involvement in sending to Britain seeds of Virginian May wheat, or the arrival in America of the perennial chicory, introduced to Britain from France by Young, and sent on to Washington by the London society of agriculture:

> I mention these things, to show the nature of the correspondence which is carried on between societies instituted for the benevolent purpose of communicating to all parts of the world whatever useful is discovered in any one of them. These societies are always in peace, however their nations may be at war. Like the

---

[16]   *Journal of Continental Congress*, vol. IV, quoted in Gray, *History of Agriculture*, 738.

[17]   Jefferson to Robert R. Livingston, 16 February 1801, in Jefferson, *The Writings*, ed. Bergh, vol. VII, 492–3; Thomas Jefferson, 'Scheme for a System of Agricultural Societies, March 1811', in *ibid.*, vol. XVII, 405.

republic of letters, they form a great fraternity spreading over the whole earth, and their correspondence is never interrupted by any civilized nation.[18]

The first agricultural society, whose echoes reverberated beyond America and which made a mark on the country's political and cultural scene, was the Philadelphia Society for the Promotion of Agriculture, situated in what was the prime grain-producing area before 1800. Philadelphia, where it was founded, was the most cosmopolitan American city and had the strongest French presence even before the wave of emigration in the aftermath of the revolt in Santo Domingo.[19]

International openness and progressive republicanism characterized the membership of the Philadelphia Society from its inception on 11 February 1785. Of its 23 founder members, four – George Clymer, Robert Morris, Benjamin Rush and James Wilson – had signed the Declaration of Independence, four were members of the convention that had drafted the Constitution of the United States and two, Logan and Morris, were senators. From the outset, Washington and Franklin took an active part in the society, and in 1791 John Vaughan, who corresponded with Du Pont de Nemours, became its treasurer.[20]

The inflow of French economic thought passed both through institutional channels and through the compelling presence of figures like Franklin and Logan. In 1789 Abbot Tessier, of the Académie des Sciences and the Académie de Médecine in Paris, presented the Philadelphia Agricultural Society (via the mediation of François de Marbois) a series of questions on the state of agriculture in the United States. The positive outcome of this exchange prompted the society to continue this type of agronomic enquiry.[21] As time went by the notion that

---

[18]   Jefferson to John Hollins, 19 February 1809, in Jefferson, *The Writings*, ed. Bergh, vol. XII, 253.

[19]   Cf. May, *The Enlightenment in America*.

[20]   Cf. Lucius F. Ellsworth, "The Philadelphia Society for the Promotion of Agriculture and Agricultural Reform," *Agricultural History*, 42 (1968): 189–99; Simon Baatz, *"'Venerate the Plough': A History of the Philadelphia Society for Promoting Agriculture, 1785–1985* (Philadelphia: PSPA, 1985).

[21]   *American Museum or Universal Magazine*, V (April 1789): 374–82. In the same months the magazine – one of the most influential channels through which the agricultural societies influenced public opinion – had published other articles in favour of agricultural improvements as a means to improve the post-war economy ('An Address to the public, from the South Carolina Society for promoting and improving agriculture and other rural concerns', *ibid*. (January 1789): 41–42). The magazine also clearly promoted the idea of the exclusive productivity of agriculture: 'Mechanic arts may be justly considered, as the offspring of that plenty, which agriculture begets' ('Whether it be [sic] most beneficial to the United States, to promote agriculture, or to encourage the mechanic arts and manufactures? From a discourse pronounced by John Morgan, M.D.F.R.S., at a meeting of the Shandean Society of New-Bern, North Carolina, march 15, 1789', *ibid*. (July 1789), 72).

patriotism presupposed the improvement of agriculture persisted, for agriculture was deemed the basis of the country's liberty and independence.[22]

The double binomial of agriculture-patriotism and agriculture-science was taken to be a guideline for society.[23] Agriculture and democracy, agriculture and political radicalism were not, however, concepts shared universally, particularly after the adoption of the constitution in 1787, which induced many members to assume more conservative positions against the new order. The exception was Logan, and his membership of agricultural societies and his activities exemplified the effectiveness they had as political instruments with which to influence the government.

George Logan: Agricultural Societies and Political Radicalism

British practice and French theory marked George Logan's activities as an agronomist and, as we have seen, the theoretical framework of his plans for technical innovation was provided by Physiocracy. He was a founding member of the Philadelphia Society, and through him Jeffersonian democratic ideology made a powerful impact on the agricultural societies. His Quaker radicalism caused him to be disillusioned by the conservative turn in the society after 1787, to such a degree that he broke from it in 1790. That was the year of Jefferson's return to America, the beginning of the clash between Republicans and Federalists over the farmer/republic combination, and the rise of the Revolution in France.

On 4 August 1788, Logan founded the Philadelphia County Society for the Promotion of Agriculture and Domestic Manufactures, on a conception of an agricultural society profoundly different from British and French ones.[24] Made up exclusively of farmers, it subordinated the cosmopolitan vocation to the political project of transforming agricultural societies into centres of democratic practice, where farmers could organize themselves on a national scale for the defence of their rights, coordinating their efforts through correspondence committees as

---

[22]   *Memoirs of the Philadelphia Society for promoting agriculture*, vol. II (Philadelphia: Johnson and Warner, 1811): vi–vii; 'it would evidence an increase of a spirit of patriotism, in this diffusing a knowledge of the art, by which the great body of our citizens, in this agricultural country, not only gain a plentiful subsistence, but contribute to that of others' (*ibid.*, vol. III (1814): iii).

[23]   'A Discourse on agriculture, by Richard Peters, president at the request of the Society' (*Memoirs of the Philadelphia Society for promoting agriculture*, vol. IV (1818), ix); the influences of the author of this essay were Montesquieu, who 'has, with truth, observed, that "countries are not cultivated in proportion of their fertility, but to their liberty"', and Sully, who had defined 'both tillage and pasturage … the two breast of the state' (*ibid.*, xiii, xxi).

[24]   'Constitution of the Philadelphia County Society for the promotion of agriculture and domestic manufactures', *American Museum*, V (February 1789): 161–3.

the committees of patriots had done during the Revolution.[25] The improvement programme he put forward was aimed at the class of farmers that could bear the costs of modernizing agriculture. Crop rotation, he said in his speech to the Philadelphia Society:

> is not calculated for a poor tenantry, but for an independent yeomanry – such as our American farmers ought to be – gentlemen cultivating their own estates, and living under the protection of a just and enlightened government. In this situation the industrious husbandman ploughs his fields with pleasure and alacrity, well knowing that after giving to the government a fixed and certain proportion of the net produce of his farm, he will be protected in the full enjoyment of the remainder.[26]

Logan's endeavours as an agronomist, which were matched by his political radicalism, found resistance in the Philadelphia Society, which in 1791 rejected the project for crop rotation that he had presented in December 1790 in response to a question posed by the society five years earlier. He had answered the society's call by assembling the results of his experiments on the subject, but the society objected to his scheme because it was not 'agreeable to the English mode of farming'. Whereas the crop rotation that he proposed was based on the British approach, his theoretical framework was manifestly Physiocratic, to justify the preference for reaching agreements with large landowners who were able to ensure large investments, the 'primitive, instrumental, annual expenses'. The relationship between agriculture and government nevertheless remained strong, in so far as, despite private owners having to take on the expense of technical improvements, 'the final success, of rendering the soil the most productive possible, depends on the government of the country'. A clear source of inspiration was the new era of liberty that had begun in France, where the centrality of agriculture was already fully acknowledged.[27]

Faced with the rejection of the Philadelphia Society, whose political motivations were obvious, Logan became convinced that there was a national plan, of which the constitution was an instrument, to favour traders and financial speculators at the expense of farmers. From 1790, his increasingly radicalized language was placed at the service of the political campaign he orchestrated with Jefferson, which made him one of the most resolute ideologists of agrarian democracy. The Philadelphia County Society became a democratic test-bed for his proposals.

Five weeks after the publication of Hamilton's *Report on Public Credit*, Logan sent the Philadelphia County Society a series of arguments that formed the basis of

---

[25]   *National Gazette* (20 February 1792); George Logan, 'To the Philadelphia Society for promoting Agriculture', *Independent Gazetteer and agricultural Repository* (5 March 1791).

[26]   Logan, 'To the Philadelphia Society'

[27]   George Logan, *Fourteen Agricultural Experiments, to Ascertain the Best Rotation of Crops: Addressed to the Philadelphia Agricultural Society* (Philadelphia: Bailey, 1797).

his *Letters Addressed to the Yeonmanry of the United States*.[28] Thus began his duel with Hamilton, based on Physiocratic principles. Logan's American radicalism was linked to French revolutionary radicalism and his agrarianism caused him to entrench his political positions.

In 1800, he introduced a new project for establishing a society for the promotion of agriculture, the arts and manufactures, expressing the hope that others might be founded and work together. In it agriculture and patriotism remained synonymous, and America constituted an alternative to the European economic models.[29] Logan's commitment to the agricultural societies never wavered. In 1803, alongside James Madison, he became the vice-president of the American Board of Agriculture, which was based on the British pattern, to coordinate the agricultural societies on a national level. However, his hopes for the organization were dashed when it failed to meet the real needs of American farmers.

In 1802 he abandoned politics and his role as senator and returned to being a farmer. He gave his support to Du Pont de Nemours and Livingston for the importing of merino sheep into America and was among the founders of the Merino Society of the Middle States of North America. This was an enterprise that he considered at once economic and patriotic, since it fortified the autonomy of the American economy.

In 1818, towards the end of his life, he returned, as vice president, to the Philadelphia Society from which he had distanced himself, and to which he now gave renewed vigour. There, in the face of the Tariff of 1816 and the revival of the Bank of the United States, he reaffirmed his belief in the centrality of the farmer in the republican value of agriculture – a science 'reducible to fixed, unalterable principles' – denouncing once again the protraction, in spite of the efforts of the agricultural societies, of errors and of ignorance: 'attributable to banking and manufacturing establishments, under the protection of government, absorbing a portion of capital that might be employed to greater advantage in agricultural improvements'.[30]

Thomas Jefferson: Between Local Engagement and National Politics

In the post-revolutionary period agriculture in the Southern States progressed, and its modernization was aided by the birth of the first agricultural societies. In 1785 the South Carolina Agricultural Society was established in Charleston, with

---

[28]   Logan's ideas for the Philadelphia County Society were published in the *Independent Gazetteer* on 20 February and 6 March 1790.

[29]   George Logan, *A Letter to the Citizens of Pennsylvania, on the Necessity of Promoting Agriculture, Manufactures, and the Useful Arts* (Philadelphia: Patterson and Cochran, 1 May 1800).

[30]   George Logan, *An Address on the Errors of Husbandry in the United States*, Philadelphia (1818), quoted in Tolles, *George Logan of Philadelphia*, 315.

Washington as president and Jefferson as vice president, and in 1787 the Kentucky Society for Promoting Useful Knowledge was founded.[31] A strong impetus for the creation of new societies came later, after the shift towards isolationism which preceded the War of 1812 and which signalled the decline of the British approach to agronomy.

Jefferson's work in Virginia took place in this setting, leading, on 5 May 1817, to the founding in Charlottesville of the Albemarle Agricultural Society, the most active of the South and among the most important in America. As President of the United States for two terms, he testified by his presence and actions to the political usefulness of progress and the distribution of information in the field of agriculture. 'There is certainly a much greater abundance of material for Agricultural Societies than Philosophical', he wrote in a letter to Livingston in 1801.[32] For Jefferson, his work in the agricultural societies was an opportunity to verify and implement a policy of local and decentralized participation centred on the social figure of the farmer.

As a landowner, in his youth he had followed the example of other southern farmers and exhausted his lands in Virginia – in the counties of Albemarle, Bedford and Campbell – with the incessant cultivation of tobacco and grain. Later, when aware of his mistakes, he became an agricultural experimenter and launched a restoration programme based on crop rotation, the use of manure and artificial fertilizers.[33]

In accordance with his agrarian ideology, he considered the expanding of awareness of agricultural science to be a priority on an economic and political level, as well as a way of consolidating Republican support. In the initial stages of the Revolution, his work in Virginia for the abolition of the entail and the custom of primogeniture was aimed at increasing the number of farmers and small landholdings in the belief of the importance of creating a social fabric based on tillers of the soil, figures who were economically vibrant and politically independent.

After his two presidential terms, his return to a more direct local action, which occupied him in the formation of the agricultural society of Albemarle, coincided with his plans for the establishment of the University of Virginia. For this he sought Du Pont de Nemours's help and he worked towards the creation of a chair in agricultural science, with the aim of having the occupation of the cultivator recognized as a specialized profession:

> In every College and University, a professorship of agriculture, and the class of
> its students, might be honored as the first. Young men closing their academical
> education with this, as the crown of all other sciences, fascinated with its
> solid charms, and at a time when they are to choose an occupation, instead of

[31] Cf. Gray, *History of Agriculture*, vol. II, 779 ff.; Timothy H. Breen, *Tobacco Culture: The Mentality of the Great Tidewater Planters on the Eve of Revolution*, 2nd ed. (Princeton: Princeton University Press, 2001).

[32] Jefferson to Robert R. Livingston, 16 February 1801, in Jefferson, *The Writings*, ed. Ford, vol. VII, 493.

[33] Cf. Miller, 'Jefferson as an Agriculturist'; *Thomas Jefferson's Farm Book*.

crowding the other classes, would return to the farms of their fathers, their own, or those of other, and replenish and invigorate a calling, now languishing under contempt and oppression.[34]

In this picture of pragmatic thinking, which constantly paralleled the attention he paid to economic theory, in the final years of his life Jefferson was able to resume his interest in farming practice. In his library, next to the rich collection of Physiocratic texts, he kept memoirs and transactions of proceedings from several agricultural societies.[35]

The project for a system of agricultural societies, formulated in 1811, and his commitment to the creation of the society of agriculture in Albemarle, in 1817, bear cogent witness to the tenaciousness of his interest in the central role of agriculture, in a moment in which he had made the idea of a necessary balance between economic activities and the need for growth in manufacturing in the United States his own. Faced with the Tariff of 1816 and the revival of the Bank of the United States, for him, as for Logan, direct engagement in the agricultural societies had political implications.

This was the spirit that led to the setting up of the Agricultural Society of Albemarle, whose members included Joseph C. Cabell (who worked with Jefferson for the establishment of the University of Virginia),[36] Ruffin (the editor of the *Farmer's Register* and a leading agricultural experimenter), and James Madison, who became its first president.

In his inaugural address, Madison offered a synthesis of the subject matter and objectives of the American agricultural societies, summed up in the primacy of agriculture and the educational usefulness of the agricultural societies.[37] In his depiction of human history, agriculture was placed at the apex of civilization. Hindrances to the entrance of new techniques were therefore perceived to be obstacles to the progress of the entire American economy. Compared to the colonial period, the urgency for change was now felt more strongly: while the situation in the past had been characterized by the low cost of land and the high cost of labour, 'labor is now comparatively cheaper and land dearer'.[38] In the face of the exhaustion of the land, Madison returned in his speech to the various points of the programme highlighted by Jefferson: 'rotation of crops', 'calendars of work',

---

[34]   Jefferson to David Williams, 14 November 1803, in Jefferson, *The Writings*, ed. Bergh, vol. IX, 429–30.

[35]   *Catalogue of the Library of Thomas Jefferson*, vol. I, nos. 216, 768, 769, 772, 774, 1195, 1264, vol. III, nos. 2370, 2371, 2372, 2373, 2374, 2375, 2377, 2432, 2433, 2436, 3551, 3617.

[36]   Cf. *Early History of the University of Virginia, as contained in the letters of Thomas Jefferson and Joseph C. Cabell* (Richmond: J.W. Randolph, 1856).

[37]   James Madison, 'Address to the Agricultural Society of Abemarle Virginia', in James Madison, *Letters and Other Writings*, 4 vols. (New York: R. Worlongton, 1884): vol. III, 64.

[38]   Madison, 'Address to the Agricultural Society of Abemarle Virginia', 76–7.

'farm buildings and conveniences, enclosures, roads, fuel, timber', 'manures, plaster, green dressings, fallows, and other means of ameliorating the soil'.[39]

Jefferson's name continued to be cited as the undisputed point of reference for every discussion of agrarian issues. In 1819 the Agricultural Society of Prince George's County repeated 'a maxim often attributed to Mr. Jefferson, but justly belonging to the French economists before his time, namely, that every person should be left to pursue his own business, in his own way'.[40] In such ways French economic culture and agrarian ideology were channelled through him.

From 1820 James Garnett, president of the Virginia Agricultural Society of Fredericksburg, denounced the violation of 'true republican principles', which had been caused by an increase of duty on foreign goods. He pointed out, with typically Physiocratic argument, that in the final analysis the cost of the duty fell on the 'agriculturists', who constituted the majority of the population, and that a policy of protectionist tariffs contradicted the principles of political economy, that 'according to the natural progress of society in every country favourably situated for agriculture, the class of Manufactures is the last to spring up'. He quoted passages from Thomas Cooper, in which he spoke of the 'tillers of the earth, the fountain head of all wealth, of all power, and of all prosperity', and he referred to Franklin and his fight against protectionism.[41]

Skinner's *American Farmer*, in which these various interventions were published, made itself the voice of the American agricultural societies in the early 1820s. Jefferson and Taylor were now the unquestioned points of reference. In 1820 a letter from Jefferson appeared in which he claimed that the agriculture of countries like France and Italy was closer to that of the United States, on account of their climate and geographic conditions, and that therefore they, rather than Britain, should be taken as comparisons:

> There is probably no better husbandry known at present, than that of England. But that is, for the climate and productions of England. Their books lay for us a foundation of good general principles; but we ought, for their application, to look more than we have done into the practices of countries, and climates,

---

[39]   Jefferson, 'Scheme for a System of Agricultural Societies', 406–7.

[40]   'Address of the Vice-President of the Agricultural Society of Prince George's County', *American Farmer*, vol. I, no. 16 (Friday 16 July 1919): 121.

[41]   'Remonstrance of the Virginia Agricultural Society of Fredericksburg Read in Congress, January 3d 1820', *American Farmer*, vol. I, no. 42 (14 January 1820): 333. Cf. Thomas Cooper, 'Political Arithmetic', in *The Emporium of Arts and Sciences*, new series, vol. I, no. 1 (June 1813): 178 and 'Congressional Report of the Committee on Agriculture, on the Memorial of the Delegates of the United Agricultural Societies of Sundry Counties in the State of Virginia, February, 2, 1821', *American Farmer*, vol. II, no. 50 (9 March 1821): 394.

more homogeneous with our own. I speak as a Southern man. The Agriculture of France and Italy is good, and has been better at this time.[42]

There followed a list of authors and works for a library of agronomy, which included Fabbroni and Lastri, Duhamel, De Serres and Rozier, alongside Young and Tull, and Taylor's *Arator*.

John Taylor: Agricultural Societies in the Service of the Doctrine of the States

The same issue of the *American Farmer* published a suggestion by John Taylor of texts to form part of an agricultural library, including: Young, who 'alone seems to me to occupy the station among agriculturists, which Bacon does among philosophers', the records of the Agricultural Society of Philadelphia, Tull, Sinclair and his own *Arator*. [43] Ruffin emphasized how it 'opened the eyes of many in this part of the country to see that agriculture ought to be and did embrace more than simply cutting down trees, grubbing and plowing land'.[44] The following year Taylor published – again in the *American Farmer*, which was the organ that gave voice to his campaigns – 'A Letter on the United Agricultural Societies of Virginia'. In this he stressed, from a patriotic perspective, the need for coordination between the agricultural societies.[45] The whole debate was charged with political urgency: it was against the banks, the financial and mercantile powers, the monopolies that crushed the interests of agriculture , the public debt that imposed new taxes and despotism that conflicted with the republican system.

Like Jefferson, Franklin and Logan, Taylor was an agricultural experimenter and one of the leading American agronomists at a time in which traditional methods were wearing out lands in the South.[46] He championed the introduction of crop rotation, and, in opposition to monoculture farming based on tobacco, promoted the use of fertilizers and supported the interests of the large landholdings, which alone could ensure the investment of capital required for the modernization of agriculture.

His commitment to an agrarian economy and his involvement in the agricultural societies served as an exemplar at a time when a strong call was being made for the exercise of local power and links between states and the federal government. He was a member of the Philadelphia Society and the Richmond Agricultural

---

[42]   *American Farmer*, vol. II, (June 16, 1820): 93. A year later the journal republished a letter from Jefferson of 1788 addressed to the Agricultural Society of South Carolina, in which he gave an account of his observations during his journey to France and Italy and of his cultivation of olives, capers and figs (*ibid.*, vol. III (7 December 1821): 294–5).

[43]   *American Farmer*, vol. II (16 June 1820): 93.

[44]   *Farmer's Register*, II, 12–14.

[45]   *American Farmer*, vol. III (20 July 1821): 131.

[46]   Cf. Grampp, 'John Taylor: Economist of Southern Agrarianism'; MacLeod, 'The Political Economy of John Taylor of Caroline'.

Society (of which he became president in 1817), and he was the first president of the Virginia Agricultural Society, as well as an associated correspondent of many others. He was active in bringing in British methods to the United States, though well aware of America's uniqueness, which exposed 'the incongruity of English books upon Agriculture, with the climates, soils and habits of the United States. This incongruity, by drawing ridicule upon imitators, too often extinguishes a patriotic ardor, and checks instead of advancing improvements'.[47]

Other aspects of America's singularity were its particular political context and the relationship between agriculture and republic. The decline of the fertility of its agriculture was precipitated not only by the lack of improvements but also, and essentially, by Hamilton's policies and the British model, because of which the endorsement of manufacturing appeared merely a pretext for the creation of a 'monied interest, aristocracy or despot'.[48]

As we have seen, Taylor launched his campaigns against Hamilton and his economic policy in the early 1790s, with a series of incendiary pamphlets lambasting the banks, public debt, financial interests and fiscal policies.[49] His engagement as a man of the South and a rich plantation owner – at a time of the collapse of grain exports to Europe, which lasted until his death in 1826 – linked to the preservation of values of an agrarian society of large landowners, set him apart from the radicalism of Jefferson and Logan. Agriculture and republican freedom coexisted in his vision for the nation as an entity, both physical and moral, in which the government was subordinate to the economy. In his thought the nation was at once moral and natural, in its agrarian essence, which expressed itself through politics. The political environment in which the agricultural societies could operate was therefore important.[50]

Taylor shared the criticisms of Jefferson and many other Americans of the theories of Malthus, which were held to have been written for European situations and were therefore irrelevant to America, given its wide availability of land, but he also held Malthus's skills in high regard: 'the ablest of the English economists. He vindicated to a great extent the doctrines of Adam Smith', and later turned to him when defying arguments against the American tariff policy:

> He observes, that the fertility of land, either natural or acquired, may be said to
> be the only source of permanently high returns of capital. In the earlier periods
> of history, monopolies of commerce and manufactures produced brilliant effects,

---

[47]   John Taylor, *Arator; Being a Series of Agricultural Essays, Practical and Political; in Sixty One Numbers* (Georgetown: J.M. and J.B. Carter, 1813): 4.

[48]   *Arator; Being a Series of Agricultural Essays ... in Sixty One Numbers*, 18–19.

[49]   Cf. above, p. 153.

[50]   Taylor, *An Inquiry*, 395; Taylor, *Arator; Being a Series of Agricultural Essays, Practical and Political; in Sixty Four Numbers*, 4th ed. (Petersburg: 1818): 42.

but in modern Europe there is no possibility of large permanent returns being received from any other capitals, than those employed on land.[51]

Because of its unique circumstances, the United States had to adhere to a development project based on agriculture and economic freedom, as an alternative to the British way.

The agricultural societies were thus at the heart of an economic and political project for the local exercise of democracy and the realization of agrarian liberalism, as well as the articulation of a republican ideology espoused by an economic and intellectual elite whose interests Taylor represented, with his practical commitment and his political philosophy, as they found expression in the South.

Over a period of almost half a century and against a backdrop of profound political and economic change, both national and international, the American agricultural societies thus fed on the European economic culture of a long eighteenth century. Based on the model of similar institutions that emerged in several countries of Europe, they were the answer to the need to promote progress in agriculture and the spread of knowledge, in the Enlightenment awareness that economics was a science, whose purpose was to improve the material conditions of life. Like the economic societies of Europe, their response was made according to the specific reality in which they existed. The dynamic between the states and the national government brought about experiences that revealed how local elites and centralized power interacted. In this picture of the creation of a single market, the agricultural societies in the North and South had, despite their differing circumstances, similar characteristics.

Working within plans for economic development that pitted Jefferson's Republicans against Hamilton's Federalists, the societies became politically useful. British agriculture and agronomic literature were the essential benchmarks while, at the same time, French economic culture and Physiocracy, with its rigorous theory and agrarian model in particular, worked through some of the societies' exponents to raise awareness of an American national identity in opposition to Britain. In the panorama of eighteenth-century revolutionary events, which gave rise to the new state, the American agricultural societies were an outward manifestation of republican adherence and the consolidation of the new national reality.

---

[51]   Taylor, *Arator; Being a Series of Agricultural Essays ... in Sixty Four Numbers*, 160. On the American reactions to Malthus, cf. George J. Cady, 'The early American reaction to the theory of Malthus', *Journal of Political Economy*, 39 (1931): 601–32; Joseph J. Spengler, 'Malthusianism in the Late Eighteenth Century America', *American Economic Review*, 25 (1935): 697–707; Drew R. McCoy, 'Jefferson and Madison on Malthus: Population Growth in Jeffersonian Political Economy', *The Virginia Magazine of History and Biography*, 88 (1980)|: 259–76.

The Teaching of Economics

From Jefferson to Hamilton, from Gallatin to Tench Coxe, and from Franklin to Logan and to Taylor, the most complete reflections on political economy were published not in economic treatises but in pamphlets and other writings relating to political struggle. From their earliest days Americans had a political approach to economics and, at the same time, the opportunities offered by their exceptional environment determined their practical rather than speculative character.[52] With few exceptions, the works of political economy produced in the United States up to the opening three decades of the nineteenth century were conceived as textbooks by authors who taught in the colleges and universities, and so had nothing original to offer in terms of economic analysis.

The political value of teaching economics and the revolutionary potential of education, in the wake of an eighteenth-century Enlightenment tradition whose major American exponent was Jefferson and that survived the turn of the century, quickly led to the inclusion of economics in educational syllabuses. The usefulness of such teaching for a democracy like the United States was clearer than it was for other countries: 'Ought not the study of it, then, to be earlier and more extensive known, in our country especially? The protection of enterprise, and of wealth in some shape, forms the sole aim of all civil legislation'.[53]

On a popular level, following the success of Franklin's *Poor Richard's Almanack*, almanacs performed an educational function throughout the century, being aimed primarily at farmers. They conveyed a 'freehold concept' marked by the natural law's notion that the possession and cultivation of land was the most productive activity, the true source of wealth, the guarantor of independence and the foundation of democracy to consolidate national pride: 'I eat, drink, and sleep, and do what I please, the King in his Palace can only do these'.[54] From almanacs emerged an agrarian nationalism that unleashed the patriotic pride which

---

[52]   Beginning with Charles Dunbar's 1876 article, which, a hundred years after independence, denied that American economic literature had made any contribution to the development of political economy, the originality of American thought has been contested for a long time. Cf. for example: Charles F. Dunbar, 'Economic Science in America 1776–1876', *The North American Review*, vol. 122, no. 250 (January 1876): 124–54 (later republished in Charles Dunbar, *Economic Essays*, ed. O.M.W. Sprange (New York: Macmillan, 1904)); Joseph A. Schumpeter, *History of Economic Analysis* (New York: Oxford University Press, 1954): 514–19; Frank A. Fetter, 'The Early History of Political Economy in the United States', *Proceedings of the American Philosophical Society*, 87 (1943): 51–60; William J. Barber, 'The Position of the United States in the International Marketplace for Economic Ideas (1776–1900)', in *Political Economy and National Realities*, ed. Manuela Albertone and Alberto Masoero (Turin: Fondazione Luigi Einaudi, 1994): 255–67.

[53]   *North American Review*, vol. 25, no. 57 (October 1827): 409–10.

[54]   'The Almanack for 1761', in Nathaniel Ames, *The Essays, Humor, and Poems of Nathaniel Ames, Father and Son, of Dedham, Massachusetts, from their Almanacks, 1726–1775*, ed. Samuel Briggs (Cleveland, OH, 1891): 318. Cf also 'The Almanack for 1764',

contributed to the affirmation of the superiority of America and of its distinction from Europe. In the 1760s Nathaniel Ames's almanac was the template for a type of publication that served as a bridge between a cosmopolitan culture, through references to Locke, Voltaire, Hume and the classics, and a localized knowledge, which was directed at the education of a class of farmers:

> The Kingdoms of the Earth, and the Glory of the World will be transplanted into America: But the Study and Practice of Agriculture must go Hand in Hand with our Increase; for all the Policy and Learning in the World will not enable us to become a rich, flourishing and Happy People, without the Knowledge and Practice of Agriculture: The vast and noble Scene of Nature infinitely excel the pitiful Shifts of Policy. The Lands are here taken from a State of Nature, and we improve them by the Strength of Nature: when one Piece of Land is worn out, we throw it by: But the Art of Husbandry teaches us how to make these Lands continue fertile, and produce Crops by Management and Manure, and how to adapt the Manure to its proper Soil.[55]

As we have seen, the economic societies also had an important role to play as centres for the promulgation of knowledge, mainly about agriculture, but also for the stimulation of manufacturing. In 1790 the first American dictionary of agriculture was published with the intention of presenting technical knowledge adapted to the American experience and to its independence. An important figure was Jared Eliot, and the British agricultural model was deemed inapplicable to America. From this prospect the development of farming was presented, in the dictionary's entry on 'Agriculture', as a necessity, albeit one without a firm theoretical foundation.[56]

The formal teaching of political economics began later, at the beginning of the new century. It resulted from the interest of educators and leading public figures, who anticipated rather than articulated a need of society that was being felt in places where there existed monetary problems linked to banking, tariffs or foreign trade.[57] Ever since the colonial era college courses had followed precedents set

---

in *ibid.*, 355). Cf. Chester E. Eisinger, 'The Farmer in the Eighteenth Century Almanac', *Agricultural History*, 28 (1954): 107–12.

[55]   Nathaniel Ames, 'The Almanack for 1764', in *The Essays, Humor, and Poems of Nathaniel Ames*, 355. Other almanacs appeared towards the end of the century: Eben W. Judd's *The United States Almanack for 1786*, Robert B. Thomas's *The Farmer's Almanack 1796*, Richard Saunders's *Poor Richard Improved 1800*.

[56]   Samuel Deane, *The New-England Farmer; or, Georgical Dictionary* (Worcester, MA: I. Thomas, 1790): 9.

[57]   For an overview of the spread of economics teaching in the United States, cf. Edwin R.A. Seligman, 'The Early Teaching of Economics in the United States', in *Economics Essays: Contributed in Honour of John Bates Clark*, ed. Jacob H. Hollander (New York: The MacMillan Company, 1927): 283–321; Michael J.L. O'Connor, *Origins of Academic*

by English universities, and political economy was usually included under moral philosophy. Sometimes, however, despite the differences of the subjects, it was included in the preparation for the teaching of the law of nature and of nations, part of the training of public administrators. The first course entitled Political Economy was held in 1801 at the William and Mary College, albeit Bishop James Madison, the college's president and a professor of philosophy, had from 1784 given lessons in economics, using the *Wealth of Nations* as his textbook.

One should nevertheless distinguish between the title of courses and the material they dealt with. From the second half of the eighteenth century economic themes were studied within the range of political science, political arithmetic, jurisprudence and moral philosophy or, more specifically, that of geography, natural history and chemistry. Only after the War of 1812, and the difficulties of the American postwar economy and the Industrial Revolution in Britain, were the chairs in political economy instituted (between 1818 and 1828) to become part of the academic curricula. It was the colleges of the South – in an agrarian setting where the interests of agriculture predominated – which paid most attention to this. Whereas in the colleges of the North there was a moral aim to the teaching of political economy, in the South the civil value of economic science was central, as the curricula of the William and Mary College, South Carolina College and the University of Virginia attest.[58] When commenting on the ethical approach of economic questions, Francis Wayland – a theologian, professor of moral philosophy and, from 1828, the head teacher of political economy at Brown University – wrote in his *Elements of Political Economy*: 'The principles of Political Economy are so closely analogous to those of Moral Philosophy, that almost every question in the one, may be argued on grounds belonging to the other'. That notwithstanding, he made clear his desire to confront these questions only on their economic foundations.[59]

In 1818 John McVickar was appointed professor of moral philosophy and political economy at Columbia College, and his textbook, *Elements of Political Economy* (1837), became widely disseminated. The second chair – the first in any Southern state – was occupied by Thomas Cooper, who was professor of chemistry and political economy from 1824 at South Carolina College. The University of Virginia began to teach political economy in 1826, some nine years after Jefferson had included the subject in his proposals for the university. In 1819 the charter of the university provided for the inclusion of the discipline, which was put under the charge of the School of Law. The first chair, which Jefferson had

---

Economics in the United States (New York: Columbia University Press, 1944); William Barber, *Breaking the Academic Mould: Economists and American Higher Learning in the Nineteenth Century* (Middletown, CT: Wesleyan University Press, 1988).

[58]   Cf. Elbert V. Wills, 'Political Economy in the Early American College Curriculum', *The South Atlantic Quarterly*, 24/2 (1925): 131–53.

[59]   Francis Wayland, *Elements of Political Economy* (Boston: Gould and Lincoln, 1855), IV.

wanted for Cooper, who had asked to launch courses on political economy, was later included within the School of Moral Philosophy and given to George Tucker, who accentuated practicality in his teaching, as part of training for public service.[60]

In the years in which the American depression of 1819, which ensued from the postwar crisis, set in motion the protectionist movement on which the American system was worked out, the teaching of free trade prevailed in the American universities. The textbooks used were either European works or works that set out imported knowledge, which was, however, presented and revised in the light of America's specificity. The contents of the courses conformed to classical economic theory: Smith, Say, Malthus and Ricardo, the latter two being less influential than Say owing to the conspicuous difference between the British and American environmental realities. This situation favoured the spread of French economic thought, from Physiocracy to Say, both in the context of the history of economic theories and because of the social dimension of the French approach, aimed at moulding the national consciousness and an American culture independent from Britain, one of the objectives of the teaching of political economy.

Textbooks of Political Economy

Thomas Cooper was the first to make a clear-cut separation between the teaching of political economy and that of moral philosophy, seeing economic science as a subject suited for preparing students for participation in national life. His convinced agrarianism and his political engagement did not slacken, even after the period of open disagreement, when he fulfilled the role of professor at South Carolina College, which he took up in the 1820s.[61] His originality was manifest in the framework of a reflection that was guided – apart from the changes that led him to review his liberal positions in the final years of his life – by classical economics in which Physiocracy featured prominently. He continued to see Physiocracy as the foundation of the science of political economy and as a theory of the importance of agriculture, which remained valid, despite the limits of some of its principles, for providing the political dimension of an economic discourse.

This particular dimension led Cooper to give the French economic tradition a place in his textbooks: Say, Garnier, Destutt de Tracy and Ganilh were thus

---

[60]   In his letter to Priestley of 18 January 1800, in which he outlined his plan for the creation of a new university that would not be tied to any religious group, Jefferson intended to include agriculture and commerce among the subjects (Thomas Jefferson, *The Writings*, ed. Peterson, 1071). Presenting to Peter Carr, on 7 September 1814, his plan for the general reorganization of education in Virginia, he included in the 'general schools' political economy under the section of philosophy (Conant, *Thomas Jefferson and the Development of American Public Education*, 114). For Jefferson's various educational projects cf. also Honeywell, *The Educational Work of Thomas Jefferson*.

[61]   Cf. below, pp. 230–35.

included alongside British authors in order to reject protectionist ideas. In the *Lectures in the Elements of Political Economy*, of 1826 – the first work written as a textbook by an American, the preface of which argued for the need in America for courses on political economy – considerable space was given over to a detailed description of Quesnay's arguments concerning the primacy of agriculture and the harmony between economic activities: 'He contended strenuously for perfect freedom of employment among all classes, as the only means of encouraging that mutual competition which would lead every man to employ his faculties with the most Energy, and most effect, to the mutual benefit of all classes'.[62] Cooper also recognized the enduring merits of the French economists: 'This system of Dr. Quesnay got rid at once of all the evils of the mercantile and manufacturing system', even if he did point out the errors made by Physiocratic authors 'in ranking the merchant and the manufacturer among the non producers' and declaring value to be linked to land and not to labour.[63]

As we have seen, the William and Mary College played a pioneering part in the teaching of political economy, and in fact became characterized by it when, in 1827, Thomas Dew was appointed Professor of History, Metaphysics and Political Law. In 1829 he published a handbook, *Lectures on the restrictive System delivered to the Senior Political Class of the William and Mary College*, and in 1836 was elected president of the college. His *Lectures* became an authority in the exposition of the economic hypothesis used in the opposition of the South to protectionist theories, although it should not be forgotten that, in the debate that opened up in Virginia during 1831–2, he became the first major economist to defend slavery as a means of social control rather than on the basis of economic arguments.

For Dew the purpose of a systematic account of the developments of economic science was to demonstrate the repercussions of protectionist politics for an agrarian economy. He identified four different systems that had characterized thinking on the accumulation of wealth: the 'mercantile system' whereby wealth consisted in money and the State played an active role in the economy, the objective of which was to attain an active trade balance; the 'manufacturing system', a variation of the mercantile system, in which prosperity depended on manufacturing, which relied on protectionist measures; the 'agricultural system', which was opposed to the manufacturing system and in which wealth was derived from land; or 'the *produit net*, as Dr. Quesnai termed it'.[64] He gave a detailed description only of the last-named, by presenting the principles of Physiocracy, which came to equate to the fourth system, 'the free trade system, whose advocates contend that upon purely politico-economical principles, the prosperity and happiness of the world,

[62]   Thomas Cooper, *Lectures on the Elements of Political Economy* (Columbia, SC: D.E. Sweeny, 1826): 8.

[63]   Cooper, *Lectures on the Elements of Political Economy*, 8.

[64]   Thomas Dew, *Lectures on the Restrictive System Delivered to the Senior Political Class of the William and Mary College* (Richmond: S. Shepherd and Co., 1829), 1.

and of each nation, would be greatest when each nation traded with others freely and fairly'.[65]

In Dew's history of economic ideas, delivered in terms of gradual progress, Smith was placed with the Physiocrats for having been heavily influenced by their approach and their mistakes: 'Dr. Smith seems never to have thoroughly seen the errors of the economists; the veil was only in part lifted from his eyes. Hence his constant predilection for agriculture, and his preference for the home trade over the foreign'.[66] In the continuous increment of economic science, Smith's ideas were held to have been rendered obsolete by political changes resulting from the American and French Revolutions, which had brought about new forms of government and fresh ideas favouring the advancement of political economy along scientific lines.[67] Indeed, here Dew made reference to economic ideas that came out of the French Revolution – those of Say and Destutt de Tracy – to bolster his claims about free trade, which clashed with the protectionist school of Mathew Carey. As a Virginian, Dew feared that national unity would fracture under the protectionist pressures of the manufacturing North and his work did in fact influence subsequent tariff reductions.

The first American edition of the *Wealth of Nations* was published in 1789 and, as we have seen, from 1784 it became a text used in American colleges and universities. British classical economics was represented by the widely read *Outlines of Political Economy* by McVickar of Columbia College. His work was reprinted in 1825 as part of McCulloch's article in the *Encyclopedia Britannica* and was the core text at Columbia for many decades and the first textbook edited by an American cleric.[68] In this picture of free trade and the Ricardian theory of wages, the reconstruction of the path of economics gave ample space to the Physiocratic authors:

> The celebrated M. Quesnay, a physician attached to the court of Louis XV, has the unquestionable merit of being the first who attempted to investigate and analyze the sources of wealth, with the intention of ascertaining the fundamental principles of Political Economy, and who gave it a systematic form, and raised it to the rank of a science.[69]

---

[65]   Dew, *Lectures on the Restrictive System*, 2.

[66]   Dew, *Lectures on the Restrictive System*, 16

[67]   Dew, *Lectures on the Restrictive System*, 16. Say was probably the modern economist to whom Dew referred to here in support of his argument. Cf. Jean-Baptiste Say, *Histoire abrégée des progrès de l'économie politique*, in Say, *Cours complet d'économie politique pratique*, Edition variorum des deux éditions (1828–1840), ed. Emmanuel Blanc, Pierre-Henry Goutte, Gilles Jacoud, Jean-Pierre Potier, Michèle Sacquin, Jean-Michel Servet, Philippe Steiner, André Tiran, 2 vols. (Paris: Economica, 2010), vol. II, 1271.

[68]   Cf. Michael O'Connor, *Origins of Academic Economics*, 154–5.

[69]   John McVickar, *Outlines of Political Economy, Being a Republication of the Article upon that Subject Contained in the Edinburgh Supplement to the Encyclopedia Britannica* (New York: Wilder and Campbell, 1825): 35.

Apart from Quesnay, the article also referred to Mirabeau, Le Mercier de la Rivière ('commentator of this system'), Baudeau and Du Pont de Nemours, recommending the latter's *Notice sur les économistes* (included in his edition of the works of Turgot) and providing a list of his major works. The group also included Condorcet, Raynal and Turgot, whose *Réflexions sur la formation et la distribution des richesses* was considered to be the best work of political economy prior to Smith.[70] Even though Physiocracy had not arrived at a proper understanding of income and value, the contribution that it had made in favour of free trade was appreciated. The originality of Quesnay was emphasized and, although Locke might have been a noteworthy authority, 'there is an immeasurable difference between the suggestion of Locke and the well digested system of Quesnay'.[71]

Alongside these works by British or American authors the most widespread was Say's *Traité d'économie politique*, which appeared in the American edition edited by Clement Biddle in 1821.[72] It was adopted by Yale and Harvard as early as 1825, was reprinted until 1880 and was the first European text edited and annotated for educational purposes and one of the first textbooks widely available, having appeared in an English translation published in Britain by Charles R. Prinsep in 1821, the same year as the American edition.[73]

The educational task that Say ascribed to political economy, and the perception that his treatise served well as a textbook, meant that it was perfectly placed to make inroads into American academia.[74] Say dominated the American book market and through his influence on Henry Carey helped to shape the first complete American theoretical system.[75] He extolled the harmony of social interests, had an optimistic view of economic prosperity, understood the reciprocity and interdependence of the various economic sectors and, in keeping with the French tradition, paid more attention than British economists did to problems of distribution and saw no threat in Malthusian theories – all of which made him well suited to American circumstances. For fifteen years, his book was a core text of universities in the North, and he himself was appreciated for his Calvinist roots and criticism of Napoleon, and not only for his support of free trade. The dissemination of his

---

[70]   McVickar, *Outlines of Political Economy*, 39.

[71]   McVickar, *Outlines of Political Economy*, 38.

[72]   Jean- Baptiste Say, *A Treatise on Political Economy* (Boston: Wells and Lilly, 1821), which includes a translation of the introduction and additional notes by Clement C. Biddle. On the events leading to the publication in America, cf. below, p. 263 ff.

[73]   Detailed information on the adoption of Say's book can be found in Michael J. L. O'Connor, *Origins of Academic Economics*, 120–35.

[74]   On the methodological and educational value of Say's economic work, cf. André Tiran, 'Jean-Baptiste Say: l'écriture et ses pièges', in *Governare il mondo: L'economia come linguaggio della politica nell'Europa del Settecento*, 103–22.

[75]   On Say's influence on Henry Carey's thought, cf. Ernest Teilhac, *Histoire de la pensée économique aux Etats-Unis au dix-neuvième siècle* (Paris: Recueil Sirey, 1928): 94–111.

ideas in the South, where his positions against slavery met with resistance, took much longer.

As we will see, Jefferson played an important role in the publication of Say, whom he had wanted as a professor at the University of Virginia, and organized a careful editorial strategy aimed at introducing French economic thought to America for anti-British and anti-Ricardian purposes.[76] For the same reason he encouraged the spread of the ideas of Destutt de Tracy, who was less successful than Say partly because of the radicalism of his philosophical positions. Jefferson had wanted to see de Tracy's *Treatise on Political Economy* – published in 1817 in an edition on which Jefferson collaborated – adopted as the textbook for the University of Virginia, but Tucker used the works of Smith and Say instead.

Another important vehicle for the ideas of Say in America was Jane Marcet's *Conversations on political economy*, which was published in London in 1816 and in American editions in Philadelphia (1817), New York (1820) and Boston (1828).[77] Cooper used the work as a textbook for the first year of his lessons at the College of South Carolina and in other colleges, before the English translation of Say's *Traité* in 1821. And it was used as the text through which to make known Say, who was easier to understand than Smith.

Say's *Catéchisme d'économie politique* had anticipated the educational literary form of Marcet by only a year. *Conversations* was written as a series of questions and answers and was one of the first vulgarizations of political economy. Its dominant themes were that of the harmony of the economy, of the right distinction between rich and poor, of the benefit of accumulated capital for the lower classes, and of the legitimacy of property, although it rejected slavery and defended working conditions in factories. The work was translated into French,[78] and Say admired its author, the daughter of a Swiss merchant living in London, to whom he wrote:

> You have worked much more efficiently than I to popularize and to spread extremely useful ideas; and you will succeed Madame, since you have built on the strength of science. ... It is not possible to stay closer to the truth with more charm; to clothe much indisputable principles with a more elegant style. I am an old soldier who asks only to die in your light.[79]

---

[76] Cf.below, p. 267.

[77] Jane Haldimand Marcet, *Conversations on Political Economy, in Which the Elements of that Science are Familiarly Explained* (London: Hurst, Rees, Orne, and Brown, 1816); cf. also the recent edition, *Conversations on the Nature of Political Economy*, ed. Evelyn L. Forget (New Brunswick: Transaction, 2009).

[78] Jane Haldimand Marcet, *Conversations sur l'économie politique, dans lesquelles on expose d'une manière familière les éléments de cette science*, trans. from English (Geneva: J.J. Paschoud, 1817).

[79] Quoted in Bette Polkinghorn, 'A Communication: An Unpublished Letter of J.-B. Say', *Eastern Economic Journal* 11 (1985): 167–70.

They shared the same pedagogical vocation, and Marcet, who declared in her preface that she had followed Smith, Say, Malthus and Sismondi, quoted untranslated passages from the 'excellent treatise on political economy'. Many similarities with Say can be recognized in the *Conversations*. Marcet concurred with Say's theory of value, which was opposed to that of British classical economists, and the *Conversations* thereby became an avenue for propagating French economic thought in America at the popular level.

Economic Knowledge

During the years in which French economic thought began its entry into American academic circles, resumed discussions on Physiocracy or Physiocratic themes also travelled across the Atlantic from France and Britain. The first two decades of the nineteenth century were the years when, in France, Physiocratic theories were reconsidered in the light of Smith's interpretations and then consigned once and for all to the history of economic thought as a passing phase.[80] Harsh criticism against the dogmatism of Physiocratic principles was made by Say and Destutt de Tracy, while the elderly Du Pont de Nemours, in the most intense period of his relationship with Jefferson, argued that there was a line of continuity of French economic thought in the study of the economy and restated the relationship between economics and politics as put forward by the Physiocrats. Then, in 1817, he intervened directly in the British debate with his *Examen du livre de M. Malthus*.

Charles Ganilh discussed the Physiocratic theories in great detail, albeit while criticizing them, and he declared that the apologia Germain Garnier had made for them in his notes to the 1802 French translation of Smith warranted close attention.[81] Ganilh was translated into English, and Cooper, who referred to him in his *Lectures*, included his name among those, such as the French authors Say, Garnier and Destutt de Tracy, who had contributed to the advancement of the science of economics.[82] Apart from the limits of their theories, Ganilh recognized that the Physiocrats 'flattered the pride of landowners, that important class entitled to so much regard and consideration', an approach to which the Americans were particularly susceptible.[83] The French economists undoubtedly remained the

---

[80]   Cf. Philippe Steiner, 'Quels principes pour l'économie politique? Charles Ganilh, Germain Garnier, Jean-Baptiste Say et la critique de la physiocratie', in *La diffusion internationale de la physiocratie (XVIIIe–XIXe)*, ed. Bernard Delmas, Thierry Demals and Philippe Steiner (Grenoble: Presses Universitaires, 1995): 209–30.

[81]   Charles Ganilh, *An Inquiry Into the Various Systems of Political Economy*, trans. from French by D. Boileau (London: H. Colburn, 1812): 75 (1st French edition Paris: Xhrouet, Déterville, Lenormant, Petit, 1809).

[82]   Thomas Cooper, *Lectures on the Elements of Political Economy*, 2nd ed. (New York: A.M. Kelley, 1830): 18–19.

[83]   Ganilh, *An Inquiry*, 64.

founders of the 'agricultural system', even if no British author still referred to them. The one exception was William Spence who, with his *Britain Independent of Commerce*, shared their idea that land was the source of all wealth.[84]

It was in fact around Spence's work that there developed a discussion which, from Mill to Torrens to Malthus, following the position taken by the *Edinburgh Review*, reignited the debate on Physiocracy, whose outdated and unoriginal recovery Spence was accused of using in his extolment of a policy which focused on agriculture in defence of the British response to the blockade by Napoleon.[85]

The authority of the *Edinburgh Review* was recognized in the United States. Jefferson praised the periodical, 'the ablest critics of the age,'[86] and subscribed to the American reprint published in New York and Boston in 1809.[87] The presence in America of the publication, which aimed to raise awareness of political economy, provided another avenue through which to keep alive interest in eighteenth-century French economic thought. Among the earliest initiatives of the group that was to make up the *Edinburgh Review* was the draft 1800 project (later abandoned) to produce an edition of the works of Turgot, an author who continued to arouse interest and who was also known through Condorcet's *Vie de Turgot*, which the British public could read in an English translation.[88] Members of the group were involved in a debate, echoed in the pages of the journal, which in its criticisms of Smith re-posited Physiocratic ideas in a new context. Francis Horner, one of the promoters of the Turgot project, believed that there was a superstitious veneration of Smith and his mistakes and, in the *Edinburgh Review*, advanced his criticism and expressed his appreciation of Physiocratic authors,[89] whom he defended from the accusation of being among those to blame for the French Revolution, noting instead the progressive aspects of the Revolution.

While they had been overtaken on the level of economic analysis, Physiocratic ideas, conceived as a theorization of the primacy of agriculture, still circulated in the early nineteenth century. In his response to Mill's *Commerce defended*, Spence wrote: 'I thought important to insist upon the truth of the main tenet of

---

[84]   Ganilh, *An Inquiry*, 75.

[85]   Thomas R. Malthus, 'Spence on Commerce', *Edinburgh Review* (11 January 1808): 429–48; D. Buchanan and Francis Jeffrey, 'Spence on Agriculture and Commerce', *ibid.* (14 April 1809): 50–60.

[86]   Jefferson to John Waldo, Monticello, 16 August 1813, in Jefferson, *The Writings*, ed. Peterson, 1295.

[87]   On the *Edinburgh Review* see Biancamaria Fontana, *Rethinking the Politics of Commercial Society: The Edinburgh Review, 1802–1832* (Cambridge: Cambridge University Press, 1985).

[88]   Cf. below, pp. 206–8.

[89]   Francis Horner, 'Canard's *Principes d'Economie politique*', *Edinburgh Review* (1 January 1803): 431–50.

the Economists, that the soil is the grand source of wealth',[90] even though he considered 'this axiom' to be unfeasible. He recognized manufacturing as an important reason for the prosperity of agriculture and asserted his independence of the 'French economists': 'there can exist no reason why I should embrace the conclusions of another, merely because I admit the truth of his premises'.[91] Spence cited Malthus, a source not suspected of harbouring any sympathy for the Physiocrats, in support of their conviction that agriculture was the primary origin of wealth, and pointed to Franklin as a believer of their principle that agricultural work was the measure of all other labour.[92]

In *Britain independent of commerce* Spence had written: 'Dr. Smith, though in words he denied this doctrine of the Economists, and though he declined "entering into the disagreeable discussion of the metaphysical arguments by which they support their very ingenious theory," has, in fact, virtually admitted its truth'.[93] The entire work laid out the Physiocratic theories in full, highlighting how their underestimation of the role of manufacturing would only apply to a country like the United States, where land was cheap and agriculture had no need to be stimulated by manufacturing.[94] He quoted Condorcet and Godwin as extollers of a golden age in which the small landowner was able to satisfy all his spiritual needs.[95]

William Cobbett, Priestley's adversary, published in his *Political Register* extracts from Spence and the debate around his work, and placed this line of thought in direct relation with the policies pursued by America during Jefferson's presidency of the same years:

> 'perish commerce' is perhaps the motto of the American president. … During his residence in France he became enamoured of the doctrines of the Oeconomists and Turgot, and he wishes, pitably, to try the experiment of a nation relinquishing foreign commerce, living upon the produce of its own territories, and confirming itself to the pursuit of agriculture. If such be his wishes, we know not that he

---

[90] William Spence, *Agriculture the source of the Wealth of Britain; a reply to the objections urged by Mr Mill, the Edinburgh reviewers and others against the doctrines of the pamphlet, entitled "Britain independent of commerce"* (London: T. Cadell, W. Davies, 1808), 6. Cf. James Mill, *Commerce Defended. An Answer to the Arguments by Which Mr Spence, Mr Cobbett and Others Have Attempted to Prove That Commerce is Not a Source of National Wealth* (London: C. and R. Baldwin, 1808).

[91] Spence, *Agriculture the source of the Wealth of Britain*, 9.

[92] Spence, *Agriculture the source of the Wealth of Britain*, 46, 58.

[93] William Spence, *Britain independent of commerce; or Proofs deduced from an investigation into the true causes of the wealth of nations, that our riches, prosperity and power are derived from resources inherent in ourselves and would not be affected, even though our commerce were annihilated*, 6th ed., corrected and enlarged (London: W. Savage for T. Cadell and W. Davies, 1808): 41.

[94] Spence, *Britain independent of commerce*, 16.

[95] Spence, *Britain independent of commerce*, 24.

could have found out a more likely means of realizing them than by going to war with this country.[96]

The indirect presence of French economic culture and the agrarian economic model developed by the Physiocrats thus arrived at the first systematic American theories of political economy. Lauderdale was a decisive influence on the reflections of Daniel Raymond who, in his *Thoughts on Political Economy* of 1820, outlined the first American treatise in opposition to the British classical school.[97] He derived from Lauderdale's *Inquiry into the Nature and Origin of Public Wealth* the distinction between individual and national wealth, which formed the basis of his concept of the American system. He had a thorough knowledge of Smith, Malthus, Ricardo, Ganilh and Say and it was through Lauderdale that he indirectly engaged with the Physiocrats.

In Lauderdale's critique of the mercantile system and the assimilation of money to wealth, expressed in his *Inquiry*, there were long and frequent references to the writings of the Physiocrats, including Quesnay's *Maximes*, Mirabeau's *Philosophie rurale*, the *Physiocratie* and Turgot' *Traité sur la formation de la richesse*, making particular mention of Turgot's theory of capital and the role of savings.[98] Lauderdale's work also contained as an appendix an excerpt from a speech by Butré to the Société d'agriculture in Paris.[99] He recognized that theories on the prevalence of trade as a source of wealth had been dominant in Britain. The Physiocrats in France, and Smith in Britain, had refuted these theories, although the French economists had not been convincing in their argument that net produce was the only form of profit and Smith had not taken a firm position.[100] There was nevertheless another possible reading to justify such theories:

> If we reject the doctrine of the Oeconomists, it is in vain we look for a decided and precise opinion upon the origin of wealth, in any modern work on public

---

[96]   *Political Register*, XII (12 December 1807): 918. In a letter to the newspaper, Spence, defending himself from the accusation of plagiarism made against him by Cobbett, acknowledged that he had followed the ideas of the Physiocrats, 'I profess merely to place these doctrines in a new point of view, to restrict them in some respects, to elucidate them more fully in others, and to deduce some conclusions from them, which, as far as I knew, were novel'. (*Ibid.*, 922).

[97]   On Raymond and Lauderdale, cf. Charles P. Neill, *Daniel Raymond: An Early Chapter in the History of Economic Theory* (Baltimore: The Johns Hopkins Press, 1897).

[98]   James Maitland, Earl of Lauderdale, *Inquiry into the Nature and Origin of Public Wealth, and into the Means and Causes of its Increase* (Edinburgh: A. Constable and Co.; London: T.N. Longman and O. Rees, 1804): 125–27, 158, 210.

[99]   *Extract form the Apology made for the distinction betwixt the Great and the Little Mode of Cultivation, by M. Butré, of the Societies of Agriculture of Paris and Orleans* (Lauderdale, *Inquiry into the Nature and Origin of Public Wealth*, 474–7).

[100]   Lauderdale, *Inquiry into the Nature and Origin of Public Wealth*, 114–16.

oeconomy, and it is impossible not to think, that the anxiety of the oeconomists to overthrow that system, which regards commerce as the sole source of opulence, has led them, in rejecting labour and capital as original sources of wealth, beyond the bounds that reason authorises.[101]

The political implications of this reading of Physiocracy were not ignored: 'The liberal doctrines to which this theory led, by inculcating the impropriety of all legislative restraints, or interference in commercial transaction, must command approbation'.[102]

The American System, a unique doctrine that combined external protectionism and internal free trade, was developed as a means of distancing the country from the roots of the British theoretical tradition, against the backdrop of the embargo acts and war blockades of 1808 to 1815. By paralysing trade and provoking the increase of manufactured goods, these led to the growth of manufacturing in New England. The post-war depression of 1816 to 1820 brought about a movement calling for higher tariffs in defence of domestic manufacturers. In keeping with an approach centred on economic protection, which harked back to Hamilton and Tench Coxe,[103] Carey launched the American school, influencing with his nationalist philosophy the Americanization of American textbooks, at the same time as free trade theories dominated the early teachings of political economy.[104]

Carey's protectionist theories were rejected by academic circles, which mostly followed classical British thought: Cooper, Tucker, McVickar and Francis Wayland – all of whom held teaching roles in political economy and were authors of textbooks – belonged to the free trade school, even if not all of them accepted in full the Mill–Ricardo approach, which from 1800 to 1825 was elaborated in the particular circumstances of Britain. American conditions were different, and the reception of British thought occurred within the context of an appreciation of the profound dissimilarity of American and British authors. Many Americans, whether they were protectionists or supporters of free trade, repudiated the distinction made between capital and land, income and interest. Given its widespread availability, land in America was considered, like other forms of wealth, to be an object of

---

[101]   Lauderdale, *Inquiry into the Nature and Origin of Public Wealth*, 120.

[102]   Lauderdale, *Inquiry into the Nature and Origin of Public Wealth*, 120–21.

[103]   On Tench Coxe as a precursor of the American system, and on his friendship with Jefferson, cf. Jacob E. Cooke, 'Tench Coxe, American Economist: the Limitation of Economic Thought in the Early National Era," *Pennsylvania History*, 42 (1976): 267–89. On Coxe, a Loyalist, then Federalist, then Republican supporter of agriculture, but one convinced that the development of manufacturing guaranteed a nationwide market, cf. Tench Coxe, 'An Address to the Assembly of the friends of American Manufacturers', *American Museum*, II (1787): 253–5; Tench Coxe, *A view of the United States of America. In a series of papers written at various times, in the years between 1787 and 1794* (Philadelphia: 1794).

[104]   James N. Green, *Mathew Carey, Publisher and Patriot* (Philadelphia: The Library Company of Philadelphia, 1985).

trade and a form of capital.[105] The endurance of French economic thought should be viewed against this background. At the same time, the religious sensibility of America contributed to the vision of a harmony of interests between economic activities, which spurned the pessimism of the British, from Malthus to Ricardo. Thus elements of the language and culture of the eighteenth century survived in a totally transformed theoretical context, compared to that of the previous century.

Raymond maintained that the foundations of political economy were not to be found in universal doctrines but rather in national needs, and that Americans found themselves in a more favourable situation than Europeans for the study of political economy.[106] For Raymond, who leaned heavily on Lauderdale, 'no argument is necessary to prove that the earth is the only source of private as well as public wealth'.[107] The notion of the superiority of tillers of the soil had roots that spread far back in time, yet were still close to Franklin: 'Agriculturists are a superior class of men to manufacturers. They enjoy more vigorous health, and possess more personal courage. They have more elevated liberal minds. It is more congenial to man's nature, to be abroad in the fields'.[108] From this perspective, Raymond attributed a role to the Physiocrats that was not only historic:

> The theory of the Economists as to the source of wealth comes nearer to the truth than any other. They say, 'Let the sovereign and the nation always remember that the earth is the sole source of riches and it is agriculture that multiplies those riches.' Now if they had said 'labour' instead of 'agriculture' they would have been right.[109]

Raymond's doctrine interpreted the opposition between the American and European economies, expressed in a reaction to the classical school. Americans remained tied for longer to the eighteenth-century natural economy, which had its most complete formulation in the agrarianism of the Physiocrats. Raymond was interested in an economy marked by prosperity and development, calling for its protection, and, in his dynamism, he opposed Malthus and Ricardo with a critique that was original compared to European ideas. His starting point was

---

[105]   On the American critiques of the Malthus–Ricardo theory, cf. John R. Turner, *The Ricardian Rent Theory in Early Economics* (New York: New York University Press, 1921).

[106]   Daniel Raymond, *The Elements of Political Economy*, 2 vols., 2nd ed. (Baltimore: F. Lucas, E.J. Coale, 1823): vol. I, 397; 'Whenever the true foundations of this science shall be laid, they will be laid in America. As our country has had the high honour of laying the true foundations of civil government, it must also have the honour of laying the true foundations of political economy.' (*Ibid.*, 395).

[107]   Raymond, *The Elements*, vol. I, 92.

[108]   Raymond, *The Elements*, vol. I, 215–16.

[109]   Raymond, *The Elements*, vol. I, 96–7. The exact reference is to the third of the *Maximes générales du gouvernement économique d'un royaume agricole* by Quesnay of the first volume of the Leyde edition (1768) of *Physiocratie*.

the distinction, taken from Lauderdale, between national and individual interests, which led him (still following Lauderdale) to consider Smith's ideas to be ill defined and vacillating, and those of Say, who still confused the two levels, to be insufficient.[110] This viewpoint aligned him with the Physiocrats, albeit by way of Lauderdale, and led him to admire their ideas, in spite of the limitation of their theory of value and of the exclusive productivity of agricultural labour.[111] He was close to them and to Smith in distinguishing between land, the source of wealth, and labour, which was its cause, subordinating labour to the land.[112] Yet he was by then quite distant from the eighteenth-century context of Physiocracy: 'the Economists mistook the interests of the agriculturists for the interests of the nation' and the partisans of the trade system had done the same by prioritizing the interests of the merchants.[113]

Raymond held that Smith had never entirely freed himself from the influence of the Physiocrats, and that their differences were in fact divergent developments of the same principle.[114] He also believed that if land was the only source of wealth, then agricultural labour was the only productive work, superior to all others from a social, political and economic point of view. If in his theory agriculture dominated both production and distribution, he nevertheless distinguished himself from the Physiocrats by recognizing that income followed the law of supply and demand, that there had to be a balance between income and wages, and that the state had to intervene to ensure economic balance by dint of a protectionist policy applicable to all activities. Even if they had come close to discovering the true source of wealth, for Raymond the Physiocrats had still been far from defining the basics of economics, since they had misconstrued the distinction between 'source' and 'cause'. In this he again recalled Lauderdale, and his idea that land, labour and capital were the three sources of wealth.[115]

Even Henry Carey, the American economist, whose fame crossed the Atlantic,[116] still put forward his reflections within the coordinates of eighteenth-century economic naturalism. The development of an American economic theory meant that he, too, was opposed to the Malthus–Ricardo line of thinking, disassociating

---

[110]   Raymond, *The Elements*, vol. I, 63, 155–6, 158, 161, 163–4, 172–3.

[111]   Raymond, *The Elements*, vol. I, 84. Teilhac believed Raymond's ideas went back as far as Physiocracy, seeing a line that went from the French economists, through Raymond, up to the socialism of Otto Effertz (Teilhac, *Histoire de la pensée économique*, 48–49); cf. Otto Effertz, *Le principe pono-physiocratique et son application à la question sociale* (Paris: Rivière, 1913).

[112]   Raymond, *The Elements*, vol. I, ch. V, 'The Source and Cause of Wealth', 89 ff.

[113]   Raymond, *The Elements*, vol. I, 158.

[114]   Raymond, *The Elements*, vol. I, ch. XVII, 'The Agricultural System contrasted with "The Wealth of Nations"', 370 ff.

[115]   Raymond, *The Elements*, vol. I, 97.

[116]   Cf. Abraham D.H. Kaplan, *Henry Charles Carey: A Study in American Economic Thought* (Baltimore: The Johns Hopkins Press, 1931).

Smith from the same tradition of thought. It was just this reference to a natural order, and the need to understand it, that served as an introduction to his critical discussion of Malthus and Ricardo: 'the existence of a simple and beautiful law of nature, governing man in all his efforts for the maintenance and improvement of his condition, a law so powerful and universal that escape from it is impossible, but which, nevertheless, has therefore remained unnoticed'.[117]

For Carey, the greatest theorist of the American System, who started out as a liberalist, Physiocracy and the tradition of French naturalism still had value, in a context far behind in time and space: 'The political economist examines and states what are the laws of nature, and indicates what are the disturbing causes which have in so many cases interfered with their action'.[118] All the same, he shared Smith's subordination of foreign trade to domestic trade, seeing it as a reinforcement of agriculture.[119] Economic science and American optimism worked together to defy British economic orthodoxy. For him, too, the land was a form of capital and the natural order of cultivation went from the poorest lands to the richest, in opposition to Ricardo's theory of income and as the American reality bore witness.

Carey was indebted to the sociology of Comte, the naturalism of the Physiocrats and Say's harmony and his 'économie politique pratique', for his interpretation of the relationship between economics and politics and his vision of economics as a social science. He drew upon Say for the attention given to the consumer and to distribution, despite the differences of their positions.[120] In his *Principles of Political Economy* he recognized that Say attributed importance, in relation to production, to natural agents, citing the passage from the *Treatise* that criticized Smith's principle that labour alone was the measure of wealth, and underlined the contrast between Smith and Physiocratic theory, according to which labour did not produce value. He reported the judgement of Say, which considered that both positions had been reduced to rigid systems, while observation of the facts showed that several factors interacted with one another, while recognizing, with Say's own words, that 'the chief, though by no means the only one, is land capable of cultivation'.[121]

Carey helped to spread Say's ideas. It was he who, in 1817, with his father, Mathew, was the first to publish an American edition of the *Catéchisme d'économie politique*.[122] His protectionism, intended to benefit both manufacturers and agriculture, was connected to the idea of agriculture as the essence of social

---

[117]   Henry Carey, *The Past, the Present and the Future* (Philadelphia: Carey and Hart, 1848): 5.

[118]   Henry Carey, *Principles of Political Economy*, vol. I (Philadelphia: Carey, Lea and Blanchard, 1837): xiv.

[119]   Carey, *Principles of Political Economy*, vol. I, 95.

[120]   On Carey and Say, cf. Teilhac, *Histoire de la pensée économique*, 55–111.

[121]   Carey, *Principles of Political Economy*, 218.

[122]   Jean-Baptiste Say, *Catechism of political economy, or familiar conversations on the manner in which wealth is produced, distributed and consumed in society, By J.B. Say, professor of political economy in the Athénée Royal of Paris, Knight of St Wolodomir of*

science, and was fuelled by his interest in French economic thought, which persisted in America in the early nineteenth century as the search for national identity and an American political and economic culture.

In the setting of a country of exceptional characteristics and facing increasing needs, agriculture was a topic that engaged enlightened American public opinion influenced by a cosmopolitan culture. Two different economic models and economic cultures were competing with one another. The American economic societies paid great attention to a French agricultural system they believed fitted American conditions better than British agronomic practice. American academia was up-to-date with the most recent developments, despite the fact that the teaching of political economy had begun late and only came after the progress of economic science. Nevertheless the attention paid to French economic ideas persisted not only within an historical perspective, but as the expression of an alternative economic thought to that of Britain, as the success as a university textbook of Say's *Treatise on Political Economy* proved. This attitude existed within an ever-changing political scenario. From the outbreak of the American Revolution to the first decades of the nineteenth-century America was a protagonist in a transatlantic exchange of ideas in which the economic foundations of French political rationalism fostered revolutionary ideas throughout France and America but which also accepted contributions from strands of English radicalism.

Russia, member of the societies of Zurich, Bologna, etc..., and author of a treatise of political economy, trans. from French by John Richter (Philadelphia: M. Carey and Son, 1817).

Chapter 7
The English Jacobins:
A Three-Way Interrelation Between France, Britain and America

Just as the years that Thomas Jefferson spent in France accelerated his detachment from the British political tradition, spread by Montesquieu's Anglophilia, so Benjamin Franklin's stay led him to find in French economic thought, and Physiocracy in particular, the theoretical tools that marked a turning point in his own economic views and led to reject the English model. However, during their stays in Europe both men also forged decisive links with members of the English radical religious dissent and when, in the 1790s, many Dissenters helped to swell the tide of politically and religiously motivated emigration to America, thereby having a significant impact on the conflict between Federalists and Republicans by supporting Jefferson's rise to the presidency, English radicalism and the American political struggle became intertwined.

It is hard to estimate to what degree such links helped the development of republican agrarian democracy, and how much the Dissenters contributed the Americans' 'rhetoric of accusation', which was aimed at creating a society fundamentally different from that of Great Britain, in keeping with the aspirations of the Founding Fathers, and was characterized by its opposition to British corruption,[1] its denunciation of pauperism, its middle class opposition to aristocracy and the accumulation of property, its exaltation of the agrarian model and free trade, and its rejection of privilege and deference.[2] The difficulty in gauging the extent of the English radicals' influence arises from the sheer number of personal and intellectual exchanges, the diversity of currents of religious dissent and individual personalities, and the distinction that must be made between the old Commonwealth radicalism of the 1760s and 1770s and the new radicalism of the 1790s.[3]

---

[1] Cf. John P. Diggins, *The Lost Soul of American Politics* (New York: Basic Books, 1984).

[2] Cf. Frank Lambert, *The Founding Fathers and the Place of Religion in America* (Princeton: Princeton University Press, 2003).

[3] Cf. James E. Bradley, *Religion, Revolution and English Radicalism* (Cambridge: Cambridge University Press, 1990); Knud Haakonssen, ed., *Enlightenment and Religion: Rational Dissent in Eighteenth-Century Britain* (Cambridge: Cambridge University Press, 1996); Peter Clark, *British Clubs and Societies 1580–1800: The Origins of an*

Despite this complexity, it is nevertheless possible to identify certain elements that characterized this relationship. From the free market of religion to the free market of economy, the confluence of economic and political thought marked the democratic evolution of those English Dissenters who either became American, moved to America or looked to the American example. The moral dimension of economic life, the goal of bringing about an economic revolution that would make it possible to overcome the conflict between the right to bread and the right to work,[4] and the centrality of a commercial society capable of reconciling trade and agriculture, offered Jefferson and Jeffersonian ideology a form of radicalism that combined democracy and economic development. The criticisms made by the English radicals countered the British economic model and its mercantilist policies with a vision of a republican political economy and the correlation between economic freedom and the abolition of privilege.[5]

These positions were characterized and nurtured by a cosmopolitan openness that makes it possible to follow, within the international circulation of ideas over many years, a triangulation between France, Britain and America in an exchange flowing not in one direction only but between different environments and cultures. In the complexity of this interchange, certain individuals, whose ideas and experiences can be followed through different stages of evolution, supported a radical republican tradition based on the relationship between economics and politics, which had been developed in part by French economic authors before 1789 and had been further developed by political practices that had emerged after the outbreak of the French Revolution. The democratic maturation of the American Republicans' political project was stimulated by the encounter between strands of English radicalism and the social dimension of French economic thinking, a point of contact that has been less explored than the better-known connection with the 'country' ideology. France occupied a central position in the critical and comparative reflection on Britain, and the French Revolution marked a decisive moment that, in the course of the struggles between the Federalists and the Republicans of the 1790s, brought to the fore the incompatibility of the political

---

Associational World (Oxford: Clarendon Press, 2000). Among the different historiographic interpretations, cf. Colin Bonwick, *English Radicals and the American Revolution* (Chapel Hill: University of North Carolina Press, 1977), one that accentuates the conservatism of English radicalism. For a reading that highlights the radical ideology, cf. George Rude, *Wilkes and Liberty: A Social Study of 1763 to 1774* (Oxford: Clarendon Press, 1962); John Brewer, *Party Ideology and Popular Politics at the Accession of George III* (Cambridge: Cambridge University Press, 1976); Henry T. Dickinson, *British Radicalism and the French Revolution, 1789–1815* (Oxford: B. Blackwell, 1985).

[4]   In relation to this, an interesting marginal reflection on the notion of moral economy put forward by Edward Thompson is the essay by Elizabeth Fox Genovese, 'The many faces of moral economy: a Contribution to a Debate', *Past and Present*, 58 (1973): 161–8.

[5]   Cf. Thomas Cooper, *A Manual of Political Economy* (Washington: Duff Green, 1834): 48.

and economic models of France and Britain. Among the English religious and political dissent groupings, the American Revolution opened up new expectations, and the French Revolution led to an acceleration of their radicalism, which was at the root of the political emigration that was also favoured for the practical opportunities offered by America.

Reconciling religious radicalism and a scientific approach to politics and economics, Joseph Priestley, Richard Price, Thomas Paine, Richard Gem, Thomas Cooper and William Duane looked with interest to the rationalism of French economic thought and its political implications. Their names were variously linked with those of Turgot, Condorcet, Du Pont de Nemours, Morellet and the Count of Mirabeau, and they were able to rely on Franklin and Jefferson as points of reference through their personal and intellectual contacts. While keeping in mind the broader framework of British intellectual and political life in the eighteenth century, from the debate on the corruption of the British monarchy to the movement for parliamentary reform and the network of the English societies, we will concentrate here on these specific links with French ideas.

The economic ideas put forward by these authors were at the heart of the discussions on both sides of the Atlantic.[6] The debate on economic freedom that was conveyed to America by Paine, Priestley and Cooper, thus represents a further route by which to follow the adoption of French economic culture and the way this grasped the continuity of economic thought from Physiocracy to Smith and brought about a democratic evolution through the experience of two Revolutions: 'It is a perversion of terms', Paine wrote in the *Rights of Man*, attacking corporations and privileged government concessions, 'to say, that a charter gives rights. It operates by a contrary effect, that of taking rights away. Rights are inherently in all the inhabitants; but charters, by annulling those rights in the majority, leave the right by exclusion in the hands of few'.[7]

The British and Irish emigration to America of the 1790s occurred alongside the political revolution that resulted in Jefferson becoming President of the United States in 1800. The campaigns for economic freedom, waged by authors such as Priestley and Cooper, took place in the closing years of the century, within the context of American trade that was prospering thanks to exceptional international circumstances.[8] The situation made Jeffersonians fear an imbalance towards trade, a fear reinforced by the Federalists' demands for protective measures during this phase of business expansion, which reopened the debate on political economy. At that time, the Jeffersonians enjoyed the support of entrepreneurs who wanted more

---

[6] In this sense, Jefferson's agrarianism has also been interpreted as the synthesis, carried out by Priestley, between British ideas and Physiocracy. Cf. Grampp, 'A Re-examination of Jeffersonian Economics', 272.

[7] Thomas Paine, *Rights of Man*, in *The Writings*, ed. Moncure D. Conway, 4 vols. (New York: Burt Franklin, 1969): vol. II, 242.

[8] Cf. McCoy, *The Elusive Republic*.

room to manoeuvre. The work of Cooper and Priestley on their arrival in 1794 took place within this setting, assuming from the outset a strong political value.

Already, however, in the face of the American economic downturn of the 1780s a debate had got under way on the relationship between trade, agriculture and luxury, to which in 1784 Price added his *Observations on the importance of the American Revolution*, urging Americans not to focus on foreign trade, which brought with it luxury, corruption and war. The model of a self-sufficient Rousseauian-style republic combined in Price with a picture of the American colonies characterized as societies of independent planters with only a few industries, as Smith had described in Book IV of the *Wealth of Nations*, using data and information provided by Franklin. This corresponded to the 'middle state of civilisation' concept, which Price – who was, with Franklin, in contact with Smith[9] – had developed in 1776 in the *Observations on Civil Liberty*, published in the same year of Smith's work and likewise making reference to Franklin's demographic calculation of a doubling of the American population every 25 years:

> Our American Colonies, particularly the Northern ones, have been for some time in the very happiest state of society; or, in the middle state of civilisation, between its first rude and its last refined and corrupt state. Old countries consist, generally, of three classes of people; a Gentry; a Yeomanry; and a Peasantry. The Colonies consist only of a body of Yeomanry supported by agriculture, and all independent, and nearly upon the level.[10]

Franklin: An International Circulation of Ideas within Religion and Science

At the centre of this triangulation between France, Britain and America, and its ability to deliver original economic reflection and radical thought, was Benjamin Franklin. With Price, Priestley and Cooper, he frequented the London's Club of Honest Whigs, which was active from 1764 to the Revolution. This was a typical eighteenth-century coffee house that served as a centre for scientific, religious and political discussions, and for support for the cause of the American colonies, being frequented by non-conformist artisans, ministers of religion and intellectuals.[11] By that time, its members belonged to the third generation of political and social opposition in the Commonwealth tradition. The attacks they made against the corruption of the British political system and the proposed parliamentary reform were connected to the religious Dissenters' demands for civil and political rights.

---

[9]   Cf. *Memoirs of Dr. George Logan of Stenton*, 46–47.

[10]   Richard Price, *Observations on the Nature of Civil Liberty, the Principles of Government, and the Justice and Policy of the War with America* (London: T. Cadell, 1776): 70–71.

[11]   Cf. Hans, 'Franklin, Jefferson, and the English Radicals at the End of the Eighteenth-Century'; Crane, 'The Club of Honest Whigs: Friends of Science and Liberty'.

The debate on freedom thus went beyond religion, and the counter-positioning of virtue and corruption assumed a value at once ethical and economic, through a network of contacts and international personal relationships. Common to these figures was a vision of religion that permeated their idea of political morality and the social process. Moreover, their exaltation of the individual's political centrality and of his rationalism, implied a non-confrontational view of society. Based on ethical principles, their political theories, notwithstanding the diversity of their positions, were thus aimed at creating an economically and politically virtuous society.

The moral dimension of economics – of industriousness as a form of moral education – linked Franklin to these circles of religious dissent right from the time of his arrival in London in 1764, when he became one of the founders of the Honest Whigs.[12] Being in contact with Physiocratic groups, he brought with him their theories, to be used as anti-British and anti-mercantilist means of supporting the American cause. In 1774, as we have seen, he founded the Society of Thirteen with David Williams, who, under Franklin's patronage, published *A Liturgy on the Universal Principles of Religion and Morality* in 1776.[13] Barbeu Du Bourg, the Physiocratic author who edited the first French edition of Franklin's writings, made contact with Williams in 1768 for the purpose of publishing one of his articles on deism. The society was connected by an international network,[14] and Jefferson also had the chance to participate, through his relationship with his Parisian doctor, Richard Gem, in a milieu in which Physiocratic theories were mixed with religious dissent, the hidden hyphen of this circulation of ideas.[15]

Support for the revolt of the American colonies, and then for the French Revolution, was consistent with the spirit that animated these groups and their expectations: America opened up new opportunities, while France gave impetus to the radicalization of their positions. On 28 November 1792, Joel Barlow was among the signatories, on behalf of the Constitutional Whigs, of the appeal presented to

---

[12]   Jay to Franklin, Bath, 26 December 1783, in Franklin, *The Works*, vol. X, 47.

[13]   David Williams was in the United States at the start of 1806, the period in which Paine attempted to establish a deist church in America following a project by Franklin and Williams, and he began the publication of the *Theophilanthropist* (cf. Hans, 'Franklin, Jefferson, and the English Radicals', 417). On Paine and theophilanthropy, cf. Jack Fruchtman, *Thomas Paine and the Religion of Nature* (Baltimore: The Johns Hopkins University Press, 1993).

[14]   Giovanni Fabbroni, who linked radicalism and religious dissent, scientific culture, diplomacy and economic circles, was a friend of Jefferson and Franklin and acted as a go-between between British and French circles. He facilitated the exchange of letters between Paris and London at the end of the 1770s, making known the technico-scientific discoveries of Price and Priestley (Fabbroni to Jefferson, London, 1 November 1779) in Jefferson, *The Papers*, vol. III, 148–9). On Fabbroni cf. Renato Pasta, *Scienza, politica e rivoluzione: l'opera di Giovanni Fabbroni (1752–1822) intellettuale e funzionario al servizio dei Lorena* (Florence: Olschki, 1989).

[15]   Jefferson to Madison, Paris, 12 January 1789, in Jefferson, *The Papers*, vol. XIV, 437. On Gem, cf. above pp. 94–5.

the Convention for an alliance between the peoples of America, France and Britain to bring peace to Europe and the world and to extend the reign of reason.[16]

Among the Dissenters of the Honest Whigs, scientists and doctors were the most represented professions. Franklin shared his scientific experiments on electricity and chemistry with Priestley and Price. Similarly, the scientific inquiry that characterized their discussions made Franklin a valuable interlocutor, who introduced them to the scientific and rationalist economic approach of French authors. At the same time, the contact with English radicalism reinforced Franklin's convictions on the unnatural basis of property, through a development of Locke's critiques of an unlimited accumulation of land, a political instrument by which to reshape society.[17]

As part of the transformation that took place within British society between 1775 and 1815, reflections on land sparked off a radical discussion on property and equality. Consequently, the distinction between natural and civil rights, and the legitimacy of property as a civil right, lay at the centre of a line of thought that led from Franklin to Jefferson and Priestley via Turgot, and which would culminate in Paine's *Agrarian Justice*.[18]

In the context of natural right and the existence of a natural order, in which the link between economy and politics was emphasized, the social dimension of French economic theory, from the Physiocrats onwards, was a point of reference, even though for the Physiocrats property had a natural origin. It was on these foundations of property that the political rationalism spread by Condorcet was acknowledged, with all its radical implications, by Priestley in 1788 (via Turgot) in his *Lectures on History and General Policy*:

> That all persons should have the absolute disposal of their property during their own lives, and while they have the use of their understanding, was never disputed. But it is a question among politicians, how far this privilege should extend? ... some, and among them is Mr. Turgot, says, there should be no testament, 'a man should have no power of disposing of his property after his death'.[19]

---

[16]   *Archives parlementaires de 1787 à 1860. Première Série (1787–1799)*, vol. LIII, 636–7.

[17]   Franklin to Robert Morris, Passy, 25 December 1783, in Franklin, *The Writings*, vol. IX, 138.

[18]   On the meaning of *Agrarian Justice* to British agrarianism, and its distance from the positions of William Spence, cf. James Eayrs, 'The Political Ideas of the English Agrarians, 1775–1815', *The Canadian Journal of Economics and Political Science*, 18/3 (1952): 287–302.

[19]   Joseph Priestley, *Lectures on History and General Policy* (Birmingham: Pearson and Rollason, 1788): 278. This book reproposed, as a means of attack against privilege, the arguments developed by Turgot in the entry 'Fondation' of the *Encylopédie*: 'It is well observed by Mr. Turgot that all hereditary distinctions, if they have any civil effect, and confer any right, and all personal prerogatives, if they are not the necessary consequence of

To this, Priestley added a note: 'See *Vie de Mr. Turgot* (by Condorcet), 1786, p. 234.' These were the same thoughts about the limits of the burdens that one generation should bequeath to the next, an issue on which Jefferson would be encouraged to reflect by Gem, his English doctor and a Physiocrat, the following year.

The authoritative position held by Turgot's and Condorcet's work within English Dissenter circles resulted in the translation of the *Vie de Turgot*, in 1787, the year after Condorcet had published the life of his master, a watershed in the recognition of the political value and republican implications of economic thought, in which he himself was involved.[20] The translation matured in the coteries close to Sir William Petty, Marquis of Lansdowne, Earl of Shelburne, who was another important link between French and British circles. Priestley was Shelburne's librarian from 1772, and was among his retinue when he journeyed to Paris in 1774, where both had contact with Turgot and the salons of the city.

Shelburne had already visited Paris, and on that occasion, in 1771, he had met both Turgot and André Morellet,[21] to whom he acknowledged his intellectual debt: 'your conversation and your knowledge have made an essential contribution to extending and *liberalising* my ideas'.[22] Through his friendship with Morellet, Shelburne discovered political economy and modified some of his views, dedicating himself to pressing the British government to adopt a policy of economic freedom and increased trade with France.[23] This intense relationship, to which their lengthy correspondence bore witness, led Morellet to visit Shelburne in England where, in the latter's residence in Bowood, he had occasion to meet with Franklin, Priestley and Price.[24] Shelburne sent Priestley's and Price's political and scientific writings to Morellet, who did his best to have them translated.[25] In return, Morellet

---

exercising a public function, are a diminution of the natural rights of other men'. In a note: 'Life of Mr. Turgot.,' 307. (*ibid.*, 308).

[20]   Condorcet, *The Life of M. Turgot*, 340–41. French. ed., *Vie de Turgot*, vol. V, 209–10.

[21]   Edmond Fitzmaurice, *Life of William, Earl of Shelburne*, 3 vols. (London: Macmillan, 1876). Cf. also Nigel Aston and Clarissa Campbell Orr, eds, *An Enlightenment Statesman in Whig Britain: Lord Shelburne in Context, 1737–1805* (Woodbridge: Boydell and Brewer, 2011); Dorothy Medlin and Arlene P. Shy, 'Enlightened exchange: the correspondence of André Morellet and Lord Shelburne', in *British–French Exchanges in the Eighteenth Century*, ed. Kathleen Hardesty Doig and Dorothy Medlin (Cambridge: Cambridge Scholars, 2007): 34–82.

[22]   Shelburne to Morellet, 23 March 1783, in André Morellet, *Mémoires inédits sur le dix-huitième siècle et la Révolution française*, 2 vols. (Paris: Ladvocat, 1822): vol. I, 276.

[23]   Morellet, *Mémoires inédits*, 277–8.

[24]   Morellet, *Mémoires inédits*, 201.

[25]   Morellet to Shelburne, 1 March 1775 and 18 February 1777 (Morellet, *Lettres de l'abbé Morellet à lord Shelburne, depuis marquis de Lansdowne, 1772–1803* (Paris: Plon, 1898): 66 and 111). In the letter of 3 November 1772 (13–14) Morellet announced that Trudaine was busy with the translation of a work by Priestley on fixed air (probably *De Aere fixo* of September 1772); in that of 1 March 1775 he had also asked Shelburne to tell Priestley that he was translating *The First Principles of Government* (66). Cf. Joseph

sent him, Condillac's *Le commerce et le gouvernement*: 'an elementary work of economics, whose notions are generally correct and its principles sane. You will find freedom of trade supported throughout it, and you should make Doctor Price read it'. Morellet maintained that his English interlocutors would appreciate the rationalism of the French approach.[26] The same conviction led him to believe that his correspondent, like him, would not have appreciated the 'Scottish subtlety' and the superfluity of the arguments in the first volume of the *Wealth of Nations*.[27]

In his letters to Shelburne Morellet always remembered Priestley and Price. Economic and political reflections were mixed and in both cases free trade was dependent on a positive outcome of the American Revolution.[28] He kept Shelburne up to date – and, with him, also his Dissenter friends – on the hopes and difficulties of Turgot's ministry, denouncing 'the foolish jealousy of trade' from the British government:

> If Turgot's administration only lasts a few years, the effects will be so striking that the whole of Europe will open its eyes, which will be good for everyone. This is always my cosmopolitan policy, my Lord. ... Alas it is because of this cosmopolitanism that your government is behaving in a manner so absurd and so unjust to the Americans. Your ministers have not seen that enslaving and ruining the Americans they will waste a rich source of wealth and benefits.[29]

Morellet was pleased with Shelburne's assessment of the *Vie de Turgot*, 'Your opinion of the work of M. de Condorcet is perfect', even though he did not share his view that Turgot was more an author than a man of politics.[30]

In fact it was to Shelburne, who had made it his business to have the English edition of the *Life of Turgot* published, that the translator, most likely Benjamin Vaughan, interested in the French *Économistes*,[31] dedicated the work, praising Turgot's 'anxious search after political truth' and also observing that his ideas on

---

Priestley, *Manière d'imprégner l'eau d'air fixe... par M. Joseph Priestley: ouvrage traduit de l'anglois par M****, extrait du 'Journal d'observations sur la physique, sur l'histoire naturelle et sur les arts et métiers' par M. l'abbé Rozier (n.p., n.d.).

[26]   Morellet to Shelburne, 12 March 1776, in Morellet, *Lettres*, 105. Cf. Etienne Bonnot de Condillac, *Le commerce et le gouvernement, considerés relativement l'un à l'autre. Ouvrage élémentaire* (Amsterdam, et se trouve à Paris: chez Jombert & Cellot, 1776).

[27]   Morellet to Shelburne, 12 March 1776, in Morellet, *Lettres*, 105.

[28]   Morellet to Shelburne, 30 December 1777, Morellet, *Lettres*, 135; 26 November 1774, *ibid.*, 51.

[29]   Morellet to Shelburne, 12 March 1776, Morellet, *Lettres*, 102–103.

[30]   Morellet to Shelburne, 9 December 1786, Morellet, *Lettres*, 217.

[31]   On Vaughan as the translator of Condorcet's *Vie de Turgot* and Turgot's *Réflexions sur la Formation et Distribution des Richesses* I am grateful to Giancarlo De Vivo and Gabriel Sabbagh for the learned unpublished article they provided. Cf. also Peter D. Groenewegen, *The Economics of A.R.J. Turgot* (The Hague: Nijhoff, 1977).

the economy, his project for provincial assemblies (put forward on his behalf by Du Pont de Nemours), and his fiscal reform represented 'pacific systems', which began to attract interest 11 years after his death.[32] The idea of the existence of a truth about principles of government, which came from political rationalism rather than from history and the traditional British political culture, was revisited in the preface to the translation, which stressed how such principles, which led to 'political perfection', could be useful also for Ireland and Britain.[33]

The explicit recognition that one of the reasons that had led to the publication in English of Condorcet's work had been Turgot's commitment to freedom in matters of religion, a stance that had to be applied equally to politics, demonstrates that religious Dissenters were involved with the project right from the start.[34] These positions were the same as what would be expressed a few years later by Price in his famous sermon *On the Love of Our Country*, which led Burke to launch the debate on the French Revolution.[35] The translation initiative was not intended to end with the publication of Condorcet's book alone: if it was well received by the British public, then work on writings by Turgot would then be initiated. Thus, the political and cultural project had a specific, concomitant editorial programme.[36]

A series of appendices were added to the text by Condorcet: the translation of the entry 'Fondation' of the *Encyclopédie*; Price's appraisal of Turgot's *Lettre*, taken from the *Observations on the importance of the American Revolution*; and several pages and comments by Condorcet, taken from the *Vie de Turgot*, on the rights of testament and 'direct tax upon the landed interest' as an alternative to purchase tax. Each appendix was provided so 'that those who are interested in studying it may find it separate',[37] and thus the objective of underscoring the more radical elements of Turgot was made explicit. The volume also included a brief observation on the *Mémoires sur la vie, l'administration et les ouvrages de m. Turgot*, recalled by Condorcet in his introductory note, and the translator made a point of mentioning their paternity, attributed to Du Pont De Nemours, 'who is particularly known through Europe, as the respectable author of the "*Ephemerides du citoyen*," and who on every account is held in high esteem in France'.[38]

Condorcet's strategy to offer the reflections on economy that had originated from Physiocrat authors through Turgot's original scheme and its radical implications was

---

[32] Condorcet, *The Life of M. Turgot*, v.

[33] Condorcet, *The Life of M. Turgot*, xi.

[34] Condorcet, *The Life of M. Turgot*, xiii.

[35] Cf. below, p. 220.

[36] 1793 saw the first publication in book form of the translation of the *Réflexions sur la Formation et la Distribution des Richesses* (Anne-Robert-Jacques Turgot, *Reflections on the formation and distribution of Wealth* (London: J. Good, 1793)).

[37] Condorcet, *The Life of M. Turgot*, 398.

[38] Condorcet, *The Life of M. Turgot*, 416. With the significant indication of Philadelphia as the place of publication, the *Mémoires* on Turgot by Du Pont de Nemours appeared in 1782.

accepted in full by the milieu that wished to submit the same proposal to the British public and political scene of those years. Turgot was pivotal to the dissemination of this maturation of the Physiocratic perspective, which made possible the reconciliation of the unity and rationality of the law with the conventional nature of property.

The Honest Whigs' interest in Turgot, and the political rationalism to which he belonged, clearly emerged from a letter by Jonathan Shipley, Bishop of St Asaph, who was a member of the club. He thanked Price for his *Observations*, as an important contribution to political thought. And with regard to the ideas contained in the *Lettre au Docteur Price*, he wrote: 'I agree with Turgot in almost every one of his propositions and wish they were as practicable as they are true'. America could offer an opportunity for these ideas to become reality, because there 'the common People have property and have been much better educated than ours'.[39]

In a different frame of mind, in a letter written to Price in 1789, John Adams had deplored the way in which Americans had been burdened by the 'erroneous opinions of Government, which have been propagated among them by some of their ill informed favorites and various writings which were very popular among them', including Paine, Macaulay and Turgot.[40]

The erroneous opinions of the government that Adams singled out revolved around the relationship between the land and political participation, property and distribution of wealth, the economy and politics, which impacted the Americans right where the cultural hotbed of English radicalism and the scientific coordinates of French economic ideas made contact. And at this very point of collision was Franklin.

During his stays in Europe, Franklin spent fifteen years in England and more than eight in France, at which time he was in contact with the Dissenters, the Physiocrats and the salon of Mme Helvétius. His American democratic republicanism, of an economic matrix and characterized by frugality and industry, took shape in these experiences, synthesizing the evangelical principles and the ideal of middle-class wellbeing and social levelling that precluded both extreme wealth and extreme poverty. This non-hierarchical model, which promoted equality and opportunity, material progress and education, and economic and political freedom, by means of a scientist vocation and providentialist naturalism, was reinforced by his cosmopolitan membership of the Freemasons, which drew together religion, science and economics, and lay at the heart of the network of the American colonies' partisans: Brissot, Cabanis, Condorcet, La Rochefoucauld, Du Pont de Nemours, Destutt de Tracy, Franklin, Jefferson, Paine, Price and Priestley were all members of the Loge des Neuf Soeurs and, at the same time,

---

[39]   Jonathan Shipley to Price, Chilbolton, 21 October 1784, in Richard Price, *Correspondence*, eds. Bernard Peach and David. O. Thomas, 3 vols. (Durham, NC: Duke University Press, 1991–4): vol. II, 242–43.

[40]   Letter from Adams to Price, 20 May 1789, quoted in David Thomas, *The Honest Mind: The Thought and Work of Richard Price* (Oxford: Clarendon Press, 1997): 275.

the American Philosophical Society.[41] Franklin shared with David Williams – a friend of Brissot who was appointed to the Convention of French Citizenship and contributed to the Girondin draft constitution of 1793 – the endeavour of creating a religion of nature that was compatible with the naturalism of French economic thinking, the principles of which Franklin brought to the discussions of the Society of the Thirteen. Support for the revolt of the colonies in the climate of British anti-Americanism eventually led to the dissolution of the Society of Thirty.

The English radical groups that Franklin frequented were united by a political interest in religion and the scientific dimension of the social process. Franklin became acquainted with Price in London in 1757, and with Priestley in 1766. These and his many other British friendships – from Hume to Lord Kames, to representatives of the Church of England[42] – as well as his close relations with some leading figures of religious dissent, were dictated by his two motivations, science and politics.

Franklin admired Price's mathematical abilities, which were put to use in the study of tables of mortality and insurance, apprehending the relationship between political radicalism and the application of the sciences to questions relating to social wellbeing. Price, in keeping with Jefferson's principle that a generation had no right to offload its burdens onto the next, sought to find a way of extinguishing public debt. The *Observations on reversionary payments* and the theory of compound interest, known in France, were coloured by his Dissenter ethics and the vision of a state regulator of energies as well as a utilitarianism that respected the rights of the individual and encouraged him to provide for himself. This vision was close to Franklin's.[43]

From 1729, with *A Modest Inquiry into the nature and necessity of a paper currency*, Franklin had reflected on the link between agriculture and commerce, developing and consolidating his thoughts while in contact with British circles. Price regularly corresponded with him, and the two discussed the economy of America, the prosperity of which, Franklin wrote in 1785, 'is the happy consequence of our

---

[41]   Cf. Nicholas Hans, 'UNESCO of the Eighteenth Century. La loge des Neuf Soeurs and its Venerable Master, Benjamin Franklin', *Proceedings of the American Philosophical Society*, 98 (1953): 513–24, which underlines how many members of the lodge later took part under the Directory in the movement of theophilanthropy, whose origins were linked to the deist society of Franklin and David Williams, who was also a member.

[42]   Cf. Leonard W. Labaree, "Benjamin Franklin's British Friendships," *Proceedings of the American Philosophical Society*, 108 (1964): 423–8.

[43]   Richard Price, *Observations on reversionary payments* (London: Cadell, 1771); cf. Henri Laboucheix, *Richard Price, théoricien de la révolution américaine, le philosophe et le sociologue, le pamphlétaire et l'orateur* (Paris: Didier, 1970); Manuela Albertone, *Moneta e politica in Francia: Dalla Cassa di sconto agli assegnati (1776–1792)* (Bologna: Il Mulino, 1992).

commerce being open to all the world, and no longer a monopoly to Britain'.[44] For his part, in the same years Price perceived a revolutionary thought rising out of the mutual exchange between Europe and America and in 1787 he wrote:

> In this part of the world there is a spirit rising, which must in time produce great effects. I refer principally to what is now passing in Holland, Brabant, and France. This spirit originated in America; and, should it appear, that is there terminated in a state of society more favourable to peace, virtue, science, and liberty, and consequently to human happiness and dignity, than has ever yet been known, infinite good will be done. Indeed, a general fermentation seems to be taking place through Europe. In consequence of the attention created by the American war, and the dissemination of writings explaining the nature and end of civil government, the minds of men are becoming more enlightened; and the silly despots of the world are likely to be forced to respect human rights, and to take care not to govern too much, lest they should not govern at all.[45]

For Franklin, Price remained the main channel of communication with the English radicals. For Price, Franklin represented the entry point into French circles; he turned to him when seeking permission to publish the *Lettre* by Turgot in his *Observations*,[46] which Franklin duly gave him with the consent of Du Pont de Nemours who 'has the Care of the Papers left by that great Man'.[47]

Franklin's close links with the Honest Whigs also passed through Priestley.[48] The two shared an interest in the study of electricity and, when Priestley arrived in London in 1766, Franklin urged him to revise and publish the drafts of his *History of Electricity*, which appeared in 1767. Science and politics were bound together: thus, in 1774 Franklin revised a text on the relations between Britain and the American colonies,[49] published anonymously by Priestley, and also became the

---

[44]   Franklin to Price, Passy, 1 February 1785, in Benjamin Franklin, *The Writings*, vol. IX, 286.

[45]   Price to Franklin, Hackney, 26 September 1787, in Franklin, *The Works*, vol. X, 21.

[46]   'Should you think, that no ill consequences can result, from publishing this letter, to any family that M. Turgot may have left, and that his death has freed me from any obligation to keep it secret, I will order to be printed off, and sent it to America with my pamphlet. Should you think the contrary, it shall be suppressed, and I shall depend on your being so good as to destroy the copy sent you'. (Price to Franklin, Newington-Green, 12 July 1784, in Franklin, *The Works*, vol. X, 106).

[47]   Franklin to Price, Passy, 2 August 1784, in Price, *Correspondence*, 223.

[48]   Priestley to Franklin, London, 13 February 1776, in Franklin, *The Works*, vol. VIII, 173.

[49]   Joseph Priestley, *An address to Protestant Dissenters of all denominations on the approaching election of Members of Parliament, with respect to the state of public liberty in general, and of American affairs in particular* (London: Joseph Johnson, 1774).

promoter of his work, sending to Barbeu Du Bourg, along with many appreciative comments, a copy of the *Essay on the First Principles of Government*.[50]

Thomas Paine: Economy, Democracy and Social Justice

It took the two end-of-century Revolutions to link the two aspects, economic and political, of the discussions from which later emerged a transatlantic group of intellectuals and cosmopolitan revolutionaries; the French Revolution hastened this radicalization, triggering a new wave of departures for America. Thomas Paine became the hub and focal point of this international group, through which the English radical societies of the 1790s synthesized their criticisms of Britain and their enthusiasm for the French Revolution and the myth of America. His influence on the emigration of those years was decisive, channelling the surge of English radicals towards America after the events that unfolded in France in 1793.[51]

Paine embodied the radicalism of the British middle classes, and he used his Quaker rhetoric to spread, in America, the notion of a harmony of economic activities within the framework of a society that considered trade to be subservient to agriculture, thereby invigorating the American agrarian ideal. His radicalism combined a democratizing, but not levelling, form of egalitarianism with the economic development of a market society, thus contributing to the maturation of Jeffersonian political economics. From the *Common Sense* to *Agrarian Justice* he represented a turning point, placing the economic debate at the heart of revolutionary thought. Thus he brought about a revolution in favour of free trade and through which political economics was considered a means of ensuring that rights became the key objective of a society motivated by a common interest consciously pursued by all its members, a society in which individuals were not in competition but whose conduct was governed by reason rather than egoism.[52] This approach drew Paine close to the economic political rationalism of the French.[53] Through his personal relationships with French groups, particularly with Condorcet, the notion of the republic – understood as a democratic representative

---

[50]   Franklin to Barbeu Du Bourg, London, 22 September 1769, in Franklin, *The Papers*, vol. XVI, 205.

[51]   Michael Durey, 'Thomas Paine's Apostles: Radical Emigrés and the Triumph of Jeffersonian Republicanism', *The William and Mary Quarterly*, 44 (1987): 661–88.

[52]   On Paine's intellectual and political arguments in support of social democracy, cf. John Keane, *Tom Paine: A Political Life* (London: Bloomsbury, 1995).

[53]   Here I intend to concentrate on the tradition of natural law, which led Paine to collaborate with Condorcet. The tradition persisted despite the development of his ideas, which culminated in *Agrarian Justice*. For a different reading of Paine from a utilitarian perspective, cf. David Wooton, 'The Republican Tradition: From Commonwealth to Common Sense', in *Republicanism, Liberty and Commercial Society*, ed. David Wootton (Stanford: Stanford University Press, 1994): 1–41.

government – followed, in his reflections, a course that drew its inspiration from French thought. This idea was consolidated by his contacts with Franklin and Jefferson, and, as his writings show, underwent a progressive radicalization during the years of the French Revolution.[54]

At the heart of the debate, which was modified under the weight of personal experiences, political upheavals and economic and social changes in the different circumstances of Britain, France and America, the importance of economics over politics was emphasized more and more in Paine's thought.[55] Property, land, taxation, political representation and social justice were the elements around which revolved a cosmopolitan project to redefine society. With the force of the sermon well known to Americans, and with an attitude that challenged traditional authority (an attitude established in America since the Great Awakening), Paine's *Common Sense*, although still oriented towards a debate on government rather than property, on politics rather than economics, marked the distinction between government – seen as an inevitable evil – and society, and thus stood for the displacement of the concept of deference by that of representation.

At this point Paine's ideas were still steeped in the British political tradition, even though they went beyond the usual British contrast between trade and virtue. He took to America the economic and social tensions of the English radicals that were linked to his roots as a son of a Quaker smallholder.[56] In his work, which helped to make Americans aware of the incompatibility of republic and monarchy, the exclusion of any privilege of birth implied a vindication of the right of future generations not to be bound by choices of the past.

Paine arrived in America in 1774, and was presented to Philadelphia circles by letters of introduction from Franklin, who he had met in London that same year. In 1775 he became the editor of the *Pennsylvania Magazine*, in which, under the pseudonym of Amicus, he published a series of articles about welfare that he developed further after the French Revolution.[57]

---

[54]   For a perspective of Paine and this thread of English radicalism, seen as the means to go beyond the debate on American republicanism as an opposition between court party and country party, cf. Durey, 'Thomas Paine's Apostles', 661–87. A reading that pays attention to the links with the French groups is that of Richard Whatmore, which contrasts Paine's modern republicanism with the interpretations that tend to circumscribe him to a British dimension (Richard Whatmore, 'A gigantic manliness: Thomas Paine's republicanism in the 1790s', in: *Economy, Polity and Society: British Intellectual History, 1750–1950*, ed. Stefan Collini, Richard Whatmore and Brian Young (Cambridge: Cambridge University Press, 2000): 135–57).

[55]   Cf. Joseph Dorfman, 'The Economic Philosophy of Thomas Paine', *Political Science Quarterly*, 53 (1938): 372–86.

[56]   Thomas Paine, *Common Sense*, in Paine, *The Writings*, vol. I, 71, 79.

[57]   Cf. Alfred O. Aldridge, *Thomas Paine's American Ideology* (Newark: University of Delaware Press, 1984).

The radicalization of his thought was enhanced by acquaintances he made in France through Jefferson, whom he had come to know in America after the success of *Common Sense*, and Franklin, who considered him his 'adopted political son'[58] and also admired his versatility as a scientist, inventor, diplomat, politician and writer. Having made contact with Franklin in 1787 in order to visit Europe to present his model of a bridge, he was introduced by him into Parisian circles, where, alongside Jefferson, Lafayette, Condorcet and Gem, he took part in debates on the American constitution and approached French political rationalism inspired by Physiocracy, which identified natural law with those of economics.

This setting encouraged his radical reflection on property. In his letter to Jefferson, of 1788, he made the distinction between natural rights and civil rights for the first time, inserting property among the latter.[59] In the second part of the *Rights of Man* he then distinguished between property derived from work and unjust property that was obtained by inheritance. And he completed the elaboration of this distinction in *Agrarian Justice*. Property was included within the 'rights of Compact', since it was useful not by virtue of the qualities of a person, but under the guarantee of society, and he pointed out that 'the word liberty is often mistakenly put for security'.[60]

Previously, in his earliest interventions on American matters, he had defined land as a source of wealth, linking, as a good disciple of Franklin, the increase of land value to population growth. In 1780, in a pamphlet in which he sided with Congress on Virginia's expansionist claims on lands towards the West, he recognized the economic centrality of agriculture and the role of government in the safeguarding of property:

> Lands are the real reaches of the habitable world, and the natural funds of America. The funds of the other countries are, in general, artificially constructed; the creature of necessity and contrivance; dependent upon credit, and always exposed to hazard and uncertainty. But lands can neither be annihilated nor lose their value; on the contrary, they universally rise with population, and rapidly so; when under the security of effectual government.[61]

---

[58]　Cf. Moncure D. Conway, *The Life of Thomas Paine*, 2 vols. (London: Routledge, 1996): Appendix B, 468.

[59]　Paine to Jefferson, March 1788, in Jefferson, *The Papers*, vol. XIII, 4–5. On the questions relating to the precise dating of the letter between February and May 1788, cf. the note on the letter in the *Papers* (*ibid.*, 6–7) and Adrienne Koch, *Jefferson and Madison: The Great Collaboration* (New York: A.A. Knopf, 1950): 83.

[60]　Paine to Jefferson, March 1788, *The Papers*, vol. XIII, 5.

[61]　Thomas Paine, *Public good, being an Examination into the claim of Virginia to vacant Western Territory*, in Thomas Paine, *Political Writings*, 2 vols. (Charlestown, MA: G. Davidson, 1824): vol. I, 298–9.

In the *Rights of Man* he made an explicit claim for the prime importance of agriculture, whose interests he deemed superior to those of other economic activities.[62] This was set in a new radicalization of his discourse that bound the economic dimension tightly to that of politics and was resultant upon contact with the French Revolution. He placed land at the heart of his reflection on property, which touched on the issues of taxation and political participation. 'The aristocracy are not the farmers who work the land, and raise the produce, but are the mere consumers of the rent; and when compared with the active world, are the drones, a seraglio of males, who neither collect the honey nor form the hive, but exist only for lazy enjoyment';[63] hence taxes should be levied on 'landed property'. He proposed a progressive tax on income from landed property, confiscating that above £20,000 per year. This was a way of restricting the power of the aristocracy and of ensuring a more equal distribution of wealth. The rejection of the aristocracy and privilege, and the demand – made also by Jefferson – that the right of primogeniture be abolished,[64] were intended to sever the link between ownership and voting, while at the same time giving security to property, since denying the vote to a section of the nation led to attacks on property itself.

He would revisit this idea during discussions on the Constitution of the Year III, when, opposing the creation of a census regime, he resumed the same argument, namely that the best way to safeguard property was to avoid making it the reason for a debate on the inequality of rights.[65] Linking the right to vote to the payment of taxes and not to property was suggested as the way to break loose from the presumptions of privilege.[66]

His radical thinking on property, which shifted the focus from goods to the individual, was also the basis of his defence of the entitlements of generations in *Rights of Man*, 'Man has not property in man'.[67] This was his response to the support for the authority of tradition and the past made by Burke, who placed Paine – together with Jefferson, who shared and developed the same principle while in contact with his French counterparts, from Gem to Condorcet[68] – at the heart of revolutionary ideology: 'Every generation is equal in rights to generations

---

[62]   Thomas Paine, *Rights of Man. Second Part*, in Paine, *The Writings*, vol. II, 470.

[63]   Paine, *Rights of Man. Second Part*, in *The Writings*, vol. II, 471.

[64]   Paine, *Rights of Man. First Part*, in Paine, *The Writings*, vol. II, 321.

[65]   Paine, *Dissertation on the first principle of government (1795)*, in Paine, *The Writings*, vol. III, 269.

[66]   Paine, *Letter addressed to the addressers on the late proclamation (1792)*, in Paine, *The Writings*, vol. III, 88.

[67]   Paine, *Rights of Man. First Part*, in Paine, *The Writings*, vol. II, 278.

[68]   In the letter to Monroe of 10 July 1791, Jefferson recognized that he professed the same principles as Paine (Jefferson, *The Papers*, vol. XX, 297). Cf. also Jefferson to John Adams, Philadelphia, 30 August 1791, *ibid.*, 310. On Jefferson, his idea that 'the earth belongs to the living' and the discussion on the attribution of the concept to him or to Paine, cf. above, p. 93 ff.

which preceded it, by the same rule that every individual is born equal in rights with his contemporary'.[69]

The economic aspect of rights were reinforced in Paine alongside Franklin, Jefferson, Condorcet and the circles in which the economic fundamentals of political representation developed by the Physiocrats, from Du Pont de Nemours's *Mémoire sur les Municipalités* to Condorcet's *Essai sur les assemblées provinciales*, had been the starting point for focusing attention on society and individuals.[70] The success of the *Rights of Man* and the cosmopolitan life of Paine had transformed this perspective into a joint transatlantic patrimony.

In keeping with this tradition of economic and political rationalism, Paine highlighted the relationship between democracy and economic growth in which monarchy had no place, a position which led him to identify natural law with the laws of economics,[71] as opposed to seeing it a conception of voluntary and contractual society. The sole objective of state intervention, as he was to declare in *Agrarian Justice*, was that of guaranteeing the natural functioning of rights. The economy was closely identified with the rights of man and republic, and America was the archetype: 'I see in America the generality of people living in a style of plenty unknown in monarchical countries'.[72] The principle of citizenship, seen as a grouping of economic interests, which the Physiocrats were among the first to advance, here arrived at a formulation that was fuelled by the effect of the two Revolutions.

In Paine the idea of agriculture's centrality ran parallel with a perception of trade as a civilizing force, re-echoing the rhetoric of certain sermons.[73] He was convinced that a developed economy could ensure the rights of individuals, in other words ensure the common economic good, which was the republic. Related to his idea of republican equality, an expression of economic prosperity, was the ideal of a middle class, to which he himself belonged, and which justified itself in economic terms. Rejecting a society divided between an exploitative ruling

---

[69]   Thomas Paine, *Rights of Man. First Part*, in Paine, *The Writings*, vol. II, 304. In 1786, in *Dissertations on Government; the Affairs of the Bank; and Paper Money* (Paine, *The Writings*, vol. II, 165), Paine expressed the idea that a generation did not have the right to condition the choices of the next, without however linking it to a radicalization of his positions. The occasion was the controversy over the Bank of North America, which was determined to preserve the perpetual charter it had received from Congress in 1781. Against the accusations of monopoly aimed at the bank, Franklin, who, like Paine, held shares in it, had persuaded him to come to its defence.

[70]   On the economic foundations of political representation and Physiocratic reflection, cf. Keith M. Baker, 'Representation', in *The French Revolution and the Creation of Modern Political Culture*. Vol. I: *The Political Culture of the Old Regime*, ed. Keith M. Baker (Oxford:, Pergamon Press, 1987): 469–92; Manuela Albertone, 'Il proprietario terriero'".

[71]   On a reading of Physiocracy as an original elaboration of natural law conducted in economic terms, cf. Catherine Larrère, *L'invention de l'économie au XVIIIe siècle. Du droit naturel à la physiocratie* (Paris: PUF, 1992).

[72]   Thomas Paine, *Rights of Man. First Part*, in Paine, *The Writings*, II, 367.

[73]   Thomas Paine, *Rights of Man. Second Part*, in Paine, *The Writings*, II, 456.

class and the exploited dispossessed, he extolled the productive class as the only virtuous one. In 1807, after his return to America, he had an article published in the *Public Advisor* in which he defined himself as the 'Farmer of thoughts'; he placed class and political representation in direct association and sketched an outline of the different classes. These formed the 'new system, that of representation', in which one can still discern, in its already mature economic thinking, distant Physiocratic memories of the idea that everything derives from the earth:

> the first useful class of citizens are the farmers and cultivators. These may be called citizens of the first necessity, because every thing comes originally from the earth.
>
> After these follow the various orders of manufacturers and mechanics of every kind. These differ from the first class in this particular, that they contribute to the accommodation rather than to the first necessities of life.
>
> Next follow those called merchants and shopkeepers. These are occasionally convenient but not important. They produce nothing themselves as the two first classes do, but employ their time in exchanging one thing for another and living by the profits.[74]

In a conception of the economy that viewed activities and classes as interdependent, Paine aimed at a social justice that did not impede the creation and circulation of wealth. From the *Rights of Man* to *Agrarian Justice*, this economic and political project was constantly stimulated by the French Revolution.

In the winter of 1789–90, he was in France, collaborating closely with Condorcet.[75] In November, Burke's *Reflections on the French Revolution* was published, and Paine, who was in London, immediately responded with the first part of the *Rights of Man*, which appeared on 13 March 1791, dedicated to Washington.[76] He returned to Paris and entrusted the translation of the work to Lanthenas, and his contribution, together with that of Condorcet, was crucial, after Varennes, in speeding France along the road of republicanism.[77] At the start of

---

[74]   *Public Adviser*, 30 May 1807. Whatmore has underlined that the theme of the criticisms against British mixed government, which were not widely disseminated in Britain, was central to the Physiocrats' anti-British polemic in the 1760s and 1770s (Cf. Richard Whatmore, 'A gigantic manliness', 148–9).

[75]   Alfred O. Aldridge, 'Condorcet et Paine: Leurs rapports intellectuels', *Revue de littérature comparée*, 32 (1958): 47–65.

[76]   The preface to the American edition stated that the work had found approval with the Secretary of State, though Jefferson, in his letter to Madison of 5 September 1791, complained that the note in his hand had been used against his knowledge (Thomas Jefferson, *The Papers* vol. XX, 293; Thomas Paine, *Rights of Man*, 2nd ed. (Philadelphia: Samuel Harrison Smith, 1791): 4).

[77]   Regarding the influence of Paine on Condorcet and his wife, Etienne Dumont wrote: 'Payne had given them the most erroneous ideas in England; I often fought against

July 1791 he was one of the five founders of the Société des Républicains (the others being Condorcet, Bonneville, Lanthenas and Duchatelet) and of the *Républicain ou le Défenseur du gouvernement représentatif*. The first issue opened with a letter by Paine, translated by Condorcet, which extolled the republic and attacked Montesquieu's arguments on the inadequacy of the republican system for large states.[78] On 1 July the same collaboration and author produced the manifesto, posted on the streets of Paris, which urged the abolition of the monarchy.[79] To the attacks addressed to the manifesto Duchatelet responded on 4 July with an article published in the *Patriote français* – perhaps in fact written by Paine – which cited Price in support of the republic and, with him, the ideas of Franklin and Rousseau.[80]

In 1792 the second part of the *Rights of Man* was published, and it proved a turning point in the radicalization of revolutionary thought. In August Paine was awarded French citizenship, in September he was elected to the National Convention and the next month became a member of the Constitution Committee, alongside Condorcet, Sieyes, Brissot, Pétion and Vergniaud, the originators of the draft *Girondin* constitution. Like Condorcet, he voted against the death sentence of the King. On 27 December 1793 he was arrested while occupied with writing the *Age of Reason*, a work inspired by the intellectual environment around him and by the formulation of a deism in which the laws of science were a revelation of a benevolent nature that expressed itself in Franklin's 'wise and economical sayings'.[81] The work was attacked in America, his deism being interpreted as atheism; Priestley responded critically to it while Jefferson stood aloof for fear of compromising his race for the presidency.

After his release from prison in November 1794, Paine's disillusionment with the French Revolution[82] – which had contributed to the feelings of those English radicals who had opted for emigration to America – and his resentments towards the American government, which he felt had abandoned him,[83] as well as his pessimism regarding the future of America, distanced him from Jefferson. In response to receiving the second part of the *Rights of Man*, Jefferson acknowledged that Paine's pen was mightier than the sword against those who might have wished

---

them but in vain. America seemed to them the model of good government, and it seemed to them easy to transport the federal system to France'. Etienne Dumont, *Souvenirs sur Mirabeau et sur les deux premières assemblées législatives* (Paris: PUF, 1950): 179.

[78]   Cf. Hélène Delsaux, *Condorcet journaliste* (Paris: Honoré Champion, 1931): 49–61.

[79]   Cf. Dumont, *Souvenirs sur Mirabeau*, 175.

[80]   *Patriote François*, no. 695, 4 July 1791, 24–5.

[81]   Thomas Paine, *The Age of Reason*, in Paine, *The Writings*, vol. IV, 35.

[82]   Paine to Jefferson, 20 April 1793, in Paine, *The Papers*, vol. XXV, 576–7.

[83]   On the presumed responsibility of Gouverneur Morris for Paine's arrest and the subsequent accusations of betrayal made by Paine against Washington, cf. Conway, *The Life of Thomas Paine*.

for the return of monarchy.[84] However, ten years would elapse before Jefferson would resume replying to the letters that Paine continued to send him.

Still, the evolution of his radicalism in *Agrarian Justice*, and the social implications of his discourse on property, by which he intended to promote social justice without hindering the creation and circulation of wealth, were not unlike Jefferson's and were vitalized by a political debate on the economy, which was consolidated by contact with the same French thinkers known to Jefferson.[85] Jefferson appreciated *Agrarian Justice*,[86] which reconciled economic liberty and republic with a new idea of 'moral economy'.[87] It was within this that Paine developed the main points of a welfare policy, which was to be one of the chief objectives of a republican state, and which he had introduced in the second part of the *Rights of Man*. In a different context, he intended to oppose the communist project of Babeuf's *Conspiracy of the Equals*.[88]

Paine accepted Locke's idea of an original common ownership of land, but resolutely opposed agrarian law, with a redistributive social policy aimed at limiting ownership through the laws of succession – a subject to which Turgot had made a major contribution from France, as acknowledged in British debates – and setting up a national fund for the young and the elderly, as a form of compensation made by society for all who had been deprived of the natural right to land by the formation of private property. Betterment connected to the land justified property, rather than the ownership of it, according to Paine. All owners of cultivated land thus owed a 'ground rent' to the community, on which was based the proposed social fund of £15 a year for those aged under 21 years and £10 for those over 50. For Paine the culmination of eighteenth-century reflection on land and property was a non-levelling egalitarianism that could harmonize equality and liberty. 'France has had the glory to add to the word of freedom, that of equality', he wrote, addressing his thoughts at the Directory. He differentiated between two

---

[84]   Jefferson to Paine, 19 June 1792, in Paine, *The Papers*, vol. XX, 312. Cf. also Paine to Jefferson, 13 February 1792, *ibid.*, vol. XXIII, 115.

[85]   Jefferson to Madison, Fontainebleau, 28 October 1785, in Jefferson, *The Papers*, vol. VIII, 682.

[86]   Jefferson to Madison (Philadelphia: 15 June 1797), Jefferson, *The Papers*, vol. XXIX, 434.

[87]   Cf. Eric Foner, *Tom Paine and Revolutionary America* (New York: Oxford University Press, 1976).

[88]   The work was published first in French, in 1796, and a year later in English (Thomas Paine, *La Justice agraire opposée à la loi et monopole agraire, ou Plan d'amélioration du sort des hommes* (Paris: chez les marchands de nouveautés, an V de la République); Thomas Paine, *Agrarian justice, opposed to agrarian law, and to agrarian monopoly, being a plan for ameliorating the condition of man* (Paris, London: W. Adlard, J. Adlard, undated). In 1797 another French translation emerged, which explained how Paine's unexpected departure prevented him from reviewing the translated text (Thomas Paine, *Thomas Paine à la Législature et au Directoire, ou la Justice agraire opposée à la loi et aux privilèges agraires* (Paris: la citoyenne Rigouleau, 1797)).

types of property: 'natural property', which included land, water and air, and 'artificial or acquired property' for which equality was impossible. He therefore chose to focus the discussion on natural equality within which he placed the right to vote, according to which every man was born with 'legitimate rights of some kind of property or equivalent compensation'.[89]

Through the maturation of a thought that had become progressively radicalized in his growing interest in economics as an instrument of social justice, Paine's anti-British spirit and efforts to draw France and America closer together remained unchanged. He supported the foreign policy of the Directory, writing *The Decline and Fall of the English System of Finance* in 1796, at the request of the French. Prior to that, in 1782, the French government had considered using his critiques of Raynal, in his *Letter to the Abbé Raynal, on the affairs of North America*, as a propaganda weapon against Britain; Mazzei took up these critiques in his *Observations sur l'Histoire philosophique des Deux Indes*.[90] Returning to the United States in 1802, Paine resumed contacts with Jefferson, who consulted him at the time of the Louisiana Purchase.[91]

Notwithstanding the marginalisation of his later years, Paine remained a reference point for British emigration and, through the elaboration of a republican ideology that galvanized both the Americans and the French, brought about a defining moment in English radicalism, provoking in both Britain and in America a transition from the circulation of ideas of the 1760s and 1770s to the practical political action of the 1790s. In opposition to the language of Burke's economics, which defended the commercial tradition of the Whigs, in the *Rights of Man* Paine used the language of political economy in its most radical sense to support his convictions about how individuals could live naturally in a developed economy so as to ensure the rights of all.

Richard Price and the Ideal of the American Farmer

At the root of several of the debates that most marked the political ideas of the closing years of the eighteenth century stood the Dissenter, moral philosopher and

---

[89]   Paine, *A la Législature et au Directoire*, 6–7.

[90]   Drawing on Paine, Mazzei inserted the *Observations* as the third volume of the *Recherches historiques et politiques sur les Etats-Unis de l'Amérique septentrionale*. Cf. Darnell Abel, 'The Significance of the Letter to the Abbé Raynal in the Progress of Thomas Paine's Thought', *The Pennsylvania Magazine of History and Biography*, 66/2 (April 1942): 176–90; Alfred O. Aldridge, 'La signification historique, diplomatique et littéraire de la "Lettre addressée à l'Abbé Raynal" de Thomas Paine', *Etudes anglaises*, 8/3 (July–September 1955): 223–32; Carlo Borghero, 'Raynal, Paine e la rivoluzione americana', in *La politica della ragione: Studi sull'illuminismo francese*, ed. Paolo Casini (Bologna: Il Mulino, 1978): 349–81.

[91]   Paine to Jefferson, 25 December 1802, in Paine, *The Writings*, vol. III, 379–80.

author of economic works, Richard Price. In 1784 he published his *Observations on the Importance of the American Revolution*, which was born of his desire to publish the *Letter* Turgot had sent him.[92] On 4 November 1789 he delivered the sermon, *A Discourse on the Love of Our Country*, to which Burke replied with the *Reflections on the Revolution in France*, sparking a reaction from Paine and a clash between their irreconcilable political cultures.[93]

Linked to Lord Shelburne, a member of the Club of Honest Whigs and in contact with Franklin, Morellet, Turgot, Du Pont de Nemours, Condorcet[94] and the Count of Mirabeau, Price was close to French political culture, which Burke accused him of tapping into.[95] Price's support for the French Revolution – whose developments he was however unable to follow – animated his preaching and had its source in the distinctive traits of his ethics and religious commitment. These were based on a political theory of the free agency of man, an idea that descended from a Rousseauian exaltation of the inner light, which transcended the sensual psychology of Locke. Although far from Priestley's determinism, Price, in opposition to Hume and Hutcheson,[96] nevertheless held reason to be the basis of ethics and freedom and believed in the existence of a moral order.

It was in fact one of his works on morality, the *Review of the Principal Questions of Morals*, published in 1757 and appreciated by both Franklin and Shelburne, that introduced him to the intellectual and political circles of English radicals. His political writings were linked to those on financial questions – insurance and the public debt – and from 1771 onwards they won him wide renown in Britain and beyond, in particular his *Appeal to the Public on the Subject of the National Debt*, an expression of his unusual combination of religious commitment and scientific outlook.

---

[92]   Richard Price to Arthur Lee, Newington Green, 18 January 1779, in Richard Price, *Correspondence*, vol. II, 36; Richard Price, *Observations on the importance of the American Revolution* (London: 1784). Cf. David Thomas, *The Honest mind*, 263–4.

[93]   Burke, *Reflections on the Revolution in France*, ed. Conor C. O'Brien (Harmondsworth: Penguin, 1973): 91.

[94]   Amongst Condorcet's papers, there is the manuscript text of his open letter, written after 4 November 1790 and before 19 April 1791, the date of Price's death, in response to an article in the *Mercure*, in which Price was attacked and Burke was praised. Regarding Price, Condorcet wrote: 'Mr. Price is a respectable old man with a life devoted entirely to the service of humanity. All of his works express the wish and the hope of seeing freedom, peace and virtue settle on the earth. ... A stranger to all parties, a friend of all men'. Regarding Burke, he noted in the footnotes: 'Mr. Burke is of a different character, he has become known worldwide for his work on rhetoric, since attached to a party that has not long had power for long and is distinguished by such pedantry'. (Bibliothèque de l'Institut de France, Paris: *Papiers Condorcet*, MS 860, 216–17).

[95]   Edmund Burke, *Reflections*, 93.

[96]   On Price, considered a classic in the radical intuitionism in ethics, cf. Thomas, *The Honest Mind*.

This same passion for free civil and religious self-determination led him to oppose the war with the American colonies. Beginning with the success of the *Observations on the Nature of Civil Liberty, the Principles of Government, and the Justice and Policy of the War with America*, of 1776, which declared that freedom and equality derived from natural law and not the Magna Carta,[97] his name, and with it all English radicalism, became bound to the American cause. In 1778 he turned down an invitation to move to America to help administer the finances of the new states, but his political commitment to the construction of the new nation did not weaken.[98]

When the American Revolution erupted, the intellectuals who coalesced around Turgot already possessed the conceptual framework in which to insert the American experience, namely the rejection of the British constitution and of Montesquieu's balance of powers, along with a scientific consideration of the economy posited on land value and the priority of agriculture. It was around the unpublished letter to him from Turgot – whose subsequent publication prompted the response of the *Defence of the Constitutions of Government of the United States of America* by John Adams – that Price organized a written campaign in support of the new nation, already well under way in 1779, and centred on the ideal of the American farmer.

With the support of Franklin and Du Pont de Nemours, the *Observations on the Importance of the American Revolution* became a project that was linked to the intensification and the radicalization, influenced by events in America, of the economic and political discussions in France during the 1780s.[99] Franklin introduced the Count of Mirabeau to English radical groups, presenting him to Price,[100] who enlisted the collaboration of this vital link with French circles. Mirabeau translated Turgot's letter for the second English edition of the *Observations* of 1785, which was published together with the French original.[101] In the same year, an appendix to his *Considérations sur l'ordre de Cincinnatus* included, as well as the *Lettre* by Turgot, the translation of Price's work.[102]

Price did not share Turgot's unicameral ideas and criticisms of the separation of powers and the British political model; he remained a British subject and never

---

[97]   Price had already outlined an analysis of American society in the third edition of the *Treatise on Reversionary Payments*, of 1773.

[98]   Laboucheix, *Richard Price*.

[99]   Cf. Edoardo Tortarolo, *Illuminismo e rivoluzioni*.

[100]   Franklin to Price, 7 September 1784, cf. above, pp. 133–4.

[101]   Richard Price, *Observations on the importance of the American Revolution* (Dublin: L. White, 1785). In the letter to Ezra Stiles, Newington Green, 15 October 1884, Price gave notice that the Count of Mirabeau, 'an excellent writer' was working on the translation in English of Turgot's *Lettre* (Price, *Correspondence*, vol. II, 236).

[102]   Honoré-Gabriel Riquetti, Count of Mirabeau, *Considérations sur l'Ordre de Cincinnatus, ou Imitation d'un pamphlet anglo-américain* (London: Johnson and Rotterdam: C.R. Hake, 1785).

desired the abolition of the monarchy.[103] Nevertheless, he admired the American experience and the economic opportunities it offered. The ideal of the farmer described in his *Observations* was consistent with his economic convictions, which focused on a model of development established on agriculture. He was critical of the commercial economy and called for the strengthening of the agrarian middle classes, translating the demands of the English middle classes, expressed by a part of radical circles, into the reality of America. Agriculture was thus considered a support for a social form of democratic levelling, and his appreciation of American rural life was based on its absence of hierarchies. He hoped that America could remain that way, as far from luxury as from poverty, and serve as an example to others.[104] The natural economy of America was in conflict with the artificial economy typified by Britain.

Even for Price American events induced an evolution and radicalisation of positions: if twenty years before the Revolution he had expressed in the *Review of Morals* a conventional view of property, in the *Observations* his argument on equality had become more radical. He cited Plato, More and Wallace and their proposals for shared ownership of goods and the abolition of property:

> Such theories are in speculation pleasing, nor perhaps are they wholly impracticable. Some approaches to them may hereafter be made; and schemes of government may take place, which shall leave so little, besides personal merit, to be a means of distinction, as to exclude from society most of the causes of evil. But be this it will, it is out of doubt that there is an equality in society which is essential to liberty, and which every State that would continue virtuous and happy ought as far as possible to maintain.[105]

Rousseauian ideas influenced his opinion of foreign trade and luxury: when American trade suffered a downturn in the mid-1780s these were the object of severe criticism. Despite the fact that trade per se favoured the relationships between individuals,[106] an economic policy founded on foreign trade was ill suited to the vastness and climate of America and could even prove harmful if it drove Americans to adopt protectionist measures and abandon their natural state of simplicity and equality.[107] His arguments for the uniqueness of the American reality consequently offered strong hints to the proponents of a Spartan model of republic. At the same time, the idea, which he shared with Turgot, that the American Revolution represented a step forward in the progress of the Enlightenment, pervaded the whole work.

---

[103] On Price's appreciation of Adams' *Defence*, cf. Thomas, *The Honest Mind*, 277.
[104] Price, *Observations* (Dublin: L. White, 1785): 69–70.
[105] Price, *Observations* (Dublin: L. White, 1785): 71.
[106] Price, *Observations* (Dublin: L. White, 1785): 74–5.
[107] Price, *Observations* (Dublin: L. White, 1785): 77.

Discussing with Jefferson the question of what powers to give Congress – when sending him his *Observations* via Franklin – Price underlined the correlation of the political and economic dimensions: precisely because the United States was a democracy, and therefore had the character of its people reflected in its form of government, the coastal states' propensity for luxury and trade was dangerous, since it could engender corrupt and tyrannical administrations. This was a critique of an English Dissenter, which conformed to the *country* political tradition, but also applied the principles of eighteenth-century economics. It was a direct echo of Turgot, made in the conviction, as Price said to Jefferson, that Americans must not allow their government to become a replica of European ones.[108]

The French Revolution impelled Price along the path of maturation. For him Franklin and Jefferson were sources of information and privileged interlocutors, to whom he could express his enthusiasm and hopes.[109] In the Autumn of 1788 he applauded French efforts to draft a free constitution,[110] and on 4 May 1789 he followed with interest the progress of civil and religious liberty, even though he believed it would be difficult to achieve, in France, a political representation that gave voice to the small landowners.[111] For him, as for Jefferson, there was a link between the American and French Revolutions and a mutual exchange between the political cultures of the two countries:

> What gratitude is due to the Americans States for the resistance and diffusion of just sentiments on the subject of government which have led the way to this revolution? How honourable is it to the memory of Mr Turgot? What pleasure must his friends and Count Mirabeau receive from the reflection that they have contributed to it by their writings and exertions? Dr Price wishes that his congratulations on this occasion may be communicated to M. Du Pont, Abbé Morlaix, and the marquis Condorcet, all of whom have honoured him much by their attention and by the presents they have sent him of their valuable publications.[112]

---

[108] Price to Jefferson, Newington Green, 21 March 1785, in Jefferson, *The Papers*, vol. VIII, 52–4.

[109] In the letter to Price of 8 January 1789, Jefferson expressed his conviction that the Revolution in America had contributed to freeing France from despotism (Jefferson, *The Papers*, vol. XIV, 420).

[110] Price to Jefferson, Hackney, 26 October 1788, Jefferson, *The Papers*, vol. XIV, 38.

[111] Price to Jefferson, Hackney, 4 May 1789, Jefferson, *The Papers*, vol. XV, 90.

[112] Price to the Count of Mirabeau, 4 July 1789, in Richard Price, *Correspondence*, vol. III, 230.

Joseph Priestley: The French Revolution and the American Model

Even though he never left England, Price shared the international vocation of the English liberal Jacobins that boosted the 'Jacobin connection' of the radical emigration to America.[113] Those who comprised this tide of migration varied in both provenance and position, but they also had some strong unifying points: support for the Jeffersonians, attentiveness to the relationship between economics and politics and adherence to Paine's democratic ideology and modern republicanism, all of which persuaded them to leave the British Commonwealth tradition. For them, America was the testing ground for a discussion about economic liberty and the Republican brand of equality. Their criticisms of Britain were directed not only at the monarchy, but also at its privilege-based economic policy. The English strand of radicalism, which proposed a less hierarchical model of society that promoted equality and material progress, went beyond Harrington and Sidney and spoke the language of Locke, Turgot, Condorcet and Smith.

A number of the radical emigrants brought, into the America of the Revd. Samuel Williams,[114] ideas that reconciled religion and economics, as well as a moral vision of the economy that shared the Puritan principles of ethics.[115] Their interest in economic science reflected a range of values that underlay a social project that – uniting British, French and American debates, in the 1790s – ran alongside the Republicans' political struggle against the Federalists' principle of deference.

The emigrants took with them the conceptions of British democratic societies inspired by Paine. In the midst of the economic difficulties of the 1790s the need to face up to a war with France while also, following a series of bad harvests, coping with an expanding population and a concomitant demand for grain, caused discussions in Britain to lean towards protectionist policies in defence of British agriculture while deliberating future economic growth. Liberal argumentation and the potential of America stoked the radicals' criticisms of the Corn Laws, which represented aristocratic power,[116] and the British Government's repressive response to their political and economic proposals and support for the French Revolution eventually drove many of them to leave the shores of Britain.[117] In America they helped to highlight the incompatibility of the French and British systems.

In 1791 this two-pronged attack against the French Revolution and English religious dissent took a turn for the worse, when a newspaper campaign was

---

[113] Cf. Richard J. Twomey, "Jacobins and Jeffersonians: Anglo-American Radical Ideology, 1790–1810," in *The Origins of Anglo-American Radicalism*, eds. Margaret Jacob and James Jacob (London: Allen and Unwin, 1984), 284–99.

[114] Cf. above, pp. 46–51.

[115] Cf. Morgan, 'The Puritan Ethic and the American Revolution'.

[116] Cf. Chris Evans, *Debating the Revolution: Britain in 1790s* (London: I.B. Tauris, 2006).

[117] Cf. Durey, 'Thomas Paine's Apostles'.

launched against Joseph Priestley. The Birmingham Riots ensued,[118] and he was forced to flee the city. This experience was at the root of his decision, in 1794, to move with his family to America.[119]

Priestley was among the first to respond to Burke's *Reflections* and he welcomed with enthusiasm Paine's reply to it. With his own *Letters to Edmund Burke* he addressed the issue of the French Revolution, with regard to its political dimension and religious freedom, by mounting a defence of Price's *A Discourse on the Love of Our Country*.[120] Despite the opposing philosophical foundations of their religious dissent – for Price, man was a free agent, while for Priestley, freedom found expression in the circumstance of need[121] – the two men, engaged in spreading a rational Christianity, moved in the same cosmopolitan environment. And both were close to French circles, where economic analysis and policy planning intertwined under the stimulus of events in America.

Priestley, who was a theologian, chemist and political theorist, was also part of the international scientific community, which in France was centred upon the Physiocrats, Turgot and Condorcet. He was in Paris with Lord Shelburne in 1774,[122]

---

[118]   In 1791 the crowd set fire to Priestley's home on the outskirts of Birmingham, where the Francophiles had organized a banquet to celebrate the 14th of July. In the name of the Académie des Sciences, Condorcet expressed French solidarity towards Priestley in an open letter that was published in the *Patriote François*, no. 729 (4 August 1791), 161–2, and in the *Moniteur universel*, no. 217 (5 August 1791), 302, in which he praised his membership of an ideal European league for the triumph of freedom with the use of reason alone. Priestley's response to the 'friends of philosophy' was published in the *Patriote François*, no. 239 (27 August 1791), 500.

[119]   Cf. Caroline Robbins, 'Honest Heretic: Joseph Priestley in America, 1794–1804', *Proceedings of the American Philosophical Society*, 106 (1962): 60–76; Colin Bonwick, 'Joseph Priestley: Emigrant and Jeffersonian', *Enlightenment and Dissent*, no. 2 (1983): 3–22;Cf. also Anne Holt, *A Life of Joseph Priestley* (London: Oxford University Press, 1931); Jenny Graham, *Revolutionary in Exile: the Emigration of Joseph Priestley to America, 1794–1804* (Philadelphia: American Philosophical Society, 1995).

[120]   Joseph Priestley, *Letters to the right honourable Edmund Burke, occasioned by his 'Reflections on the revolution in France'* (London: J. Johnson, 1791). Madison, when sending a copy to Jefferson wrote to him: 'You will see by a note on page 56 how your idea of limiting the right to bind posterity is germinating under extravagant doctrines of Burke on that subject' (Madison to Jefferson, New York, 1 May 1791, in Jefferson, *The Papers*, vol. XX, 336).

[121]   Price to Jefferson, 3 August 1789 (Jefferson, *The Papers*, vol. XV, 330). Cf. Richard Price and Joseph Priestley, *A free discussion of the doctrines of materialism and philosophical necessity, in a correspondence between Dr. Price, and Dr. Priestley* (London: J. Johnson and T. Cadell, 1778). Cf. Laboucheix, *Richard Price*; Jack Fruchtman, *The Apocalyptic Politics of Richard Price and Joseph Priestley: A Study in the Late Eighteenth-Century English Republican Millennialism* (Philadelphia: The American Philosophical Society, 1983).

[122]   On Priestley's and Lavoisier's dispute on the paternity of their discoveries in chemistry, cf. Charles C. Gillispie, *Science and Polity in France at the End of the Old Regime* (Princeton: Princeton University Press, 1980).

and there he spent time with Turgot and other Parisian intellectuals, though he did not feel completely at ease with them.[123]

He was a member of the Club of Honest Whigs, and Franklin had an important influence on him. Their collaboration deepened into a common political commitment when the revolt of the American colonies became a revolution. Priestley shared his research on electricity with Franklin, his passion for science being born of a desire to understand the unity of God's universe. For him Franklin was also a channel through which he could communicate with the French economists, whose theories on the existence of a necessary natural order were in tune with the determinism of his philosophical universe. In 1768, the year in which Franklin was in London and drew closer to Physiocracy, Priestley published *An Essay on the First Principles of Government* in which he criticized the British taxation of the American colonies.[124] Only a third of the work actually dealt with the foundations of government, its nub being education and religious freedom; even so, his approach was political and recognized education as a means by which to understand the order of God through the exercise of personal freedom.[125]

Locke was the explicit point of reference, and it was in fact his premises that prompted Priestley to share Franklin's radical views of property and their democratic implications.[126] If society was called upon to legitimize property, individual freedom was a prerequisite for the development of agriculture.[127] From Locke to Priestley, here was the exposition of a British tradition of liberty, the evolvement of which was nourished by eighteenth-century economic thinking. In 1769, in *The Present State of Liberty in Great Britain and her Colonies*, Priestley advocated a policy of encouragement for agriculture in the colonies and manufacturing in Britain, citing Franklin's testimony to the House of Commons in 1765 to support the thesis that a dearth of labour in America benefited British manufactured goods.[128]

Twenty years later, in 1788, during the ferment of French discussions of the American experience, Priestley highlighted the interconnections between

---

[123]   Cf. Morellet's letter to Lord Shelburne of 10 February 1775, in which Morellet also addressed Priestley, 'although he did not find it in Paris the ' it is so' ... and he never wanted to say 'there are some good things". (Morellet, *Lettres à lord Shelburne*, 63).

[124]   In 1774 Franklin reviewed an anonymous pamphlet by Priestley against the war, *An Address to Protestant Dissenters... with Respect to the State of Public Liberty in General and of American Affairs in Particular*.

[125]   Joseph Priestley, *An Essay on the First Principles of Government, and of the Nature of Political, Civil and Religious Liberty*, 2nd ed. (London: J. Johnson, 1771): 85.

[126]   Priestley, *Essay*, 41.

[127]   Priestley, *Essay*, 69. In support of his assertion Priestley cited Poivre's *Voyages d'un philosophe*, published in the same year.

[128]   Joseph Priestley, *The present state of Liberty in Great Britain and her Colonies*, in Joseph Priestley, *The Theological and Miscellaneous Works*, ed. John Towill Rutt, 25 vols. (London: Smallfield, 1817–1831): vol. XXII, 397–8.

agriculture, more stable economic activities and trade, in the *Lectures on History and General Policy*, which acknowledged the by then mature economic ideas of the *Wealth of Nations* and the radical implications of Turgot's and Condorcet's political rationalism. This was not a discourse revolving around Price's agrarian ideal, but one that rejected the predominance of commercial interests.

With this intellectual baggage, Priestley moved to America full of hope, even though he continued to consider himself a British subject. His republicanism consisted of recognizing the sovereignty of the people, although he was to change his position on the organization of political power. In 1791, with *A Political Dialogue on the General Principles of Government*, he approved the unicameral model of Pennsylvania (where he had established himself) and France, condemning the British system of checks and balances. He later came close to Adams and, in the 1803 revision of the *Lectures on History*, shifted to the acceptance of the two-house system and suffrage linked to property and education. His republicanism was articulated not so much in constitutional forms as in its social dimension, and in the attention he gave to the correlation of economics and politics, perceived as sciences. This was directed at fulfilling the best interests of the nation, represented by the middle classes to which he himself belonged, and on which his thoughts on the limits to impose on the excessive accumulation of property were targeted.

Thomas Cooper, who was close to Priestley not only as a fellow exile, discerned the thread of radical thought being unwound in the cosmopolitan circulation of ideas: 'The doctrines of the perfectibility of the species, or at least its continually increasing tendency to improvement and to happiness, which Franklin and Price, and Condorcet and Godwin have lately supported, was advanced prior to their intimations of this cheering theory, by Dr. Priestley'.[129] He was referring to the 1768 essay on the principles of government, which had anticipated by ten years the principles of American independence.[130] Cooper made this pronouncement in 1806, as a response to the theories of Malthus. In Cooper's opinion, Priestley's views matched republican principles, which had long remained impracticable: 'On this rock M. Turgot split. This was forseen and well understood by Dr. Priestley'.[131] Given the political landscape in post-revolution France, it was evident to Priestley, Cooper stated – and thereby expressed his own belief – that only in America would the republican system be successful.[132]

Priestley was part of the American intellectual community from 1786, the year in which he was affiliated to the American Philosophical Society. When he arrived

---

[129] John Priestley, *Memoirs of Dr. Joseph Priestley to the year 1795, written by himself, with a continuation, to the time of his decease, by his son Joseph Priestley, and Observations on his writings by Thomas Cooper and the Rev. William Christie*, 2 vols. (London: J. Johnson, 1806): vol. I, 345.

[130] John Priestley, *Memoirs of Dr. Joseph Priestley*, 358.

[131] John Priestley, *Memoirs of Dr. Joseph Priestley*, 363.

[132] John Priestley, *Memoirs of Dr. Joseph Priestley*, 366–7. Cf. Joseph Priestley, *Lectures on History and General Policy* (London: 1826): 39.

in America, he settled in Pennsylvania. However, although the religious tolerance, the absence of slavery and the plenitude of land appeared to offer him assurances, he did not settle easily into American society, and his expectations were not entirely fulfilled. At the time of his arrival, apprehension about the developments of the French Revolution was being used as a political weapon in the clash between the Federalists and Republicans, and this brought about a change in the attitude towards France. These were the years of the Alien and Sedition Laws,[133] and of the Quasi-War with France. As an immigrant, under suspicion for his Unitarianism, his Francophilia and his links with Cooper – who had made the *Northumberland Gazette* an organ at the disposal of the Republicans – he became the target of William Cobbett, who in his attacks made a connection between religious dissent and direct support for the French Revolution. Like Cooper, Priestley risked expulsion, and only Jefferson's victory in the race for the presidency ensured his political protection, which made him a key figure of the English political emigration to America.[134]

In 1799, his *Letters to the Inhabitants of Northumberland* was issued as more than a defence against the accusations launched by Cobbett in his *Porcupine's Gazette*,[135] for in the text his international economic and political culture was exhibited in a reflection on the nexus of economics, politics and society, and on the rational foundations of modern republicanism. This put the work at the service of the Republicans. Having reflected long and hard on property, he acknowledged its centrality to the wider picture of natural harmony and order, the manifestation of divine providence, of which the economy was an expression.

Made up of twelve letters, his work was intended to help promote the prosperity of the country, to which everyone, foreigner or native, was expected to commit himself. He claimed to be proud of being an Englishman in America, the refuge of political, civil and religious freedom, where he had relocated his property and his family.[136] Obliged to defend himself against the accusation of being French – in September 1792 he had been given citizenship by the National Assembly – he disabused his readers of the idea that a French citizen was perforce an enemy of America. Against the Federalists, who branded Francophiles as democrats, he took issue with the negative eighteenth-century interpretation of the term democracy, which for them connoted anarchy, recommending a modern

---

[133]   Cf. James M. Smith, *Freedom's Fetters: The Alien and Sedition Laws and American Civil Liberties* (Ithaca, NY: Cornell University Press, 1956).

[134]   Jefferson to Priestley, Washington, 21 March 1801, in Jefferson, *The Papers*, vol. XXXIII, 393–4.

[135]   Cobbett also published a pamphlet against him in 1794, *Observations on the Emigration of Dr. Joseph Priestley.*

[136]   Joseph Priestley, *Letters to the Inhabitants of Northumberland and its Neighbourhood, on Subjects interesting to the Author and to them. The Second Edition with Additions; to which is added A Letter to a Friend in Paris, relating to Mr. Liancourt's Travels in the North American States* (Philadelphia: John Bioren, 1801): Letter I, 3.

definition: 'Pray consider what *democracy* really means. It signifies nothing more than *the government of the people*' and he likened it to the equality of rights and opportunity, as distinct from the 'equalization of all property'.[137]

Priestley distanced himself from France in 1794, yet in his work he mentioned his French contacts, 'as Mr. Turgot, Mr. Neckar, Mr. Brissot, Mr. Pethion, and the Duc de Rochfocault', his friendship with Franklin and his cosmopolitan culture.[138] The French Revolution was the expression of a political culture, to which he had come close and shared: thus, he defended Cooper from the accusation of being an 'English Jacobin, but this is merely a term of reproach. The principles that Mr. Cooper has maintained are clearly those of the American Constitution', and dismissed the accusations of Cobbet that Jefferson's administration 'will be conducted on the principles of Jacobinism, which tho' he does not define'.[139]

The criticisms of the British political system echoed the discussions of the late 1780s, inspired by John Stevens and amplified in France and beyond by the success of the *Recherches sur les Etats-Unis* by the Mazzei, Condorcet and Du Pont de Nemours group. For Priestley, as for Stevens, there was no real division of powers in Britain and, although still sympathetic to limited monarchy, he recognized the tendency of monarchic power to degenerate into despotism and so declared in favour of the American republic, founded on the rights of man and popular sovereignty.[140]

In the last letter, 'On the Policy of America with Respect to Foreign Nations' he summarized his economic stance. He opposed all forms of protectionism and was on the side of free trade, warning against favouring the interests of the mercantile classes.[141] He did not discuss at length the balance between economic activities and the role of agriculture, but merely aligned himself with the opinions professed by Cooper in *Political Arithmetic*.

Priestley had already indicated the economic policies that he had in mind for America in the *Maxims of Political Arithmetic*, published in the *Aurora* of 26 and 27 February 1798 and included in the 1801 edition of the *Letters*. It was in a nation's interest that every individual member managed his property in the most productive way, and it gained further advantage by following 'the wants of nature'.[142] This was made manifest in the harmony of the interests between different classes and between states' economies at international level. Trade was

---

[137] Priestley, *Letters to the Inhabitants of Northumberland*, Letter II, 9–10.

[138] Priestley, *Letters to the Inhabitants of Northumberland*, Letter III, 14.

[139] Priestley, *Letters to the Inhabitants of Northumberland*, Letter III, 20; Letter VI, 37.

[140] Priestley, *Letters to the Inhabitants of Northumberland*, Letter V, 24, 29; Letter X, 62.

[141] Priestley, *Letters to the Inhabitants of Northumberland*, Letter XII, 78.

[142] Priestley, *Letters to the Inhabitants of Northumberland*, *Maxims of Political Arithmetic*, 81–2.

considered a factor of communication and mutual benefit for the nations and as such was incompatible with any protectionist policy.[143]

In the interdependence of economies worldwide and in accordance with America's particular circumstances and commitment to peace, Priestley advocated an economic policy centred on a commercialized agriculture, considering agriculture and trade to be complementary rather than in opposition.[144]

Thomas Cooper and the Science of Economics

Priestley had come to represent a relationship with France more focused on the fundamentals of its political culture than on the events of the Revolution, concerning which he made certain distinctions. He shared these views with Thomas Cooper, to whom he was linked in America by way of a strong political partnership. Through Cooper it was possible to understand the nexus between economics and politics, a bond marked by percipience that was concerned more with the social project than wealth increase, and placed at the service of American agrarian ideology.

A materialist in philosophy and a Unitarian in theology, a revolutionary and economist, Cooper encapsulated the course of an entire movement of eighteenth-century cosmopolitan culture. In 1792 he was in Paris and close to the Jacobins, seeking to establish contact between the French club and the Manchester Constitutional Society, of which he was the leading figure.[145] For this reason he was censured by Burke, to whom he responded with a pamphlet lambasting the world of privilege.[146]

The hostility of the British government towards democratic societies and their support for the French Revolution led Cooper to migrate to America with Priestley in 1794, and to settle near him in Northumberland, Pennsylvania. It was then that he wrote *Some information respecting America* in order to encourage others to follow his path, taking into account the economic prospects and political guarantees

---

[143]   Priestley, *Letters to the Inhabitants of Northumberland, Maxims of Political Arithmetic*, 86.

[144]   Priestley, *Letters to the Inhabitants of Northumberland, Maxims of Political Arithmetic*, 87.

[145]   *Société des Amis de la Constitution, séante aux Jacobins, à Paris. Discours de MM. Cooper et Watt, Députés de la Société constitutionnelle de Manchester, prononcé à la société des amis de la constitution, séante à Paris, le 13 avril 1792, et imprimé, avec la réponse du président, par ordre de cette société* (De l'Imprimerie du patriote François, place du Théâtre Italien): 2. Responding to the petition presented to the Jacobins, Carra sang the praises of the revolutionary forces of three countries, Britain in 1688, France and America (*Ibid., Réponse de Carra*, 4).

[146]   Thomas Cooper, *A Reply to Mr. Burke's Invective against Mr. Cooper, and Mr. Watt, in the House of Commons, on 30th of April 1792* (Manchester: M. Falkner & Co., 1792).

that the new state had to offer. The wide availability of land in America was the greatest attraction for an Englishmen of middling means in search of religious freedom, Cooper said. Even if the objective of his work, in line with a very rich literature, was to provide practical information on the territory and its climate, it also included reflections on the agrarian vocation of the American economy and on the superiority of agriculture.[147] His critical attitude towards manufacturing was influenced by the social impact of the British industrial revolution:

> I detest the manufacturing system; observing the fallacious prosperity it induces, its instability, and its evil effect on the happiness and the morals of the bulk of the people. You must on this system have a large portion of the people converted into mere machine, ignorant, debauched, and brutal, that the surplus value of their labour of 12 or 14 hours a day, may go into the pockets and supply the luxuries of rich, commercial, and manufacturing capitalists.[148]

In America there was no great disproportion between the farmers. Cooper described how the term 'farmer' was used in America, where it was synonymous with 'landowner', 'equal in rank to any other rank in the state, having a voice in the appointment of his legislators', comparing it to general British usage, which indicated a socially inferior status, 'a tenant, holding of some lord'.[149] In this idealisation of the levelling of social conditions he placed also the political guarantees: 'the government is the government of the people, and for the people'.[150] Even before entering into the American political struggle, he had a clear idea of the political and economic project of the Federalists, 'rather leaning to British than to French politics', and the contrasting one of their opponents, 'rather lean to the French theory, though not to the French practice of politics'.[151]

On his arrival in America, Cooper allied himself to Jefferson's cause, and in the 1799–1800 supported his presidential campaign – as did Priestley – by disseminating his political-economic thoughts through his column in the *Sunbury and Northumberland Gazette*, of which he had become editor. His political commitment went hand in hand with a profound knowledge of economic science;

---

[147] Thomas Cooper, *Some information respecting America* (London: J. Johnson, 1794): 1–2.

[148] Cooper, *Some information respecting America*, 77–8.

[149] Cooper, *Some information respecting America*, 72.

[150] Cooper, *Some information respecting America*, 52–3.

[151] Cooper, *Some information respecting America*, 67–9. The French translation of the work, *Renseignements sur l'Amérique* (Hambourg: Pierre François Fauche, 1795), included an introduction by the translator, who, in the thermidorian climate, judged the work addressed to all emigrants, 'to the discontented of all classes and all countries, to the outlawed royalists and the suffering republicans' (XII).

he was one of the first American economists and among the first American university professors of political economy.[152]

He launched his liberal campaign in 1799 with the *Political Essays*, conceived as a means of criticizing government policy and giving support to Jefferson. The work was characterized, in the name of Republican principles and popular sovereignty, by an extolment of agriculture and free trade and a denouncement of protectionism. The essays confirmed his reputation as a political publicist and scholar of economics. In the collection of articles, all of which had been published previously in his newspaper, he drew his readers' attention to the backwardness of American political economic thinking, compared to that of the British and French. Among those who had made the greatest effort to explain how the agricultural and commercial systems differed had been 'the French *Economistes*, a class of Philosophers in the truest acceptation of this word; but whom the conceited and ignorant partizans of the present day, and this enlightened country, pretend to ridicule'.[153] The Physiocrats always held an important place in his thoughts, as the founders of the science of economics, but more so as theorists of the agrarian system.

He made a distinction between domestic trade, working for agriculture, and foreign trade, which required the underpinning of protectionist bonds, generated wars, and provided for a strong central government.[154] In support of his assertions he made mention – in addition to Priestley – of Smith, Young, the Marquis of Casaux and, in particular, the many Physiocratic arguments that Americans had come to know through 'Logan's publication in this country, containing a concise but just view of the more prominent evils of this system'.[155] His position on foreign trade would later be modified by events. His economic knowledge was vast and mature, but in a scheme aimed at illustrating the character and independence of the American economy, Physiocracy was ever present. America would remain for a long time a country insufficiently cultivated and under-populated, 'if any profession is to be fostered, let it be the Tiller of the earth, the mountain head of all wealth, and all power, and all property'.[156]

His work as an economist continued beyond his years of political engagement. The decision to abandon his post as a state judge, which he held from 1804 to 1811, and to devote himself to teaching, coincided with a decline towards conservatism in his positions, which led him eventually to distance himself from Jefferson and become a staunch defender of the rights of the Southern states and slavery in a way similar to that of other Republicans, who had sown the seeds of secession.

---

[152]   Cf. Dumas Malone, *The Public Life of Thomas Cooper 1783–1839* (New Haven: Yale University Press, 1926): 89.

[153]   Thomas Cooper, *Political Essays originally inserted in the Northumberland Gazette* (Northumberland: Andrew Kennedy, 1799), 42.

[154]   Cooper, *Political Essays*, 43.

[155]   Cooper, *Political Essays*, 55.

[156]   Cooper, *Political Essays*, 56.

As a journalist and professor, Cooper sought to popularize the science of economy. From 1813 to 1814, he was the editor of the *Emporium of Arts and Sciences*, which aimed to be a practical medium for the promotion of scientific and technical education. In defence of the domestic market and economic independence from Britain, he came to support protective measures as a spur to American manufacturing. With a change of position, similar to that of Jefferson and linked to the events that led to the War of 1812, he declared himself in favour of the development of manufacturing on the proviso that it operated in favour of agrarian interests. Albeit motivated by belief in economic freedom, his aversion to Britain, and that of other radicals, encouraged the notion of American self-sufficiency, which would lead to the 'American System'.

Convinced that the agricultural surplus would be able to absorb the products,[157] Cooper announced his support for the advancement of manufacturing in the *Prospectus* of the *Emporium of Arts and Sciences*. His intention was to compare this defence of manufactured goods with the doctrines of Ganilh and his *Inquiry into the various systems of political economy*.[158] He made numerous references to the works of authors interested in political economy, such as Davenant, Gee, Child, Hume and Steuart. It was Quesnay who first advocated agriculture for its exclusive productivity, and Cooper wrote at length on the 'new Sect, the Economistes', the members of which included Mirabeau and his son, Turgot, Condorcet, Mercier de La Rivière, and, to a lesser degree, the Marquis of Casaux, Herrenschwand, Garnier and Canard.[159] As Priestley had done in his *Memoirs*, published a few years earlier, Cooper made clear his full awareness of the existence of a Physiocratic tradition. In the very same years that French intellectuals resumed discussions on Smith to set themselves apart from the Physiocrats, by then finally consigned to economic history, Cooper declared the *Wealth of Nations* to be 'the book on the subject of political economy' that elaborated Physiocratic principles. Since then, he claimed, British authors 'have adopted the leading principles of the economistes', albeit while holding different positions on the productivity of manufacturing and trade, and he quoted in that regard Young, Crumpe, Anderson, Vaughan and Lauderdale. He specified that he had yet to see Say's *Traité d'économie politique*, of which he called for a translation,[160] and endorsed William Spence's views on the *sine qua non* of agriculture, referring to his *Britain Independent of Commerce*.[161]

---

[157]   *Emporium of Arts and Sciences*, new series, vol. I (Philadelphia, 1813): no. 1 (June), *Prospectus*, 1–10.

[158]   Charles Ganilh, *An Inquiry into the various systems of Political Economy*, trans. from French by D. Boileau, (London: 1812).

[159]   *Emporium of Arts and Sciences*, 12.

[160]   *Emporium of Arts and Sciences*, 13.

[161]   William Spence, *Britain independent of commerce: or, proofs deduced from an investigation into the true causes of the wealth of nations, that our riches, prosperity, and power, are derived from resources inherent in ourselves and would not be affected, even*

Cooper did not consider his refocused perspective on foreign trade and manufacturing a repudiation of his original positions. Thus in the *Emporium of arts and sciences* he republished *Political Arithmetic* and his extolment of agriculture, as well as *Foreign Commerce*, published in 1799 in the *Northumberland Gazette*. He explained how the war had led him to modify his ideas, without however retreating from his credo.[162]

In addition to his work as a journalist, he transmitted his liberal and free market beliefs through his activities as a professor and author of manuals on political economy. His aspiration was to collate and systematize information on the subject, which he deemed still to be scarce among Americans. He was one of the first professors of political economy in America and the first in a state of the South. By virtue of his interest in chemistry, which derived from his friendship with Priestley, he was professor of applied chemistry and mineralogy at the University of Pennsylvania between 1816 and 1819. Jefferson called him to the University of Virginia, and Cooper hoped that he could teach political economy there, but the opposition of Presbyterian clergy induced him to move to South Carolina College, where from 1820 he taught chemistry and political economy. His interest in economics was directly related to his scientific background.

He collated his lessons, and his manuals became textbooks that enjoyed a wide circulation in American universities. The *Lectures in the Elements of Political Economy* of 1826 and *A Manual of Political Economy* of 1833 were not original in terms of theory, but rather were intended to impart a political education via economics.[163] For him the handbook exposition of the principles of economic science fitted well Republican ideology, which intended to combine individual liberty and equality of rights.[164]

The coordinates of his treatises were provided by the classical economists: he cited Smith, Ricardo and Mill. However, he also gave a detailed description of the Physiocrats, considering their work to be the starting point of the science of economics; but even so, he criticized their principle of the exclusive productivity of agriculture, while crediting the merit of their censure of mercantilism.[165] Physiocratic reasoning recurred in the negative references to Colbert[166] and in the idea that the mercantile system was the source of conflicts and in the legitimization

---

though our commerce were annihilated, 6th ed., corrected and enlarged (London: W. Savage for T. Cadell and W. Davies, 1808; originally published, 1807). Cf. above, pp. 190–91.

[162]   *Emporium of Arts and Sciences, Foreign Commerce*, 161–2.

[163]   Thomas Cooper, *Lectures on the Elements of Political Economy*, 2nd. ed. (New York: A.M. Kelley, 1830): iv.

[164]   Thomas Cooper, *A Manual of Political Economy* (Washington: Duff Green, 1834): 48.

[165]   Cooper, *Lectures on the Elements of Political Economy*, 2nd. ed. (New York: A.M. Kelley, 1830): 14.

[166]   'The prayer of the citizens to their legislature, is that of the merchant to Colbert; "let us alone"'. (Cooper, *Lectures on the Elements of Political Economy* (Columbia: Doyle E. Sweeny, 1826): 117.)

of defensive war alone.[167] He placed Turgot and Condorcet among the Physiocratic authors – in accordance with eighteenth-century opinion – and he underscored the link between free trade and liberalism in French economic thought: 'Dr. Quesnay was followed in the same career, by the Marquis Mirabeau the elder, M. Mercier de la Riviere, M. Du Pont de Nemours, M. Turgot, and his biographer Condorcet. They did much to introduce the genuine principles of free trade, and liberal notions that characterize the modern science of Political Economy'.[168]

Cooper always remained a convinced agrarian and he continued to believe that working the land offered greater profitability compared to other activities. Moreover, the superiority of agriculture over manufacturing was confirmed by the negative impact, which he had observed, of the industrial revolution, 'a system in England very hurtful to the body and to the mind', which he never wanted to see in America.[169]

Even *A Manual of Political Economy* took up convinced agrarian positions, which echoed Physiocratic arguments regarding the value of agriculture and the direct relationship between education and the wealth of the country, a subject to which he dedicated an entire chapter,[170] albeit in the context of an economic culture that by then belonged to classical economics. His interest in French authors never waned. When opposing protectionist measures and taxes imposed by the Congress he cited Smith, Malthus, Ricardo, McCulloch and Mills, but also Say, Garnier, Destutt de Tracy and Ganilh.[171] He acknowledged the value of trade exchange, but continued to argue for the uniqueness of agriculture: 'Agriculture alone, adds, by direct result, to the quantity of consumable produce. ... Manufacture adds nothing in bulk, but otherwise, to the raw material. But altering the form, they add exchangeable value to that which had none before'.[172]

---

[167]   Cooper, *Lectures on the Elements of Political Economy* (Columbia: Doyle E. Sweeny, 1826): 20.

[168]   Cooper, *Lectures on the Elements of Political Economy*, 2nd. ed. (New York: A.M. Kelley, 1830): 14.

[169]   Cooper, *Lectures on the Elements of Political Economy* (Columbia: Doyle E. Sweeny, 1826): 131. He also took up the subject in *A Manual of Political Economy*, denouncing the exploitation of children in factories (Thomas Cooper, *A Manual of Political Economy* (Washington: Duff Green, 1834): 47–8).

[170]   Cooper, *Lectures on the Elements of Political Economy* (Columbia: Doyle E. Sweeny, 1826): 99 ff.

[171]   Cooper, *A Manual of Political Economy*, 59.

[172]   Cooper, *Lectures on the Elements of Political Economy* (Columbia: Doyle E. Sweeny, 1826),:45–6.

Thomas Jefferson: Political Action and Intellectual Dialogue

During his presidential campaign, Thomas Jefferson arranged for the distribution in Virginia of dozens of copies of Priestley's *Letters to the Inhabitants of Northumberland* and Cooper's *Political Arithmetic*. 'The Papers of political arithmetic', he wrote to Priestley in January 1800, 'both in your & Mr. Cooper's pamphlets, are the most precious gifts that can be made to us; for we are running navigation mad, & commerce mad, & navy mad, which is worst of all'.[173] In the same letter he asked Priestley to make a contribution towards the creation of the University of Virginia, which he intended would have a place for all sciences of use to Americans, including agriculture, commerce and the science of politics; he invited him to visit him and, as an enticement, announced the imminent arrival of Du Pont de Nemours, who he had asked to draw up the plan for the university, which was close to his heart.[174]

The political and scientific value of education and the formative role of economic science studies were interests that the elderly Physiocrat, Priestley, and Jefferson had in common. Education was equally important to Cooper, for whom teaching was a form of political engagement; Jefferson wrote to him, offering him a professorship at the university and saying that he had sent him a copy of Destutt de Tracy's volume on logic from the *Elémens d'idéologie*. He showed great appreciation of Cooper's work on political economy and as an editor, which was invaluable for Americans, 'misled from their true interests by the infection of English prejudices, and illicit attachments to English interests and connections. I look to you for this effort'.[175]

The anti-British arguments in Priestley's and Cooper's reflections on the economy, taken up again after their arrival in America during a heated moment in the political life of the new state, provided potent weapons for Jefferson and the Republicans and contributed to their victory. The emigration of English radicals to America coincided with the period in which the Jeffersonians placed political economy at the foundation of their Republican ideology. By dint of their writings and the support of newspapers, in which they were given leading positions, the exponents of this emigration came to provide a crucial bridge with American public opinion.[176]

Jefferson's political and cultural project could thus count on several prominent figures among the English radicals who had become journalists: William Duane,

---

[173]   Jefferson to Priestley, Philadelphia, 18 January 1800, in Jefferson, *The Writings*, ed. Peterson (1984): 1069; Jefferson to Philip Norborne Nicholas, Philadelphia, 7 April 1800, in Jefferson, *The Papers*, vol. XXI, 485.

[174]   Jefferson to Priestley, Philadelphia, 18 January 1800, *The Writings*, ed. Peterson (1984): 1070–71.

[175]   Jefferson to Cooper, Monticello, 16 January 1814, in Jefferson, *The Writings*, ed. Bergh, vol. XIV, 61.

[176]   The newspapers of the English emigrés represented between 15 to 20 per cent of the Republican press (cf. Durey, 'Thomas Paine's Apostles', 683).

after the death of Benjamin Franklin Bache in 1798, transformed the *Aurora* into a national newspaper and, as editor, featured prominently in Jefferson's publication strategy of translations of French post-Physiocratic thought, especially Say and Destutt de Tracy.[177] Again, James Carey, with the *Virginia Gazette*, and Mathew Carey, with *American Museum*, spread the Republican agrarian ideology; Priestley first published his *Maxims of Political Arithmetic* in the *Aurora* and Cooper used the *Sunbury & Northumberland Gazette* and the *Emporium of Arts and Sciences* as the organs of his political campaigns and the dissemination of economics.

Priestley and Cooper were two important interlocutors for Jefferson, representative of the world of English radicalism with which, through Franklin's mediation, he had come into contact during his stay in Europe. Despite the discretion required of his official position, he had also come to know the Honest Whigs, and his personal doctor in Paris, Richard Gem, came from the ranks of the Dissenters.[178] There was also a political incentive, related to his diplomatic remit, to the search for contacts within the few British circles sympathetic to political and economic relations with the new state.[179] In the Britain of the Dissenters Jefferson's success was due also to his *Religious Freedom*, a politically valuable discourse on rights, the English edition of which was edited by Price himself.[180]

Jefferson met Price for the first time in London in 1786, by which time he already knew and admired his *Observations on the importance of the American Revolution*, which Price had sent to him via Franklin.[181] At the same time he was aware that the pages on the abolition of slavery, a subject on which they agreed, would not win many converts in the South; however, he went on to claim that progress had been made in Virginia on the slavery issue, and he invited Price to bring his ideas to the students of William and Mary College.[182]

Despite declining the invitation, Price was always aware of having in Jefferson a partner with whom to share his radicalism.[183] More than a conversation between two authors, their correspondence was a rich political dialogue. Jefferson discussed the

---

[177]   James Tagg, *Benjamin Franklin Bache and the Philadelphia 'Aurora'* (Philadelphia: University of Pennsylvania Press, 1991).

[178]   Cf. Hans, 'Franklin, Jefferson, and the English Radicals'.

[179]   In 1786, complaining to Henry Lee of the difficulty of finding support for concluding a trade treaty between the United States and Britain, he wrote: 'I can scarcely consider as a party the Marquis of Lansdowne, and a half dozen characters about him, such as Dr. Price etc. who are impressed with the utility of a friendly connection with us' (Jefferson to Henry Lee, London, 22 April 1786, in Jefferson, *The Papers*, vol. IX, 398).

[180]   Thomas Jefferson, *An Act for Establishing Religious Freedom, Passed in the Assembly of Virginia in the Beginning of the Year 1786*, introduction by R. P. (London: 1786).

[181]   Jefferson to Price, Paris, 1 February 1785, in Jefferson, *The Papers*, vol. VII, 630.

[182]   Jefferson to Price, Paris, 7 August 1785, Jefferson, *The Papers*, vol. VII, 356–7.

[183]   Price to Jefferson, Newington Green, 24 October 1785, Jefferson, *The Papers*, vol. VII, 668; Price to Jefferson, Newington Green, 2 July 1785, Jefferson, *The Papers*, vol. VII, 258.

powers of the American Congress with the English Dissenter and, in the face of the latter's apprehension of an excessively strong central government, he skilfully considered the pros and cons and defended the American decisions. The Revolution in France was another topic of their exchange of views and enthusiasm, and Price followed its initial phases through the news sent to him by the well-connected Jefferson.[184]

With Priestley resident in America, Jefferson had a permanent intellectual contact with those English and French circles, which infused each other, that had played a vital part in the broadening of his political understanding while in Europe. He had wanted to gather around him both Priestley and Du Pont de Nemours, united by the choice of the United States as their political asylum, as he wrote in 1800. In the same letter, he expressed his rejection of the cult of the past in government, in religion and in learning, a position that he knew to be shared by the rationalism of the Physiocrat and the Dissenter, who continued to be his interlocutors.[185]

In May 1800 Priestley replied to Jefferson's invitation to collaborate in the creation of the University of Virginia by sending him some guidelines, *Hints concerning public education*. Written from a social standpoint, they were aimed at providing students with a complete, but diversified, instruction. The teaching included 'liberal education' as well as 'Chemistry, including the theory of Agriculture'.[186] In 1807, when debating the principles of civil society and government, Jefferson recommended, along with Locke, Sidney and the *Federalist*, Priestley's *Essay on the First Principles of Government*.[187]

After Priestley's death, in 1804, Cooper became an important political and intellectual interlocutor for Jefferson, with whom he discussed, more so than with Priestley, political economy.[188] Malthus's principles were the subject of an exchange of letters, the two men concurring that his theories were pessimistic and unsuited to the American reality. The correspondence shows that Cooper belonged to Jefferson's inner circle, and it was as such that he took part in debates at George Logan's home on issues of economic theory, which had direct political implications for America, impacting on its emigration policy. The debaters were

---

[184]   Jefferson to Price, Paris, 1 February 1785, Jefferson, *The Papers*, vol. VII, 630–31; Price to Jefferson, 3 August 1789, Jefferson, *The Papers*, vol. XV, 329.

[185]   Jefferson to Priestley, Philadelphia, 27 January 1800, in Jefferson, *The Writings*, ed. D. Peterson, 1073.

[186]   The plan is enclosed with Priestley's letter to Jefferson, Northumberland, 8 May 1800, in *The Correspondance of Jefferson and Du Pont de Nemours*, ed. Gilbert Chinard (Baltimore: The Johns Hopkins Press, 1931): 15–18.

[187]   Jefferson to John Norvell, 11 June 1807, in Jefferson, *The Writings*, vol. XI, 222–3.

[188]   Jefferson to Joseph Cabell, 1 March 1819, quoted in Malone, *Jefferson and his time*, vol. VI, 368.

unanimous in criticizing the lack of weight given by Malthus to emigration as a means of addressing demographic pressures.[189]

Jefferson appreciated Cooper's expertise – the fruit of a wide-ranging culture not circumscribed by specialization – which he wanted to be of service to the University of Virginia. It was while he was president of the American Philosophical Society that Cooper joined in 1802, and Jefferson consulted him for the organizational plans of the university.[190] He also urged Cooper to read the French authors, whom he considered in keeping with his serious approach to the science. And when Cooper sent him the text of his chemistry lessons, in which he recommended students to read 'the books of metaphysics', Jefferson suggested the inclusion of Destutt de Tracy's *Elémens d'idéologie* and the *Rapports du Physique et du moral de l'homme* by Cabanis. He also invited Cooper to read the *Commentaire sur l'"Esprit des Lois' de Montesquieu*, adding, 'I hope it will become the elementary book of the youth at all our colleges'.[191]

Jefferson was able to make good use of diverse lines of argument from the economic reflections of English radicalism during different periods of American politics. It is not possible to trace a uniformity of positions: in the economic crisis of the 1780s, the ideal of the self-sufficient farmer and the attacks by Price on luxury and trade strengthened the Jeffersonians, whereas in the 1790s it was Priestley's and Cooper's critique of foreign trade that reinforced Republican opposition to the financial and protectionist trade policies of the Federalists; that critical analysis also enhanced Republican principles when measured against Federalist policies which they considered to be dangerously close to monarchy. And all things considered, it was Paine's discourse on trade and agriculture, and its reworking by Priestley and Cooper, that helped to lay the foundation of a dynamic vision of the American agrarian model.

In essence, the arrival of English radicals in the 1790s contributed to the rejection of the British economic model and the positive value of a society in which economic exchange strengthened democracy while the balance between activities promoted the centrality of land and the motivating force of agriculture came to conjoin in the agrarian ideology of the Republicans. At the same time, the economic culture of France and the Revolution of 1789 constituted a common point of orientation through the circulation of ideas and literature and the unfolding of personal relationships and individual destinies between France, Britain and America.

---

[189] Cooper to Jefferson, 16 February 1804 and Jefferson's reply of 24 February, *Jefferson Papers*, Library of Congress, cited in Drew R. McCoy, 'Jefferson and Madison on Malthus. Population growth in Jeffersonian Political Economy', *The Virginia Magazine of History and Biography*, 88 (1980): 259–76, here 266–7.

[190] Jefferson to Cooper, 25 August 1814, in Jefferson, *The Writings*, vol. XIV, 173–4.

[191] Jefferson to Cooper, Monticello, 10 July 1812, Jefferson, *The Writings*, vol. XIII, 177–78; Monticello, 16 January 1814, *ibid.*, vol. XIV, 62–63. On Jefferson's attempts to publish Tracy's work, cf. below Chapter 8.

Among the different factors that combined to shape American national identity, the French contribution to economics reinforced the Republican economic and political project in opposition to the British model. While Britain remained a target of their attacks in the struggle against the Federalists, the Republicans were nevertheless enriched by the contributions of the British radical immigrants to the United States. Republicanism, religion and economic thought became intertwined through the connections with the English Dissenters that we have followed here. The long-running interest in French economic thought, from the ideologists of the agrarian democracy and the American economic societies, and from within the academic culture and the circles of British radical emigration highlights the resilience of the intellectual heritage and personal links which were in no way static but were enriched by mutual exchanges, with Jefferson continuing to play a central and dynamic role.

Chapter 8
A Long Eighteenth Century

From the second half of the eighteenth century to the early nineteenth America's reception of French economic thought was characterized by a perception of its continuity from the Physiocrats to Jean-Baptiste Say. The years 1800 to 1820 were marked by a series of significant moments: it was the period in which Say developed his ideas; 1807 to 1813 were, for Say and French intellectual circles, the most oppressive phase of the Napoleonic Empire;[1] 1802 to 1820 were the years in which the various interpretations of Smith's *The Wealth of Nations* were debated, and a reconsideration of Physiocracy led to its final rejection.[2] In America, 1800 to 1809 were the years of Thomas Jefferson's presidency; in 1811 the concession of privilege to the Bank of the United States came to an end; and in 1812 the United States went to war with Britain. In the years of the pre-Ricardian debates, America witnessed a series of initiatives aimed at disseminating French economic thought in order to halt the spread of British ideas.

At the heart of these critical points in time stood the pragmatist Jefferson, who was able to grasp the full breadth of the social approach of post-Physiocratic French economic thought. His detection of a thread that ran through a national economic tradition resulted from his rejection of all forms of dogmatism and from his personal contacts: the continuity was represented by the *Idéologues*, the group that kept alive the legacy of eighteenth-century political and economic reflection, which had passed through the experience of the Revolution, and which forged a link between Europe and America, and between the French and American Revolutions – a kind of Euro-American movement that expedited the passage of the American myth and the model of the United States from the eighteenth to the nineteenth centuries.[3]

---

[1]   A new interpretation of Say's thoughts on economics, seen as a modern expression of the republican language, can be found in Richard Whatmore, *Republicanism and the French Revolution: An Intellectual History of Jean-Baptiste Say's Political Economy* (Oxford: Oxford University Press, 2000).

[2]   Cf. Philippe Steiner, 'Quels principes pour l'économie politique? Charles Ganilh, Germain Garnier, Jean-Baptiste Say et la critique de la physiocratie', in *La diffusion internationale de la physiocratie (XVIIIe–XIXe)*, ed. Bernard Delmas, Thierry Demals and Philippe Steiner (Grenoble: Presses Universitaires, 1995): 209–30. ; Kenneth E. Carpenter, *The Dissemination of the Wealth of Nations in French and in France, 1776–1843* (New York: The Bibliographical Society of America, 2002).

[3]   Cf. Moravia, *Il tramonto dell'illuminismo*; Moravia, *Il pensiero degli Idéologues*. On the importance of the revolution for French authors, cf. Sophie-Anne Leterrier, *L'institution*

Say had already understood the contribution the two Revolutions made to the progress of economic science: 'Two great events, independently of men, have been the teachers of mankind: the revolution of North America, and that of France. Speculative politics and political economy have made important collections of right ideas, and these same two events have supplanted more than one error'.[4]

It was not by chance that an American, Benjamin Franklin, played the key role of bridge between the Physiocratic tradition and the *Idéologue* circles:[5] he who frequented the salon of Madame Helvétius in Auteuil, whose realism and simplicity made him a symbol of the average man, anticipating Say's middle class; who was a legend in Europe; and was, with Jefferson, the most European of Americans.[6] And Jefferson shared Say's belief that the study of political economy was vital to the stabilisation of the democratic revolutions. The success of Say's *Traité d'économie politique* in America was proof of this.

Behind this web woven around the circulation of Say's *Traité* it is possible to reconstruct Jefferson's version of French ideas – innovative for having been made by an American and a statesman – which highlighted the interaction between his reception of economic culture and his contribution to debates in France. It was the sometimes-tortuous path of a reflection on the relationship between economics and politics, which spread from France to the United States and then back to France enriched by American realism and pragmatism. The interaction took place through the association between personalities at the crossroads of ideas circulating between the eighteenth and the early nineteenth centuries: Jefferson, Du Pont de Nemours, Say and Destutt de Tracy.

The criss-crossing exchange of their correspondence and contacts, for which Jefferson was the core organizer and Say the theoretical authority, make it possible to determine, by paying close attention to the sequence of events, new lines of interpretation: indeed, it is possible to trace the indirect path along which Say's works advanced into the United States and to specify how Jefferson defined the relationship between agriculture and manufacturing, linking it not only to his political realism but also to his theoretical reflection. It is possible, moreover, to apprehend the full scope of the part performed by Du Pont de Nemours in the transformation of Physiocracy at the beginning of the nineteenth century. This allowed him, through his rapport with Jefferson, and beyond the controversy of his letters to Say, to arrive at a partial modification of positions, which drew him closer to post-Physiocratic economic thinking.

---

des sciences morales: l'Académie des sciences morales et politiques, 1795–1850 (Paris: L'Harmattan, 1995). A recent reading of the comparative reactions of contemporaries to the two revolutions is the essay by Richard Whatmore, 'The French and North American Revolutions in Comparative perspective', in *Rethinking the Atlantic World*, 219–28.

[4]   Jean-Baptiste Say, *Histoire abrégée des progrès de l'économie politique*, in Say, *Cours complet d'économie politique*, vol. II, 1271, in *Œuvres complètes*.

[5]   Cf. Aldridge, *Benjamin Franklin et ses contemporains*.

[6]   Cf. Gordon S. Wood, *The Americanization of Benjamin Franklin*.

A Continuing Dialogue: Jefferson and Du Pont de Nemours

Du Pont consistently carried out the role of intermediary between French circles and Jefferson, following the return of the latter to the United States at the end of 1789. Du Pont was Jefferson's living link with the Physiocrats, particularly after he had decided to move to America, where he arrived in January 1800, the year in which Jefferson won the presidency. The two men's acquaintance dated back to the time of Jefferson's sojourn in Paris: 'During your ambassadorship you saw me fight on behalf of your country, and for the principles of liberality, of sincere friendship between the two nations, and against every financial and commercial prejudice which our government had at that time'.[7] Du Pont had already demonstrated his zeal for America during the drafting of the 1778 trade treaty between France and the United States, on which he worked with Franklin.[8] After the *coup d'etat* of 18 Fructidor, Year V, which persuaded him to leave France, America became his asylum of liberty.[9] Two years later, in May 1802, he returned for a brief mission in Paris, where however he remained until 1815.

During his first two years in America he worked with Jefferson on two important issues: the Louisiana Purchase, of 1803,[10] and the founding of the University of Virginia. Public education was an interest he had in common with Jefferson, who had written the *Bill for the More General Diffusion of Knowledge*[11] and the elderly Physiocrat had served as secretary for the Education Commission of Poland in 1774. In July 1800 he sent Jefferson a comprehensive project for national education that showed how his pedagogical career had been enriched by a sociological approach adapted to the reality of American democracy.[12] From the

---

[7]   Du Pont de Nemours to Jefferson, Paris, 27 August 1798, in *Correspondence Between Thomas Jefferson and Pierre-Samuel du Pont de Nemours 1798–1817*, ed. Dumas Malone, trans. Linwood Lehman (Boston: Houghton Mifflin, 1930): 1. The French original is in *The Correspondence of Jefferson and Du Pont de Nemours*, ed. Gilbert Chinard (Baltimore: The Johns Hopkins Press, 1931): 6.

[8]   On the role played in 1798 by Du Pont's first son, Victor, General Consul to Philadelphia, in convincing the Directory to change its anti-American politics, thus helping to avoid war between the two countries, cf. William Carr, *Ces étonnants Du Pont de Nemours* (Paris: Editions de Trevise, 1967).

[9]   Du Pont de Nemours to Jefferson, 27 August 1798, *Correspondence*, 2 (The French original is in *The Correspondence*, 7). For details of the decision made by Du Pont and his family to move to the United States, cf. Mark Thompson, 'Causes and Circumstances of the Du Pont Family's Emigration', *French Historical Studies*, 6 (Spring 1969): 59–77.

[10]   On Du Pont's important role as an intermediary between Jefferson and the French government, cf. the detailed narration in Gilbert Chinard's introduction to *The Correspondence of Jefferson and Du Pont de Nemours*, xxvii–xliv.

[11]   Thomas Jefferson, *A Bill for the More General Diffusion of Knowledge*, in Jefferson, *The Papers*, vol. II, 526–34. Cf. Honeywell, *The Educational Work of Thomas Jefferson*.

[12]   Pierre-Samuel Du Pont de Nemours, *Sur l'éducation nationale dans les Etats-Unis d'Amérique*, 2nd ed. (Paris: Le Normant, 1812). The first edition was published in Good Stay.

Physiocrats to the *Idéologues*, the importance of education and the educational usefulness of political economics were a compelling point of interest that helped maintain Jefferson's interest in French ideas.

During his first stay, Du Pont kept up an exchange of letters with Jefferson, which revealed the compatibility of their ideas: Du Pont expressed his dislike for Hamilton and his economic policies, while Jefferson wrote of his distrust of Bonaparte.[13] Furthermore, as President, Jefferson was a supporter of agrarian interests, much like his Physiocratic confidant.[14]

On 1 February 1804 Jefferson thanked Say for the gift of his *Traité d'économie politique*, which he received while engrossed in reading the second edition of Malthus's *Essay on the Principle of Population*. His letter was written as a sort of dialogue with the French economist.[15] With his hallmark pragmatism, he argued that if political economy was applied to very different realities, like those of European nations and the United States, it would have different outcomes. The increased production of subsistence goods, which followed an arithmetic progression in Europe and a geometric one in America, owing to its abundance of land, precluded Malthus's analysis from having a universal relevance, confining it to Europe alone. This same European reality imposed a balance between agriculture and manufacturing, which Jefferson doubted could be advantageous to the United States.[16] For Jefferson, a reader of Physiocracy, the primacy of agriculture was indisputable. He therefore hoped that reading Say would yield an answer to his questions: 'Perhaps, as worthy the attention of the author of the *Traité d'économie politique*, I shall find them answered in that work. If they are not, the reason will have been that you wrote for Europe; while I shall have asked them because I think for America'.[17]

Reading Malthus gave him a fresh opportunity for reflection on Physiocracy. He shared the critical reception of the Americans of the pessimistic analysis of the

---

Jefferson, having become president, refocused on the university project only later, much to Du Pont's regret. The English translation of his project was not published until the twentieth century (*National education in the United States of America* (Newark: University of Delaware Press, 1923)). Cf. Philip A. Bruce, *History of the University of Virginia 1818–1919*, 5 vols. (New York: Macmillan, 1920–1921): vol. I, 63–4, which showed how Du Pont based his educational proposals on Jefferson's plan of 1779, further proof of the ways in which the two men influenced each other.

[13]   Du Pont de Nemours to Jefferson, New York, 17 December 1801, in *Correspondence*, 33 (The French original is in *The Correspondence*, 33); Jefferson to Du Pont, Washington, 18 January 1802, *Correspondence*, 41 (the French original is in *The Correspondence*, 37).

[14]   *Correspondence*, 40 (the French original is in *The Correspondence*, 36); cf. also Du Pont de Nemours to Jefferson, Paris, 23 July 1808, *ibid.*, 131.

[15]   Say to Jefferson, 3 November 1803, in Gilbert Chinard, *Jefferson et les Idéologues d'après sa correspondance inédite* (Baltimore: The Johns Hopkins Press; Paris: PUF, 1925): 14–15.

[16]   Jefferson to Say, 1 February 1804, in Jefferson, *Writings*, ed. Peterson, 1144.

[17]   Jefferson to Say, 1 February 1804, Jefferson, *Writings*, ed. Peterson, 1144.

Essay on Population, and this reinforced his sense of national identity. However, he appreciated the more Physiocratic tone of the second edition with its defence of the agricultural system and its attacks on mercantilism and British policies, which in his eyes secured Malthus a role in the discourse on political economics that ran from the Physiocrats to Say: 'A work of sound logic, in which some of the opinions of Adam Smith, as well as of the economists, are ably examined. I was pleased, on turning to some chapters where you treat the same questions, to find his opinions corroborated by yours'.[18]

In the 1803 edition Malthus had cited Du Pont de Nemours and his arguments in favour of high cereal prices,[19] and it was probably Du Pont who confirmed Jefferson's Physiocratic interpretation of Malthus; after his return to the United States he published his *Examen du livre de M. Malthus*: 'Mr. Malthus's book is a long, but clever and curious commentary on this maxim of French economists: *the measure of subsistence is that of the population*'.[20] His belief in Malthus's superiority to Smith was also shared by Jefferson: 'Malthus, even more profound and tenacious than Smith, on the correct principles relating to the administration of agriculture, manufacturing and trade'.[21]

After Physiocracy: Jefferson and the Reception of French Economic Thought

We have seen how, during the violent political clashes of the closing decade of the eighteenth century, Jefferson set his project of agrarian democracy against Hamilton's federalist programme. Becoming president, Jefferson's political realism and his commitment to reconciliation led him to soften his positions; he remained a stalwart supporter of the primacy of agriculture, but, in the end, faced with external pressures such as the Embargo and later the War of 1812, conceded that manufacturing should be developed, albeit subordinately, to support agricultural

---

[18]   Jefferson to Say, Washington, 1 February 1804, in Jefferson, *Writings*, ed. Peterson, 1143; in the same period he had also expressed his appreciation for Malthus's work to Joseph Priestley (Jefferson to Priestley, 29 January 1804, in Thomas Jefferson, *The Writings*, ed. Bergh, vol. X, 447–8). Cf. Bernard Semmel, 'Malthus: "Physiocracy" and the Commercial System', *The Economic History Review*, 17 (1965): 522–35; Samuel Hollander, 'Malthus as a Physiocrat: Surplus Versus Scarcity', in *La diffusion internationale de la Physiocratie*, 79–116.

[19]   Thomas R. Malthus, *An Essay on the Principle of Population*, 2nd. ed. (London: printed for J. Johnson by T. Bensley): 458.

[20]   Pierre-Samuel Du Pont de Nemours, *Examen du livre de M. Malthus sur le Principe de Population; auquel on a joint la traduction de quatre chapitres de ce livre supprimés dans l'édition française; et une Lettre à M. Say sur son Traité d'économie politique* (Philadelphia: P. M. Lafourcade, 1817): 2.

[21]   Du Pont de Nemours, *Examen*, 30.

interests.[22] An analysis of his correspondence with his French interlocutors allows us to follow the flow of his ideas and to judge how economic ideas influenced his actions as a politician.

By 1809 Jefferson was convinced of the validity of the principle of balance between economic activities. A month after leaving the presidency he wrote: 'An equilibrium of agriculture, manufacturers, and commerce, is certainly become essential to our independence', though his conception of industrial development was limited to domestic consumption and the redistribution of agricultural surplus.[23] In 1815, when thanking Say for the second edition of the *Traité*, and after the experience of the war, he declared: 'The question proposed in my letter of February 1st, 1804, has since become a "question viseuse"', since the problem was now reduced to a dilemma: 'This fact, therefore, solves the question by reducing it to its ultimate form, whether profit or preservation is the first interest of a State? We are consequently become manufacturers'.[24] The systematization of data concerning the real mechanisms of the economy was the main reason for the new edition of his work, which Say dedicated to Jefferson's pragmatism.[25]

The liberal attitude that led Say to consider the United States the best governed country and the one in which the presence of the state was least apparent, accorded with his preference for the federal system, of which America set the standard.[26] The expectations linked to the reality of a federal republic, and the difficulties encountered by his own country, induced Say to plan to resettle in the United States and establish, in a more promising environment, a cotton factory in combination with an agrarian enterprise. Jefferson was enthusiastic about Say's intention to settle in Charlottesville, Virginia, near Monticello, and even hoped to raise the

---

[22]   On Jefferson's change of position, cf. Grampp, 'A Re-examination of Jeffersonian Economics'.

[23]   Jefferson to John Jay, Monticello, 7 April 1809, in Jefferson, *The Writings*, ed. Bergh, vol. XII, 271; cf. also Jefferson to Thomas Leiper (Washington: 21 January 1809), *ibid.*, 238.

[24]   Jefferson to Say, Monticello, 2 March 1815, in Jefferson, *The Writings*, ed. Bergh, vol. XIV, 258–9; Say to Jefferson, Paris, 14 June 1814, Library of Congress, The Thomas Jefferson Papers. Series 1. General Correspondence, 1651–1827.

[25]   Say to Jefferson, Paris, 14 June 1814, Library of Congress, The Thomas Jefferson Papers. Series 1. General Correspondence, 1651–1827. Thanking Say, Jefferson wrote: 'I rejoice that the book, of which you were so kind to send me a copy, is becoming known here, begins to be much read, and really see in that circumstance chiefly a prospect, however distant, that our rulers will come in time to understand the subject and to apply the remedy which is in their power only. A shorter work of Mr. Tracy's on the same subject is in course of publication, and will co-operate with yours to the same end' (Jefferson to Say, Monticello, 14 May 1817, in Jefferson, *The Writings*, ed. Bergh, vol. XIX, 249).

[26]   Jean-Baptiste Say, *Cours complet*, vol. II, 1239.

funds needed to engage him as a teacher.[27] The dialogue with Say once again gave Jefferson cause to reflect on America and Europe and on America's individuality.

In response to Say's request for information about Virginia, the value of land and the likelihood of success, Jefferson sent details of the types of crops farmed there, the systems of crop rotation and the climate, and he praised the benefits of the region, likening its fertility to that of Champagne or Burgundy.[28] He also described the opportunities offered by a 'rational and republican society'. Unfortunately, the depreciation of the American dollar resulting from the printing of paper currency during the War of 1812 made it impossible to determine the price of land and so, in his letter to Say of 2 March 1815, he decried American government policy, financial speculation and the power of the banks, knowing well that Say held the same views.[29] He attributed the dire situation not only to forces opposed to agrarian interests, but also to the backwardness of American economic thought, which had allowed the government to take on loans without imposing taxes for their repayment:

> Mr Say will be surprised to find, that forty years after the development of sound financial principles by Adam Smith and the Economists, and a dozen years after he has given them to us in a corrected, dense and lucid form, there should be so much ignorance of them in our country.[30]

Faced with the high American inflation after the War of 1812, Jefferson used Say's attacks against public debt and the monopoly of the banks as a political weapon, in the same way as he had turned to the Physiocrats when contesting Hamilton's financial policies. In 1817, in a letter to Say thanking him for having sent the third edition of the *Traité*, he expressed his hope that the work of the French economist might help America's governors to widen their knowledge of political economy and use the tools provided by the new science.[31]

Apart from the political circumstances, Jefferson's interest in Say and in post-Physiocratic French thought had ideological motivations, which involved cultural affinities. Though Say had broken with the *Économistes*, his *Traité* still stood also in the Physiocratic tradition, for its denial of the centrality of money and

---

[27] Jefferson to Joseph C. Cabell, 5 January 1815, in *Early History of the University of Virginia,* 36.

[28] Jefferson to Jean-Baptiste Say, 2 March 1815, in Jefferson, *The Writings*, ed. Bergh, vol. XIV, 260–63.

[29] Jefferson, *The Writings*, ed. Bergh, vol. XIV, 264–65.

[30] Jefferson to José Correa de Serra, 27 December 1814, in Jefferson, *The Writings*, ed. Bergh, vol. XIV, 224.

[31] Jefferson to Jean-Baptiste Say, 14 May 1817, in Jefferson, *The Writings*, ed. Bergh, vol. XIV, vol. XIX, 249.

public debt, and it also accorded with Jefferson's views.[32] In addition to holding a common set of beliefs, Jefferson and Say also approached their different situations in the same way, seeking to stabilize their republics and safeguard the legacy of their Revolutions. Say provided the ideology of American democratic agrarianism with a scientific evaluation of the economy that was directed not towards an élite, but towards the middle class that emerged from the Revolution. This was a path similar to that taken by the American Republicans who, by extolling the farmer as an independent and virtuous property owner, had equated the interests of the agrarian class with the general interest. The American notion of virtue, conceived as a unity of interests, contained a new ethical dimension relating to the economy, which Say addressed in his *Olbie*.

For Jefferson and Say, in their different countries, this was a matter of affirming the central role of the economy within Republican freedom, which implied the need to educate the people. The imperative of education in Say's work dated back to the Physiocratic view of the need to understand economic laws as a science of society. This was the same perspective that prompted Jefferson to seek the help of Du Pont at the time of the creation of the University of Virginia.

In contact with French circles Jefferson fortified his national identity. Reading Malthus and Say, he reflected on the importance of verifying the principles of political economy put forward in Europe in the exceptional environment of America. If his relationship with Du Pont de Nemours allowed him to feel the still vital presence of Physiocracy, the experimental value of Say's practical political economy offered responses to the pragmatism of the politician and to the issues that he had to confront during his two terms as president, during a tempestuous period in international affairs.

Jefferson was not directly concerned with Say's methodological reflection on political economy,[33] which favoured procedures rather than theoretical breakthroughs, but he nonetheless knew how to make use of the practical import of the distinction between economics and politics, the primacy of the economy over politics, the social approach, the importance of teaching economic science, and the rejection of systems, especially those resulting from British thinking. For his part, Say was interested in the empirical approach and realism of the Americans, just as Jefferson appreciated the French tradition that had separated itself from all forms of dogmatism. For this reason, soon after the end of his presidency, he began work on propagating French post-Physiocratic economic thought in America, as

---

[32]   In his handwritten pages Say also openly recognized his debt towards the Physiocrats: 'I esteem them', he wrote in a letter to Du Pont de Nemours, in which he assured Du Pont that he would use his critiques for the third edition of his *Traité*, 'I love them; they are the ones that gave me the taste for these subjects; it is in their writings that I began to study them '. (Jean-Baptiste Say to Du Pont de Nemours, 23 June 1814, Eleutherian Mills Historical Library, *Winterthur Manuscripts*.)

[33]   Cf. Edgar Allix, "La méthode et la conception de l'économie politique dans l'oeuvre de J.-B. Say', *Revue d'histoire économique et sociale* (1911): 321–60.

part of a continuous whole embracing the eighteenth-century tradition enriched by the outcome of the Revolution and the impulses of liberal opposition of the *Idéologues*, some of whom were among his interlocutors.

On 12 June 1809, through the mediation of Lafayette to whom he was related,[34] Destutt de Tracy sent to Jefferson the manuscript of his *Commentaire sur Montesquieu*, asking him to publish it in English, but to do so anonymously.[35] Jefferson had retired from the presidency three months earlier, and his decision not to present his candidature again had been admired in France, where it had been compared to Bonaparte's conduct. Ten months later, on 12 August 1810, he sent Tracy's manuscript to William Duane, editor of *Aurore*, along with the English translation – of his own hand – of Book XI on civil liberties and the constitution, proposing an American edition.

Jefferson shared the *Commentaire*'s criticisms of the *Esprit des lois*.[36] The repudiation of Montesquieu's relativism and his attention to history and tradition, explicated by the *Commentaire*, could be traced back to the political rationalism of the Physiocrats, which Jefferson had first discovered during his stay in France and found again in the *Idéologues*.[37] He did not approve of all Tracy's claims, yet believed that his work countered well the false opinions of the *Esprit del lois* and the British model, since he defended the rational foundations of representative government.[38] He assured the publisher that Tracy's book was a valuable political work and that it brought Montesquieu down 'to his just level, as his predilection for monarchy, and the English monarchy in particular, has done mischief everywhere, and here also' and reminded him of how Hamilton had invoked his authority.[39]

Between 1809 and 1811 Jefferson was actively engaged in revising the translation, which he followed step by step so as not to let the author down, 'knowing his precision of idea, and his attention to the choice of words, for expressing them'.[40] He suggested the English title and wrote the introductory dedication in the form of a letter from a Frenchman who had fled from Robespierre

---

[34] Destutt de Tracy's daughter had married Lafayette's son, George Washington.

[35] Destutt de Tracy to Jefferson, Auteuil, 12 June 1809, in Chinard, *Jefferson et les Idéologues*, 43–4.

[36] Jefferson to Duane, Monticello, 12 August 1810, in Chinard, *Jefferson et les Idéologues*, 57.

[37] Gilbert Chinard, *Pensées choisies de Montesquieu tirées du 'Common-Place Book' de Thomas Jefferson* (Paris: les Belles Lettres, 1925); cf. also Moravia, *Il tramonto dell'illuminismo*. On Jefferson's change of opinions on Montesqueiu, cf. above, pp. 91–2.

[38] Jefferson to Duane, Monticello, 12 August 1810 in Chinard, *Jefferson et les Idéologues*, 55.

[39] Jefferson to Duane, Monticello, 16 September 1810, Chinard, *Jefferson et les Idéologues*, 59–60.

[40] Jefferson to Duane, Monticello, 25 October 1810, Chinard, *Jefferson et les Idéologues*, 61 and also 18 January 1811, 65.

to the United States. American public opinion was presented as ready to profit from the correction of Montesquieu's errors.[41]

On 26 January 1811 Jefferson was finally able to inform Tracy that the translation was completed, in a letter in which he admonished him for his preference of a form of executive power entrusted to several people. Here all the differences between the statesman, with his pragmatism, and the *Idéologue*, whose goal was to establish fixed principles, were plain to see. The different states guaranteed a plurality of political subjects in America – which did not exist in France – without weakening executive power. Jefferson did not wish to export the American model, but regretted the failure to organize the provincial assemblies proposed by the Physiocrats, which could have saved France from both the weakness of the Directory and the dominance of a single leader. He did not, however, call into question the value of Tracy's work.[42] In July 1811, the *Commentary and Review of Montesquieu's Spirit of Laws* was finally published.[43]

Described as the bedrock of Jeffersonian democracy and 'the handbook of the perfect American democrat',[44] the *Commentaire* presented a large number of political and economic ideas that Jefferson made his own: the repudiation of Montesquieu's relativism and the British system, the reproof of a strong executive power and government interference in society, the exaltation of popular sovereignty and representative government, the attacks against colonialism, the legitimacy of defensive war alone, the separation of church and state, and the necessity of

[41]   *The author, To his fellow citizens of the United States of America*, in Chinard, *Jefferson et les Idéologues*, 64.

[42]   'The republican government of France was lost without a struggle, because the party of '*un et indivisible*' has prevailed; no provincial organizations existed to which the people might rally under authority of the laws' (Jefferson to Destutt de Tracy, Monticello, 26 January 1811, in Jefferson, *The Writings*, ed. Bergh, vol. XIII, 20).

[43]   Antoine-Louis-Claude Destutt de Tracy, *A commentary and Review of Montesquieu's Spirit of Laws. Prepared for press from the original manuscript, in the hands of the publishers. To which are annexed, Observations on the thirty-first book, by the late M. Condorcet: and two letters of Helvétius, on the merits of the same work* (Philadephia: W. Duane, 1811). A French edition, *Commentaire sur l''Esprit des lois' de Montesquieu, suivi d'observations inédites de Condorcet sur le vingt-neuvième livre du dit ouvrage* (Liège: Desoer, 1817), was published without the author's permission and reprinted in 1819 (cf. Tracy to Jefferson, 11 April 1818, in Chinard, *Jefferson et les Idéologues*, 180). Tracy later published the original text (Paris: Delaunay, Mongie aîné, 1819). One reads in the French 'Editor's notice': 'This work was published in English in Philadelphia in 1811, under the auspices of the celebrated Mr. Jefferson, former President of the United States; it served as a textbook in the William and Mary College in the State of Virginia, and in many others. A distinguished French scholar had begun to translate it in 1812: this translation was not completed' (*Commentaire sur l'Esprit des lois de Montesquieu; édition entièrement conforme à celle publiée à Liège en 1817* (Paris: Delaunay, 1819), v). On the allusion to Du Pont de Nemours, who began the translation, cf. below, p. 255.

[44]   Chinard, *Jefferson et les Idéologues*, 45–6.

public education. Tracy acknowledged that a modern democracy required a vast territory and that the United States, and not Britain, was the first to have achieved a separation of powers. From an economic point of view, Jefferson shared the criticisms of the burden of taxation, public debt and the monopoly of the banks, which, in 1811, during the expiry of the Bank of the United States' charter, offered him a valuable weapon for political warfare.

Jefferson also appreciated Tracy's psychological interpretation of the economy as a global discourse that was not limited to the scientific analysis of wealth creation. Tracy's science of ideas allowed him to comprehend the interconnectedness of politics and economics, considered scientifically and brought back to their natural foundations.[45]

Jefferson knew the French texts of the *Idéologie*. In 1802 he received from Cabanis his *Rapports du physique et du moral de l'homme*,[46] and on 21 October 1811 Tracy sent him, in response to the copy that he had received of his *Review of Montesquieu*, the first three volumes of the *Eléments d'idéologie*.[47] With his critiques of Montesquieu's economic arguments, Tracy provided a better understanding of the political significance of economic principles, which he drew directly from Say and his *Traité*, 'the best work on political economy, that has yet appeared', including[48] the tripartite division of political economy and the links between production, distribution and consumption, the idea of the productivity of trade, and production perceived as the creation of utility.

Du Pont de Nemours's Revealing Mistake

The most telling evidence of the similarity of Tracy's and Jefferson's positions was provided by Du Pont de Nemours, who mistakenly believed that Jefferson was the author of the *Commentary and Review of Montesquieu's Spirit of Laws*.

---

[45]   Jefferson to J. Adams, 11 January 1817, in Chinard, *Jefferson et les Idéologues*, 259.

[46]   Chinard, *Jefferson et les Idéologues*, 23–6.

[47]   Destutt de Tracy to Jefferson (Paris: 21 October 1811), in Chinard, *Jefferson et les Idéologues*, 88.

[48]   Destutt de Tracy, *Review of Montesquieu*, 87–188. Despite having been critical of Tracy's ideas, particularly those relating to the theory of value, Say appreciated Tracy, who: 'demonstrated the important relationships that link economics to methods of understanding and the laws of morality'. (Say, *Histoire abrégée*, 570). On Tracy, considered 'one of the Say's school', cf. Ricardo's letter to Malthus, 16 December 1822, in David Ricardo, *Letters, 1821–1823*, ed. Piero Sraffa, vol. IX (Cambridge: Cambridge University Press, 1962): 248. Cf. Edgard Allix, 'Destutt de Tracy, économiste', *Revue d'économie politique*, 26 (1912): 424–51; Emmet Kennedy, *A Philosophe in the Age of revolution: Destutt de Tracy and the Origins of 'Ideology'* (Philadelphia: The American Philosophical Society, 1978); Brian W. Head, *Ideology and Social Science: Destutt de Tracy and French Liberalism* (Dordrecht: M. Nijhoff, 1985).

Du Pont's return to France, intended to be for only a few months, was extended partly because of his plan to edit the works of Turgot.[49] In June 1809 he sent Jefferson the volumes which had already appeared,[50] intensifying his dialogue with the former president who, from his refuge in Monticello, had been able to resume more easily his contact with his French interlocutors. Urged on by Jefferson, who informed him of the American government's decision to promote industrial expansion in response to the continental blockade, Du Pont wrote a small treatise on finance, which he sent to Jefferson on 14 September 1810.[51]

Du Pont held that the development of manufacturing would bring about changes in the finances of the United States. His objective was to convince Americans to abandon the system of duties, to avoid indirect taxes and to organize their fiscal system on a single land tax. The structure of his work adhered to the Physiocratic perspective, beginning with a strong criticism of the British system of taxation and the interests of traders: 'they put in their tax on their invoices said your excellent and wise Franklin';[52] the work also attacked Hamilton's economic policy, which attempted to reproduce the British model in America. An entire section was devoted to the history of the 'state financial systems' of the Egyptians, the Jews and the Chinese 'the worst of the three would still be better than the English system because it would not hinder with excises and duties the freedom of work and actions as the English system does'.[53] The only valuable tax was, in his opinion, the *Système domanial de Finances à partage de Revenu*, the Physiocratic land tax, which enabled the guarantee of capital to nascent manufacturing companies, protecting 'the middle class'.[54] These pages were inspired by a Du Pont

---

[49]   Anne-Robert-Jacques Turgot, *Oeuvres de mr Turgot, précédées et accompagnées de mémoires et de notes sur sa vie, son administration et ses ouvrages*, 9 vols. (Paris: A. Belin et Delance, 1808–1811).

[50]   Du Pont de Nemours to Jefferson, Paris, 12 June 1809, in *Correspondence*, 146. Cf. also Du Pont de Nemours to Madison, Paris, 11 July 1809, *ibid.*, 149.

[51]   Du Pont de Nemours to Jefferson, Paris, 14 September 1810, in *Correspondence*, 158; Du Pont had already announced his work in the letters of 20 January and of 10 April, *ibid.*, 154, 157. The handwritten text is kept in the Eleutherian Mills Historical Library, *Memoir on the finances of the United States, entitled lettre à Thomas Jefferson ancien Président des Etats-Unis d'Amérique. Juillet 1810, Papers of Pierre Samuel Du Pont de Nemours, The Winterthur Manuscripts*, series B, no. 44; it is comprised of 87 pages written by a copyist, with handwritten corrections by Du Pont.

[52]   Pierre-Samuel Du Pont de Nemours, *Memoir on the finances of the United States*, sheet 12. Du Pont published in volume IX of Turgot's *Oeuvres*, the *Comparaison de l'impôt sur le revenu des propriétaires, et de l'impôt sur les consommations* (393–414). In a note, he stated that Turgot began the work at Franklin's request but did not complete it. Franklin aimed to save the United States from the British model, which Hamilton had followed, preferring indirect taxes and the 'English system to the opinions of the French Philosophes' (393).

[53]   Du Pont de Nemours, *Memoir on the finances of the United States*, sheet 23.

[54]   Du Pont de Nemours, *Memoir on the finances of the United States*, sheet 16.

who had read Say, and who took into account the American situation, yet remained profoundly Physiocratic:

> Do not take anything from the English other than their trustworthiness and punctuality in making payment, which will ensure you credit if you ever need it. Take from the French, and before them since you allow them time, the happy idea of giving the body politic a proportional share of the net revenue from land that increases and decreases with them.[55]

Du Pont now had a clear perception of an original reception of French economic thought in the United States and of America's opportunity to receive an enriched reflection of its own specificity in exchange:

> You will thus render service to France herself as the old friendship cannot be forgotten by Americans who are thankful and proud of their independence to which the French have been fortunate to make a strong contribution. You will be honourable, it is most desirable for the two nations that you return to France your own insights confirmed by an experience of undoubted success that can be demonstrated in advance by calculations for which evidence is tangible.[56]

With America's unique situation in mind, Du Pont underlined the difficulty of arriving at a fair appraisal of land value due to its abundance, and the absence of the social figure of the *fermier*, who could not be compared to the American farmer, 'the cultivator who owns land that he doesn't rent'.[57] He rejected indirect taxes[58] and the system of duties. He presented his findings as being designed to ensure the use of funds allocated to manufacturing, but his conclusion was an enunciation of the principles of Physiocracy, albeit one that had been enriched by his updated readings.[59]

His letters to Jefferson, written more or less in the same period as his drafting of the dissertation on finance, revolve around the same ideas, which they often reproduced almost word for word. Jefferson appreciated the work – which in 1815 he still hoped to have translated,[60] for its sound Physiocratic reasoning: 'your observations ... bear the stamps of logic and eloquence which mark everything coming from you, and place the doctrines of the Economists in their strongest

---

[55] Du Pont de Nemours, *Memoir on the finances of the United States*, sheet 39.

[56] Du Pont de Nemours, *Memoir on the finances of the United States*, sheet 39.

[57] Du Pont de Nemours, *Memoir on the finances of the United States*, sheets 46–7.

[58] Du Pont de Nemours, *Memoir on the finances of the United States*, sheet 47.

[59] Du Pont de Nemours, *Memoir on the finances of the United States*, sheets 68–9.

[60] Jefferson to Du Pont, Monticello, 28 February 1815, in Jefferson, *The Writings*, ed. Bergh, vol. XIV, 257. In his letter to Jefferson of 12 September 1811 (*Correpondence*, 172). Du Pont alluded to the translator, Paterson, who Jefferson also wanted to translate the *Essai sur l'éducation nationale* and the *Table raisonnée des principes de l'Economie politique*.

point of view'.[61] Nevertheless, he defended with his realism the economic policy of the American government, and he did not share Du Pont's belief that the financial system needed to be modified in view of manufacturing expansion. He also stressed the difference between the southern states, which operated the land tax, and those of the northeast, which applied duties, the validity of which he acknowledged: 'because it falls exclusively on the rich, and with the equal partition of intestate's states, constitutes the best agrarian law'.[62]

The dialogue between Jefferson and Du Pont continued throughout 1812, becoming more intense when Du Pont began to read the *Review of Montesquieu*, thinking it had been penned by Jefferson. Others thought the work had come from one of Du Pont's sons, but Du Pont had no doubts: 'You put in a little dedication as if it were offered by a French national in the United States ... but there is no French person in America or even in France who might have followed so many threads with such a rigorous logic of the first order and in such amazing depth'.[63]

His analysis focused mainly on chapter XIII, 'Des rapports que la levée des tributs et la grandeur des revenues publics ont avec la liberté' (On the relations that the raising of tributes and the size of public revenues have with freedom).[64] He took up once more the arguments he had set out in his work on finance, refusing to accept that the land tax was a burden on owners.[65] He strongly affirmed the role of the state, which he did not believe was disadvantageous to the interests of individuals,[66] and this set him apart from Jefferson's approach and that of the *Review of Montesquieu*. His approach to economics was taken from the core of Physiocratic thought,[67] enriched by authors of his time; he still did not have a precise notion of capital, but spoke of 'useful labour', of 'worker's wages', of 'profit', and of 'services' offered 'to agricultural entrepreneurs'. He connected Malthus to Physiocracy with the same arguments that he would later employ in his *Examen*,[68] in support of his theory of the primacy of agriculture.[69] He bolstered his arguments by making direct reference to Jefferson's letter on the difficulty of applying the land tax to the northeastern states: a propos of manufactured products, he wrote, discussing the commentary to Montesquieu, '*riches are gathered and preserved,* I would reply to the profound thinker Jefferson*, not produced.*'[70] While

---

[61]   Jefferson to Du Pont, Monticello, 15 April 1811, in Jefferson, *The Writings*, ed. Bergh, vol. XIII, 37–8.

[62]   Jefferson, *The Writings*, ed. Bergh, vol. XIII, 39.

[63]   Du Pont to Jefferson, 25 January 1812, in *Correspondence*, 179–80.

[64]   *Correspondence*, 180.

[65]   Destutt de Tracy, *Commentary and Review of Montesquieu*, 160–61.

[66]   'The existence of a government is one of society's first needs' (Du Pont to Jefferson, 25 January 1812, in *Correspondence*, 182).

[67]   'It is this that constitutes the whole *Théorie de l'Impôt*'. (*Correspondence*, 189).

[68]   *Correspondence*, 184. Cf. Du Pont, *Examen du livre de M. Malthus*, 2.

[69]   Du Pont to Jefferson, 25 January 1812, in *Correspondence,* 186.

[70]   *Correspondence*, 185, 189.

remaining true to his principles, Du Pont rated the *Review of Montesquieu* highly and concluded that the principles of the economic science that it had set out pointed to a way of strengthening the American republic:

> Your book is a good consolidation of this government which exists only imperfectly in England but perfectly only here ... Jefferson was not made to stop where Smith and Mr Say stopped! Although both men, especially the former, are men of eminent merit, he has a more profound mind and a stronger back than them.[71]

Du Pont also discussed in detail book XI, 'Des lois qui forment la liberté politique dans son rapport avec la constitution' (On the laws that form political freedom in their relationship to the constitution) – translated by Jefferson – clarifying his political position and the distance that separated his liberalism from Jefferson's democracy. The land tax legitimized the exclusion of other social classes from the 'Exercise of Sovereignty' reserved for landowners.[72] He nevertheless appreciated the book, in which 'American wisdom is united to French gaiety, as in Franklin's books', so much that he decided to translate it.[73]

This correspondence, and the misunderstanding on which it was based, thus offer a precious testimony, which allows us to see the persistence of Physiocracy and how it encountered economic science in the early nineteenth century. At the same time, it is also possible to clarify, through the affinity between Jefferson and

---

[71]   *Correspondence*, 190, 193. In another letter Du Pont denied the statement made by the *Review of Montesquieu* (217) according to which 'Smith is the first to have remarked that our faculties are our only original property', arguing for the primacy of his *Table raisonnée des principes de l'Economie politique*. He also underlined Smith's debt towards Physiocracy, 'he was, like me, a disciple of Quesnay, and he does not hide it'. He praised him only for the originality of his principle of the division of labour, even if he underlined the risks of 'creating a class of weak, unhealthy and unintelligent people' and hoped that similar misfortunes could be avoided in America. (Du Pont to Jefferson, 17 May 1812, *ibid.*, 196–98).

[72]   Du Pont to Jefferson, 14 April 1812, *Correspondence*, 194.

[73]   *Correspondence*, 195. Jefferson wrote to William Duane regarding this matter: 'A copy which I sent to France was under translation by one of the ablest men of that country' (Jefferson to Duane, 4 April 1813, in Jefferson, *The Writings* ed. Bergh, vol. XIII, 230), and to Tracy a few months later: 'One of the best judges and best men of the age has ascribed it to myself; and has for some time been employed in translating it into French' (Jefferson to Tracy, 28 November 1813, *ibid.*, vol. XIV, 12). On the information given in the 1819 French edition of the *Commentaire* (see above, p. 250) Du Pont had written to Tracy in 1816: 'You had plenty to laugh about in your philosophical, mysterious and mystifying self, but you will not be angry when you see the enthusiasm that I took and that I preserve for this great work whose first eleven chapters I have translated into French'. (Handwritten letter by Du Pont to Tracy, Paris, 14 August 1816, Eleutherian Mills Historical Library, *Papers of Pierre Samuel Du Pont de Nemours*, The *Winterthur Manuscipts*, series A, Correspondence).

the circle of *Idéologues*, the nature of the reaction to French economic culture in the United States.

From Physiocracy to Idéologie: Du Pont de Nemours and Ideas in Movement

Du Pont always admired Destutt de Tracy, regarding him to be the father of *Idéologie*. Tracy's systematic approach, in some ways deductive, was closer to that of the Physiocrats than was Say's,[74] despite the criticisms that he made of the *Économistes*, which led Du Pont to appreciate his economic principles. Although Tracy was linked to Say, his objective of placing economic reflection within the wider context of social science helped to clarify the connection between economics and politics and was better suited to Du Pont's point of view. Discussing in 1816 the *Commentaire* with its real author, Du Pont wrote:

> If you had written this book thirty years ago, you would been at the top of our Philosophy, our Literature and our Political Economy, way above Say even though he does have great merit, and he tries to cut the grass under our feet with Smith's sickle, a little sharp but shorter than three quarters. Instead it will take another thirty years and two or three revolutions before this important book reaches its full usefulness, its full glory.[75]

Therefore, being closer to Tracy, in his famous letter to Say of 22 April 1815 in which he attacked the author of the *Traité d'économie politique*, Du Pont placed his own *Table raisonnée des principes de l'Economie Politique* in opposition to Say's economic science.[76] While recognizing his merits, Du Pont never liked Say, chiefly because of his approach to economics and the difference of their arguments, a difference that he also stressed with regard to Tracy. In the letter he reminded Say that he was 'by way of Smith, a child of Quesnay and grandson of the Great Turgot ... your brilliance is vast; do not imprison it within the ideas and the language of the English'. He reproved him primarily for having abandoned an overview of the economy and for having overlooked the relationship between economics and politics, which he claimed was a distinctive characteristic of French thought and

---

[74]   On Tracy and Say cf. Moravia, *Il tramonto dell'illuminismo*; Philippe Steiner, 'L'économie politique pratique contre les systèmes: quelques remarques sur la méthode de J.-B. Say', *Revue d'économie politique*, 100 (1990): 664–87.

[75]   Du Pont's handwritten letter to Tracy, Paris, 14 August 1816. This letter is also an important help to understanding Du Pont's political ideas during this time and his idea of republic, which identified with the representative government.

[76]   Du Pont to Say, 22 April 1814, in *Collection des principaux économistes, Physiocrates*, ed. E. Daire, vol. II (Paris: Guillaumin, 1846): 397. Du Pont reprinted the letter in an appendix to his *Examen du livre de M. Malthus*, 117–59.

of Physiocracy in particular: 'You have narrowed too much the path of political economy by treating it only as the *science of wealth*. It is the *science of natural law* applied, as it should be, to civilised societies. It is the *science of constitutions*'.[77] In his letters to Say, Du Pont repeated, more or less exactly, ideas from his work on finance and his correspondence with Jefferson, as well as assertions he made in the *Examen du livre de M. Malthus* and in his notes to Turgot's *Oeuvres*.[78] His tone was severe and revealed the full extent of his concern: in his eyes Say represented a break with the Physiocratic tradition, and his analysis marked a change of direction in French thought.

While giving credit to the Physiocrats for their discourse on freedom and their contribution to economic science, Say repeatedly made clear his move away from them.[79] He concurred with the criticisms they levelled at Montesquieu and their passion for America, which led him to edit works by Franklin.[80] Even so, he never had a close relationship with the last Physiocrat. From one of his letters we learn that prior to 1814 he had never met Du Pont,[81] of whom, in his works, he made detailed criticisms;[82] and in his correspondence he always defended his independence, notwithstanding the homage paid to the elderly economist. In versions of his letters to Du Pont – either unpublished or variations of the published copies[83] – Say's tone was more direct and his argument more nuanced,

---

[77]   Du Pont to Say, 22 April 1814, in *Collection des principaux économistes, Physiocrates*, 397.

[78]   *Collection des principaux économistes, Physiocrates*, 394–424. The same letters, written between 1815 and 1816, are reproduced, with small variations of style and spelling, in Jean-Baptiste Say, *Oeuvres diverses*, ed. Charles Comte, Eugène Daire and Horace Say (Paris: Guillaumin, 1848), 361–97; this edition also contains Du Pont's letter to Say of 20 June 1814. On Say and Du Pont, cf. Philippe Steiner, 'Politique et économie politique chez Jean-Baptiste Say', *Revue française d'Histoire des Idées Politiques*, no. 5 (1997): 38–40.

[79]   In addition to the different editions of the *Traité*, cf. *Cours complet d'économie politique*.

[80]   *La Décade philosophique littéraire et politique par une société de républicains*, ed. Pierre-Louis Ginguené, 42 vols. (Paris, 1794–1804)., 10 Frimaire an X, 443–4 and Jean-Baptiste Say, *Traité d'économie politique*, ed. André Tiran, 2 vols., in *Oeuvres Complètes* (Paris: Economica, 2006): vol. I, 28. Cf. above, p. 137.

[81]   In an unpublished letter of 5 April 1814, Say asked Du Pont for an introduction to Talleyrand, in order to obtain a ministerial post (Eleutherian Mills Historical Library, *Papers of Pierre Samuel Du Pont de Nemours*). In another letter of 1 February 1815, having returned from England, Say asked in vain for Du Pont to receive him: 'I come from England and Scotland where I saw all those involved in political economy. I presented myself to your home to talk with you without success. I reiterate my approach'. (*Ibid.*).

[82]   Say, *Histoire abrégée*, 1258; Say, *Traité*, vol. I, 96, 168, vol. II, 632, 643; Say, *Cours complet*, vol. I., 41.

[83]   Among Du Pont's correspondence preserved with the Eleutherian Mills Historical Library there are five handwritten letters by Say (5 April, 23 June, 12 July 1814; 1 February, 15 November 1815). The structure of the letter of 15 November 1815, and the style and the

his approach experimental, and the opposition that he highlighted between the *Économistes* and the *Smithistes*, with whom he placed himself,[84] had the accents of a difficult dialogue: 'I am an ally of the Economistes; but without agreeing with them on all points':[85]

> You tell me about it: If you had looked at this from another angle, if you had started from the point of view where Quesnay stood, that of *justice* regulating the *right* of every man: Hey, my worthy master, this is exactly what I boast. This is my whole merit; I probably have neither the spirit nor the knowledge of Quesnay, and if I had looked from his standpoint I would probably not have seen more than him. I broke the lens and stood in the middle of its debris. The right which is everything in the eyes of humanity could not affect my education; I wanted to see how rightly or wrongly riches are created or destroyed. Do not judge me by the laws you have established, as this is precisely what characterises the sectarian spirit; judge me by the only rules whose influence I recognise: The nature of things, such as they are. If I say something is so and it is not, I am wrong, but I am not wrong for having studied it in my way.[86]

Along with his intellectual independence, Say also professed to an idea of progress in economic science, which Du Pont could not accept, since he believed that it was through evidence that Physiocracy had arrived at the truth of political economics:

> I have no other advantage than that of having come later, to have been raised for trade, having created and managed several industrial establishments. Yet I have in common with all of them the love of the public good and of the greatest

---

tone of the discussion, are different to the published version. The handwritten letter focuses on the value of production and is the prompt reply to Du Pont's letter of 22 April 1815, while the published text deals in the main with public revenues and is a more organized reflection. This latter text is published with small stylistic changes in the Daire *Collection des principaux économistes, Physiocrates* (416–20) without a date, while in Say's *Oeuvres diverses* (387–92) it is dated 15 November 1815. On Say's intention to make public his correspondence as a response to the polemic with the Ricardo school, which would explain the changes carried out on his letters, cf. the documentation used by Philippe Steiner and the interpretation given in his introduction to Jean-Baptiste Say, *Cours d'économie politique et autres essais* (Paris: Flammarion, 1996): 15, note 13.

[84]   Say to Du Pont, 15 November 1815, *Papers of Pierre Samuel Du Pont de Nemours*, Correspondence, sheet 2. Some passages of this letter are published in Philippe Steiner, 'L'économie politique pratique', 673; Steiner, 'Politique et économie politique', 39.

[85]   Say to Du Pont, 15 November 1815, *Papers of Pierre Samuel Du Pont de Nemours*, Correspondence, sheet 7.

[86]   *Papers of Pierre Samuel Du Pont de Nemours*, Correspondence, sheets. 3–4. Cf. Du Pont to Say, 22 April 1815, *Collection des principaux économistes, Physiocrates*, 370.

freedom in the use of our resources. If this is what makes an economist, then I am one, and I always will be.[87]

Say's observation of reality and his anti-dogmatic attitude had attracted the interest of Jefferson, who with his pragmatism had looked to the *Traité* for an answer to the questions concerning the American situation. This same approach distanced him from Du Pont:

> What do you do as a disciple like him, who approaches fifty and who admits that as he studied he becomes less clever? Also, discarding all issues of rights, origin, previous state, I merely described in my work the train that things follow, as we can see them. I put to use what, in the Economistes, in Smith and others, seemed to me to be part of the exposition that occupied me. When it seemed to me that on important subject their explanation of the nature of the thing was inexact or misrepresented, I said so frankly, and I find no ill in those that treat me in the same way. I have been mistaken as much and more than those I have fought with as they have had more knowledge and spirit than I.[88]

Although his tone may have been more severe and dogmatic, Du Pont took up in his letters to Say many of the contentions he had made in his correspondence with Jefferson, appealing to the same Physiocratic principles and the same state financial system, the 'constitution domaniale des finances à partage des revenus'.

A Commerce of Ideas Between France and America

While remaining true to his promise not to disclose the identity of Tracy, Jefferson finally confessed to Du Pont that he was not the author of the *Review of Montesquieu*.[89] Faced with upheavals in international trade that had suffered as a result of the War of 1812 with Britain, in the course of his discussion with Du Pont on the economic principles in the *Review*, Jefferson's attitude towards the relationship between economics and politics and the interdependence of different economic activities had been reinforced by the 'methodical' and 'detailed' exposition of the *Traité de la volonté*. Tracy, encouraged by the publication of the *Review of Montesquieu*, had in fact sent Jefferson on 15 November 1811 the *Traité de la volonté*, asking him to arrange for it to be published in English.[90] He was

---

[87] Say to Du Pont, 23 June 1814, *Papers of Pierre Samuel Du Pont de Nemours*, Correspondence, sheet 2.

[88] Say to Du Pont, 23 June 1814, *Papers of Pierre Samuel Du Pont de Nemours*, Correspondence, sheet 2.

[89] Jefferson to Du Pont, 29 November 1813, in *Correspondence*, 206.

[90] Destutt de Tracy to Jefferson, 15 November 1811, in Chinard, *Jefferson et les Idéologues*, 99–101. Cf. also the letter of 21 October 1811, in which Tracy announced

aware of how close his ideas were to Jefferson's positions and that they created the 'illusion that seduced' his compatriot Du Pont.[91]

Jefferson worked on this new publishing venture for six years, during which time, in particular after his return to America, Du Pont performed the role of his intermediary with Tracy.[92] Naturally, Tracy was eager to see his work published and, given its clarity and didactic structure, as well as the fact that it belonged to a same economic tradition, Jefferson deemed it to be a point of arrival :

> It may be considered as a review of the principles of the Economists, of Smith, and of Say, or rather an elementary book on the same subject. As Smith had corrected some principles of the economists and Say some of Smith's; so Tracy has done as the whole. He has in my opinion corrected fundamental errors in all of them, and by simplifying principles has brought the subject within a narrow compass.[93]

While the soundest principles of politics were contained in the *Review of Montesquieu*, for Jefferson the correct principles of political economy were summarized in the *Traité de la volonté*,[94] which was based on the economic chapters of the *Commentaire*. Tracy's defence of the lower classes, his attention to the contrariety of distribution and production, which derived from his reflections on Malthus,[95] the problem of inequality of wealth, which he strongly emphasized in his liberal analysis of the economy, were all elements of a scientific approach that did not ignore real facts and which chimed with the ideas of Jefferson. For the latter, Du Pont, Say and Tracy constituted a body of anti-Hamiltonian principles that he could use at a time when the United States suffered from the depreciation of their paper currency and were divided by bitter debates on the banks and public funds. Tracy included in the *Treatise on Political Economy* – the English title that Jefferson had suggested to Duane – all the arguments against financial wealth, which harked back to the Physiocrats. In particular, on the question of the legitimacy of public debt, he appealed to the same radical arguments used by Jefferson on the rights of generations not to be obliged to pay the debts of their

---

his work, in the context of his *Idéologie* and of a rigorous approach to the science of government, to 'prevent me from falling into these ramblings and inconsistencies which Montesquieu was unable to avoid despite his genius'. (*ibid.*, 88).

[91]   Destutt de Tracy to Jefferson, Paris, 14 July 1814, Chinard, *Jefferson et les Idéologues*, 125.

[92]   For all the details of this intermediary role, which Du Pont shared with Lafayette, cf. Gilbert Chinard, *Jefferson et les Idéologues*.

[93]   Jefferson to William Duane, 22 January 1813, Chinard, *Jefferson et les Idéologues*, 105–6.

[94]   Jefferson to Joseph Milligan, 25 October 1818, in Jefferson, *The Writings*, ed. Bergh, vol. XIX, 263.

[95]   Destutt de Tracy to Jefferson, Paris, 11 April 1818, in Chinard, *Jefferson et les Idéologues*, 181.

fathers.[96] Jefferson hoped that Tracy's work might become a textbook for every American student and man of state, so that they would know about a 'science in which of all others we have blundered most'.[97]

In 1813 Jefferson urged Duane to publish a translation of both Say's and Tracy's works.[98] This was the period in which he had become convinced of the unavoidable growth of manufacturing in the United States, despite still believing in the supremacy of agriculture.[99] As we have seen, a few years later, in his famous letter to Benjamin Austin of 9 January 1816, he would explain that he had come to accept manufacturing development in order to ensure the economic independence of his country. In May 1815, Du Pont returned to the United States and immediately resumed his dialogue with Jefferson. In January 1816 he sent President James Madison his dissertation *Sur l'agriculture et les manufactures aux Etats-Unis*, which contained all the wealth of his discussions of those years, the political science of his time filtered through Jefferson's mediation, and the Physiocracy that had survived to the beginning of the nineteenth century. Jefferson considered Du Pont a link in the evolutionary chain of the science of political economy: 'first developed by the economists, since commented and dilated by Smith, Say, yourself, and the luminous reviewer of Montesquieu',[100] and he shared the perspective of Du Pont's work on manufacturing that was based on the balance of economic activities and the development of it in the service to agriculture.

'Agriculture is a manufacture like any other, although of still greater importance since it provides subsistence and raw materials',[101] wrote Du Pont, who had abandoned his dogmatic tone, appealing instead to 'good sense' and the 'happy medium'. In support of his discourse on the need to provide the United States with a system of manufacturing as a boost to agriculture, Du Pont proposed a set of principles that constituted an updating of economic science: he spoke of

---

[96]   Destutt de Tracy, *Traité d'économie politique* (Paris: Bouguet et Levi, 1823): ch. XII, 'Des dépenses du government' (On government expenses), 313.

[97]   Jefferson to Destutt de Tracy, Monticello, 24 November 1818, in Chinard, *Jefferson et les Idéologues*, 183. 'The most profound ignorance of which threatened irreparable disaster during the late war, and by the parasite institution of banks is now consuming the public industry' (Jefferson to Albert Gallatin, Monticello, 24 November 1818, *ibid.*, 182). Cf. also Thomas Ritchie to Jefferson (Richmond: 9 October 1814), *ibid.*, 128.

[98]   Jefferson to Duane, Monticello, 4 April 1813, in Jefferson, *The Writings*, ed. Bergh, vol. XIII, 229.

[99]   Jefferson to John Melish, Monticello, 13 January 1813, in Jefferson, *The Writings*, ed. Bergh, vol. XIII, 207–8.

[100]   Jefferson to Du Pont de Nemours, Monticello, 28 February 1815, in Jefferson. *The Writings*, ed . Bergh, vol. XIV, 256.

[101]   Pierre-Samuel Du Pont de Nemours, *Sur l'agriculture et les manufactures aux Etats-Unis*, in *Correpondence*, 240.

outlets ('débouchés')[102] and services, and distinguished between producers and consumers, as well as between workers' wages and entrepreneurs' capital, while dealing with 'Agriculture, where everything begins and to which everything returns'.[103] His dissertation carried an almost word-for-word reiteration of criticisms expressed in the *Examen du livre de M. Malthus* concerning the inordinate stimulation of industry in Britain.[104] He nevertheless showed the same appreciation that Jefferson had for Malthus while sharing also the assessment of America's exceptional geography, which contradicted the Malthusian theory on the relationship of population and subsistence. Du Pont elaborated this idea in his *Examen*, published the following year. Following the same economic culture, which from the Physiocrats arrived at Jefferson, Du Pont disapproved of promoting manufacturing, which, in keeping with the British system, would perforce resort to monopolies and tariffs, and legitimize state involvement in the economy.[105]

For Du Pont, the interrelation of economic activities was also to be seen in the unique character of the American economy: in his *Observations sommaires sur l'utilité des encouragemens à donner aux manufactures américaines*, addressed to Jefferson on 31 March 1816, he gave an analysis of the value of manufactured products that was aimed at demonstrating how all forms of spending benefited agriculture, framing a policy which asserted that all activities, particularly industry, were dangerous when elevated above agriculture.[106] After his return to the United States, Du Pont thus modified his positions, partly because of the influence of his discussions with Jefferson.

For all that, when, during the same months, Du Pont was asked by the new republics of South America for an opinion on their draft constitutions, he and Jefferson made clear their different political positions, thereby revealing the gulf between his liberalism and the former president's democratic spirit. His idea of political participation being restricted solely to landowners – in accordance with principles set out in 1775 in the *Mémoire sur les municipalités* – was derived from the Physiocratic 'evidence'.[107] In contrast, for Jefferson political participation represented the essence of a republican government.[108] This different definition

---

[102]   *Ibid.* Du Pont here speaks of agriculture, but he used the same arguments in relation to every branch of production (*Sur l'agriculture*, 242–3).

[103]   *Sur l'agriculture*, 241.

[104]   *Sur l'agriculture*. Cf. Du Pont, *Examen*, 19.

[105]   Du Pont, *Sur l'agriculture*, 246–7.

[106]   Du Pont, *Observations sommaires sur l'utilité des encouragemens à donner aux manufactures américaines*, in *Correspondence*, 254–5.

[107]   Du Pont de Nemours to Jefferson, 12 May 1816, in *Correspondence*, 26.

[108]   Jefferson to Du Pont de Nemours, Poplar Forest, 24 April 1816, in *Correspondence*, 258.

of republic, which Jefferson likened to representative democracy, showed the measure of his distance from Du Pont:

> We both of us act and think from the same motive. We both consider the people as our children, and love them with parental affection. But you love them as infants whom you are afraid to trust without nurses, and I as adults, whom I freely leave to self government.[109]

Making the American Economic Culture: A Network of Translations

While discussing these issues, Jefferson worked on the revision of the translation of Tracy's *Traité de la volonté* and was sorry for the lateness of its publication, as he wrote to Du Pont, talking about their mutual friend.[110] Jefferson shared in full Du Pont's zeal for the dissemination of French economic thought as a corrective to the British model. He arranged for the William and Mary College to adopt the *Review of Montesquieu*, while also recommending the *Traités* of Say and Tracy.[111]

He encouraged the translation of Say[112] and took part in the publishing project that resulted in the first American edition of the *Traité d'économie politique*, the goal of which was to exert a definite influence on American political culture: 'There is no branch of science of which our countrymen seem so ignorant as Political Economy. The bulk and prolixity of Smith forbid venturing on him'.[113] Joseph Cabell, a member of the Senate of Virginia, had borrowed a copy of Say's work from Jefferson, and his careful and comparative reading of it convinced him of Say's superiority over Smith and led him to translate the *Traité*.[114] John Smith, President of the William and Mary College, buoyed up by Jefferson and

---

[109] *Correspondence*, 258.

[110] 'I found the translation a very bad one indeed, done by one who understood neither French nor English, and I proceeded too far before it became evident that I could have translated it myself in less time than the revisal cost me. I devoted to it five hours a day for between two and three months'. (Jefferson to Du Pont de Nemours, Monticello, 3 August 1816, *Correspondence*, 269–70). Cf. Du Pont de Nemours to Destutt de Tracy, 14 August 1816.

[111] Jefferson to John Minor, 30 August 1814, in Jefferson, *The Writings*, ed. Ford, vol. IX, 483; Cabell to Jefferson, 4 August 1816, in *Early History of the University of Virginia*, 69.

[112] 'It is a pity that Say's work should not, as well as Tracy's, be made known to our countrymen by a good translation. It would supplant Smith's book altogether, because shorter, clearer and sounder' (Jefferson to William Duane, 4 April 1813, in Jefferson, *The Writings*, ed. Bergh, vol. XIII, 231); cf. also Jefferson to Joseph C. Cabell, 28 February 1816, in *Early History of the University of Virginia.*, 62.

[113] Jefferson, *The Writings*, ed. Bergh, vol. XIII, 231.

[114] Joseph C. Cabell to Jefferson, 29 November 1813, *Early History of the University of Virginia*, 12; cf. also Cabell to Jefferson, 21 February and 4 July 1816, *ibid.*, 60, 64.

the English translation of the *Catéchisme d'économie politique*, wanted to use the work as a textbook, but health problems and misinformation about an edition published in Britain caused the project to fail.[115]

In March 1821 the first English translation of the *Traité* was at last published in London, edited by Charles R. Prinsep and based on the fourth French edition,[116] and the following December an American edition of the same translation was published in Boston by Clement C. Biddle. In his preface, Prinsep, a convinced Ricardian, placed Say within a tradition of thought that went back to Turgot, deeming him the foremost foreign economist. He considered the *Traité*, together with the works of Smith and Steward, as the only attempts to develop a complete systematization of political economy.[117] Prinsep added a series of notes, in which he criticized Say's theories of value and wealth, comparing them to Ricardo's ideas.

The American edition, which included Say's introduction (omitted by Prinsep) and a preface by the American editor, together with the English one and notes by Biddle, was the result of an American project by the editor and the printers in Boston to make an impact on the circulation of economic ideas.[118]

Biddle, a native of Philadelphia, was the acknowledged leader of free-trade advocates in America, even though he hailed from a city at the heart of protectionist circles. With the publication of Say's *Traité* he sought to link American economic liberalism to French post-Physiocratic thought for the purpose of stimulating a critical discussion of theories that came from Britain. The progressive reworking of his translation in the later editions, which he edited after 1821, bore witness to this growing awareness of the relationship between the French and American economic cultures.[119]

---

[115]   Cabell to Jefferson, 4 August 1816, 12 January 1817, *Early History of the University of Virginia*, 69, 72.

[116]   Jean-Baptiste Say, *A Treatise on Political Economy; or The production, distribution and consumption of Wealth*. Translated from the fourth edition of the French by C.R. Prinsep, M.A. with notes by the translator (London: Longman, Hurst, Rees, Orme and Brown, 1821).

[117]   Jean-Baptiste Say, *A Treatise on Political Economy; or The production, distribution and consumption of Wealth*. Translated from the fourth edition of the French by C.R. Prinsep, M.A. with notes by the translator. To which is added a translation of the introduction, and additional notes by Clement C. Biddle, in two volumes (Boston: Wells and Lilly, 1821): vol. I, 'Advertisement by the English Editor', xiii–xix.

[118]   As part of their efforts in favour of economic liberalism, Wells and Lilly were also editors of the *North American Review*, a periodical working for the support of trade freedom edited by Edward Everett, brother of Alexander Everett, the American economist who was one of Say's correspondents.

[119]   The first two American editions of the *Traité* were published in Boston by Wells and Lilly in 1821 and 1824. Starting with the third (1827), the work was published in Philadelphia by J. Grigg. Biddle's introduction was progressively enlarged up to the third edition of 1827. After the sixth edition of 1834 there were only some reprints, with the

According to Biddle, no work of political economy after Smith had been worthy of attention until Say's *Traité*, 'the most methodical, comprehensive, and best digested treatise on the elements of Political Economy', which had become a textbook of almost all European universities.[120] 'The true nature of value' was owed to Say, his critiques of Ricardo had been decisive, his *Lettres à Malthus* had put an end to every discussion on the *Principles of Political Economy*; 'In distinguishing re-productive from un-productive consumption, M. Say has exhibited the exact nature of capital and its agency in production, and hence has shown why economy is a source of national wealth'.[121] Biddle believed that Say's *Discours préliminaire*, which had appeared in English for the first time, was methodologically valuable in so far as it provided economic science with an historical context and had a philosophical approach that made it an educational tool for use in the study of political economics. From a theoretical point of view, Biddle maintained it was necessary to correct the presentation of Say's thought that Prinsep had offered English readers, since he had wrongly criticized Say's theory of utility value, proposing Ricardo instead. For this reason, Biddle decided to omit Prinsep's notes from the American edition.[122] Starting with the second edition, he challenged Prinsep with the refutation of the twentieth chapter of Ricardo's *Principles* in Say's notes to the French translation, in which he had demonstrated that the 'fallacies contained in Mr. Ricardo's theory of Value' had originated from Ricardo's anxiety to confer 'consistency to the loose and inaccurate assertion of Dr. Smith, that exchangeable value is entirely derived from human labour'.[123]

From the third American edition of the *Traité*, from which Biddle had removed Prinsep's 'Advertisement', the compass of the American editor was enlarged by a discourse on economic liberalism, which did justice to Ricardo, giving him due credit for having brought Smith and Say closer together through their common defence of economic freedom. The progress of economic science had followed this path, exposing the unsoundness of mercantilist principles: after Smith, freedom of trade had been adopted and its precepts imparted in both Britain and the continent;

---

indication 'New American Edition'. The *National Union Catalogue* shows 27 editions and reprints of the *Traité* between 1821 and 1880.

[120] In the 'Advertisement' to the second edition, Biddle added, 'the two former American editions of the following translation have also been introduced into several of the most respectable of our own seminaries of learning' (Jean-Baptiste Say, *A Treatise*, 2nd. American Edition, two volumes bound in one (Boston: Wells and Lilly, 1824): vol. I, v).

[121] Jean-Baptiste Say, *A Treatise* (1821), vol. I, viii–ix.

[122] Jean-Baptiste Say, *A Treatise* (1821), vol. I, x.

[123] Jean-Baptiste Say, *A Treatise* (1824), vol. I, viii. The later editions include the same additions, except for small stylistic changes. Cf. David Ricardo, *Des principes de l'économie politique*, in *Oeuvres complètes de David Ricardo... augmentées des notes de Jean-Baptiste Say, de nouvelles notes et de commentaires par Malthus, Sismondi, mm. Rossi, Blanqui etc...* (Paris: Guillaumin, 1847): 247–63.

and Biddle named, among others, Dugald Stewart, Ricardo, Malthus, Lauderdale, Bentham, Mills, MacCulloch, Say, Sismondi, Garnier, Destutt de Tracy and Ganilh.[124]

Biddle recognised the leading role played by America in this assimilation of economic science into economic liberalism. It had in fact been Franklin's works that, before the *Wealth of Nations*, had anticipated 'the great principle of freedom of trade'.[125] Moreover, the United States, with their experience of revolution and their political regime, were a favourable environment for economic freedom. Say himself, in a letter to Biddle, which was quoted in his preface, reinforced this view:

> Where should we expect sound doctrine to be better received than amongst a nation that supports and illustrates the value of free principles, by the most striking examples. The old states of Europe are cankered with prejudices and bad habits; it is America who will teach them the height of prosperity which may be reached when governments follow the counsels of reason and do not cost too much.[126]

The sixth edition was improved on the basis of the fifth French edition of 1826 (the last to be completed in Say's lifetime), which preserved the translation by Prinsep. Translated too were the data regarding money, weights and measures used in the French edition, with the corresponding American values, in order to make the work more useful and easier to study for American students of political economy.[127] Biddle also added new notes to update statistics on Europe and the United States. This latest edition was the first after Say's death, inducing Biddle to consider the results of the economist's work in a broader dimension, placing him and Smith among the authors who had made the greatest contribution to the advancement of the nations of Europe and America.[128] Thus, he reproduced the homage published in the *London Political Examiner* on 25 November 1832, in which the editor of the periodical, Fonblanque, underlined the full breadth of Say's scientific and methodological approach, which had never merely addressed the issue of political economy, but had always taken account of the need to study the diverse aspects of a country's prosperity.[129]

The notes added to the American edition of the *Traité* were marked by a convinced economic liberalism and paid attention to the Physiocratic tradition. The principle of the spontaneous rebalancing of activities in a regime of economic

---

[124]   Jean-Baptiste Say, *A Treatise*, 3rd American Edition (Philadelphia: J. Grigg, 1827): xiii, xv.

[125]   Say, *A Treatise*, 3rd American Edition xvi.

[126]   Say, *A Treatise*, 3rd American Edition, xvi–xvii. In his preface Biddle published in a note another passage of a letter he had received from Say, in which the French author expressed appreciation for his initiative (*Ibid.*, xvii).

[127]   Jean-Baptiste Say, *A Treatise* (Philadelphia: Grigg and Elliot, 1834), iii.

[128]   Say, *A Treatise* (Philadelphia: Grigg and Elliot, 1834), iv.

[129]   Say, *A Treatise* (Philadelphia: Grigg and Elliot, 1834), iv.

freedom was put forward by Biddle in opposition to Say's thesis, whereby the value produced by trade and industry was higher than that of agriculture. Only the force of his criticisms of Physiocracy had created a false perspective in Say.[130] The freedom and security of property were lauded as the foundations of Britain's power,[131] which prompted Biddle to reject all forms of state intervention, even where Say recognized the right to limit the actions of mine owners who impoverished their lands.[132] A long note was devoted to a discussion of Say's thesis on the economic backwardness of certain French regions due to the lack of cities to act as distribution channels for the value created by agriculture. Contrarily, Biddle considered the cities to be effects of the wealth of a country and shared the opinion of the Physiocrats, criticized by Say, that manufactured goods should be imported from abroad and paid for with the raw materials of agriculture. In the name of economic freedom, he deplored any measure that removed capital from agriculture or trade to create cities or industries, and attributed the economic woes of France and other European nations to the intrusion of political power.[133]

The translation of Say's *Traité* thus fitted within Biddle and the Boston publishers' scheme to connect American thought to economic liberalism by means of an approach that favoured French economics over British thought, setting Say against Ricardo.

Jefferson personally opposed the diffusion of Ricardo in the United States. In January 1819 he wrote to the publisher Milligan, whom he had asked to have Tracy's *Traité de la volonté* translated and who had made known his intention to publish Ricardo's *Principles*, which had been reviewed in the *Edinburgh Review*:

> It is a work in my opinion which will not stand the test of time and trial. If such men as Adam Smith, Malthus, Say, and Tracy knew nothing of the nature of rent, or of the effect of Capital in prices, it is not to be proved by such muddy reasoning as that of Ricardo, or of his Edinburgh critic. Their new discoveries of the errors of great men will be like those of the errors of Newton, which almost

---

[130]   Jean-Baptiste Say, *A Treatise*, vol. I, 8, vol. II, 115. Biddle used the principle of the rebalancing to criticize Say's idea that domestic trade is more beneficial than foreign trade (*ibid.*, vol. I, 62).

[131]   Biddle, also criticizing Horner and the *Edinburgh Review* (vol. XIV, 95), expressed these ideas and criticized Britain's Navigation Act, which Say considered to be an instrument that had increased British military strength (*ibid.*, 66). In the sixth edition of the *Traité* Say agreed with Biddle and Horner on the impossibility of reaping the benefits of such a measure, nevertheless recognizing the military efficiency of the Act (Jean-Baptiste Say, *Traité*, 6th edition (Paris: Horace Say, 1841): 106).

[132]   Say, *A Treatise*, vol. I, 105.

[133]   Say, *A Treatise*, vol. II, 154.

every year produces some half sighted writer, who sees but a speck at a time of an expanded subject.[134]

The large number of American editions of Say's *Traité* is testimony to his great success in the United States. As we have seen, it became one of the most widely used educational handbooks.[135] Jefferson always preferred Tracy, especially his *Review of Montesquieu*, which he judged to be the best exposition of economic and political principles, superior to Priestley and the *Federalist*.[136] However, he equally appreciated his *Traité d'économie politique*, which he considered an expression of an economic analysis linked less directly to Smith than to Say's *Traité*.[137]

On 6 April 1816, his scrupulous editorial work being nearly finished, Jefferson sent Milligan the *Prospectus*, which he had written himself as an anonymous introduction to the *Treatise on Political Economy*.[138] This was a valuable document for understanding the reception of the French economic thought in America. In this sense, Tracy's translation fitted alongside the American edition of Say's *Traité* and shared its objective of promoting the knowledge of French political economy as a riposte to the British economists.

Following Du Pont, Jefferson traced a history of modern political economy centred entirely on French authors:

> Political Economy, in modern times, assumed the form of a regular science, first
> in the hands of the political sect in France, called the Economists. They made
> it a branch only of a comprehensive system, on the natural order of Societies.
> Quesnia [sic] first, Gournay, Le Trosne, Turgot, and Dupont de Nemours, the
> enlightened, philanthropic, and venerable citizen now of the United States, led
> the way in these developments, and gave to our enquiries the direction they have
> since observed.[139]

---

[134]   Jefferson to Joseph Milligan, Monticello, 12 January 1819, in Chinard, *Jefferson et les Idéologues*, 186. Jefferson appreciated the *Edinburgh Review*, despite considering the periodical to be the expression of a British and anti-American spirit. (Jefferson to Lafayette, Monticello, 17 May 1816, in *The letters of Lafayette and Jefferson*, with an introduction and notes by Gilbert Chinard, Chartres (Paris: Durand les Belles-Lettres and Baltimore: The Johns Hopkins Press, 1929): 382).

[135]   CF. Ernest Teilhac, *Histoire de la pensée économique*, 110.

[136]   Jefferson to Joseph Cabell, Monticello, 2 February 1816, in Jefferson, *The Writings*, Bergh, vol. XIV, 419.

[137]   His letter to Joseph Cabell of 31 January 1814 called Say's work: 'a succinct, judicious digest of the tedious pages of Smith'. (Jefferson, *The Writings*, Bergh, vol. XIV, 82).

[138]   Jefferson to Joseph Milligan, 6 April 1816, in Jefferson, *The Writings*, Bergh, vol. XIV, 146–8.

[139]   Destutt de Tracy, *A Treatise on political economy, to which is prefixed a supplement to a preceding work on the understanding, or elements of ideology; with an analytical table, and an introduction on the faculty of the will*, translated from the unpublished

Thus Jefferson located the origin of political economy within the theoretical coordinates defined by Physiocracy, notwithstanding the critical discussions that had arisen around them, chiefly about the nature of taxes and wealth. Jefferson did not cast doubt on the validity of Physiocratic principles, 'whatever may be the merit of their principles of taxation, it is not wonderful they have not prevailed, not on the questioned score of correctness, but because not acceptable to the people'.[140] These were the same pragmatic lines of arguments followed in his discussions with Du Pont. He did not share the criticisms made against the Physiocrats in the resumption of discussions in France on the interpretations of Smith, which took place at the beginning of the century,[141] nor did he share the admiration of French circles for Smith:[142] 'Adam Smith, first in England, published a rational and systematic work on Political Economy; adopting generally the ground of the Economists, but differing on the subject before specified ... Hence his book admitted to be able, and of the first degree of merit, has yet been considered as prolix and tedious'.[143]

Observations about Smith's wordiness were often made, but Jefferson's opinions, particularly those in his correspondence, were of a greater severity and certainty that French thought had surpassed the *Wealth of Nations*: 'In France, John Baptist Say has the merit of producing a very superior work on the subject of Political Economy ... within half the volume of Smith's work; add to this, considerable advances in correctness, and extension of principles'.[144] Unlike the Physiocrats, Jefferson was convinced of the continual progress of the science of political economy, to which Du Pont had contributed, and the last step of which had been taken by the work of Tracy, who united 'the lights of his predecessors in the science, and with the advantages of further experience, more discussion and greater maturity of subject'.[145]

Jefferson was not inclined to abstract speculation, but his pragmatism did not preclude an appreciation of the precision and logic of the political economy of the *Idéologue*.[146] For this reason, in his 'Prospectus' he stressed the difficult work of translation that had been done and the need to preserve certain Gallicisms

---

French original (Georgetown: J. Milligan, 1817): Prospectus, iii. A comparative reading of Jefferson's Prospectus with the outline of the history of political economy traced by Du Pont in his edition of Turgot's work (vol. III, 309–20), and with the *Histoire abrégée* in Say's *Cours complet*, makes it possible to see the full extent of the affinity between Jefferson's approach and Du Pont's.

[140]   Destutt de Tracy, *A Treatise*, iii.

[141]   Du Pont had already denounced the attacks against the Physiocrats much earlier in the *Décade philosophique*: 'the habit of mocking them, while profiting from knowledge, has been engrained as they have aged, have stopped writing and have died'. (*Décade philosophique*, 20 Nivôse An IV, vol. 4, 83).

[142]   Cf. Moravia, *Il pensiero degli idéologues*.

[143]   Destutt de Tracy, *A Treatise*, iv.

[144]   Destutt de Tracy, *A Treatise*, iv.

[145]   Destutt de Tracy, *A Treatise*, iv.

[146]   Jefferson to John Adams, 14 October 1816, Chinard, *Jefferson et les Idéologues*, 241.

to render concepts that the French language could express better than English, bearing in mind the progress made by economic theory in France during the past thirty years.[147] Delays made by the American publishers prevented Jefferson from releasing the first edition of the work in English. It was not published until 1817, two years after it had appeared in France.[148]

After having received Tracy's book John Adams wrote to Jefferson, 'I am diligently and laboriously occupied in reading and hearing your "political economy"'[149] not only because he knew his zeal in spurring the publishers, but mainly because he was aware of the affinity of ideas between Jefferson and Tracy. Adams's attitude and judgement towards French political and economic culture had been harsh: 'I know', he wrote in April 1790, in a letter to Richard Price regarding the revolution in France, 'that encyclopedists and economists, Diderot and d'Alembert, Voltaire and Rousseau, have contributed to this great event more than Sidney, Locke, or Hoardly, perhaps more than the American Revolution; and I own to you, I know not what to make of a republic of thirty million atheists'.[150] In 1819 he could evaluate the radical value of Tracy's work, included in the great lineage of French economic culture: 'It is a magazine of gun powder placed under the foundations of all our mercantile institutions'.[151] Adams grasped the full significance of French economic liberalism, at a time when in the United States banks that issued unsecured paper currency proliferated, and when the country suffered from the lack of a stable currency. In spite of his underlying misgiving, he thus particularly appreciated Chapter VI, on the change of currencies, which was compared to theft: 'If this is true as I believe it is, we Americans are the most thievish people that ever existed'.[152] The similarities between the American and French economic cultures stemmed from their common revolutionary and republican experiences, which belonged to the Age of Enlightenment.[153] For him the value of this slim book, which became the manual for men of government,

---

[147]   Destutt de Tracy, *A Treatise*, iv–vii.

[148]   Destutt de Tracy, *Elémens d'idéologie. IVe et Ve parties. Traité de la volonté et de ses effets* (Paris: Vve Courcier, 1815). Tracy sent Jefferson the French edition printed 'almost without my consent', on 4 February 1816 (Chinard, *Jefferson et les Idéologues*, 165).

[149]   John Adams to Jefferson, Quincy, 24 February 1819, in Chinard, *Jefferson et les Idéologues*, 266.

[150]   Quoted in Z. Haraszti, *John Adams and the Prophets of Progress*, 81.

[151]   John Adams to Jefferson, Quincy, 2 March 1819, in Chinard, *Jefferson et les Idéologues*, 270.

[152]   Adams to Jefferson, 24 February 1819, Chinard, *Jefferson et les Idéologues*, 266. Cf. Destutt de Tracy, *A Treatise*, ch. VI, 21.

[153]   Cf. Franco Venturi, 'Destutt de Tracy e le rivoluzioni liberali', *Rivista storica italiana*, 84 (1972): 451–84. In this context Venturi looked upon Tracy and the *Idéologues* as expressions of the French culture which, between the eighteenth and nineteenth centuries, widened its interests beyond Europe. He thus believed that Tracy's decision to publish his two works in America was not linked only to prudence, but also to a desire to export his ideas (*ibid.*, 458).

lay in its condensation of the entire science of political economy, which was one alone, and which derived directly from Physiocracy:

> It is a condensation into a little globule not comparatively bigger than a nut-shell of all the sound sense and solid knowledge of the grand master Quanay [sic] and all the redoubtable knights his disciples and all their numerous huge volumes and those of Sir James Stuart and Adam Smith the chevalier Pinto and the Enciclopedists, discarding all their mysteries, paradoxes and enigmas.[154]

The two old revolutionaries, founding fathers of the American nation and political adversaries, agreed in recognizing the usefulness of French political economy as a political tool with which to act on the reality of the new state: 'I am delighted with your high approbation of Tracy's book. The evils of this deluge of paper money are not to be removed, until our citizens are generally and radically instructed in their cause and consequences'.[155]

The fortune of the French political economy was nevertheless assured by the great success of Say's *Traité*, which had managed to combine Smith's results and his science of wealth creation with the social approach of the French tradition, which was closer to American pragmatism. Both Say and Tracy censured the Physiocratic authors for their dogmatism. Jefferson admired the anti-systematic spirit of post-Physiocratic French economic thought, while acknowledging the contribution made by Physiocracy to the identification of the relationship between economics and politics, which made economics the social science par excellence. Even though he never became a theorist of political economy, he always used Physiocracy as a point of reference, often through his relationship with Du Pont de Nemours. Moreover, speaking with his French interlocutors, he contributed with his pragmatism, the expression of America's uniqueness, to renewing the link between economics and politics in the framework of the development of social science, which separated social phenomena from metaphysical notions.[156]

---

[154]   John Adams to Jefferson, Quincy, 2 March 1819, in Chinard, *Jefferson et les idéologues*, 270.

[155]   Jefferson to Adams, Monticello, 21 March 1819, Chinard, *Jefferson et les idéologues*, 272. Jefferson had wanted to include Adams's enthusiastic letter in the second edition of the *Treaty on Political Economy*, but this was never published.

[156]   When sending Jefferson one of his works in 1814, Auguste Comte wrote to him: 'This book is only the beginning of a more extensive work whose aim is to endow politics with the characteristics of a physical science, and submit, therefore, the study of social phenomena to the method now used so successfully for all other types of phenomena. ... But to know for sure whether this research is worth carrying out I must first submit the first draft to the thinkers who have most thought about this subject and to statesmen who have demonstrated the greatest capacity to understand the true nature of the present era. It is for these two reasons that I earnestly seek the judgement of Mr. Jefferson' (Isidore-Auguste-Marie-François-Xavier Comte to Jefferson, Paris, 16 July 1824, in Chinard, *Jefferson et les idéologues*, 285–6).

The exchange between France and the United States was reciprocal: Say's and Tracy's ideas found a favourable reception among the American Republicans while, with his ideas, Jefferson helped to restore the unity of the French tradition. The ideas of the elderly Du Pont de Nemours, critical of Say yet sensitive to the stimuli offered by his American friend and his reception of post-Physiocratic thought, all stand as a testimony to the movement of Physiocracy in men and in time and to the efforts of the last Physiocrat to comprehend the reality of the new American nation.

Conclusion

Both Thomas Jefferson and John Adams died on 4 July 1826, the fiftieth anniversary of the Declaration of Independence, which they had worked on together. The date not only marked the demise of two men who had played important roles in the birth of the United States but also symbolized the end of an era, the age of Enlightenment cosmopolitanism, in which ideas and people circulated and fuelled the democratic revolutions of the late eighteenth century in America and in France. It was from these that the notions of republic, democracy and political representation emerged as a heritage not identified with individual countries, but which composed the fruit of a mutual exchange between cultures with different attributes and characteristics.

In studying a century in which the acceleration of trade transformed not only the movement of goods but also the minds of people, I have sought to follow a particular form of exchange, the sharing of ideas between the two countries involved in revolution. The eighteenth century saw the birth of political economy, that is to say the formation of a science of economics with its own corpus and its own specialized language, at a time when it was believed that all areas of human enquiry could be organized into a scientific framework. Eighteenth-century economic authors elaborated their ideas as responses to their circumstances, and in the specificity of those situations political economy came to represent a modern common language that could bring about change, a lingua franca that facilitated dialogue between the two shores of the Atlantic.

Within this framework, I decided to look at American agrarian ideology from the perspective of the relationship between economics and politics, in order to observe how it came to be an expression of national identity. This occurred over a long period that started before the conflict arose between the British colonies and the motherland and continued through the early decades of the nineteenth century – in other words a long eighteenth century – to end, notionally, with the death of the second and third presidents of the United States.

The contribution of French economic thought to the plans of Jefferson's Republicans to formulate an economic and political alternative to the British model has been traced through several channels. I hope this path has made it easier to understand not only the interplay between the two cultures, but also certain specific elements of both which this comparative perspective has made more visible.

By using an approach drawn from intellectual history, I have tried to highlight the context in which individual participants operated. Hence, I have analysed how the ideologues of American agrarian democracy – Franklin, Jefferson, Logan and Taylor – transposed the French economic model, developed by the Physiocrats, into their own national reality, through their intellectual enquiry and their networks of personal contacts. I have endeavoured to describe this model and to show how the Americans found that it gave scientific legitimacy to the centrality of the landowner, a dynamic economic actor who represented the national interest and who was entitled to exercise the right of representation.

At the same time I have wanted to bring into the foreground those American characteristics that helped to create a fertile ground favourable to the circulation of ideas. I have begun this analysis with St John de Crèvecoeur because his sensibility as a Frenchman-who-became-American stands as a symbolic starting point for an agrarian myth that was evident even before the Jeffersonian political project had developed into a distinctive entity. The attention given to piecing together the conditions receptive to the idea of agriculture as a source of wealth in an exceptional geographical environment led me to retrace the distinctive traits of American agrarian ideology, the political culture of the Republicans, the role of religion, the forms and characteristics of the economic societies – of which the ideologues of agrarian democracy, who were also agronomists, were protagonists – and the shaping of public opinion through the circulation of almanacs and the republican press.

Because of their pragmatism, Franklin and Jefferson were involved with the circles of the French economists in different ways, and the generation gap allows us to evaluate how these associations varied. Franklin came into contact with the Physiocratic authors when Physiocracy was at its peak. He was an economist well able to discuss French economic theories critically, and to assimilate the idea of agriculture as a source of wealth into his flexible economic positions. Jefferson read the Physiocratic texts and found in them scientific legitimization of his political project, even when his realism in the face of changes on the international scene led him to accept a programme of manufacturing development, which, however, did not alter his certainty that only the land generated wealth.

Both Jefferson and Franklin found in the economic form of French political rationalism – from the Physiocrats to Condorcet to the *Américanistes* – not only theoretical points of reference but also immediate support, absent from Smith, for the independence of the American colonies, in the name of economic freedom and the rejection of the British model. Moreover, it was through their personal contacts with French circles that they orchestrated their campaigns in support of the American Revolution. Physiocracy represented for both not only the starting point of the science of political economy but also an alternative economic approach to that of the British model, one concerned not only with the creation of wealth but also with its distribution and the link between economics and politics. Franklin, who championed a levelling of conditions, was receptive to the arguments of Quesnay and the Marquis of Mirabeau regarding the benefits of a general raising of the material standard of living. Jefferson, an advocate of decentralized democracy, appreciated the French attempts to create a system of provincial assemblies, an expression of the more mature reformist projects of Physiocratic authors.

Jefferson was able to follow the progression of French economic thinking in the long term, through his relationship with a no longer dogmatic Du Pont de Nemours, and through his contacts with Jean-Baptiste Say, Destutt de Tracy and the *Idéologues* group motivated by the idea of countering British classical economics with post-Physiocratic thought. The presence of French economic culture and the role still assigned to Physiocracy in American academia, the success of Say's *Treatise on Political Economy* as a university textbook, the strategy of publishing translations of the works of Say and Tracy (coordinated by Jefferson to rebut Ricardo), gave manifold witness not only to the durability of American interest in French economic thought but also to its cultural importance. Smith, Steuart, Malthus and Ricardo were well known and widely debated writers, but the aspiration to distance America from the British roots of political economy meant that the Americans believed that French economic thought still deserved to play a significant role.

The winding path of the reception of these ideas, which stimulated original thinking, emerges through the many responses so far considered. Strictly speaking, Jefferson and Franklin cannot be thought of as Physiocrats, but I have tried to highlight the significance of their involvement with Physiocracy, which went beyond adherence to a rigid formulation of its principles. Moreover, I have tried to show how Physiocracy was not the source of their agrarian ideology, but rather provided confirmation for their beliefs and policies through the language and the rigour of a scientific analysis of the economic process. This becomes clear when we consider the political implications of Physiocracy, and the Physiocratic authors' strategy of radiating out to other nations through the creation of an expanding network of relationships, an economic approach conceived as a tool for policy reforms. The expansion of this network altered the initial structure of the group and its members, as the experiences and thoughts of Du Pont de Nemours demonstrate. We have followed Jefferson's dialogue with the elderly Physiocrat, who lived out his final years in the United States, and have seen how he kept faith with to his fundamental principles while responding to change and the need to keep his understanding of economics up to date.

Only by adopting this particular analytical perspective, can one identify the elements of this encounter and grasp the reasons, and also the apparent contradictions, of the mutual exchange between different cultures and contexts. One can then understand why Physiocracy, which was developed in absolutist France, aroused interest in contemporaries who were far removed from French dynamics and able to go beyond the rigidity of theoretical formulations. One can understand, too, why Jefferson, who never resolved his ambiguous attitude to slavery, approved of the geometric rigour of Physiocratic arguments in favour of free labour, and why Franklin abandoned his steadfast commitment to Petty's theory of value after meeting the Quesnay group, and, additionally, why Logan's Quaker sensitivity gave rise to an unconditional adherence to the Physiocratic natural order.

At the end of our journey, it is possible to identify some points of this encounter: the idea that wealth was derived solely from the land; a global and peaceful vision of relationships between nations based on economic freedom; the idea of a natural order expressed through economic laws, the understanding of which was realized through the spread of education; the criticism of the value of history and tradition, which was contrasted with the idea of nature; the social centrality of the landowner and his right to exercise political representation; the recognition of land ownership as an expression of individual freedom; the notion of social interest based on economic ties between individuals; a role for the state, neither absent nor obtrusive, designed to ensure the due application of economic laws; a scientific analysis of the economic process with a strong focus not only on the creation of wealth but also on its distribution; a political rationalism rooted in economics that recognized the centrality of the law and the unity of sovereignty and was not inconsistent with the decentralization of the state; the rejection of protectionism, the central role of public credit, movable wealth, banks and the role of finance, which signified the rejection not only of the economic model of Britain but also of its political constitution founded on a compromise between the interests and the balance of powers. All these elements, ordered within a scientific theory, represented a language and an economic culture that the ideologues of American agrarian democracy could exploit.

The importance of Physiocratic arguments, and the political implications of a project for economic development based on agriculture, in a setting profoundly different from that of France and long after the apogee of the Quesnay group, was attested, as we have seen, by the force of Alexander Hamilton's attacks, launched in 1791, against the Republicans and their democratic and agrarian model, attacks not detached from the denial of the principle of the exclusive productivity of the land and the notion of sterile classes. The Minister of the Treasury was convinced that Physiocracy still represented a danger to the United States.

The clash between Republicans and Federalists was partly played out around Physiocracy. George Logan was an authentic American Physiocrat. He was not alone in his attacks on Hamilton and the Federalists, which he unleashed using a battery of Physiocratic arguments, for they were part of a plan of action coordinated with Jefferson, an expression of Republican opposition to Federalist policy accused of being pro-monarchy and modelled on Britain. Logan's denunciation of moneyed interest was far removed from British country ideology, which nonetheless influenced the culture of American politics. Indeed, in the 1790s this fused with a political radicalism that took revolutionary France as a benchmark in the context of a duel in the United States in which being for or against the French Revolution sharpened the conflict and helped to define the contours of the two American political parties.

The economic form of French political rationalism also stimulated, albeit in a different way, the agrarian ideology of John Taylor, who did not share the radicalism of Logan and Jefferson despite being the theorist of states democracy and of an agrarian republic opposed to Hamilton. Taylor also read the Physiocratic authors, whose opinions on taxation he held to be more persuasive than those of Smith. But it was above all the principle of the unity of sovereignty and the critique of the balance of powers of the British model, which emerged in the disagreement between Turgot and John Adams, which fed his theory on the rights of the states, an original American formulation of the unity of sovereignty and the separation of powers.

The numerous contacts made during the long period that we have analysed in the end emphasize the reciprocity of this enriching interchange of ideas. Crèvecoeur was nourished by the culture of European Enlightenment conveyed by Raynal's *Histoire des deux Indes*. He often wavered between political positions, but with the success of his *Letters*, which he adapted for a French translation in accordance with support for the American Revolution in Parisian circles, he made known, through the eyes of an American, the agrarian myth and national identity of America, which preceded the formation of the new state.

Franklin always preserved the interest in Physiocracy in French circles, which he frequented until his return to the United States; his attendance at the salon of Madame Helvétius, alongside the future *Idéologues*, facilitated this intellectual transmission. For many years, while in Paris, he was the main source of information on America and his collaboration with the *Ephémérides du citoyen* and the *Affaires de l'Angleterre et de l'Amérique* enriched the French political debate, contributing to the programme of reforms devised by such men as Turgot and La Rochefoucauld who revolved around the Physiocratic milieu. During his stays in France and England, he also served as the lynchpin between the economic and political culture of the French circles he visited and the English Dissenters, who saw in him the embodiment of the American myth and a cosmopolitan reference point. In England, he also acted as a point of contact with French intellectual circles: Richard Price turned to him for consent to publish Turgot's *Lettre au Docteur Price* as part of a common strategy of support for the American cause and criticism of the British constitutional model. Franklin was a leading figure in the exchange of ideas between France, Britain and America.

The successful *Notes on the State of Virginia* was the first authoritative correction of erroneous information and theories about America that circulated in Europe and had been entrenched in public opinion by the success of works like Raynal's *Histoire*. When, arriving in Paris, Jefferson continued his efforts to rectify this false image by offering to contribute to the *Encyclopédie méthodique*, his actions were fortified by a new commitment to the political aims of the *Américanistes* group. His contribution was more than simply supplying information, for, in fact, he, together with American agrarian ideology and the policies of the Republicans, provided political guidance for Mazzei, Condorcet, Du Pont de Nemours and La Rochefoucauld in their opposition to the British system and their attempts to speed up changes in France. It was while he had beside him the English doctor Richard Gem and Condorcet, in an environment in which the tradition of Physiocratic political rationalism was still alive, that Jefferson worked out the principle of constitutional revision and of the right of every generation not to be burdened by earlier ones. After his return to the United States, Jefferson did not break off his dialogue with his French counterparts. And not only did he continue to implement the economic culture of post-Physiocratic France, becoming its propagator in his country, but he also contributed to its enrichment with his democracy theories, his experiences in government and his pragmatism, to which the *Décade philosophique* paid careful attention. While remaining convinced of a continuity and uniqueness in French economic thought, he admired the way in which the *Idéologues* went beyond the stringency of the Physiocrats' political economy. He helped to maintain this in his dialogue with French correspondents at a time when, in France, Physiocracy had already been relegated to the history of economic ideas. Together with Du Pont de Nemours he helped to ensure that the dimension of political economy known as the 'science des constitutions' was not lost. The compelling argument made for this link between economics and politics, which reappeared in the *Treatise on political economy* by Destutt de Tracy, led John Adams to share his lifelong rival's opinion on the benefits that American politics could draw from an English translation of the work.

The rejection of the British economic and political model, which marked the convergence of American and French economic culture, did not, however, rule out a lively British presence in and contribution to the circulation of ideas and men, which unfolded through the three-way relationship of France, Britain and America. Following the interweaving of intellectual and personal links between Franklin, Paine, Price, Priestley, Cooper, Turgot, Condorcet, Du Pont de Nemours, La Rochefoucauld, Jefferson and Gem has enabled me to spotlight a cosmopolitan network in which such men merged their identities by using the language of political economy in different national situations. Benjamin Vaughan, whose name was linked to the English translation of Condorcet's *Vie de Turgot* and who harboured an interest in Physiocracy, was in contact with Franklin and Jefferson and professed republican convictions that eventually led him to migrate to the United States. The translation took shape in the circle of Lord Shelburne, where economics, religious dissent and the desire for reforms in Britain were fuelled by an interest in French political and economic rationalism and the development of its radical implications by such writers as Turgot and Condorcet. A similar radicalization of positions encouraged the political and religious emigration from Britain to the United States. This gave Jefferson's election campaign for the presidency a decisive boost and, additionally, it enriched American agrarian ideology with economic ideas that reconciled democratic experiences and the vision of a commercial society in which different activities related harmoniously. In a period of international tension straddling the eighteenth and nineteenth century, the maturation of American agrarian ideology in the context of a commercial economy, perceived as a means of reshaping relationships between nations, continued to inform the beliefs of a generation of Americans, whose passing signalled the demise of Enlightenment cosmopolitanism, which had nurtured the formation of the national identity of the first modern republic.

Bibliography

Manuscript Sources

Académie Nationale de Médecine, Paris, Ms 81 (54), *Papiers du Dr Bourdois de la Motte*.

Archives du Ministère des Affaires Etrangères:

Etats-Unis, Mémoires et Documents, vol. 1888.

Etats-Unis, Mémoires et Documents, vol. XIV, *Correspondance consulaire de New York par St. John de Crèvecoeur 1783–1790*.

Personnel, vol. XX, *Distribution des Consulats de France dans les Etats-Unis et caractère des differens sujets qui y sont employés, 1788*.

Archives Municipales de Mantes-la-Jolie, Fonds Clerc de Landresse, *Correspondance entre J. Hector de Crévecoeur et le duc de La Rochefoucauld*.

Archives Nationales, Affaires Etrangères:

B I, 909, *New York, 1783–92*.

B III, 439, *Minutes des lettres ministerielles concernant l'Amérique 1785–1793*.

Bibliothèque de l'Institut de France, Paris: *Papiers Condorcet*, MS 860.

Eleutherian Mills Historical Library, *Winterthur Manuscripts, Papers of Pierre Samuel Du Pont de Nemours*, series A, Correspondence, series B, Writings.

Historical Society of Pennsylvania, *George Logan Papers*.

Primary Sources Contemporary Journals

Affaires de l'Angleterre et de l'Amérique, ed. Edme-Jacques Genet, Antoine Court de Gébelin and Alexandre-Louis La Rochefoucauld d'Anville, 17 vols. (Anvers, 1776–9).

American Farmer, ed. John Skinner, 15 vols. (Baltimore, 1819–34).

American Museum, or Universal magazine: containing essays on agriculture, commerce, manufactures, politics, morals and manners: sketches of national characters, natural and civil history, and biography: law information, public papers, intelligence: moral tales, ancient and modern poetry, ed. Mathew Carey and John Adams, 12 vols. (Philadelphia: 1787–92), 12 vols.

Analyse des papiers anglois, ed. Honoré-Gabriel Comte de Mirabeau (Paris, 1787–8).

Bibliothèque de l'homme public; ou analyse raisonnée des principaux ouvrages François et étrangers sur la politique en général, la législation, les finances, la police, l'agriculture, et le commerce en particulier, et le droit naturel et public, ed. Isaac-René-Guy Le Chapelier, Charles de Peyssonnel and Jean-Marie-Antoine-Nicolas Caritat de Condorcet, 14 vols. (Paris, 1790–92).

Boston Magazine, ed. John Eliot, James Freeman, Aaron Dexter, John Clarke, John Bradford, Benjamin Lincoln and Christopher Gore (Boston, 1783–6).

Chronique de Paris, ed. Aubin-Louis Millin, J.-F. Noël, Jean-Marie-Antoine-Nicolas Caritat de Condorcet and Jean-Paul Rabaud, 8 vols. (Paris, 1789–93).

Correspondance littéraire, philosophique et critique par Grimm, Diderot, Raynal, Meister, etc., ed. Maurice Tourneux, 15 vols. (Paris: Garnier, 1880).

Courier de l'Europe, Gazette anglo-française, ed. Charles Théveneau de Morande (London, 1776–92), 32 vols.

La Décade philosophique littéraire et politique par une société de républicains, ed. Pierre-Louis Ginguené, 42 vols. (Paris, 1794–1804).

Edinburgh Review, ed. Francis Jeffrey (1802–29), 250 vols. (Edinburgh, 1802–1929).

The Emporium of arts and sciences, new series, ed. Thomas Cooper (Philadelphia: 1813–14).

Ephémérides du citoyen, ou Bibliothèque raisonnée des sciences morales et politiques, ed. Nicolas Baudeau, from May 1768 Pierre-Samuel Du Pont de Nemours, 63 vols. (Paris, 1767–72).

Farmer's Register, ed. Edmund Ruffin, 11 vols. (Richmond, VA, 1833–43).

Gazette nationale ou Moniteur universel, ed. Charles-Joseph Pancoucke (Paris, 1789–1810).

Independent Gazetteer and agricultural Repository, ed. Eleazer Oswald (Philadelphia, 1794–6).

Independent Journal, ed. John McLean and Archibald McLean (New York, 1783–8).

Journal de Paris, ed. Olivier de Corancez, Jean de Romilly, Louis d'Ussieux and Antoine-Alexis Cadet de Vaux (Paris, 1777–1827).

Mémoires secrets pour servir à l'histoire de la république des lettres en France, ed. Louis Petit de Bachaumont, Mathieu-François Pidansat de Mairobert and Barthélémy-François-Joseph Moufle d'Angerville, 36 vols. (London: J. Adaneson, 1777–89).

Monthly Review, or Literary Journal, ed. Ralph Griffiths (London, 1749–1844).

National Gazette, ed. Philippe Freneau, 2 vols. (Philadelphia, 1791–3).

New York Journal, ed. Eleazer Oswald and Andrew Brown (New York, 1785–7).

Patriote François, journal libre, impartial et national, ed. Jacques-Pierre Brissot, 8 vols. (Paris, 1789–93).

Political Register, ed. William Cobbett (London and New York, 1802–35).

Worchester Magazine, ed. Isaiah Thomas (Worcester, MA, 1786–7).

Primary Sources Printed Books

Adair, James, *The History of American Indians* (London: E. and C. Dilley, 1775).

Adams, John, *A Defence of the Constitutions of Government of the United States of America* (Philadelphia: Hall and Sellers, 1787).

Ames, Nathaniel, *The Essays, Humor, and Poems of Nathaniel Ames, Father and Son, of Dedham, Massachusetts, from their Almanacks, 1726–1775*, ed. Samuel Briggs (Cleveland, OH, 1891).

Archives parlementaires de 1787 à 1860; Recueil complet des débats législatifs et politiques des chambres françaises. Première Série (1787–1799) (Paris, 1867–96) (Reprint, Nendeln, Leichtenstein: Krauss, 1969).

Ayscough, Samuel, *Remarks on the Letters from an American Farmer; or a detection of the errors of Mr. J. Hector St. John; Pointing out the pernicious Tendency of these Letters to Great Britain* (London: John Fielding, 1783).

Barbeu Du Bourg, Jacques, *Calendrier de Philadelphie, ou Constitutions de Sancho-Pança et du Bon-Homme Richard, en Pennsylvanie* (1778).

Blackstone, William, *Commentaries on the Laws of England*, 4 vols. (Oxford: Clarendon Press, 1770).

Brissot Jacques-Pierre, *Examen critique des voyages dans l'Amérique septentrionale de M. le marquis de Chastellux* (London, 1786).

—, *Mémoires (1754–1793)*, ed. Claude Perroud, 2 vols. (Paris: Picard, [1910]).

Brissot, Jacques-Pierre and Etienne Clavière, *De la France et des Etats-Unis*, preface by M. Dorigny (Paris: Editions du C.T.H.S., 1996).

Burke, Edmund, *Reflections on the Revolution in France*, ed. Conor C. O'Brien (Harmondsworth: Penguin Books, 1973).

Carey Henry, *Principles of Political Economy*, vol. I (Philadelphia: Carey, Lea and Blanchard, 1837).

—, *The Past, the Present and the Future* (Philadelphia: Carey and Hart, 1848).

Carey, Mathew, ed. *Debates and Proceedings of the General Assembly of Pennsylvania on the Memorials Praying a Repeal or Suspension of the Law Annulling the Charter of the Bank* (Philadelphia: Printed for Carey and Co. by Seddon and Pritchard, 1786).

Carver, Jonathan, *Travels through the Interior Parts of North America in the years 1766, 1767, and 1768* (London: J. Walter, 1778).

Collection des principaux économistes, Physiocrates, ed. Eugène Daire, vol. II (Paris: Guillaumin, 1846).

Condillac, Etienne Bonnot de, *Le commerce et le gouvernement, considérés relativement l'un à l'autre. Ouvrage élémentaire* (Amsterdam, et se trouve à Paris: chez Jombert & Cellot, 1776).

Condorcet, Jean-Marie-Antoine-Nicolas Caritat de, *The Life of M. Turgot, Controller General of the Finances of France, in the years 1774, 1775 and 1776* (London: J. Johnson, 1787).

—, *Déclaration des droits, traduite de l'Anglois, avec l'original à côté* (London, 1789).

—, *Oeuvres*, ed. Arthur Condorcet O'Connor and François Arago, 12 vols. (Paris: F. Didot frères, 1847–1849).

Cooper, Thomas, *A Reply to Mr. Burke's Invective against Mr. Cooper, and Mr. Watt, in the House of Commons, on 30th of April 1792* (Manchester: M. Falkner & Co., 1792).

—, *Some information respecting America* (London: J. Johnson, 1794).

—, *Renseignements sur l'Amérique* (Hambourg: Pierre François Fauche, 1795).

—, *Political Essays originally inserted in the Northumberland Gazette* (Northumberland: Andrew Kennedy, 1799).

—, *Lectures on the Elements of Political Economy* (Columbia, SC: Doyle E. Sweeny, 1826).

—, *Lectures on the Elements of Political Economy*, 2nd ed. (New York: A.M. Kelley, 1830).

—, *A Manual of Political Economy* (Washington: Duff Green, 1834).

Coxe, Tench, *A view of the United States of America. In a series of papers written at various times, in the years between 1787 and 1794* (Philadelphia: 1794).

Crevècoeur, John Hector St John de, *Traité de la culture des pommes-de-terre, Et des différens usages qu'en font les Habitans des Etats-Unis de l'Amérique* (Caen, 1782).

—, *Letters from an American Farmer: describing certain provincial situations, manners, and customs, not generally known; and conveying some idea of the late and present interior circumstances of the British Colonies in North America. Written for the information of a friend in England, by J. Hector St. John, a farmer in Pennsylvania* (London: T. Davies and L. Davies, 1782).

—, *Lettres d'un cultivateur américain, écrites à W.S. Ecuyer, depuis l'année 1770, jusqu'à 1781. Traduites de l'Anglois par ****, 2 vols (Paris: Cuchet, 1784).

—, François-Alexandre-Frédéric de La Rochefoucauld-Liancourt and Antoine-Alexis Cadet de Vaux, 'Rapport sur les usages et les avantages de la Marmite Américaine', in *Mémoires d'Agriculture, d'Economie rurale et domestique, publiés par la Société Royale d'Agriculture de Paris* (Paris: Cuchet, 1786): 107–15.

—, 'Mémoire sur la culture et les usages du Faux-Acacia dans les Etats-Unis de l'Amérique septentrionale', in *Mémoires d'Agriculture, d'Economie rurale et domestique, publiés par la Société Royale d'Agriculture de Paris* (Paris: Cuchet, 1786): 122–43.

—, *Lettres d'un cultivateur américain addressées à Wm S ... on Esqr. Depuis l'Année 1770 jusqu'en 1786, traduites de l'Anglois*, 3 vols (Paris: Cuchet, 1787).

—, *Voyage dans la Haute Pennsylvanie et dans l'état de New York, par un membre adoptif de la Nation Onéida: Traduit et publié par l'auteur des Lettres d'un Cultivateur Américain*, 3 vols. (Paris: Crapelet, Maradan, an IX (1801)).

—, *Sketches of Eighteenth Century America*, ed. Henri L. Bourdin, Ralph H. Gabriel and Stanley T. Williams (New Haven: Yale University Press, 1925).

—, *More Letters from an American Farmer: An Edition of the Essays in English Left Unpublished by Crèvecoeur*, ed. Denis D. Moore (Athens: The University of Georgia Press, 1995).

—, *Letters from an American Farmer*, ed. S. Manning (Oxford: Oxford University Press, 1997).

Cutler, Manasseh, *Description du sol, des productions etc. de cette portion des Etats-Unis située entre la Pennsylvanie, les rivières de l'Ohio et du Scioto et le lac Erié, traduite d'une brochure imprimée à Salem en Amérique en 1787* (Paris, 1789).

Deane, Samuel, *The New-England Farmer; or, Georgical Dictionary* (Worcester, MA: I. Thomas, 1790).

Démeunier, Jean-Nicolas, *Essai sur les Etats-Unis* (Paris: de l'Imprimerie de Laporte, 1786).

—, *L'Amérique indépendante, ou les différentes constitutions des treize provinces*, 3 vols. (Gand: 1790).

Destutt de Tracy, Antoine-Louis-Claude, *A commentary and Review of Montesquieu's Spirit of Laws. Prepared for press from the original manuscript, in the hands of the publishers. To which are annexed, Observations on the thirty-first book, by the late M. Condorcet: and two letters of Helvétius, on the merits of the same work* (Philadephia: W. Duane, 1811).

—, *Elémens d'idéologie. IVe et Ve parties. Traité de la volonté et de ses effets* (Paris: Vve Courcier, 1815).

—, *A Treatise on political economy, to which is prefixed a supplement to a preceding work on the understanding, or elements of ideology; with an analytical table, and an introduction on the faculty of the will, translated from the unpublished French original* (Georgetown, D.C.: J. Milligan, 1817).

—, *Commentaire sur l'"Esprit des lois" de Montesquieu, suivi d'observations inédites de Condorcet sur le vingt-neuvième livre du dit ouvrage* (Liège: Desoer,1817).

—, *Commentaire sur l'Esprit des lois de Montesquieu; édition entièrement conforme à celle publiée à Liège en 1817* (Paris: Delaunay, 1819).

Dew, Thomas, *Lectures on the Restrictive System Delivered to the Senior Political Class of the William and Mary College* (Richmond, VA: S. Shepherd and Co., 1829).

Dickinson John, *Lettres d'un fermier de Pennsylvanie aux habitants de l'Amérique septentrionale*, trans. from English (Amsterdam: aux dépens de la Compagnie, 1769).

Du Pont de Nemours, Pierre-Samuel, *Du Commerce et de la Compagnie des Indes. Seconde édition, revue, corrigée et augmentée de l'Histoire du Système de Law* (Amsterdam: chez Delalain; Paris: chez Lacombe, 1769).

—, *Lettre à la Chambre du Commerce de Normandie, Sur le Mémoire qu'elle a publié relativement au Traité de Commerce avec l'Angleterre* (Rouen, Paris: Moutard, 1788).

—, *Sur l'éducation nationale dans les Etats-Unis d'Amérique*, 2nd ed. (Paris: Le Normant, 1812).

—, *Examen du livre de M. Malthus sur le Principe de Population; auquel on a joint la traduction de quatre chapitres de ce livre supprimés dans l'édition française;*

et une Lettre à M. Say sur son Traité d'économie politique (Philadelphia: P.M. Lafourcade, 1817).

—, *National education in the United States of America* (Newark: University of Delaware Press, 1923).

Dumont, Etienne, *Souvenirs sur Mirabeau et sur les deux premières assemblées législatives* (Paris: PUF, 1950).

Eliot, Jared, *Essays upon Field Husbandry in New England and Other Papers 1748–1762* (New York: Columbia University Press, 1934).

Elliott, Jonathan, ed. *The Debates in the Several State Conventions on the Adoption of the Federal Constitution* (Philadelphia: 1826).

Franklin Benjamin, *Oeuvres de M. Franklin*, trans. from English 4th ed. by M. Barbeu Dubourg with new annotations, 2 vols. (Paris: chez Quillau, Esprit et l'Auteur, 1773).

—, *La science du Bonhomme Richard, ou Moyen facile de payer les impôts* (Philadelphia and Paris: chez Ruault, 1777).

—, *La science du bonhomme Richard; précédée d'un abrégé de la Vie de Franklin, et suivie de son Interrogatoire devant la Chambre des Communes* (Paris: Imprimerie des sciences et des arts, an II).

—, *The Works*, ed. Jared Sparks, 10 vols. (London: Benjamin Franklin Stevens, 1882).

—, *The Writings*, ed. Albert H. Smyth, 10 vols. (New York: Macmillan, 1905–7).

—, *The Papers*, ed. W.B. Willcox (New Haven: Yale University Press, 1959–).

—, *Autobiography*, ed. J.A. Leo Lemay and P.M. Zall (New York: W.W. Norton, 1986).

Ganilh, Charles, *An Inquiry Into the Various Systems of Political Economy*, trans. from French by D. Boileau (London: H. Colburn, 1812).

Godwin, William, *Of Population* (New York: August M. Kelley, 1964).

Hamilton, Alexander, *The Papers*, ed. Harold C. Syrett, 26 vols. (New York: Columbia University Press, 1961–79)

Hilliard D'Auberteuil, Michel-René, *Essais historiques et politiques sur les Anglois-Américains*, 2 vols. (Brussels and Paris: chez l'auteur, 1782).

Hume David, *Writings on economics*, ed. Eugene Rotwein (London: Nelson, 1957).

—, *Essays Moral, Political and Literary* (London: Oxford University Press, 1963).

Jefferson, Thomas, *An Act for Establishing Religious Freedom, Passed in the Assembly of Virginia in the Beginning of the Year 1786*, introduction by R.[ichard] P.[rice] (London, 1786).

—, *The Writings*, ed. Paul L. Ford, 10 vols. (New York: G.P. Putnam's Sons, 1893–9).

—, *The Writings*, ed. Andrew A. Lipscomb and Albert Ellery Bergh, 20 vols. (Washington: T. Jefferson Memorial Association, 1903).

—, *The Papers*, ed. Julian P. Boyd (Princeton: Princeton University Press, 1950–).

—, *Notes on the State of Virginia*, ed. William Peden (New York: W.W. Norton and Company, 1954).

—, *The Writings*, ed. Merrill D. Peterson (New York: Library of America, 1984).

—, *The Life and Selected Writings*, ed. Adrienne Koch and William Peden (New York: Random House, 1993).

Judd, Eben W., *The United States Almanack for 1786* (Elizabeth-Town: Shepard Collock, 1786).

La Rochefoucauld d'Anville, Louis-Alexandre, *Constitutions des Treize Etats-Unis de l'Amérique* (Philadelphia, Paris: Ph.-D. Pierres, Imprimeur ordinaire du Roi, 1783).

Lauderdale, James Maitland, Earl of, *Inquiry into the Nature and Origin of Public Wealth, and into the Means and Causes of its Increase* (Edinburgh: A. Constable and Co.; London: T.N. Longman and O. Rees, 1804).

The letters of Lafayette and Jefferson, with an introduction and notes by Gilbert Chinard, Chartres (Paris: Durand les Belles-Lettres and Baltimore: The Johns Hopkins Press, 1929).

Le Mercier de la Rivière, Pierre-Paul-François, *L'ordre naturel et essentiel des sociétés politiques*, 2 vols. (Paris: J. Nourse, Desaint, 1767).

—, *Essai sur les maximes et les loix fondamentales de la monarchie française, ou Canevas d'un code constitutionnel, pour servir de suite à l'ouvrage intitulé: 'Les voeux d'un François'* (Paris, Versailles, Vallat-La-Chapelle: Veillard, 1789).

Locke, John, *Two Treatises of Government*, ed. Peter Laslett (Cambridge: Cambridge University Press, 1960).

Logan, Deborah Norris, *Memoir of Dr. George Logan of Stenton, by his widow* (Philadelphia: The Historical Society of Pennsylvania, 1899).

Logan, George, *An Address on the Natural and Social Order of the World, as Intended to Produce Universal Good; Delivered Before the Tammany Society, at their Anniversary on 12th of May 1798* (Philadelphia: B. Franklin Bache, 1789).

—, *Letters Addressed to the Yeomanry of the United States: Shewing the Necessity of Confining the Public Revenue to a Fixed Proportion of Net Produce of Land; and the Bad Policy and Injustice of Every Species of Indirect Taxation and Commercial Regulations* (Philadelphia: E. Oswald, 1791).

—, *Five Letters Addressed to the Yeomanry of the United States, Containing Some Observations on Funding and Bank Systems* (Philadelphia, 1793).

—, *Fourteen Agricultural Experiments, to Ascertain the Best Rotation of Crops: Addressed to the Philadelphia Agricultural Society* (Philadelphia: Bailey, 1797).

—, *A Letter to the Citizens of Pennsylvania, on the Necessity of Promoting Agriculture, Manufactures, and the Useful Arts* (Philadelphia: Patterson and Cochran, 1 May 1800).

Lolme, Jean-Louis de, *Constitution de l'Angleterre* (Amsterdam: E. Van Harrevelt, 1774).

McVickar, John, *Outlines of Political Economy, Being a Republication of the Article upon that Subject Contained in the Edinburgh Supplement to the Encyclopedia Britannica* (New York: Wilder and Campbell, 1825).

Madison, James, *Letters and Other Writings*, 4 vols. (New York: R. Worlongton, 1884).

Malthus, Thomas R., *An Essay on the Principle of Population*, 2nd. ed. (London: printed for J. Johnson by T. Bensley, 1803).

—, *An Essay on the Principle of Population* (London: Macmillan, 1966).

Marcet, Jane Haldimand, *Conversations on Political Economy, in Which the Elements of that Science are Familiarly Explained* (London: Hurst, Rees, Orne, and Brown, 1816).

—, *Conversations sur l'économie politique, dans lesquelles on expose d'une manière familière les éléments de cette science, trans. from English* (Geneva: J.J. Paschoud, 1817).

—, *Conversations on the Nature of Political Economy*, ed. Evelyn L. Forget (New Brunswick: Transaction, 2009).

Mazzei, Filippo, *Recherches historiques et politiques sur les Etats-Unis de l'Amérique septentrionale*, 4 vols. (Colle-Paris: Froullé, 1788).

—, *Lettere di Filippo Mazzei alla corte di Polonia (1788–1792)*, ed. Raffaele Ciampini, vol. I: July 1788–March 1790 (Bologna: Zanichelli, 1937).

—, *Memoirs of the Life and Peregrinations of the Florentine Philip Mazzei, 1730–1816* (New York: Columbia University Press, 1942).

Memoirs of the Philadelphia Society for promoting agriculture (Philadelphia: Johnson and Warner, 1811 (vol. II), 1814 (vol. III), 1818 (vol. IV))

Mill, James, *Commerce defended. An Answer to the arguments by which Mr Spence, Mr Cobbett and others have attempted to prove that commerce is not a source of national wealth* (London: C. and R. Baldwin, 1808).

Mirabeau, Honoré-Gabriel Riquetti, Comte de, *Considérations sur l'Ordre de Cincinnatus, ou Imitation d'un pamphlet anglo-américain* (London: Johnson and Rotterdam: C.R. Hake, 1785).

Mirabeau, Victor Riquetti, Marquis de, *L'Ami des hommes, ou Traité de la population*, 1st ed. (Avignon: 1758–1760).

—, *L'Ami des Hommes, ou Traité de la population*, 5th edition, 6 vols. (Hambourg: Chrétien Hérold, 1760–62).

—, *Les économiques*, 3 vols. (Amsterdam: 1769–71).

— and François Quesnay, *Philosophie rurale, ou Economie générale et politique de l'agriculture*, 3 vols. (Amsterdam: chez les Libraires associés, 1763).

—, *Traité de la monarchie*, ed. Gino Longhitano (Paris: L'Harmattan, 1999).

Morellet André, *Mémoires inédits sur le dix-huitième siècle et la Révolution française*, 2 vols. (Paris: Ladvocat, 1822).

—, *Lettres de l'abbé Morellet à lord Shelburne, depuis marquis de Lansdowne, 1772–1803* (Paris: Plon, 1898).

Morris, Gouverneur, *Diary of the French Revolution*, ed. Beatrice Carey Davenport, 2 vols. (Boston: Houghton Mifflin Company 1939).

Mousnier, Jean-Joseph, *Exposé de ma conduite dans l'assemblée nationale; et motifs de mon retour en Dauphiné* (Paris: chez Desenne, 1789).

Necker, Jacques, *Oeuvres*, 4 vols. (Lausanne: J.-P. Heubach et Compagnie, 1786).

Paine, Thomas, *A Letter addressed to the abbé Raynal on the affairs of North America in which the Mistakes in the abbé's account of the revolution of America are corrected and cleared up* (Philadelphia, 1782).

—, *Rights of Man*, 2nd ed. (Philadelphia: Samuel Harrison Smith, 1791).

—, *Thomas Paine à la Législature et au Directoire, ou la Justice agraire opposée à la loi et aux privilèges agraires* (Paris: la citoyenne Rigouleau, 1797).

—, *La Justice agraire opposée à la loi et monopole agraire, ou Plan d'amélioration du sort des hommes* (Paris: chez les marchands de nouveautés, an V de la République).

—, *Political Writings*, 2 vols. (Charlestown, MA: G. Davidson, 1824).

—, *The Writings*, ed. Moncure D. Conway, 4 vols. (New York: Burt Franklin, 1969).

—, *Rights of Man*, ed. Henry Collins (Harmondsworth: Penguin Books, 1971).

—, *Agrarian justice, opposed to agrarian law, and to agrarian monopoly, being a plan for ameliorating the condition of man* (Paris, London: W. Adlard, J. Adlard, undated).

Parmentier, Antoine-Augustin, *Traité de la culture et les usages des pommes de terre, de la patate et du tapinambour* (Paris: Barrois, 1789).

Petty, William, *A Treatise of Taxes and Contributions* (London: N. Brooke, 1662).

Price Richard, *Observations on reversionary payments* (London: Cadell, 1771).

—, *Observations on the Nature of Civil Liberty, the Principles of Government, and the Justice and Policy of the War with America* (London: T. Cadell, 1776).

—, *Observations on the Importance of the American Revolution and the Means of Making it a Benefit to the World. To Which is Added a Letter from m. Turgot ... with an Appendix, Containing a Translation of the Will of m. Fortuné Ricard* (Dublin: L. White, 1785).

—, *Correspondence*, ed. Bernard Peach and David. O. Thomas, 3 vols. (Durham, NC: Duke University Press, 1991–4).

— and Joseph Priestley, *A free discussion of the doctrines of materialism and philosophical necessity, in a correspondence between Dr. Price, and Dr. Priestley* (London: J. Johnson and T. Cadell, 1778).

Priestley Joseph, *An Essay on the First Principles of Government, and of the Nature of Political, Civil and Religious Liberty*, 2nd ed. (London: J. Johnson, 1771).

—, *An address to Protestant Dissenters of all denominations on the approaching election of Members of Parliament, with respect to the state of public liberty in general, and of American affairs in particular* (London: Joseph Johnson, 1774).

—, *Lectures on History and General Policy* (Birmingham: Pearson and Rollason, 1788).

—, *Letters to the right honourable Edmund Burke, occasioned by his 'Reflections on the revolution in France'* (London: J. Johnson, 1791).

—, *Letters to the Inhabitants of Northumberland and its Neighbourhood, on Subjects interesting to the Author and to them. The Second Edition with Additions; to which is added A Letter to a Friend in Paris, relating to Mr. Liancourt's Travels in the North American States* (Philadelphia: John Bioren, 1801).

—, *Memoirs of Dr. Joseph Priestley to the year 1795, written by himself, with a continuation, to the time of his decease, by his son Joseph Priestley, and*

Observations on his writings by Thomas Cooper and the Rev. William Christie, 2 vols. (London: J. Johnson, 1806).

—, *The Theological and Miscellaneous Works*, ed. John Towill Rutt, 25 vols. (London: Smallfield, 1817–1831).

—, *Lectures on History and General Policy* (London, 1826).

—, *Manière d'imprégner l'eau d'air fixe... par M. Joseph Priestley: ouvrage traduit de l'anglois par M****, extrait du 'Journal d'observations sur la physique, sur l'histoire naturelle et sur les arts et métiers' par M. l'abbé Rozier (n.p., n.d.).

Quesnay, François, *Oeuvres économiques complètes et autres textes*, ed. Christine Théré, Loïc Charles and Jean-Claude Perrot, 2 vols. (Paris: INED., 2005).

Ramsay, Allan, *Thoughts on the Origin and nature of Government, Occasioned by the Late Disputes between Great Britain and Her Colonies: written in the Year 1766* (London: T. Becket, 1769).

Raymond, Daniel, *The Elements of Political Economy*, 2 vols., 2nd ed. (Baltimore: F. Lucas and E.J. Coale, 1823).

Raynal Guillaume-Thomas-François, *Histoire philosophique et politique des établissemens & du commerce des européens dans les deux Indes*, 6 vols. (Amsterdam: 1770).

—, *Histoire philosophique et politique des établissemens et du commerce des Européens dans les deux Indes*, 4 vols. (Geneva: J. Pellet, 1780).

Recueil des loix constitutives des colonies angloises, confédérées sous la dénomination d'Etats-Unis de l'Amérique-Septentrionale ... Dédié à M. le Docteur Franklin (Philadelphia, Paris: chez Cellot et Jombert, 1778).

Ricardo, David, *Des principes de l'économie politique,* in *Oeuvres complètes* (Paris: Guillaumin, 1847)

—, *Oeuvres complètes... augmentées de notes de Jean-Baptiste Say, de nouvelles notes et de commentaires par Malthus, Sismondi, mm. Rossi, Blanqui etc...* (Paris: Guillaumin, 1847).

—, *The Works and Correspondence*, ed. Piero Sraffa and Maurice H. Dobb, 11 vols. (Cambridge: Cambridge University Press, 1951–73).

Rogers, Robert, *A Concise Account of North America* (London: J. Millan, 1765).

Romilly, Samuel, *Memoirs of the Life of Sir Samuel Romilly*, 3rd ed., 2 vols. (London: J. Murray, 1841).

Rules and Regulations of the Massachusetts Society for Promoting Agriculture (Boston: Thomas Fleet, 1796).

Say, Jean-Baptiste, *Traité d'économie politique, ou Simple exposition de la manière dont se forment, se distribuent et se consomment les richesses*, 2 vols. (Paris: Imprimerie de Crapele-Deterville, 1803).

—, *Catechism of political economy, or familiar conversations on the manner in which wealth is produced, distributed and consumed in society, By J.B. Say, professor of political economy in the Athénée Royal of Paris, Knight of St Wolodomir of Russia, member of the societies of Zurich, Bologna, etc..., and author of a treatise of political economy*, trans. from French by John Richter (Philadelphia: M. Carey and Son, 1817).

—, *A Treatise on Political Economy; or The production, distribution and consumption of Wealth*, translated from the fourth edition of the French by C.R. Prinsep, M.A. with notes by the translator (London: Longman, Hurst, Rees, Orme and Brown, 1821).

—, *A Treatise on Political Economy; or The production, distribution and consumption of Wealth*, translated from the fourth edition of the French by C.R. Prinsep, M.A. with notes by the translator. To which is added a translation of the introduction, and additional notes by Clement C. Biddle, in two volumes (Boston: Wells and Lilly, 1821).

—, *A Treatise on Political Economy*, 2nd American Edition, two volumes bound in one (Boston: Wells and Lilly, 1824).

—, *A Treatise on Political Economy*, 3rd American Edition (Philadelphia: J. Grigg, 1827).

—, *A Treatise on Political Economy* (Philadelphia: Grigg and Elliot, 1834).

—, *Traité d'économie politique*, 6th edition (Paris: Horace Say, 1841).

—, *Oeuvres diverses*, ed. Charles Comte, Eugène Daire and Horace Say (Paris: Guillaumin, 1848).

—, Œuvres *complètes*, ed. Emmanuel Blanc, Pierre-Henri Gouttes, Gilles Jacoud, Claude Mouchot, Jean-Pierre Potier, Michèle Saquin, Jean-Michel Servet, Philippe Steiner and André Tiran (Paris: Economica, 2003–).

Smith, Adam, *An inquiry into the nature and causes of the Wealth of Nations*, ed., Roy H. Campbell and Andrew S. Skinner, 2 vols. (Oxford: Clarendon Press, 1976).

—, *The Correspondence*, ed. Ernest Campbell Mossner and Ian Simpson Ross (Oxford: Clarendon Press, 1977).

—, *Lectures on Jurisprudence*, ed. Ronald. L. Meek, David D. Raphael and Peter G. Stein (Oxford: Clarendon Press, 1978).

Smith William, *An historical account of the expedition against the Ohio Indians, in the year 1764* (Philadelphia: W. Bradford, 1765).

Société des Amis de la Constitution, séante aux Jacobins, à Paris. Discours de MM. Cooper et Watt, Députés de la Société constitutionnelle de Manchester, prononcé à la société des amis de la constitution, séante à Paris, le 13 avril 1792, et imprimé, avec la réponse du président, par ordre de cette société (De l'Imprimerie du patriote François, place du Théâtre Italien).

Spence, William, *Britain independent of commerce; or Proofs deduced from an investigation into the true causes of the wealth of nations, that our riches, prosperity and power are derived from resources inherent in ourselves and would not be affected, even though our commerce were annihilated*, 6th ed., corrected and enlarged (London: W. Savage for T. Cadell and W. Davies, 1808).

—, *Agriculture the source of the Wealth of Britain; a reply to the objections urged by Mr Mill, the Edinburgh reviewers and others against the doctrines of the* pamphlet, entitled 'Britain independent of commerce' (London: T. Cadell, W. Davies, 1808).

Stevens, John, *Examen du gouvernement d'Angleterre, comparé aux constitutions des Etats-Unis. Où l'on réfute quelques assertions contenues dans l'ouvrage de m. Adams intitulé: 'Apologie des constitutions des Etats-Unis d'Amérique', et dans celui de m. Delolme intitulé: 'De la constitution d'Angleterre'. Par Un cultivateur de New-Jersey* (London and Paris: Froullé, 1789).

Stork, William, *An Account of East Florida, with A journal kept by John Batram of Philadelphia, botanist to His Majesty for the Floridas* (London: W. Nicoll and G. Woodfall, 1766).

Tatham, William, *Communications Concerning the Agriculture and Commerce of the United States* (London: J. Ridgway, 1800).

Taylor, John, *A Definition of Parties: or the Political Effects of the Paper System Considered* (Philadelphia: Francis Bailey, 1794).

—, *An Enquiry into the Principles and Tendency of Certain Public Measures* (Philadelphia: Dodson, 1794).

—, *An Argument Respecting the Constitutionality of the Carriage Tax; Which Subject was Discussed at Richmond, in Virginia, in May 1795* (Richmond: A. Davis, 1795).

—, *Defence of the Measures of the Administration of Thomas Jefferson* (Washington: Samuel H. Smith, 1804).

—, *Arator; being a series of agricultural essays, practical and political; in sixty one numbers* (Georgetown: J.M. and J.B. Carter, 1813).

—, *An Inquiry into the Principles and Policy of the Government of the United States* (Fredericksburg: Green and Cady, 1814).

—, *Arator, Being a Series of Agricultural Essays, Practical and Political*; in sixty four *numbers*, 4th ed. (Petersburg: 1818).

—, *Construction Construed and Constitutions Vindicated* (Richmond: Shepherd & Pollard, 1820).

—, *Correspondence*, in *The John P. Branch Historical Papers of Randolph-Macon College*, vol. II (June 1908), nos. 3–4, 253–353.

—, *Arator*, ed. Melvin E. Bradford (Indianapolis: Liberty Classics, 1977).

—, *Tyranny Unmasked*, ed. F. Thornton Miller (Indianapolis: Liberty Fund, 1992).

Toqueville, Alexis de, *L'ancien régime et la Révolution* (Paris: Gallimard, 1981; 1st ed. 1856).

Turgot, Anne-Robert-Jacques, *Reflections on the formation and distribution of Wealth* (London: J. Good, 1793).

—, *Oeuvres de mr Turgot, précédées et accompagnées de mémoires et de notes sur sa vie, son administration et ses ouvrages*, 9 vols. (Paris: A. Belin et Delance, 1808–11).

—, *Oeuvres*, ed. Gustave Schelle, 5 vols. (Paris: Alcan, 1913–23).

—, *Réflexions sur la formation et la distribution des richesses* (Paris: Flammarion, 1997).

Washington, George, *Letters on Agriculture*, ed. Franklin Knight (Washington: The editor; Philadelphia: W.S. Martien, 1847).

—, *Writings*, ed. John Rhodehamel (New York: Literary Classics of the United States, 1997).

Wayland, Francis, *Elements of Political Economy* (Boston: Gould and Lincoln, 1855).

Williams, Samuel, *A Discourse on the Love of our Country; delivered on a Day of Thanksgiving, 15 December 1774* (Salem: S. and E. Nall, 1775).

—, *The Influence of Christianity on Civil Society, Represented in a Discourse Delivered November 10, 1779* (Boston: John Boyle, 1780).

—, *The Natural and Civil History of Vermont*, 2 vols. (Burlington, VT: Samuel Mills, 1809).

Secondary Works Periodicals

Abel, Darnell, 'The Significance of the Letter to the Abbé Raynal in the Progress of Thomas Paine's Thought', *The Pennsylvania Magazine of History and Biography*, 66/2 (April 1942): 176–90.

Adams, Percy G., 'Crèvecoeur and Franklin', *Pennsylvania History*, 14 (1947): 273–9.

—, 'The historical value of Crèvecoeur's "Voyage dans la Haute Pensylvanie et dans New York"', *American Literature*, 25/2 (May 1953): 155–68.

Albertone Manuela, 'Du Pont de Nemours et l'instruction publique pendant la Révolution: De la science économique à la formation du citoyen'. In *Les Physiocrates et la Révolution française*, Revue française d'Histoire des Idées Politiques, no. 20 (2004): 353–71.

Aldridge, Alfred O., 'Franklin as Demographer', *The Journal of Economic History*, 9 (1949): 25–44.

—, 'Jacques Barbeu-Dubourg, a French disciple of Benjamin Franklin', *Proceedings of the American Philosophical Society*, 95 (1951): 331–92.

—, 'La signification historique, diplomatique et littéraire de la "Lettre addressée à l'abbé Raynal" de Thomas Paine', *Etudes anglaises*, 8 (1955): 223–32.

—, 'Condorcet et Paine: Leurs rapports intellectuels', *Revue de littérature comparée*, 32 (1958): 47–65.

Allain, Mathé, 'La révolution américaine dans "l'Histoire philosophique" de l'abbé Raynal', *Studies on Voltaire and the Eighteenth Century*, no. 263 (Oxford: Voltaire Foundation, 1989): 277.

Allix, Edgar, 'La méthode et la conception de l'économie politique dans l'oeuvre de J.-B. Say', *Revue d'histoire économique et sociale* (1911): 321–60.

—, 'Destutt de Tracy, économiste', *Revue d'économie politique*, 26 (1912): 424–51.

Appleby, Joyce, 'The Jefferson–Adams Rupture and the First French Translation of John Adams' *Defence*', *The American Historical Review*, 73/4 (April 1968): 1084–91.

—, 'America as a Model for the Radical French Reformers of 1789', *The William and Mary Quarterly*, 3d ser., 28 (1971): 267–86.

—, 'The New Republican Synthesis and the Changing Political Ideas of John Adams', *American Quarterly*, 25 (1973): 578–95.

—, 'Liberalism and the American Revolution', *New England Quarterly*, 49 (1976): 3–26.

—, 'Commercial farming and the "Agrarian Myth" in Early Republic', *Journal of American History*, 68/4 (1982): 833–49.

—, 'What is Still American in the Political Philosophy of Thomas Jefferson?', *The William and Mary Quarterly*, 3d ser., 39 (1982): 287–309.

—, 'Republicanism in Old and New Contexts', *The William and Mary Quarterly*, 3d ser., 43 (1986): 20–34.

—, 'How Revolutionary Was the Revolution? A Discussion of Gordon S. Wood's "The Radicalism of American Revolution"', *The William and Mary Quarterly*, 3d ser., 51 (1994): 677–83.

Arch, Steven, 'The Progressive Steps of the Narrator in Crèvecoeur's Letters from an American Farmer', *Studies in American Fiction*, 18 (1990): 145–58.

Ashworth, John, 'The Jeffersonians: Classical Republicans or Liberal Capitalists?' *Journal of American Studies*, 18/3 (1984): 425–35.

Bailor, Keith M., 'John Taylor of Caroline: Continuity, Change and Discontinuity in Virginia's Sentiments Toward Slavery, 1790–1820', *Virginia Magazine of History and Biography*, 75 (1967): 290–304.

Barnett, Claribel R., '"The Agricultural Museum": An Early American Agricultural Periodical', *Agricultural History*, 2 (1928): 99–102.

Beidler, Philip D., 'Franklin's and Crèvecoeur's "Literary" Americans', *Early American Literature*, 13/1 (Spring 1978): 50–63.

Bonwick, Colin, 'Joseph Priestley: Emigrant and Jeffersonian', *Enlightenment and Dissent*, no. 2 (1983): 3–22.

Branson, Roy, 'James Madison and the Scottish Enlightenment', *Journal of the History of Ideas*, 40 (1979): 235–50.

Bridgman, Richard, 'Jefferson's Farmer before Jefferson', *American Quarterly*, 14 (1962): 567–77.

Buel, Richard, 'Democracy and the American Revolution: A Frame of Reference', *The William and Mary Quarterly*, 3d ser., 21 (1964): 165–90.

Cady, George J., 'The Early American Reaction to the Theory of Malthus', *Journal of Political Economy*, 39 (1931): 601–32.

Carew-Miller, Anna, 'The Language of Domesticity in Crèvecoeur's "Letters from an American Farmer"', *Early American Literature Newsletter*, 28 (1993): 242–54.

Charles, Loïc and Philippe Steiner, 'Entre Montesquieu et Rousseau: La physiocratie parmi les origines intellectuelles de la Révolution française', *Etudes Jean-Jacques Rousseau*, no. 11 (1999): 89–159.

Cheney, Paul B., 'Les économistes français et l'image de l'Amérique: L'essor du commerce transatlantique et l'effondrement du "gouvernement féodal"', *Dix-huitièmes siècle*, no. 33 (2001): 231–45.

Chevignard, Bernard, 'Les souvenirs de Saint John de Crèvecoeur sur Madame d'Houdetot', *Dix-huitième siècle*, 14 (1982): 243–62.

—, 'St. John de Crèvecoeur à New York en 1779–1780', *Annales de Normandie*, 33/2 (1983): 162.

—, 'St. John de Crèvecoeur in the looking Glass: "Letters from an American Farmer" and the Making of a man of Letters', *Early American Literature*, 19/2 (Fall 1984): 173–90.

—, 'Une pomme de terre à la sauce américaine: le "Traité de la Culture des Pommes-de-terre" de Saint-John de Crèvecoeur (1782)', *Mémoires de l'Académie des sciences, arts et belles lettres de Dijon*, 131 (1992): 45–55.

Chinard, Gilbert, 'Notes on the French Translations of the "Forms of Government or Constitutions of the several United States" 1778 and 1783', *The American Philosophical Society Year Book* (1943): 88–106.

—, 'Eighteenth Century Theories on America as a Human Habitat', *Proceedings of the American Philosophical Society*, 91 (1947): 27–57.

—, 'Adventures in a Library', *The Newberry Library Bulletin*, 2d ser., no. 8 (March 1952): 223–38.

Colbourn, H. Trevor, 'Thomas Jefferson's Use of the Past', *The William and Mary Quarterly*, 3d ser., 15 (1958): 56–70.

Cooke, Jacob E., 'Tench Coxe, American Economist: the Limitation of Economic Thought in the Early National Era', *Pennsylvania History*, 42 (1976): 267–89.

Crane, Verner, 'The Club of Honest Whigs: Friends of Science and Liberty', *The William and Mary Quarterly*, 3d ser., 23 (1966): 210–33.

Craven, Avery O., 'The Agricultural Reformers of the Ante-bellum South', *The American Historical Review*, 33/2 (January 1928): 302–14.

'*The Creation of the American Republic, 1776–1787*: A Symposium of Views and Reviews', *The William and Mary Quarterly*, 3d ser., 44 (1987): 549–640.

Dauer, Manning J., 'John Taylor: Democrat or Aristocrat?', *The Journal of Politics*, 6 (1944): 381–403.

Degros, Maurice, 'L'administration des Consulats sous la Révolution', *Revue d'histoire diplomatique* (1982): 68–111.

Dodd, William, 'John Taylor of Caroline, Prophet of Secession', *The John P. Branch Historical Papers of Randolph-Macon College*, II/3–4 (June 1908): 214–52.

Dorfman, Joseph, 'The Economic Philosophy of Thomas Paine', *Political Science Quarterly*, 53 (1938): 372–86.

Drell, Bernard, 'John Taylor of Caroline and the Preservation of an Old Social Order', *The Virginia Magazine of History and Biography*, 46 (1938): 285–98.

Dunbar, Charles F., 'Economic Science in America 1776–1876', *The North American Review*, vol. 122, no. 250 (January 1876): 124–54.

Durey, Michael, 'Thomas Paine's Apostles: Radical Emigrés and the Triumph of Jeffersonian Republicanism', *The William and Mary Quarterly*, 3d ser., 44 (1987): 661–88.

Eayrs, James, 'The Political Ideas of the English Agrarians, 1775–1815', *The Canadian Journal of Economics and Political Science*, 18/3 (1952): 287–302.

Echeverria, Durand, 'French Publications of the Declaration of Independence and the American Constitutions, 1776–1783', *The Papers of the Bibliographical Society of America*, 47 (Fourth Quarter, 1953): 313–38.

—, 'Condorcet's "The Influence of the American Revolution on Europe"', *The William and Mary Quarterly*, 3d. ser., 25 (1968): 85–7.

Eisinger, Chester E., 'The Influence of Natural Rights and Physiocratic Doctrines on American Agrarian Thought During the Revolutionary Period', *Agricultural History*, 21 (1947): 13–23.

—, 'The Farmer in the Eighteenth Century Almanac', *Agricultural History*, 28 (1954): 107–12.

Eliot, Thomas D., 'The relations between Adam Smith and Benjamin Franklin before 1776', *Political Science Quarterly*, 39 (1924): 67–97.

Ellsworth, Lucius F., 'The Philadelphia Society for the Promotion of Agriculture and Agricultural Reform', *Agricultural History*, 42 (1968): 189–99.

Faÿ, Bernard, 'Franklin et Mirabeau collaborateurs', *Revue de littérature comparée*, 8 (1928): 5–28.

Fetter, Frank A., 'The Early History of Political Economy in the United States', *Proceedings of the American Philosophical Society*, 87 (1943): 51–60.

Ford, Paul L., 'Affaires de l'Angleterre et de l'Amérique', *The Pennsylvania Magazine of History and Biography*, 13/2 (July 1889): 222–6.

Formisano, Ronald P., 'Deferential-Participant Politics: The Early Republic's Political Culture, 1789–1840', *American Political Science Review*, 68/2 (1974): 473–87.

Genovese, Elizabeth Fox, 'The many faces of moral economy: a Contribution to a Debate', *Past and Present*, 58 (1973): 161–8.

Goggi, Gianluigi, 'Filangieri e "L'Ami des hommes" di Mirabeau', *Italianistica: Rivista di letteratura italiana*, 10/2 (May–August 1981): 188–214.

Grampp, William D., 'John Taylor: Economist of Southern Agrarianism', *The Southern Economic Journal*, 11/3 (1945): 255–68.

—, 'A Re-examination of Jeffersonian Economics', *The Southern Economic Journal*, 12/3 (1946): 263–82.

Grasso, Christopher, 'The Experimental Philosophy of Farming: Jared Eliot and the Cultivation of Connecticut', *The William and Mary Quarterly*, 3rd ser., 50 (1993): 502–28.

Griswold, Whitney, 'Three puritans on prosperity', *New England Quarterly*, 7 (1934): 475–93.

Hans, Nicholas, 'UNESCO of the Eighteenth Century: La loge des Neuf Soeurs and its Venerable Master, Benjamin Franklin', *Proceedings of the American Philosophical Society*, 97 (1953): 513–24.

Hans, Nicolas, 'Franklin, Jefferson, and the English Radicals at the End of the Eighteenth Century', *Proceedings of the American Philosophical Society*, 98 (1954): 406–26.

Henline, Ruth, 'A Study of Notes on the State of Virginia as an Evidence of Jefferson's Reaction against the Theories of the French Naturalists', *Virginia Magazine of History and Biography*, 55 (July 1947): 233–46.

Henretta, James A., 'Families and Farms: "Mentalité" in Pre-Industrial America', *The William and Mary Quarterly*, 3d ser., 35 (1978): 3–32.

Hofstadter, Richard, 'Parrington and the Jeffersonian Tradition', *Journal of the History of Ideas* 2 (1941): 391–400.

Holbo, Christine, 'Imagination, Commerce and the Politics of Associationism in Crèvecoeur's "Letters from an American Farmer"', *Early American History*, 32 (1997): 20–65.

Hutson, James H., 'Country, Court and Constitution: Antifederalism and the Historians', *The William and Mary Quarterly*, 3d. ser. 38 (1981): 337–68.

Jehlen, Myra, 'J. Hector St. John Crèvecoeur: A Monarcho-Anarchist in Revolutionary America', *American Quarterly*, 31 (1979): 204–22.

Katz, Stanley N., 'Thomas Jefferson and the Right to Property in Revolutionary America', *Journal of Law and Economics*, 19 (1976): 467–88.

Kessler, Sanford, 'Tocqueville's Puritans: Christianity and the American Founding', *The Journal of Politics*, 54/3 (1992): 776–92.

Kirby, John B., 'Early American Politics – The Search for Ideology: an Historiographical Analysis and Critique of the Concept of "Deference"', *Journal of Politics*, 32 (1970): 808–38.

Kloppenberg, James T., 'The Virtues of Liberalism: Christianity, Republicanism, and Ethics in Early American Political Discourse', *Journal of American History*, 74/1 (1987): 9–33.

Kramnick, Isaac, 'Republican Revisionism Revisited', *The American Historical Review*, 87/3 (June 1982): 629–64.

—, '"The Great National Discussion": The Discourse of Politics in 1787', *The William and Mary Quarterly*, 3d ser., 45 (1988): 3–32.

Kulikoff, Allan, 'The Transition to Capitalism in Rural America', *The William and Mary Quarterly*, 3d ser., 46 (1989): 120–44.

Kwass, Michael, 'Consumption and the World of Ideas: Consumer Revolution and the Moral Economy of the Marquis de Mirabeau', *Eighteenth Century Studies*, 37/2 (2004): 187–213.

Labaree, Leonard W., 'Benjamin Franklin's British Friendships', *Proceedings of the American Philosophical Society*, 108 (1964), 423–8.

Lemay, Edna H., 'L'Amérique dans les écrits d'un Parisien franc-comtois: 1776–1795', *Annales de Bretagne et des Pays de l'Ouest*, 84 (1977): 307–315.

Loher, Rodney C., 'The Influence of English Agriculture on American Agriculture, 1775–1825', *Agriculture History*, 11 (January 1937): 3–15.

McConnell, Grant, 'John Taylor and the Democratic Tradition', *The Western Political Quarterly*, 4/1 (1951): 17–31.

McCoy, Drew R., 'Jefferson and Madison on Malthus: Population Growth in Jeffersonian Political Economy', *The Virginia Magazine of History and Biography*, 88 (1980): 259–76.

Machor, James, 'The Garden City in America: Crèvecoeur's Letters and the Urban–Pastoral Context', *American Studies*, 23/1 (1982), 69–83.

Macleod, Duncan, 'The Political Economy of John Taylor of Caroline', *Journal of American Studies*, 14/3 (1980): 387–405.

Maza, Sarah, 'Luxury, Morality, and Social Change: Why there was no Middle-Class Consciousness in Pre-Revolutionary France', *The Journal of Modern History*, 69 (1997): 199–229.

Medlin, Dorothy, 'André Morellet, Translator of Liberal Thought', *Studies on Voltaire and the Eighteenth Century*, no. 174 (1978): 189–201.

—, 'Thomas Jefferson, André Morellet, and the French Version of "Notes on the State of Virginia"', *The William and Mary Quarterly*, 3d ser., 35 (1978): 85–99.

Miller, August C., 'Jefferson as an Agriculturist', *Agricultural History*, 16 (1942): 65–78.

Mirri, Mario, 'Per una ricerca sui rapporti fra 'economisti' e riformatori toscani: L'abate Niccoli a Parigi', *Annali dell'Istituto Giangiacomo Feltrinelli*, 2 (1959): 55–115.

Mohr, James C. 'Calculated Disillusionment: Crèvecoeur's Letters Reconsidered', *South Atlantic Quarterly*, 69 (1970): 354–63.

Morgan, Edmund S., 'The Puritan Ethic and the American Revolution', *The William and Mary Quarterly*, 3d ser. 24 (1967): 3–43.

Onuf, Peter S., 'Liberty, Development, and Union: Visions of the West in the 1780s', *The William and Mary Quarterly*, 3d ser., 43 (1986): 179–213.

Philbrick, Nathaniel, 'The Nantucket Sequence in Crèvecoeur's *Letters from an American Farmer*', *New England Quarterly*, 64 (1991): 414–32.

Plotkin, Norman A., 'Saint-John de Crèvecoeur Rediscovered: Critic or Paneygyrist?', *French Historical Studies*, 3 (1964): 390–404.

Polkinghorn, Bette, 'A Communication: An Unpublished Letter of J.-B. Say', *Eastern Economic Journal*, 11 (1985): 167–70.

Post, David M., 'Jeffersonian Revisions of Locke: Education, Property-Rights, and Liberty', *Journal of the History of Ideas*, 47 (1986): 147–57.

Rapping, Elayne A., 'Theory and Experience in Crèvecoeur's America', *American Quarterly*, 19 (1967): 707–18.

Robbins, Caroline, 'Honest Heretic: Joseph Priestley in America, 1794–1804', *Proceedings of the American Philosophical Society*, 106 (1962): 60–76.

Robinson, David, 'Crèvecoeur's James: the Education of an American Farmer', *Journal of English and Germanic Philology*, 80/4 (1981): 552–70.

Rosengarten, Joseph G., 'The Early French Members of the American Philosophical Society', *Proceedings of the American Philosophical Society*, 46 (1907): 87–93.

Ross, Earle D., 'Benjamin Franklin as an Eighteenth-Century Agricultural Leader', *Journal of Political Economy*, 37 (1929): 52–72.

Ross, Ellen, 'Mandeville, Melon, and Voltaire: The Origins of the Luxury Controversy in France', *Studies on Voltaire and the Eighteenth Century*, no. 155 (1976): 1897–1912.

Semmel, Bernard, 'Malthus: "Physiocracy" and the Commercial System', *The Economic History Review*, 17 (1965): 522–35.

Shalhope, Robert E., 'Toward a Republican Synthesis: The Emergence of an Understanding of Republicanism in American Historiography', *The William and Mary Quarterly*, 3d ser., 29 (1972): 49–80.

—, 'Thomas Jefferson's Republicanism and Antebellum Southern Thought', *The Journal of Southern History*, 42/4 (November 1976), 529–56.

Skinner, Quentin, 'Meaning and Understanding in the History of Ideas', *History and Theory*, 8 (1969): 3–53.

Spengler, Joseph J., 'Malthusianism in the Late Eighteenth Century America', *American Economic Review*, 25 (1935): 697–707.

Steiner, Philippe, 'L'économie politique pratique contre les systèmes: quelques remarques sur la méthode de J.-B. Say', *Revue d'économie politique*, no. 5 (September–October 1990): 664–87.

—, 'Politique et économie politique chez Jean-Baptiste Say', *Revue française d'Histoire des Idées Politiques*, no. 5 (1997): 38–40.

—, 'Wealth and Power: Quesnay's Political Economy of the Agricultural Kingdom', *Journal of History of Economic Thought*, 24 (2002): 91–109.

Stout Harry S., 'Religion, Communications, and Ideological Origins of the American Revolution', *The William and Mary Quarterly*, 3d ser., 34 (1977): 519–41.

Théré, Christine and Loïc Charles, 'The Writing Workshop of François Quesnay and the Making of Physiocracy', *History of Political Economy*, 40/1 (2008): 1–42.

—, 'From Versailles to Paris: The Creative Communities of the Physiocratic Movement', *History of Political Economy*, 43/1 (2011): 25–58.

Thompson, Edward P., 'The Moral Economy of the English Crowd in the Eighteenth Century', *Past and Present*, 50 (1971): 76–136.

Thompson, Mark, 'Causes and Circumstances of the Du Pont Family's Emigration', *French Historical Studies*, 6 (1969): 59–77.

Tolles, Frederick B., 'Unofficial Ambassador: George Logan's Mission to France, 1798', *The William and Mary Quarterly*, 3d ser., 7 (1950): 3–25.

—, 'George Logan, Agrarian Democrat: A Survey of His Writings', *The Pennsylvania Magazine of History and Bibliography*, 75/1 (January 1951): 261–2.

—, 'George Logan and the Agricultural Revolution', *Proceedings of the American Philosophical Society*, 95 (1951): 589–96.

True, Rodney H., 'The Early Development of Agricultural Societies in the United States', *Annual Report of the American Historical Association, for the year 1920* (Washington: Government Printing Office, 1925): 295–306.

Urbinati, Nadia, 'Condorcet's Democratic Theory of Representative Government', *European Journal of Political Theory*, 3 (2004): 53–75.

Varg, Paul A., 'The Advent of Nationalism 1758–1776', *American Quarterly*, 16 (1964): 169–81.

Venturi, Franco, 'Destutt de Tracy e le rivoluzioni liberali', *Rivista storica italiana*, 84 (1972): 451–84.

Webking, Robert H., 'Melancton Smith and the "Letters from the Federal Farmer"', *The William and Mary Quarterly*, 3d ser. 44 (1987): 510–28.

Williams, D. Allan, 'The Small Farmer in Eighteenth-Century Virginia Politics', *Agricultural History*, 43 (1969): 91–102.

Williams, William A., 'The Age of Mercanitilism: An Interpretation of the American Political Economy', *The William and Mary Quarterly*, 3d ser. 15 (1958): 410–25.

Wills, Elbert V., 'Political Economy in the Early American College Curriculum', *The South Atlantic Quarterly*, 24/2 (1925): 131–53.

Wilson, Douglas L., 'The American Agricola: Jefferson's Agrarianism and the Classical Tradition', *The South Atlantic Quarterly*, 80/3 (Summer 1981): 339–54.

—, 'Jefferson vs. Hume', *The William and Mary Quarterly*, 3d ser., 46 (1989): 49–70.

Winston, Robert P., '"Strange order of Things!": the Journey to Chaos in "Letters from an American Farmer"', *Early American Literature Newsletter*, 19 (1984): 249–67.

Wood, Gordon S., 'The Authorship of the "Letters from the Federal Farmer"', *The William and Mary Quarterly*, 3d ser., 31 (1974): 299–308.

Wright, Benjamin F., 'The Philosopher of Jeffersonian Democracy', *The American Political Science Review*, 22/4 (1928): 870–92.

Secondary Works Books

Acomb, Frances, *Anglophobia in France 1763–1789: An Essay in the History of Constitutionalism and Nationalism* (Durham, NC: Duke University Press, 1950).

Albertone, Manuela, *Fisiocrati, istruzione e cultura* (Turin: Fondazione Luigi Einaudi, 1979).

—, *Una scuola per la rivoluzione: Condorcet e il dibattito sull'istruzione 1792/1794* (Naples: Guida, 1979).

—, 'Enlightenment and Revolution: The Evolution of Condorcet's Ideas on Education', in *Condorcet Studies I*, ed. Leonora Cohen Rosenfield (Atlantic Highlands, NJ: Humanities Press, 1984): 131–44.

—, *Moneta e politica in Francia: Dalla Cassa di sconto agli assegnati (1776–1792)* (Bologna: Il Mulino, 1992).

—, 'Jefferson et l'Amérique', in *Condorcet: Homme des Lumières et de la Révolution*, ed. Anne–Marie Chouillet and Pierre Crépel (Saint-Cloud: ENS Editions, 1997): 189–99.

—, 'Gerarchia sociale, repubblica e democrazia: la figura del 'farmer' nell'America del XVIII secolo', in *Il pensiero gerarchico in Europa XVIII–XIX secolo*, ed. Antonella Alimento and Cristina Cassina (Florence: Olschki, 2002): 83–109.

—, 'Il proprietario terriero nel discorso fisiocratico sulla rappresentanza', in *Fisiocrazia e proprietà terriera*, ed. Manuela Albertone, special issue of *Studi settecenteschi*, 24 (2004): 181–214.

—, '"Que l'autorité souveraine soit unique": La séparation des pouvoirs dans la pensée des physiocrates et son legs: du despotisme légal à la démocratie représentative de Condorcet', in *Les usages de la séparation des pouvoirs; The uses of the separation of powers*, ed. Sandrine Baume and Biancamaria Fontana (Paris: Michel Houdiard, 2008): 38–68.

—, 'Letture fisiocratiche della Rivoluzione americana: il manoscritto del marchese di Mirabeau sulla *Dichiarazione dei diritti della Virginia* e la risposta di Pierre-Samuel Du Pont de Nemours', in *Governare il mondo: L'economia come linguaggio della politica nell'Europa del Settecento*, ed. Manuela Albertone (Milan: Feltrinelli, 2009): 171–201.

— and Antonino De Francesco , eds, *Rethinking the Atlantic World: Europe and America in the Age of Democratic Revolutions* (London: Palgrave Macmillan, 2009).

Aldridge, Alfred O., *Benjamin Franklin et ses contemporains français* (Paris: Didier, 1963).

—, *Thomas Paine's American Ideology* (Newark: University of Delaware Press, 1984).

Alger John G., *Englishmen in the French Revolution* (London: Marston Searle and Rivington, 1889).

Allen, Oscar Hansen, *Liberalism and American Education* (New York: Octagon Press, 1965).

Appleby, Joyce, *Capitalism and a New Social Order: The Republican Vision of the 1790s* (New York: New York University Press, 1984).

—, *Liberalism and Republicanism in the Historical Imagination* (Cambridge, MA: Harvard University Press, 1992).

—, *Without Resolution: The Jeffersonian Tension in American Nationalism*, an inaugural lecture delivered before the University of Oxford on 25 April 1991 (Oxford: Clarendon Press, 1991).

Armitage, David and Michael J. Braddick, eds, *The British Atlantic World, 1500–1800* (London: Palgrave Macmillan, 2002).

Astigarraga, Jesús, *Luces y Republicanismo. Economía y política en las 'Apuntaciones al Genovesi' de Ramón de Salas* (Madrid: Centro de Estudios politicos y constitucionales, 2011).

Aston, Nigel and, Clarissa Campbell Orr eds, *An Enlightenment Statesman in Whig Britain: Lord Shelburne in Context, 1737–1805* (Woodbridge: Boydell and Brewer, 2011).

Baatz, Simon, *'Venerate the Plough': A History of the Philadelphia Society for Promoting Agriculture, 1785–1985* (Philadelphia: PSPA, 1985).

Baczko, Bronisław, *Lumières de l'utopie* (Paris: Payot, 1978).

Bailyn, Bernard, *The Ideological Origins of the American Revolution* (Cambridge, MA: Harvard University Press, 1966).

—, *To Begin the World Anew: The Genius and Ambiguities of the American Founders* (New York: Alfred A. Knopf, 2003).

Baker, Keith M., *Condorcet: From Natural Philosophy to Social Mathematics* (Chicago: University of Chicago Press, 1975).

—, ed., 'Representation', in *The French Revolution and the Creation of Modern Political Culture*. Vol. I: *The Political Culture of the Old Regime* (Oxford: Pergamon Press, 1987): 469–92.

Balinsky, Alexander, *Albert Gallatin: Fiscal Theories and Policies* (New Brunswick, NJ: Rutgers University Press, 1958).

Banning, Lance, *The Jeffersonian Persuasion: Evolution of a Party Ideology* (Ithaca: Cornell University Press, 1978).

Barber, William J., ed., *Breaking the Academic Mould: Economists and American Higher Learning in the Nineteenth Century* (Middletown, CT: Wesleyan University Press, 1988).

—, 'The Position of the United States in the International Marketplace for Economic Ideas (1776–1900)', in *Political Economy and National Realities*, ed. Manuela Albertone and Alberto Masoero (Turin: Fondazione Luigi Einaudi, 1994): 255–67.

Beard Charles A., *Economic Origins of Jeffersonian Democracy* (New York: Macmillan, 1915).

Beeman, Richard R., Stephen Botein and Edward C. Carter, eds, *Beyond Confederation: Origins of the Constitution and American National Identity* (Chapel Hill: University of North Carolina Press, 1987).

—, *The Varieties of Political Experiences in Eighteenth-Century America* (Philadelphia: University of Pennsylvania Press, 2004).

Bender, Thomas, *A Nation Among Nations: America's Place in World History* (New York: Hill and Wang, 2006).

Benhamou, Paul, 'La diffusion de l'"Histoire des deux Indes" en Amérique (1770–1820)', in *Raynal: De la polémique à l'histoire*, ed. Gilles Bancarel and Gianluigi Goggi (Oxford: Voltaire Foundation, 2000): 301–12.

Berg, Maxine, *Luxury and Pleasure in Eighteenth-Century Britain* (Oxford: Oxford University Press, 2005).

— and Helen Clifford, *Consumers and Luxury: Consumer culture in Europe 1650–1850* (Manchester: Manchester University Press, 1999).

— and Elizabeth Eger, eds, *Luxury in the Eighteenth Century: Debates, Desires and Delectable Goods* (London: Palgrave Macmillan, 2003).

Berthoff, Rowland and John M. Murrin, 'Feudalism, Communalism and the Yeoman Freeholder: The American Revolution Considered as a Social Accident', in *Essays on the American Revolution*, ed. Stephen G. Kurz and James H. Hutson (Chapel Hill: University of North Carolina Press, 1973): 256–88.

Betts, Edwin Morris, ed., *Thomas Jefferson's Farm Book* (Philadelphia: American Philosophical Society, 1953).

Bidwell, Percy W. and John I. Falconer, *History of Agriculture in the Northern United States, 1620–1860* (Clifton: A.M. Kelley, 1973) (first published 1925).

Bonwick, Colin, *English Radicals and the American Revolution* (Chapel Hill: University of North Carolina Press, 1977).

Boorstin, Daniel J., *The Lost World of Thomas Jefferson* (New York: Henry Holt and Company, 1948).

Borghero, Carlo, 'Raynal, Paine e la rivoluzione americana', in *La politica della ragione: Studi sull'illuminismo francese*, ed. Paolo Casini (Bologna: Il Mulino, 1978): 349–81.

Bouchary, Jean, *Les Compagnies financières à Paris à la fin du XVIIIe siècle*, 3 vols. (Paris: Marcel Rivière, 1940–42).

Bradley, James E., *Religion, Revolution and English Radicalism* (Cambridge: Cambridge University Press, 1990).

Breen, Timothy H., 'Ideology and Nationalism on the Eve of the American Revolution: Revisions "Once More" in Need of Revising', in *German and American Nationalism: A Comparative Perspective*, ed. Hartmut Lehmann and Hermann Wellenreuther (Oxford and New York: Berg, 1999): 33–69.

—, *Tobacco Culture: The Mentality of the Great Tidewater Planters on the Eve of Revolution*, 2nd ed. (Princeton: Princeton University Press, 2001).

—, *The Marketplace of Revolution: How Consumer Politics Shaped American Independence* (New York: Oxford University Press, 2004).

Brewer, John, *Party Ideology and Popular Politics at the Accession of George III* (Cambridge: Cambridge University Press, 1976).

— and Roy Porter, eds, *Consumption and the World of Goods* (London: Routledge, 1993).

Bruce, Philip A., *History of the University of Virginia 1818–1919*, 5 vols. (New York: Macmillan, 1920–21).

Budick, Sanford and Wolfang Iser, eds, *The Translatability of Cultures: Figurations of the Space Between* (Stanford: Stanford University Press, 1996).

Burke, Peter and Ronnie Po-chia Hsia, eds, *Cultural Translation in Early Modern Europe* (Cambridge: Cambridge University Press, 2007).

Burrows, Edwin G., *Albert Gallatin and the Political Economy of Republicanism 1761–1800* (New York: Garland, 1986).

Carey, Lewis J., *Franklin's Economic Views* (Garden City, NY: Doubleday, Doran and Company, 1928).

Carpenter, Kenneth E., *The Dissemination of the Wealth of Nations in French and in France, 1776–1843* (New York: The Bibliographical Society of America, 2002).

Carr, William, *Ces étonnants Du Pont de Nemours* (Paris: Editions de Trevise, 1967).

Cheney, Paul, *Revolutionary Commerce: Globalization and the French Monarchy* (Cambridge: Harvard University Press, 2010).

Chevignard, Bernard, 'Une Apocalypse sécularisée: Le Quakerisme selon Brissot de Warville et St. John de Crèvecoeur', in *Le Facteur religieux en Amérique du Nord: Apocalypse et autres travaux*, ed. Jean Béranger (Bordeaux: Maison des Sciences de l'Homme d'Aquitaine, 1981): 49–68.

—, 'Andrew et André: quelques variations sur le thème du "self-made man" chez Saint-John de Crèvecoeur', in *Actes du 6e Colloque du Groupe de Recherche et d'Etude Nord Américaines (GRENA). 2–4 mars 1984: 'From rags to riches':* *Le mythe du self-made man* (Aix-en- Provence: Publications de l'Université de Provence, 1984): 9–21.

Chinard, Gilbert, *Jefferson et les Idéologues d'après sa correspondance inédite* (Baltimore: The Johns Hopkins Press; Paris: PUF, 1925).

—, *Pensées choisies de Montesquieu tirées du 'Common-Place Book' de Thomas Jefferson* (Paris: les Belles Lettres, 1925).

—, *The Commonplace Book of Thomas Jefferson: A Repertory of His Ideas on Government* (Baltimore: 1926).

—, *La Déclaration des Droits de l'Homme et du Citoyen d'après ses antécédents américains* (Washington: Institut français, 1945).

—, ed., *The Correspondence of Jefferson and Du Pont de Nemours* (Baltimore: The Johns Hopkins Press, 1931).

Chouillet, Anne–Marie and Pierre Crépel eds, *Condorcet: Homme des Lumières et de la Révolution* (Saint-Cloud: ENS Editions, 1997).

Clark, Peter, *British Clubs and Societies 1580–1800: The Origins of an Associational World* (Oxford: Clarendon Press, 2000).

Colbourn, H. Trevor, *The Lamp of Experience: Whig History and the Intellectual Origins of the American Revolution* (Chapel Hill: University of North Carolina Press, 1965).

Commager, Henry Steele, *The Empire of Reason: How Europe Imagined and America Realized the Enlightenment* (Garden City, NY: Anchor Press, Doubleday, 1977).

Conant, James B., *Thomas Jefferson and the Development of American Public Education* (Berkeley: University of California Press, 1963).

Conner, Paul W., *Poor Richard's Politicks: Benjamin Franklin and his New American Order* (New York: Oxford University Press, 1965).

Conway, Moncure D., *The Life of Thomas Paine*, 2 vols. (London: Routledge, 1996).

Correspondence Between Thomas Jefferson and Pierre-Samuel du Pont de Nemours 1798–1817, ed. Dumas Malone, trans. Linwood Lehman (Boston: Houghton Mifflin, 1930).

Crèvecoeur, Robert de, *Saint John de Crèvecoeur, sa vie et ses ouvrages 1735–1813* (Paris: Librairie des Bibliophiles, 1883).

Crowley, John E., *This Sheba, Self: The Conceptualisation of Economic Life in Eighteenth-Century America* (Baltimore: The Johns Hopkins University Press, 1974).

Darnton, Robert, *George Washington's False Teeth* (New York: W.W. Norton, 2003).

Davis, David B., *The Problem of Slavery in the Age of Revolution, 1770–1823* (Ithaca: Cornell University Press, 1975).

Delmas, Bernard, Thierry Demals, and Philippe Steiner, eds, *La diffusion internationale de la physiocratie, XVIIIe–XIXe* (Grenoble: Presses Universitaires, 1995).

Delsaux, Hélène, *Condorcet journaliste* (Paris: Honoré Champion, 1931).

Dickinson, Henry T., *British Radicalism and the French Revolution, 1789–1815* (Oxford: B. Blackwell, 1985).

Diggins, John P., *The Lost Soul of American Politics: Virtue, Self-Interest, and the Foundations of Liberalism* (New York: Basic Books, 1984).

Dorfman, Joseph, *The Economic Mind in American Civilization*, 5 vols. (New York: The Viking Press, 1946).

Dorigny, Marcel, 'The Question of Slavery in the Physiocratic Texts: A Rereading of an Old Debate', in *Rethinking the Atlantic World: Europe and America in the Age of Democratic Revolutions*, ed. Manuela Albertone and Antonino De Francesco (London: Palgrave Macmillan, 2009): 147–62.

Duchet Michèle, *Diderot et l'Histoire des deux Indes, ou l'écriture fragmentaire* (Paris: Nizet, 1978).

Dunbar, Charles, *Economic Essays*, ed. O.M.W. Sprange (New York: Macmillan, 1904).

Dunn John, *Rethinking Modern Political Theory: Essays, 1979–83* (Cambridge: Cambridge University Press, 1985).

—, *The Economic Limits to Modern Politics* (Cambridge: Cambridge University Press, 1990).

Dunn, Susan, *Dominion of Memories: Jefferson, Madison and the Decline of Virginia* (New York: Basic Books, 2007).

Early History of the University of Virginia, as contained in the letters of Thomas Jefferson and Joseph C. Cabell (Richmond: J.W. Randolph, 1856).

Echeverria, Durand, *Mirage in the West: A History of the French Image of American Society to 1815* (Princeton: Princeton University Press, 1957).

Effertz, Otto, *Le principe pono-physiocratique et son application à la question sociale* (Paris: Rivière, 1913).

Eisermann, David, 'La "Raynalisation" de l'"American Farmer": la réception de l'"Histoire des deux Indes" par Crèvecoeur', in *Lectures de Raynal: L'Histoire des deux Indes en Europe et en Amérique au XVIIIe siècle: Actes du Colloque de Wolfenbüttel*, ed. Hans J. Lüsebrink and Manfred Tietz, Studies on Voltaire and the Eighteenth-Century, no. 286 (Oxford: Voltaire Foundation, 1991): 329–39.

Elliott, John H., *Empires of the Atlantic World: Britain and Spain in America 1492–1830* (New Haven: Yale University Press, 2006).

Ellis, Richard E., 'The Political Economy of Thomas Jefferson', in *Thomas Jefferson: The Man, His World, His Influence*, ed. Lally Weymouth (London: Weidenfeld and Nicolson, 1973): 81–95.

—, *American Political Cultures* (Oxford: Oxford University Press, 1993).

Evans, Chris, *Debating the Revolution: Britain in 1790s* (London: I.B. Tauris, 2006).

Faure-Soulet, Jean-François, *Economie politique et progrès au 'siècle des Lumières'* (Paris: Gauthier-Villars, 1964).

Faÿ, Bernard, *Bibliographie critique des ouvrages français relatifs aux Etats-Unis, 1770–1800* (Paris: Campion, 1924).

—, *L'esprit révolutionnaire en France et aux Etats-Unis à la fin du XVIIIe siècle* (Paris: Champion, 1925).

—, *Franklin, the Apostle of Modern Times* (Boston: Brown and Company, 1930).

Finkelman Paul, *Slavery and the Founders: Race and Liberty in the Age of Jefferson* (Armonk, NY: M.E. Sharpe, 1996).

Fitzmaurice, Edmond, *Life of William, Earl of Shelburne*, 3 vols. (London: Macmillan, 1876).

Fletcher, Stevenson W., *Pennsylvania agriculture and country life, 1640–1840* (Harrisburg: Pennsylvania Hist. and Mus. Comm., 1950).

Foner, Eric, *Free Soil, Free Labor, Free Men: The Ideology of the Republican Party Before the Civil War* (New York, Oxford: Oxford University Press, 1971).

—, *Tom Paine and Revolutionary America* (New York: Oxford University Press, 1976).

Fontana, Biancamaria, *Rethinking the Politics of Commercial Society: The Edinburgh Review, 1802–1832* (Cambridge: Cambridge University Press, 1985).

—, ed., *The Invention of the Modern Republic* (Cambridge: Cambridge University Press, 1994).

Fruchtman, Jack, *The Apocalyptic Politics of Richard Price and Joseph Priestley: A Study in the Late Eighteenth-Century English Republican Millennialism* (Philadelphia: The American Philosophical Society, 1983).

—, *Thomas Paine and the Religion of Nature* (Baltimore: The Johns Hopkins University Press, 1993).

Garlick, Richard C., *Philip Mazzei, Friend of Jefferson: His Life and Letters* (Baltimore: The Johns Hopkins Press, 1933).

Gauchet, Marcel, *La Révolution des droits de l'homme* (Paris: Gallimard, 1989).

Gillispie, Charles C., *Science and Polity in France at the End of the Old Regime* (Princeton: Princeton University Press, 1980).

Graham, Jenny, *Revolutionary in Exile: the Emigration of Joseph Priestley to America, 1794–1804* (Philadelphia: American Philosophical Society, 1995).

Gray, Lewis C., *History of Agriculture in the Southern Unites States to 1860*, 2 vols. (Clifton: A.M. Kelly, 1973; first published 1933).

Green, James N., *Mathew Carey, Publisher and Patriot* (Philadelphia: The Library Company of Philadelphia, 1985).

Groenewegen, Peter D., *The Economics of A.R.J. Turgot* (The Hague: Nijhoff, 1977).

Haakonssen, Knud ed., *Enlightenment and Religion: Rational Dissent in Eighteenth-Century Britain* (Cambridge: Cambridge University Press, 1996).

Haraszti, Zoltan, *John Adams and the Prophets of Progress* (Cambridge, MA: Harvard University Press, 1952).

Hartz, Louis, *The Liberal Tradition in America: An Interpretation of American Thought since the Revolution* (New York: Harcourt, Brace and Co., 1955).

Hatch, Nathan O., *The Democratization of American Christianity* (New Haven: Yale University Press, 1989).

Head, Brian W., *Ideology and Social Science: Destutt de Tracy and French Liberalism* (Dordrecht: M. Nijhoff, 1985).

Heimbert, Alan, *Religion and the American Mind: From the Great Awakening to the Revolution* (Cambridge, MA: Harvard University Press, 1966).

Hill, William C., *The Political Theory of John Taylor of Caroline* (Rutherford: Fairleigh Dickinson University Press, 1977).

Himmelfarb, Gertrude, *The Roads to Modernity: The British, French and American Enlightenments* (New York: Random House, 2004).

Hirschman, Albert, *Shifting Involvements: Private Interest and Public Action* (Princeton: Princeton University Press, 1982).

Hollander, Samuel, 'Malthus as a Physiocrat: Surplus Versus Scarcity', in *La diffusion internationale de la physiocratie, XVIIIe–XIXe*, ed., Bernard Delmas, Thierry Demals and Philippe Steiner (Grenoble: Presses Universitaires de Grenoble, 1995): 79–116.

Holt, Anne, *A Life of Joseph Priestley* (London: Oxford University Press, 1931).

Honeywell, Roy J., *The Educational Work of Thomas Jefferson* (Cambridge, MA: Harvard University Press, 1931).

Hont, Istvan, *Jealousy of Trade, International Competition and the Nation-State in Historical Perspective* (Cambridge MA, London: Belknap Press of Harvard University Press, 2005).

Hutson James H., *Religion and the Founding of the American Republic* (Washington: Library of Congress, 1998).

—, ed., *Religion and the New Republic: Faith in the Founding of America* (Lanham, MD: Rowman and Littlefield, 2000).

Jauss, Hans Robert, *Toward an Aesthetic of Reception* (Minneapolis: University of Minnesota Press, 1982).

—, *Question and Answer: Forms of Dialogic Understanding* (Minneapolis: University of Minnesota Press, 1989).

Jones, Colin, 'Bourgeois Revolution Revivified: 1779 and Social Change', in *Rewriting the French Revolution*, ed. Colin Lucas (Oxford: Clarendon Press, 1991): 69–118.

Jones, Howard M., *America and French Culture 1750–1848* (Chapel Hill: University of North Carolina Press, 1927).

Kaplan, Abraham D.H., *Henry Charles Carey: A Study in American economic Thought* (Baltimore: The Johns Hopkins Press, 1931).

Keane, John, *Tom Paine: A Political Life* (London: Bloomsbury, 1995).

Kennedy, Emmet, *A Philosophe in the Age of Revolution. Destutt de Tracy and the Origins of 'Ideology'* (Philadelphia: The American Philosophical Society, 1978).

Kennedy, Roger G., *Mr Jefferson's Lost Cause: Land, Farmers, Slavery and the Louisiana Purchase* (New York: Oxford University Press, 2003).

Koch, Adrienne, *The Philosophy of Thomas Jefferson* (New York: Columbia University Press, 1943).

—, *Jefferson and Madison: The Great Collaboration* (New York: A.A. Knopf, 1950).

Laboucheix, Henri, *Richard Price, théoricien de la révolution américaine, le philosophe et le sociologue, le pamphlétaire et l'orateur* (Paris: Didier, 1970).

Lambert, Frank, *The Founding Fathers and the Place of Religion in America* (Princeton: Princeton University Press, 2003).

Larrère, Catherine, *L'invention de l'économie au XVIIIe siècle: Du droit naturel à la phyisiocratie* (Paris: PUF, 1992).

Lawrence, D.H., *Studies in Classic American Literature* (New York: Doubleday, 1923).

Lee, Gordon C. ed., *Crusade against Ignorance: Thomas Jefferson on Education* (New York: Columbia University, Teachers College Press, 1961).

Lee, Tuveson E., *Redeemer Nation: The Idea of America's Millennial Role* (Chicago: University of Chicago Press, 1968).

Leterrier, Sophie-Anne, *L'institution des sciences morales: l'Académie des sciences morales et politiques, 1795–1850* (Paris: L'Harmattan, 1995).

Livesey, James, *Making Democracy in the French Revolution* (Cambridge MA: Harvard University Press, 2001).

Lopez, Claude-Anne, *Le sceptre et la foudre: Benjamin Franklin à Paris, 1776–1785* (Paris: Mercure de France, 1990).

McCoy, Drew R., *The Elusive Republic: Political Economy in Jeffersonian America* (Chapel Hill: University of North Carolina Press, 1980).

McDonald, Forrest, *Novus ordo seclorum: The Intellectual Origins of the Constitution* (Lawrence: University Press of Kansas, 1985).

Macpherson, Crawford B., *The Political Theory of Possessive Individualism: Hobbes to Locke* (Oxford: Clarendon Press, 1962).

—, *Democratic Theory* (Oxford: Clarendon Press, 1973).

Malone, Dumas, *The Public Life of Thomas Cooper 1783–1839* (New Haven: Yale University Press, 1926).

—, *Jefferson and his Time*, 6 vols. (Boston: Little, Brown and Co., 1948–81).

Martucci, Roberto, 'Les articles "américains" de Jean-Nicolas Desmeunier et le droit public moderne', in *L'Encyclopédie méthodique (1782–1832): Des Lumières au positivisme*, ed. Claude Blanckaert and Michel Ponet (Geneva: Droz, 2006): 241–64.

Marx, Leo, *The Machine in the Garden: Technology and the Pastoral Ideal in America* (New York: Oxford University Press, 1964).

Matson, Cathy D. and Peter S. Onuf, *A Union of Interests: Political and Economic Thought in Revolutionary America* (Lawrence: University Press of Kansas, 1990).

Matthews, Richard K., *The Radical Politics of Thomas Jefferson: A Revisionist View* (Lawrence: University Press of Kansas, 1984).

May, Henry, *The Enlightenment in America* (Oxford: Oxford University Press, 1976).

Medlin Dorothy and Arlene P. Shy, 'Enlightened exchange: the correspondence of André Morellet and Lord Shelburne', in *British–French Exchanges in the Eighteenth Century*, ed. Kathleen Hardesty Doig and Dorothy Medlin (Cambridge: Cambridge Scholars, 2007): 34–82.

Meek Ronald L., *The Economics of Physiocracy* (London: Allen and Unwin, 1962).

Mergey, Anthony, *L'Etat des Physiocrates: Autorité et Décentralisation* (Aix-en-Provence: Presses Universitaires d'Aix-Marseille, 2010).

Miller, Charles A., *Jefferson and Nature: An Interpretation* (Baltimore: The Johns Hopkins University Press, 1988).

Miller, John C., *The Wolf by the Ears: Thomas Jefferson and Slavery* (New York: Free Press, 1977).

Moravia Sergio, *Il tramonto dell'illuminismo: Filosofia e politica nella società francese 1770–1810* (Bari: Laterza, 1968).

—, *Il pensiero degli Idéologues: Scienza e filosofia in Francia (1780–1815)* (Florence: La Nuova Italia, 1974).

Morgan Edmund S., ed., *Puritan Political Ideas: 1558–1794* (Indianapolis: Bobbs-Merrill, 1965).

Mott, Tracy and George W. Zinke, 'Benjamin Franklin's Economic Thought: a Twentieth Century Appraisal', in *Critical Essays on Benjamin Franklin*, ed. Melvin H. Buxbaum (Boston: G. K. Hall, 1987): 111–26.

Mudge, Eugene T., *The Social Philosophy of John Taylor of Caroline: A Study in Jeffersonian Democracy* (New York: Columbia University Press, 1939).

Neill, Charles P., *Daniel Raymond: An Early Chapter in the History of Economic Theory* (Baltimore: The Johns Hopkins Press, 1897).

Nye, Russel B., 'Michel-Guillaume St. Jean de Crèvecoeur: Letters from an American Farmer', in *Landmarks of American Writing*, ed. Henning Cohen (New York: Basic Books, 1969).

O'Connor, Michael J.L., *Origins of Academic Economics in the United States* (New York: Columbia University Press, 1944).

Onuf, Peter S., 'Adam Smith and the Crisis of the American Union', in *The Atlantic Enlightenment*, ed. Susan Manning and Francis D. Cogliano (Aldershot: Ashgate, 2008): 149–64.

Pagden, Anthony, *Lords of All the World: Ideologies of Empire in Spain, Britain and France c.1500–c.1800* (New Haven: Yale University Press, 1995).

Pangle, Lorraine S. and Thomas L. Pangle, *The Learning of Liberty: The Educational Ideas of the American Founders* (Lawrence: University Press of Kansas, 1993).

Pangle, Thomas, *The Spirit of Modern Republicanism: The Moral Vision of the American Founders and the Philosophy of Locke* (Chicago: The University of Chicago Press, 1988).

Parrington, Vernon L., *Main Currents in American Thought: An Interpretation of American Literature from the Beginnings to 1920*, 3 vols. (New York: Harcourt, Brace and Co., 1927–30).

Parton, James, *Life and Times of Benjamin Franklin* (New York: Mason Brothers, 1864).

Pasta, Renato, *Scienza, politica e rivoluzione: l'opera di Giovanni Fabbroni (1752–1822) intellettuale e funzionario al servizio dei Lorena* (Florence: Olschki, 1989).

Perrot, Jean-Claude, *Une histoire intellectuelle de l'économie politique (XVIIe–XVIIIe siècle)* (Paris: Editions de l'Ecole des Hautes Etudes en Sciences Sociales, 1992).

Peterson, Merrill D., *Thomas Jefferson and the New Nation. A Biography* (New York: Oxford University Press, 1970).

Philbrick, Thomas, *St. John de Crèvecoeur* (New York: Twayne Publishers, 1970).

Pierre Crépel and Christian Gilain, eds, *Condorcet: Mathématicien, économiste, philosophe, homme politique* (Paris: Minerve, 1989).

Pocock, John, *The Machiavellian Moment: Florentine Political Thought and the Atlantic Republican Tradition* (Princeton, Oxford: Princeton University Press, 2003; first published, 1975).

Pole, Jack R., *Political Representation in England and the Origins of the American Republic* (Berkeley: University of California Press, 1969).

Porter, Roy and Mikuláš Teich, eds, *The Enlightenment in National Context* (Cambridge: Cambridge University Press, 1981).

Rahe, Paul A., *Republics Ancient and Modern: Classical Republicanism and the American Revolution* (Chapel Hill: University of North Carolina Press, 1992).

Regis, Pamela, *Describing Early America: Batram, Jefferson, Crèvecoeur and the Rhetoric of Natural History* (Dekalb: Northern Illinois University Press, 1992).

Rials, Stéphane, *La déclaration des droits de l'homme et du citoyen* (Paris: Hachette, 1988).

Rice, Howard C., *Le Cultivateur Américain: Etude sur l'oeuvre de Saint-John de Crèvecoeur* (Paris: Champion, 1932).

Risjord, Norman K., *The Old Republicans: Southern Conservatism in the Age of Jefferson* (New York: Columbia University Press, 1965).

Riskin, Jessica, *Science in the Age of Sensibility: The Sentimental Empiricists of the French Enlightenment* (Chicago,Chicago University Press, 2002).

Robertson, John, *The Case for the Enlightenment: Scotland and Naples, 1680–1760* (Cambridge: Cambridge University Press, 2005).

Roche, Daniel, *Histoire des choses banales: naissance de la consommation dans les sociétés traditionnelles (17. 19 siècle)* (Paris: Fayard, 1997).

Røge, Pernille, 'The Question of Slavery in Physiocratic Political Economy', in *Governare il mondo: L'economia come linguaggio della politica nell'Europa del Settecento*, ed. Manuela Albertone (Milan: Feltrinelli, 2009): 149–69.

Rossiter, Margaret W., 'The Organization of Agricultural Improvement in the United States 1785–1865', in *The Pursuit of Knowledge in the Early American Republic: American Scientific and Learned Societies from Colonial Times to the Civil War*, ed. Alexandra Olesen and Sanborn C. Brown (Baltimore: Johns Hopkins University Press, 1976): 284–7.

Rude, George, *Wilkes and Liberty: A Social Study of 1763 to 1774* (Oxford: Clarendon Press, 1962).

Rudolph, Frederick ed., *Essays on Education in the early Republic* (Cambridge, MA: The Belknap Press of Harvard University, 1965).

Sandoz, Ellis, *A Government of Laws: Political Theory, Religion, and the American Founding* (London: Baton Rouge, 1990).

Schelle, Gustave, *Du Pont de Nemours et l'école physiocratique* (Paris, 1888).

Schoenbrun, David, *Triumph in Paris: The Exploits of Benjamin Franklin* (New York: Harper and Row, 1976).

Schumpeter, Joseph A., *History of Economic Analysis* (New York: Oxford University Press, 1954).

Sekora, John, *Luxury: The Concept in Western Thought, Eden to Smollett* (Baltimore: John Hopkins University Press, 1977).

Seligman, Edwin R.A., 'The Early Teaching of Economics in the United States', in *Economics Essays: Contributed in Honour of John Bates Clark*, ed. Jacob H. Hollander (New York: The MacMillan Company, 1927): 283–321.

Shain, Barry A., *The Myth of American Individualism: The Protestant Origins of American Political Thought* (Princeton: Princeton University Press, 1994).

Shalhope, Robert E., *John Taylor of Caroline: Pastoral Republican* (Columbia: University of South Carolina Press, 1980).

Sharp, James R., *American Politics in the Early Republic: The New Nation in Crisis* (New Haven: Yale University Press, 1993).

Sherwood, Sidney, *Tendencies in American Economic Thought* (Baltimore: The Johns Hopkins Press, 1897).

Shklar, Judith, 'Montesquieu and the new Republicanism', in *Machiavelli and Republicanism*, ed. Gisela Bock, Quentin Skinner and Maurizio Viroli (Cambridge: Cambridge University Press, 1990): 265–79.

Simms, Henry H., *Life of John Taylor: The Story of a Brilliant Leader in the Early Virginia State Rights School* (Richmond: W. Byrd, 1932).

Sloan, Herbert E., *Principle and Interest: Thomas Jefferson and the Problem of Debt* (New York: Oxford University Press, 1995).

Smith, Henry N., *Virgin Land: The American West as Symbol and Myth* (Cambridge, MA: Harvard University Press, 1950)

Smith, James M., *Freedom's Fetters: The Alien and Sedition Laws and American Civil Liberties* (Ithaca, NY: Cornell University Press, 1956).

Sombart, Werner, *The Quintessence of Capitalism* (London: Routledge, 1998).

Sonenscher, Michael, *Before the Deluge: Public Debt, Inequality, and the Intellectual Origins of the French Revolution* (Princeton: Princeton University Press, 2007).

Sowerby, E. Millicent ed., *Catalogue of the Library of Thomas Jefferson*, 5 vols. (Washington: The Library of Congress, 1952).

Spengler, Joseph J., 'The Political Economy of Jefferson, Madison, and Adams', in *American Studies in Honour of William Kenneth Boyd*, ed. David K. Jackson (Freeport, NY: Books for Libraries Press, 1940): 2–59.

Spurlin, Paul M., *Montesquieu in America 1760–1801* (Baton Rouge: Louisiana State University Press, 1940).

—, *Rousseau in America 1760–1809* (Tuscaloosa: University of Alabama Press, 1969).

Stapelbroek, Koen, 'Neutrality and Trade in the Dutch Republic (1775–1783): Preludes to a Piecemeal Revolution', in *Rethinking the Atlantic World: Europe and America in the Age of Democratic Revolutions*, ed. Manuela Albertone and Antonino De Francesco (London: Palgrave Macmillan, 2009): 100–119.

Staughton, Lynd, *Intellectual Origins of American Radicalism* (New York: Pantheon Books, 1968).

Steel, Willis, *Benjamin Franklin of Paris 1776–1785* (New York: Minton, Boech, 1928).

Steiner Philippe, 'Quels principes pour l'économie politique? Charles Ganihl, Germain Garnier, Jean-Baptiste Say et la critique de la physiocratie', in *La diffusion internationale de la physiocratie (XVIIIe–XIXe)*, ed. Bernard Delmas, Thierry Demals and Philippe Steiner (Grenoble: Presses Universitaires, 1995): 209–30.

—, *La 'science nouvelle' de l'économie politique* (Paris: PUF, 1998).

Tagg, James, *Benjamin Franklin Bache and the Philadelphia 'Aurora'* (Philadelphia: University of Pennsylvania Press, 1991).

Tate, Adam L., *Conservatism and Southern Intellectuals, 1789–1861: Liberty, Tradition and Good Society* (Columbia: University of Missouri Press, 2005).

Teilhac, Ernest, *Histoire de la pensée économique aux Etats-Unis au dix-neuvième siècle* (Paris: Recueil Sirey, 1928).

Thomas, David, *The Honest Mind: The Thought and Work of Richard Price* (Oxford: Clarendon Press, 1977).

Thompson, Paul B. and C. Hildge, eds, *The Agrarian Roots of Pragmatism* (Nashville: Vanderbilt University Press, 2000).

Tiran, André, 'Jean-Baptiste Say: l'écriture et ses pièges', in *Governare il mondo: L'economia come linguaggio della politica nell'Europa del Settecento*, ed. Manuela Albertone (Milan: Feltrinelli, 2009): 103–22.

Tocqueville, Alexis-Henri-Charles de Clérel de, *La Démocratie en Amérique* (Paris: Gallimard, 1951).

—, *L'Ancien régime et la Révolution. 2, Fragments et notes inédites sur la Révolution*. Texte établi et annoté par André Jardin (Paris: Gallimard, 1981).

Tolles, Frederick B., *George Logan of Philadelphia* (New York: Oxford University Press, 1953).

Tortarolo, Edoardo, *Illuminismo e rivoluzioni: Biografia politica di Filippo Mazzei* (Milan: Franco Angeli, 1986).

—, 'La réception de l'"Histoire des deux Indes" aux Etats-Unis', in *Lectures de Raynal: L'Histoire des deux Indes en Europe et en Amérique au XVIIIe siècle: Actes du Colloque de Wolfenbüttel*, ed. Hans J. Lüsebrink and Manfred Tietz, Studies on Voltaire and the Eighteenth-Century, no. 286 (Oxford: Voltaire Foundation, 1991): 305–28.

Tully, James, ed., *Meaning and Context: Quentin Skinner and his Critics* (Cambridge: Polity Press, 1988).

Turner, John R., *The Ricardian Rent Theory in Early Economics* (New York: New York University Press, 1921).

Twomey, Richard J., 'Jacobins and Jeffersonians: Anglo-American Radical Ideology, 1790–1810', in *The Origins of Anglo-American Radicalism*, eds Margaret Jacob and James Jacob (London: Allen and Unwin, 1984): 284–99.

Van Doren, Carl, *Benjamin Franklin* (New York: The Viking Press, 1938).

Van Gelderen, Martin and Quentin Skinner, eds, *Republicanism: A Shared Heritage.* Vol. I: *Republicanism and Constitutionalism in Early Modern Europe*. Vol. II: *The Values of Republicanism in Early Modern Europe* (Cambridge: Cambridge University Press, 2002).

Vardi, Liana, *The Physiocrats and the World of Enlightenment* (Cambridge: Cambridge University Press, 2012).

Vaugelade, Daniel, *Franklin des deux mondes* (Paris: Editions de l'Armandier, 2007).

Venturi, Franco, *Utopia and Reform in the Enlightenment* (Cambridge: Cambridge University Press, 1971).

Vile, Maurice J., *Constitutionalism and the Separation of Powers* (Oxford: Clarendon Press, 1967).

Vossler, Otto, *Jefferson and the American Revolutionary Ideal* (Washington: University Press of America, 1980).

Walsch, Correa M., *The Political Science of John Adams* (New York: G.P. Putnam's Sons, 1915).

Walton, Craig, 'Hume and Jefferson on the uses of history', in *Philosophy and the Civilizing Arts: Essays Presented to Herbert W. Schneider*, ed. Craig Walton and John P. Anton (Athens: Ohio University Press, 1974): 103–25.

Watts, George B., *Les Affaires de l'Angleterre et de l'Amérique* (Charlotte, NC: Heritage Printers, 1965).

Wetzel, William A., *Benjamin Franklin as an Economist* (Baltimore: The Johns Hopkins' Press, 1895).

Whatmore, Richard, 'A gigantic manliness: Thomas Paine's republicanism in the 1790s', in *Economy, Polity and Society: British Intellectual History, 1750–1950*, ed. Stefan Collini, Richard Whatmore and Brian Young (Cambridge: Cambridge University Press, 2000): 135–57.

—, *Republicanism and the French Revolution: An Intellectual History of Jean-Baptiste Say's Political Economy* (Oxford: Oxford University Press, 2000).

—, 'The French and North American Revolutions in Comparative perspective', in *Rethinking the Atlantic World: Europe and America in the Age of Democratic Revolutions*, ed. Manuela Albertone and Antonino De Francesco (London: Palgrave Macmillan, 2009): 219–28.

—, *Against War and Empire: Geneva, Britain and France in the Eighteenth Century* (New Haven: Yale University Press, 2012).

White, Morton, *The Philosophy of the American Revolution* (New York: Oxford University Press, 1978).

Wilhite, Virgil G., 'Benjamin Franklin: Urban Agrarian', in *Founders of American Economic Thought and Policy* (New York: Bookman Associates, 1958): 283–319.

Wills, Garry, *Negro President: Jefferson and the Slave Power* (Boston: Houghton Mifflin, 2003).

Winch, Donald, *Riches and Poverty: An Intellectual History of Political Economy in Britain, 1750–1834* (Cambridge: Cambridge University Press, 1996).

Wood, Gordon S., *The Creation of the American Republic, 1776–1787* (Chapel Hill: The University of North Carolina Press, 1969).

—, *The American Revolution: A History* (New York: The Modern Library, 2002).

—, *The Americanization of Benjamin Franklin* (New York: The Penguin Press, 2004).

Wootton, David ed., *Republicanism, Liberty and Commercial Society, 1649–1776* (Stanford: Stanford University Press, 1994).

Zuckert, Michael P., *Natural Rights and the New Republicanism* (Princeton: Princeton University Press, 1994).

Index

Modern Economic and Social History Series

General Editor
Derek H. Aldcroft, University Fellow, Department of Economic and
Social History, University of Leicester, UK

Patrick Duffy
The Skilled Compositor, 1850–1914
An Aristocrat Among Working Men
0 7546 0255 9 (2000)

Robert Conlon and John Perkins
Wheels and Deals
The Automotive Industry in Twentieth-Century Australia
0 7546 0405 5 (2001)

Sam Mustafa
Merchants and Migrations
Germans and Americans in Connection, 1776–1835
0 7546 0590 6 (2001)

Bernard Cronin
Technology, Industrial Conflict and the Development of Technical
Education in 19th-Century England
0 7546 0313 X (2001)

Andrew Popp
Business Structure, Business Culture and the Industrial District
The Potteries, c. 1850–1914
0 7546 0176 5 (2001)

Scott Kelly
The Myth of Mr Butskell
The Politics of British Economic Policy, 1950–55
0 7546 0604 X (2002)

Michael Ferguson
The Rise of Management Consulting in Britain
0 7546 0561 2 (2002)

Alan Fowler
Lancashire Cotton Operatives and Work, 1900–1950
A Social History of Lancashire Cotton Operatives in the Twentieth Century
0 7546 0116 1 (2003)

John F. Wilson and Andrew Popp (eds)
Industrial Clusters and Regional Business Networks in England, 1750–1970
0 7546 0761 5 (2003)

John Hassan
The Seaside, Health and the Environment in England and Wales since 1800
1 84014 265 0 (2003)

Marshall J. Bastable
Arms and the State
Sir William Armstrong and the Remaking of British Naval Power, 1854–1914
0 7546 3404 3 (2004)

Robin Pearson
Insuring the Industrial Revolution
Fire Insurance in Great Britain, 1700–1850
0 7546 3363 2 (2004)

Andrew Dawson
Lives of the Philadelphia Engineers
Capital, Class and Revolution, 1830–1890
0 7546 3396 9 (2004)

Lawrence Black and Hugh Pemberton (eds)
An Affluent Society?
Britain's Post-War 'Golden Age' Revisited
0 7546 3528 7 (2004)

Joseph Harrison and David Corkill
Spain
A Modern European Economy
0 7546 0145 5 (2004)

Ross E. Catterall and Derek H. Aldcroft (eds)
Exchange Rates and Economic Policy in the 20th Century
1 84014 264 2 (2004)

Armin Grünbacher
Reconstruction and Cold War in Germany
The Kreditanstalt für Wiederaufbau (1948–1961)
0 7546 3806 5 (2004)

Till Geiger
Britain and the Economic Problem of the Cold War
The Political Economy and the Economic Impact of the
British Defence Effort, 1945–1955
0 7546 0287 7 (2004)

Anne Clendinning
Demons of Domesticity
Women and the English Gas Industry, 1889–1939
0 7546 0692 9 (2004)

Timothy Cuff
The Hidden Cost of Economic Development
The Biological Standard of Living in Antebellum Pennsylvania
0 7546 4119 8 (2005)

Julian Greaves
Industrial Reorganization and Government Policy in Interwar Britain
0 7546 0355 5 (2005)

Derek H. Aldcroft
Europe's Third World
The European Periphery in the Interwar Years
0 7546 0599 X (2006)

James P. Huzel
The Popularization of Malthus in Early Nineteenth-Century England
Martineau, Cobbett and the Pauper Press
0 7546 5427 3 (2006)

Richard Perren
Taste, Trade and Technology
The Development of the International Meat Industry since 1840
978 0 7546 3648 9 (2006)

Roger Lloyd-Jones and M.J. Lewis
Alfred Herbert Ltd and the British Machine Tool Industry,
1887–1983
978 0 7546 0523 2 (2006)

Anthony Howe and Simon Morgan (eds)
Rethinking Nineteenth-Century Liberalism
Richard Cobden Bicentenary Essays
978 0 7546 5572 5 (2006)

Espen Moe
Governance, Growth and Global Leadership
The Role of the State in Technological Progress, 1750–2000
978 0 7546 5743 9 (2007)

Peter Scott
Triumph of the South
A Regional Economic History of Early Twentieth Century Britain
978 1 84014 613 4 (2007)

David Turnock
Aspects of Independent Romania's Economic History with
Particular Reference to Transition for EU Accession
978 0 7546 5892 4 (2007)

David Oldroyd
Estates, Enterprise and Investment at the Dawn of the Industrial Revolution
Estate Management and Accounting in the North-East of England, c.1700–1780
978 0 7546 3455 3 (2007)

Ralf Roth and Günter Dinhobl (eds)
Across the Borders
Financing the World's Railways in the Nineteenth and Twentieth Centuries
978 0 7546 6029 3 (2008)

Vincent Barnett and Joachim Zweynert (eds)
Economics in Russia
Studies in Intellectual History
978 0 7546 6149 8 (2008)

Raymond E. Dumett (ed.)
Mining Tycoons in the Age of Empire, 1870–1945
Entrepreneurship, High Finance, Politics and Territorial Expansion
978 0 7546 6303 4 (2009)

Peter Dorey
British Conservatism and Trade Unionism, 1945–1964
978 0 7546 6659 2 (2009)

Shigeru Akita and Nicholas J. White (eds)
The International Order of Asia in the 1930s and 1950s
978 0 7546 5341 7 (2010)

Myrddin John Lewis, Roger Lloyd-Jones, Josephine Maltby
and Mark David Matthews
Personal Capitalism and Corporate Governance
British Manufacturing in the First Half of the Twentieth Century
978 0 7546 5587 9 (2010)

John Murphy
A Decent Provision
Australian Welfare Policy, 1870 to 1949
978 1 4094 0759 1 (2011)

Robert Lee (ed.)
Commerce and Culture
Nineteenth-Century Business Elites
978 0 7546 6398 0 (2011)

Martin Cohen
The Eclipse of 'Elegant Economy'
The Impact of the Second World War on Attitudes to Personal
Finance in Britain
978 1 4094 3972 1 (2012)

Gordon M. Winder
The American Reaper
Harvesting Networks and Technology, 1830–1910
978 1 4094 2461 1 (2012)

Julie Marfany
Land, Proto-Industry and Population in Catalonia, c. 1680–1829
An Alternative Transition to Capitalism?
978 1 4094 4465 7 (2012)

Lucia Coppolaro
The Making of a World Trading Power
The European Economic Community (EEC) in the GATT Kennedy Round
Negotiations (1963–67)
978 1 4094 3375 0 (2013)

Ralf Roth and Henry Jacolin (eds)
Eastern European Railways in Transition
Nineteenth to Twenty-first Centuries
978 1 4094 2782 7 (2013)

Manuel Pérez-García
Vicarious Consumers
Trans-National Meetings between the West and East
in the Mediterranean World (1730–1808)
978-1-4094-5685-8 (2013)